Literary St. Louis

Literary St. Louis:
A Guide

edited by
Lorin Cuoco
William H. Gass

International Writers Center,
Washington University, St. Louis

Missouri Historical Society Press

04 03 02 01 00 5 4 3 2 1

Library of Congress Cataloguing-in-Publication Data

Literary St. Louis : a guide / edited by Lorin Cuoco, William H. Gass ; images
curated by Michelle Komie ; designed by Ken Botnick ; illustrations by Emily Pyle.
    p. cm.
    Includes bibliographical references (p.) and index.
    ISBN 1-883982-35-9 (alk. paper)
    1. American literature—Missouri—Saint Louis—History and criticism.
    2. Authors, American—Homes and haunts—Missouri—Saint Louis.
    3. Literary landmarks—Missouri—Saint Louis—Guidebooks. 4. Authors,
    American—Missouri—Saint Louis—Biography. 5. Saint Louis (Mo.)—in
    literature. 6. Saint Louis (Mo.)—Guidebooks.
    I. Title: Literary Saint Louis. II. Cuoco, Lorin, 1954– III. Gass, William H.,
    1924–
    PS285.S25 L58 2000

                                        00-056626
                                         CIP

Printed in Canada

Distributed by University of Missouri Press

Financial support provided by Furthermore, the publication program of
The J. M. Kaplan Fund.

. . . and so there ain't nothing more to write about, and I am rotten glad of it, because if I'd a knowed what a trouble it was to make a book I wouldn't a tackled it and ain't agoing to no more. But I reckon I got to light out for the Territory ahead of the rest, because Aunt Sally she's going to adopt me and sivilize me and I can't stand it. I been there before.

—Huckleberry Finn

In the Author's Note to her *Collected Poems*, Marianne Moore advised that "omissions are not accidents," an editorial policy we adopted for this literary guide which has two important qualifications for inclusion—the writer must have published and perished. There are those who were born here and spent enough time in St. Louis to give it meaning in their artistic development, the largest representatives in this history; those who were born here and stayed, a smaller number; and those who came here and stayed, wrote and published books, having to do mainly with Washington University and its literary history. Other writers visited and wrote about it, some visited and didn't. We take note of a few of these.

As, alas, St. Louis is not a walking city, we have devised a driving tour. (One cannot, for example, stand on any St. Louis street and expect to hail a cab.) We have concentrated on St. Louis and environs with a south and western reach, not crossing into Illinois (except for the Alton of Elijah Lovejoy), a boundary line that I survived despite having grown up in Lebanon, Illinois, a town that boasts a visit from Charles Dickens who single-handedly saved the hotel in which he stayed, the Mermaid Inn, while he was venturing into the Looking Glass Prairie. He also visited St. Louis and scandalized the nation, but more about that later.

The sections of this book denote associations not entirely geographic. Earlier in its history downtown St. Louis was the focal point of its residents and where many of the writers lived and worked. The Downtown section describes these associations. The other sections show a more recent history when neighborhoods began to take on their own character—in addition to their own government—and to provide another distinct locale in which to live and work. As you will see from the extensive Locations List of both existing and demolished sites, writers moved frequently—this movement was usually west or out of town. The maps in each section show what stands, what has been saved and where some of the writers alighted. Keys are provided on the maps and on the Locations List.

"It is a privilege to see so much confusion," Miss Moore tells us in her poem "The Steeple-Jack." And so it was for us in preparing this volume. Sources vary—boy, do they ever—but we tried our best to confirm the facts and when we couldn't, to say so. The interpretation is all ours. Any errors are all mine.

We are grateful to all who have worked on this book for the past ten years: the researchers Lana Bittman, Jan Estep, Jane Gould, Jamie Hayes, Melanie Hersh, Monica Lewis, Naomi Mendelsohn, Betsy Merbitz, Tod Price, Jeffrey Rueppel, Pat Schlutow, Patricia Skarbinski, Matthew Strauss, Anne Townsend and Gene Wagner; and the writers Matt Bar, Todd Borlik, Max Eisenstein, Meg Hoester, Chris Lawton, Lisa Pepper and Derek Webster, who joined the editors in this task.

Mira Tanna designed our first tour, the heart of this book, in anticipation of the visitors attending our international conferences. I elevate her to sainthood. We extend our gratitude to the other staff members who worked on this book: Sally Ball and Ruthie Epstein, and in particular our left hand Michelle Komie, who as editorial assistant saw this book to completion, contributed to its writing and curated the images. This book would not have been possible without her.

We owe a debt of appreciation to the dean of Arts and Sciences, Edward Macias, for financial support of the project; to Furthermore, the publication program of The J. M. Kaplan Fund for financial assistance with printing costs; to Nancy and Ken Kranzberg for their gift of support for its design; to the designer Ken Botnick, for the pleasure of the collaboration; and to Emily Pyle for her drawings.

To libraries everywhere we give thanks, but especially to Washington University's Archivist, Carole Prietto, and Special Collections of Olin Library; to the Missouri Historical Society Library and Research Center; to the Thomas Jefferson Library at the University of Missouri for having the wisdom to retain the contents of the Mercantile Library; to the many institutions and individuals that allowed us to reproduce the images in this book and who are noted elsewhere; and to the inventor of the index.

Finally, I want to thank Bill Gass, a hero of thought, of literature and of the literary life. I do so with love and admiration in gratitude for the last ten years.

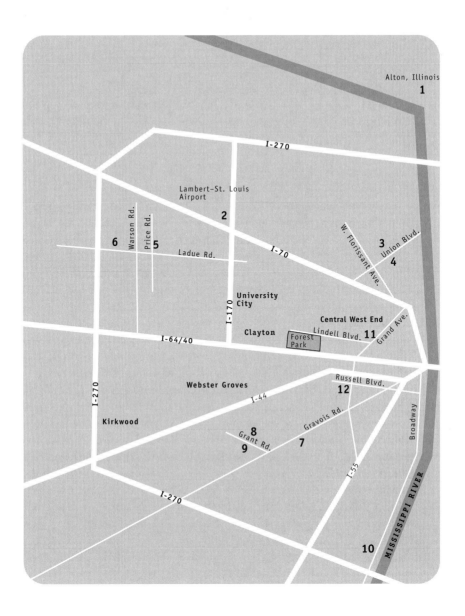

ST. LOUIS AND ENVIRONS

1 Elijah Lovejoy Monument, Monument and Fourth Streets, Alton, Illinois
2 Lambert–St. Louis International Airport, Lindbergh Boulevard
3 Calvary Cemetery, 5239 West Florissant Avenue
4 Bellefontaine Cemetery, 4947 West Florissant Avenue
5 John Burroughs School, 755 South Price Road
6 Mary Institute and Country Day School, 425 North Warson Road
7 New Mount Sinai Cemetery, 8430 Gravois Road
8 Ulysses S. Grant National Historic Site, 7400 Grant Road
9 Grant's Farm, 10501 Gravois Road
10 Jefferson Barracks, South Broadway and Grant Road
11 Saint Louis University, Grand Avenue and Lindell Boulevard
12 *Naked Truth* Monument, Compton Hill Reservoir Park, Grand Avenue and Russell Boulevard

1763 December. Pierre Laclède and Auguste Chouteau scout the west bank of the Mississippi River for the future site of a trading post.

1764 February 14. The first houses are built in St. Louis. The trading post is named for Louis IX, the French King and saint who built Notre Dame and the Sorbonne. This becomes the official founding date.

1803 May. President Thomas Jefferson purchases the Louisiana Territory from France for $15 million, doubling the size of the United States.

1804 May. Jefferson commissions Meriwether Lewis and William Clark to explore the western territories.

1806 September. Lewis and Clark return to St. Louis after their expedition.

1808 July 26. Joseph Charless, "printer to the territory," publishes the first issue of the *Missouri Gazette* (also called the *Louisiana Gazette*, and later the *Missouri Republican*), the first newspaper west of the Mississippi.

1809 The town of St. Louis is incorporated, extending to Seventh Street.

1811 August 5. William Greenleaf Eliot is born in New Bedford, Massachusetts.

1818 Bishop Louis William V. DuBourg opens St. Louis Academy near the cathedral. In 1888 the academy's Jesuit fathers move the school on Ninth and Washington to its present location in Midtown St. Louis and rename it Saint Louis University, creating the first university west of the Mississippi.

1821 Missouri becomes a state—a slave state.

1827 Pierre Jean DeSmet, s.J., arrives in St.

Louis from Belgium to begin his novitiate.

Elijah Lovejoy arrives in St. Louis.

1830 Elijah Lovejoy becomes editor and part owner of the *St. Louis Times*, where he will remain until 1832.

1833 November 27. Elijah Lovejoy publishes the first issue of the abolitionist *Observer*.

1834 November 27. William Greenleaf Eliot arrives in St. Louis to lead a new Unitarian congregation.

1835 October 31. The weekly *Anzeiger des Westens* is founded by Wilhelm Weber.

November 30. Samuel Langhorne Clemens is born in Florida, Missouri.

1836 Elijah Lovejoy moves himself and his newspaper, the *Observer*, to the free state of Illinois.

1837 November. Elijah Lovejoy is murdered in Alton, Illinois.

1838 October 1. Kate Field is born in St. Louis.

1842 Charles Dickens visits St. Louis and writes about it in *American Notes*.

1843 October 22. Charlotte Champe Stearns, mother of T. S. Eliot and author of *Easter Songs*, *Savonorola* and a biography of William Greenleaf Eliot, is born in Baltimore, Maryland.

November 25. Henry Ware Eliot, son of William Greenleaf Eliot, father of T. S. Eliot, and author of *A Brief Autobiography Written by H. W. Eliot,* is born in St. Louis.

Ulysses S. Grant is posted to Jefferson Barracks.

William T. Sherman visits St. Louis for the first time.

1846 April 9. The St. Louis Mercantile Library opens, quickly outgrows its space at the Exchange Building, and moves in September to 112 North Fourth Street.

1847 William Wells Brown publishes *Narrative of William W. Brown, A Fugitive Slave, Written by Himself.*

1850 February 8. Kate Chopin is born in St. Louis.

March 8. Austrian radical Heinrich Börnstein becomes editor of *Anzeiger des Westens.*

September 2. Eugene Field is born.

September 27. Captain William T. Sherman is posted to Jefferson Barracks and moves into the Planter's House Hotel. He'll remain in St. Louis for one year.

1852 Heinrich Börnstein's *The Mysteries of St. Louis; or, The Jesuits on the Prairies des Noyers, A Western Tale*, is published by *Anzeiger des Westens.*

1853 February 22. Wayman Crow's Charter for Eliot Seminary, named in honor of William Greenleaf Eliot, is passed by the Missouri Legislature. The name is changed to Washington University in 1857.

June. Samuel Clemens arrives in St. Louis to work as a typesetter for the *Evening News* and other publications.

Kate Field leaves St. Louis for Massachusetts.

William Wells Brown publishes his first novel, *Clotel; Or, The President's Daughter.*

February 22. William Greenleaf Eliot is elected president of Eliot Seminary.

1854 The St. Louis Mercantile Library erects a three-story building at Broadway and Locust.

1855 November 1. The newly built Gasconade Bridge collapses on opening day, killing Kate Chopin's father Thomas O'Flaherty and the Reverend John Teasdale, the grandfather of Sara Teasdale.

St. Louis High School, later known as Central High School, opens at Fifteenth and Olive Streets. First opened in 1853, it is the first public high school in Missouri—for white students only.

1856 William Greenleaf Eliot publishes *The Discipline of Sorrow.*

1857 March. The United States Supreme Court rules against Dred Scott, who sued for his freedom. He is represented by Roswell Field, the father of Eugene Field. Two months later Scott is sold for a nominal sum to Taylor Blow, the uncle of Susan Blow, who immediately frees him.

Summer. William T. Harris arrives in St. Louis.

September 27. The morning daily *Westliche Post* is founded by Carl Daenzer, former editor-in-chief at *Anzeiger des Westens.*

Samuel Clemens begins to live on and off the Mississippi River but never again in St. Louis.

1859 April 9. Samuel Clemens receives his riverboat pilot's license.

1860 Ulysses S. Grant leaves St. Louis for Galena, Illinois, and will only visit St. Louis thereafter.

1861 May. Kate Chopin is confirmed by Archbishop Peter Kenrick.

Ulysses S. Grant and William T. Sherman witness, as citizens, the surrender of pro-Confederate Missourians at Camp Jackson in Lindell's Grove, now

Saint Louis University. Heinrich Börnstein is a Union Home Guard commander.

1862 December 11. William Marion Reedy is born in St. Louis.

1863 February 2. Mark Twain is born with his first publication in the Virginia City, Nevada, *Territorial Enterprise*.

February 14. *Anzeiger des Westens* ceases publication.

Emil Preetorius becomes editor of *Westliche Post*.

1864 December 12. Paul Elmer More is born in St. Louis.

1865 February. The Public School Library Society is founded, later to become the St. Louis Public Library.

October. Joseph Pulitzer arrives in St. Louis penniless and unable to speak English.

1866 July 14. Edward Preetorius, the son of editor Emil Preetorius, is born in St. Louis.

1867 May. Mark Twain publishes his first book, *The Celebrated Jumping Frog of Calaveras County and Other Sketches*.

Carl Schurz becomes co-editor with Emil Preetorius of the *Westliche Post*.

William T. Harris launches *The Journal of Speculative Philosophy* in St. Louis.

1868 Joseph Pulitzer begins his journalism career as a reporter at the *Westliche Post*.

1869 General Ulysses S. Grant is inaugurated as the eighteenth president of the United States. Later, he is elected to a second term.

1870 Kate O'Flaherty marries Oscar Chopin, and they move to New Orleans, Louisiana.

1871 November 10. Novelist Winston Churchill is born in St. Louis.

1872 October 1. The first issue of the Roman Catholic daily *Amerika* appears. Future editors include Edward Preuss, Frederick Kenkel and Arthur Preuss.

1873 Susan Blow opens the first public kindergarten in the United States in Carondelet.

1874 June. Eads Bridge opens to the public. Wagons make the first trip across, followed by a large crowd of pedestrians, among them Kate Chopin.

July. Eads Bridge has its official opening ceremony. General William T. Sherman hammers in the final railroad spike.

1875 January 21. *Memoirs of General W. T. Sherman, By Himself* is published in two volumes.

The *Globe* and the *Missouri Democrat* merge to become the *St. Louis Globe-Democrat*. The editor, Joseph P. McCullagh, will later hire Theodore Dreiser and William Marion Reedy.

Sumner High School is established as St. Louis's first "High School for Colored Children."

1876 Home Rule Charter is instituted, defining the boundaries of St. Louis by tripling the size of the city.

1877 October 30. Irma Rombauer is born in St. Louis.

1878 December 9. Joseph Pulitzer purchases the bankrupt *Evening Dispatch* for $2,500 at an auction on the steps of the Old Courthouse. His first edition is issued December 12.

1879 Joseph Pulitzer founds the *St. Louis Post-Dispatch*.

Walt Whitman arrives in St. Louis for a three-month visit with his brother Thomas J. Whitman.

Heinrich Börnstein's *Memoirs of a Nobody* is published.

1881 January 8. John G. Neihardt is born in Sharpsburg, Illinois.

1882 Eugene Field publishes his first book, *The Tribune Primer*.

1883 May 10. Joseph Pulitzer buys the *New York World* and moves to New York.

May. Mark Twain publishes *Life on the Mississippi*.

1884 August 8. Sara Teasdale is born in St. Louis.

November 6. William Wells Brown dies in Chelsea, Massachusetts.

Ulysses S. Grant agrees to write a series of articles on the Civil War for *Century* magazine. These would become his memoirs.

Kate Chopin returns to St. Louis from New Orleans.

1885 July 18. Ulysses S. Grant delivers the second volume of his *Memoirs* to his publisher and on July 23 dies at a resort near Saratoga Springs, New York.

October 19. Fannie Hurst is born in Hamilton, Ohio.

December 1. The first volume of *Personal Memoirs of U. S. Grant* is published. The second volume is published on March 1, 1886.

October 30. Zoë Akins is born in Humansville, Missouri.

1887 January 23. William Greenleaf Eliot dies in Pass Christian, Mississippi.

June 2. Orrick Johns is born in St. Louis.

November 15. Marianne Moore is born in Kirkwood, Missouri.

Carl Schurz's two-volume *Life of Henry Clay* is published.

1888 May 22. Shirley Seifert is born in St. Peters, Missouri.

September 26. Thomas Stearns Eliot is born at 2635 Locust Street in St. Louis.

1889 January. A new six-story St. Louis Mercantile Library is built on the grounds of the old one, with a Grand Hall on the third floor.

1890 The Shelley Club becomes The Wednesday Club.

William T. Harris publishes *Hegel's Logic: A Book on the Genesis of the Categories of the Mind*.

Kate Chopin self-publishes her first novel, *At Fault*.

1891 February 14. General William T. Sherman dies in New York and is buried in Calvary Cemetery on February 21.

1892 June 21. Reinhold Niebuhr is born in Wright City, Missouri.

September 10. Heinrich Börnstein dies in Vienna.

November. Theodore Dreiser arrives in St. Louis to write for the *St. Louis Globe-Democrat*.

1893 October 4. Fannie Cook is born in St. Charles, Missouri.

William Marion Reedy becomes city editor at the *St. Louis Mirror*.

Paul Elmer More leaves St. Louis to attend graduate school at Harvard.

1894 William Marion Reedy becomes the publisher of *The Mirror*.

Theodore Dreiser moves to New York.

Marianne Moore moves to Carlisle, Pennsylvania.

Ralston Purina is founded by William H. Danforth, who will write a book titled *I Dare You.*

Union Station opens at Eighteenth and Market Streets, occupying part of Chouteau's Pond.

1895 November 4. Eugene Field dies in his Chicago home.

1896 May 19. Kate Field dies while on assignment in Hawaii.

1897 September 3. Sally Benson is born in St. Louis.

1898 Ralston Purina's Checkerboard Square building is constructed on the site of Kate Chopin's place of birth.

Winston Churchill publishes his first novel, *The Celebrity.*

Paul Elmer More publishes his first book, *A Century of Indian Epigrams Chiefly From the Sanskrit of Bhartrihari.*

1899 Kate Chopin's novel *The Awakening* is published.

1900 Theodore Dreiser publishes *Sister Carrie.*

John Neihardt self-publishes *Divine Enchantment*, a book of poems.

1902 University City is founded by Edward Gardner Lewis.

1903 June 4. Samuel Clemens receives an honorary degree from the University of Missouri–Columbia. On his return trip he stops at St. Louis to participate in ground-breaking ceremonies for the 1904 World's Fair.

1904 April 30. The Louisiana Purchase Exposition opens.

August 20. Kate Chopin dies at her home in St. Louis. The requiem mass takes place at the New Cathedral on August 24.

Thomas Wolfe moves with his family to St. Louis, where they remain until 1906.

The Phyllis Wheatley Branch of the YWCA, a segregated facility, is opened on Garrison Avenue in honor of the former slave turned poet. (Her name was actually spelled Phillis.) This moves in 1912 to 2709 Locust Street, which has since closed.

Charlotte Stearns Eliot publishes her first book, *William Greenleaf Eliot: Minister, Educator, Philanthropist.*

1905 January 14. Emily Hahn is born in St. Louis.

Zoë Akins leaves St. Louis for New York.

The Eliot family moves to 4446 Westminster and resides there until 1919. Tom Eliot leaves St. Louis to attend Milton Academy. A year later he will enter Harvard.

1906 May 14. Carl Schurz dies in New York.

1907 Sara Teasdale publishes her first book, *Sonnets to Duse and Other Poems.*

John Neihardt publishes a book of poems, *A Bundle of Myrrh*, and a collection of short stories, *The Lonesome Trail.*

1908 April 4. The cornerstone is laid for the home of The Wednesday Club at Taylor and Washington Avenues, a building designed by Theodore Link, architect of Union Station.

July 4. Joseph Stanley Pennell is born in Junction City, Kansas.

November 8. Martha Gellhorn is born in St. Louis.

1909 March 26. Tennessee Williams is born in Columbus, Mississippi.

July 29. Chester Himes is born in Jefferson City.

November 5. William T. Harris dies in Providence, Rhode Island.

November 9. Kay Thompson is born in St. Louis.

1910 April 21. Samuel Clemens dies after viewing Halley's Comet at Stormfield, New York, and is buried in Elmira. Mark Twain lives on.

June 20. Josephine Johnson is born in Kirkwood.

Fannie Hurst leaves St. Louis for New York.

1911 October 29. Joseph Pulitzer dies on his yacht off the South Carolina coast. Joseph Pulitzer II inherits the *St. Louis Post-Dispatch*.

1912 April 8. Joseph Everett Mitchell registers the name for the weekly *St. Louis Argus*, the first black newspaper in Missouri and one of the oldest in the United States.

Central Public Library unveils its new building at 1301 Olive Street, designed by Cass Gilbert.

The Sheldon Memorial is built and named for Walter L. Sheldon, founder of the Ethical Society in St. Louis.

Zoë Akins publishes her first book, *Interpretations: A Book of First Poems*.

1913 May 3. William Inge is born in Independence, Kansas.

May 30. *The Mirror* becomes *Reedy's Mirror*.

July 8. Patience Worth is born in St. Louis.

Jefferson Memorial Building, a gift from the World's Fair and the home of the Missouri Historical Society, opens in Forest Park.

1914 February 5. William S. Burroughs is born in St. Louis.

May 29-31. A Pageant and Masque is held in Forest Park to mark the one

hundred fiftieth anniversary of the founding of St. Louis.

Fannie Hurst publishes her first book, *Just Around the Corner*.

T. S. Eliot's *Prufrock and Other Observations*, his first book of poems, is published.

1917 Orrick Johns publishes his first book, *Asphalt and Other Poems*.

Patience Worth publishes her first book, *The Sorry Tale: A Story of the Time of Christ*.

1918 July. Tennessee Williams arrives in St. Louis with his mother, Miss Edwina.

Sara Teasdale receives the Pulitzer Prize in Poetry for *Love Songs*.

1919 January 7. Henry Ware Eliot dies in St. Louis.

December 4. The *St. Louis Republic*, which began as the *Missouri Gazette* in 1808, publishes its final issue, marking the end of America's longest-running newspaper. Its last owner was David R. Francis.

1920 July 28. William Marion Reedy dies in San Francisco.

Summer. Emily Hahn moves with her family to Chicago.

1921 *Poems*, Marianne Moore's first book, is published by her friends.

1922 Theodore Dreiser's *A Book About Myself* is published.

1923 October 12. John Burroughs School, one of St. Louis's first private coeducational high schools, opens in St. Louis County. Martha Gellhorn's mother, Edna, is one of its founders.

Chester Himes and his family move to St. Louis, where they remain until 1925.

1924	November 9. *Amerika* ceases publication.		Emily Hahn publishes her first book, *Seductio ad Absurdum: The Principles and Practices of Seduction—A Beginner's Handbook.*
1926	June. Emily Hahn moves back to St. Louis to work for McBride Incorporated, a lead and zinc mining company.	1931	Irma Rombauer self-publishes *The Joy of Cooking* in St. Louis.
	Charlotte Eliot publishes her dramatic poem *Savonarola*, with an introduction by her son, T. S. Eliot.	1932	William S. Burroughs leaves St. Louis to attend Harvard.
	John Neihardt becomes book editor of the *St. Louis Post-Dispatch.*	1933	January. Sara Teasdale is found dead in the bathtub of her New York home. Her death is ruled accidental, though widely thought to be by her own hand.
	Peter Taylor's family moves to St. Louis from Nashville, Tennessee, to stay until 1932.	1934	September 13. Josephine Johnson publishes *Now in November*, her first book.
	The Wednesday Club establishes its annual poetry contest.	1935	Zoë Akins receives the Pulitzer Prize in Drama for *The Old Maid.*
	Charles Lindbergh moves to St. Louis to work for Robertson Aircraft Corporation.		Josephine Johnson receives the Pulitzer Prize in Fiction for *Now in November.*
1927	May 21. Charles Lindbergh flies *The Spirit of St. Louis* on the first solo flight across the Atlantic.		Thomas Wolfe returns to visit his old home at 5095 Cates Avenue in St. Louis.
	Emily Hahn leaves St. Louis for New Mexico.	1936	Tennessee Williams enrolls at Washington University.
	T. S. Eliot becomes a British subject.		*The Joy of Cooking* by Irma Rombauer is published by Bobbs-Merrill.
1928	March 17. The weekly *St. Louis American*, the second-oldest black-owned newspaper in St. Louis, is founded by A. N. Johnson.		Martha Gellhorn publishes her first book, *The Trouble I've Seen.*
	Reinhold Niebuhr publishes his first book, *Does Civilization Need Religion?*	1937	March 9. Paul Elmer More dies in Princeton, New Jersey.
1929	September 10. Charlotte Stearns Eliot dies in Cambridge, Massachusetts.		November 15. Pearl Curran dies in Los Angeles. So does Patience Worth.
	Sara Teasdale divorces Ernst Filsinger and moves to New York.		Orrick Johns publishes his autobiography, *Time of Our Lives.*
	Thomas Wolfe publishes his first book, *Look Homeward, Angel.*		Sara Teasdale's *Collected Poems*, edited by Margaret Conklin and John Hall Wheelock, is published posthumously.
1930	October 25. Harold Brodkey is born in Staunton, Illinois.		Shirley Seifert publishes her first historical novel, *Land of Tomorrow.*

1938 June. Benjamin Thomas founds the weekly *Evening Whirl,* but none too meekly, as it becomes, as far as we know, the only rhyming newspaper under the sun.

September 15. Thomas Wolfe dies at Johns Hopkins Hospital in Baltimore, Maryland.

Fannie Cook publishes her first novel, *The Hills Grow Steeper.*

1939 Shirley Seifert's 1938 novel, *The Wayfarer,* is nominated for a Pulitzer Prize.

The *Westliche Post* ceases publication.

1943 William Inge arrives in St. Louis to become drama critic of the *St. Louis Star-Times.*

1944 Chester Himes publishes his first novel, *If He Hollers Let Him Go.*

Joseph Stanley Pennell publishes his first novel, *The History of Rome Hanks and Kindred Matters.*

1945 December 28. Theodore Dreiser dies in Hollywood, California.

1946 July 8. Orrick Johns dies by his own hand in Danbury, Connecticut.

Fannie Cook publishes *Mrs. Palmer's Honey,* which wins the George Washington Carver Award.

1947 March 12. Winston Churchill dies in Winter Park, Florida.

Harold Brodkey graduates from University City High School and leaves St. Louis to attend Harvard.

Jarvis Thurston and Mona Van Duyn launch *Perspective* at Washington University and feature the work of Stanley Elkin, John Gardner, John Morris, Howard Nemerov and Constance Urdang, among others. The journal ceases publication in 1982.

Josephine Johnson moves to Cincinnati, Ohio.

1948 T. S. Eliot receives the Nobel Prize for Literature.

Tennessee Williams receives the Pulitzer Prize in Drama for *A Streetcar Named Desire.*

1949 August 25. Fannie Cook dies at her home in University City.

1951 The *Star* and *Times* newspapers fold after uniting briefly.

1952 Marianne Moore receives the Pulitzer Prize in Poetry, National Book Award, and the Bollingen Prize for *Collected Poems.*

1953 William Inge receives the Pulitzer Prize in Drama for *Picnic.*

T. S. Eliot addresses Washington University on the centenary of its founding by his grandfather.

Junkie by William S. Burroughs, his first book, is published under the pen name of William Lee. (The unexpurgated version is published in 1977 under the title *Junky.*)

1954 Charles Lindbergh receives the Pulitzer Prize in Biography for his autobiography, *The Spirit of St. Louis.*

1955 Tennessee Williams receives the Pulitzer Prize in Drama for *Cat on a Hot Tin Roof.*

Kay Thompson publishes her first book, *Eloise.*

1958 October 29. Zoë Akins dies in Pasadena, California.

First Love and Other Sorrows, Harold Brodkey's first book, is published.

1959 William S. Burroughs publishes *Naked Lunch,* his first book under his own name, in Paris.

1960 Constance Urdang moves to St. Louis.

Stanley Elkin moves to St. Louis to join the faculty of the Department of English at Washington University.

1962 October 14. Irma Rombauer dies in St. Louis.

Naked Lunch by William S. Burroughs is published in the United States.

1963 September 26. Joseph Stanley Pennell dies in Portland, Oregon.

Stanley Elkin publishes his first book, *Boswell, A Modern Comedy.*

1965 January 4. T. S. Eliot dies in London and is buried at the Church of St. Michael in East Coker.

Constance Urdang publishes her first book of poems, *Charades and Celebrations.*

1967 January 4. A stone is unveiled as a memorial to T. S. Eliot in Poet's Corner, Westminster Abbey, on the second anniversary of his death.

John Morris moves to St. Louis to join the Department of English at Washington University.

1968 February 23. Fannie Hurst dies in New York City.

1969 Howard Nemerov moves to St. Louis to become the first Fannie Hurst Visiting Professor in English at Washington University.

1970 Emily Hahn publishes *Times and Places,* a memoir-like collection of writings.

1971 June 1. Reinhold Neibuhr dies in New York City.

September 1. Shirley Seifert dies in Kirkwood.

1972 February 5. Marianne Moore dies in Brooklyn, New York.

July 19. Sally Benson dies in Woodland Hills, California.

1973 June 10. William Inge dies of carbon monoxide poisoning in California. His death is ruled a suicide.

November 3. John G. Neihardt dies in Columbia, Missouri.

Josephine Johnson publishes her autobiography, *Seven Houses: A Memoir of Time and Places.*

The Wednesday Club moves to its new building on Ladue Road.

1974 August 26. Charles Lindbergh dies in Hana, on the Hawaiian island of Maui.

1978 Howard Nemerov wins the Pulitzer Prize and the National Book Award for *The Collected Poems of Howard Nemerov.*

1980 December 31. Marshall McLuhan dies in Toronto.

1981 Howard Nemerov receives the Bollingen Prize for Poetry.

1983 February 25. Tennessee Williams dies in New York City.

Stanley Elkin receives the National Book Critics Circle Award for *George Mills,* published in 1982.

1984 November 12. Chester Himes dies in Moraira, Spain.

1985 *Queer* by William S. Burroughs is published. It was originally written in 1952.

1986 October 26. The *St. Louis Globe-Democrat* ceases publication, leaving only one daily newspaper, the *St. Louis Post-Dispatch.*

1987 Howard Nemerov receives the National Medal for the Arts in Poetry from President Ronald Reagan.

Peter Taylor wins the Pulitzer Prize in Fiction for *A Summons to Memphis.*

1988 Howard Nemerov becomes poet laureate of the United States.

1989 T. S. Eliot, Charles Lindbergh, Joseph Pulitzer and Tennessee Williams receive stars on the St. Louis Walk of Fame.

1990 February 27. Josephine Johnson dies in Cincinnati, Ohio.

William S. Burroughs, Kate Chopin, Ulysses S. Grant and Howard Nemerov receive stars on the St. Louis Walk of Fame.

1991 July 5. Howard Nemerov dies at his home in University City.

Stanley Elkin and Eugene Field receive stars on the Walk of Fame.

1992 Elijah Lovejoy receives a star on the Walk of Fame.

1994 November 2. Peter Taylor dies in Charlottesville, Virginia.

Sara Teasdale receives a star on the Walk of Fame.

1995 May 31. Stanley Elkin dies at Barnes Hospital in St. Louis.

William Inge receives a star on the Walk of Fame.

Stanley Elkin's *Mrs. Ted Bliss* is published posthumously.

John Morris retires from Washington University and moves to North Carolina.

1996 January 26. Harold Brodkey dies in New York City.

October 8. Constance Urdang dies in St. Louis.

Marianne Moore receives a star on the Walk of Fame.

Stanley Elkin's *Mrs. Ted Bliss* receives the National Book Critics Circle Award for Fiction.

1997 February 18. Emily Hahn dies in New York City.

1998 February 15. Martha Gellhorn dies in London.

July 2. Kay Thompson dies in New York City.

August 2. William S. Burroughs dies in Lawrence, Kansas.

November 25. John Morris dies in Pittsboro, North Carolina.

Irma Rombauer receives a star on the Walk of Fame.

1999 October 29. Tennessee Williams is inducted into the University City High School Hall of Fame.

2000 William T. Sherman receives a star on the Walk of Fame.

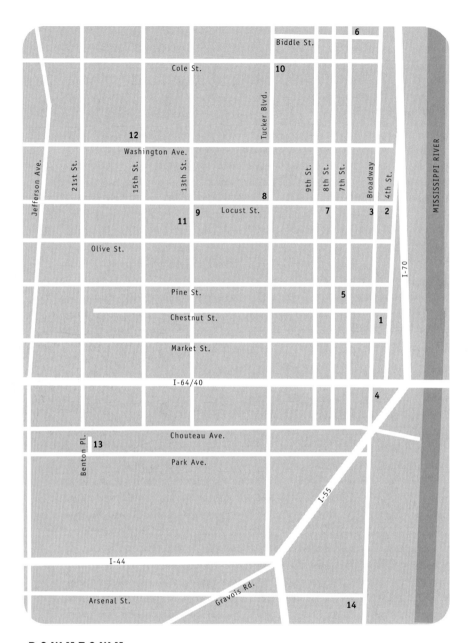

DOWNTOWN

1   Old Courthouse, 11 North Fourth Street—Joseph Pulitzer
2   Security Building, 319 North Fourth Street—Winston Churchill, WIlliam Marion Reedy
3   Mercantile Library, 501 Locust Street—Kate Chopin, William Marion Reedy, William T. Sherman
4   Eugene Field House, 634 South Broadway—Eugene Field
5   Wainwright Building, 708 Pine Street—Theodore Dreiser
6   Neighborhood Gardens, 1213 North Seventh Street—William Inge
7   Old Post Office, Eighth, Ninth, Olive and Locust Streets—Zoë Akins, Orrick Johns
8   Hotel Jefferson, Tucker Boulevard and Locust Streets—Theodore Dreiser, Tennessee Williams
9   Christ Church Cathedral, 1210 Locust Street—T. S. Eliot
10 *St. Louis Post-Dispatch*, 900 North Tucker Boulevard—John Neihardt
11 St. Louis Public Library, 1310 Olive Street—T. S. ELiot, WIlliam Marion Reedy, Mark Twain
12 1501–1509 Washington Boulevard (formerly International Shoe Company)—Tennessee Williams
13 30 Benton Place—Zoë Akins
14 Camp Jackson Memorial, South Broadway and Arsenal Street—Heinrich Börnstein

Early visitors to St. Louis would arrive by river, either carried by the Mississippi, like so much debris down from the north, or on a boat

out of breath after entering it from the Ohio and laboriously climbing the water up from Cairo, or more rarely after puffing the whole slow way from New Orleans—then a long journey. Unlike many catch-as-catch-can Creole villages they might camp in along the way, they would find a town with the design of a dream, laid out by Pierre Laclède at the edge of the easiest landing in a grid that trudged west through a series of short modest streets (that became Walnut, Chestnut, Pine) while crossing three wider ones that ran, like the towpath did, the same way the water went—streets named for their function, as was the sensible habit of the time (Church, Barn, Main).

It didn't take many new arrivals to double St. Louis's population—in 1773 it was 444 plus 193 slaves, not counting Indians—but the city was ideally located and the vibrant center of the fur trade. Moreover, after General Jackson's victory at the battle of New Orleans had reassured settlers that their lands were more or less secure, the first great wave of immigration would swell the city's census in 1820 to 4,598. By 1870 St. Louis could lay a fraudulent though plausible claim to be the fourth largest city—

1

following New York, Philadelphia and Brooklyn—while in a hundred years it would genuinely be counted the eighth largest in the nation.

There were many tales told in the struggling young outpost of the wild west—tales tall or otherwise—since the Kansas Indians would come to St. Louis on occasion to trade and to tourist, as well as mountain men to carouse, and missionaries to equip themselves for their journeys. Nevertheless, the export of literature was unlikely since most of the city's citizens couldn't write. Meriwether Lewis—who could, and would prove it through countless letters and meticulous journals—paid his compliments to Don Carlos Duhault Delassus, the Spanish commandant of St. Louis, on December 8, 1803. Through interpreters, Lewis was politely denied permission to travel up the Missouri, although higher authorities might grant passage later if properly approached. While Lewis literally cooled his heels in St. Louis through the winter, he sought out the local citizens whose knowledge of the Louisiana Territory would be most useful to him: the surveyor Antoine Soulard and the trader Auguste Chouteau, among others. He also gathered information by questionnaire, a very contemporary method whose novelty might have been one reason for its success.

The complex transfer of power, first from the Spanish to the French and then from the French to the Americans, on account of the Louisiana Purchase, appeared to remove Spanish reservations about Lewis and Clark's proposed journey; however, in Spanish eyes, the Louisiana sale looked a whole lot smaller than it did to Jefferson whose eyes grew big whenever they looked west. Nevertheless, ignorant of Spain's concerns, including the plots and sly connivance of its representatives, William Clark was able to push off by the middle of May 1804 on his and Lewis's great journal-engendering trek. What merely happens on the trail—an overturned canoe, for instance—will fade and disappear into the stream of time just as the contents of the canoe were swallowed by the water, but not the resulting narrative: the story will be read with anguish, excitement, and instruction for centuries after.

2

Other visitors, who would see to it that their travels survived in books, like the Belgian-born Pierre Jean DeSmet, first came to St. Louis to serve his Lord. He spent his novitiate in Florissant, Missouri, and was ordained in 1827. Two Flathead Indians who journeyed a long way to the settlement, because their tribe wanted a Black Robe (a Jesuit) to minister to them and save their souls, asked DeSmet to go to Montana and Idaho where they hunted—a request he fulfilled perhaps more thoroughly than the pair might have imagined. DeSmet has a high school named for him in St. Louis, but he gave his blessing to an entire town in South Dakota. Out of a life spent in the harsh wilderness of the West, DeSmet produced his widely esteemed historical books about its geography, its fickle climate, the customs of its Indian inhabitants, and the travails and triumphs of the Church's missions.

Like Lewis, Clark and DeSmet, we can say that Lieutenant John Charles Fremont got his start in St. Louis. Recently married to Jessie, daughter of Missouri senator Thomas Hart Benton, and charged by the Corps of Engineers, he arrived in St. Louis on May 22, 1842, to collect provisions and personnel for the first of his five expeditions to the Rocky Mountains, Oregon and California. Among the party was Charles Preuss, who would sketch the topographical features of the country, a hunter named Maxwell, Kit Carson, the famous guide, as well as Auguste Chouteau who would ceremonially lead them a little way out of St. Louis.

In addition to knowledge of the country, fame for Fremont, and hardship for all, these adventures through Fremont's notes and his wife Jessie's pen, yielded prose of great satisfaction and considerable information. Here is a description of the flowering prairie:

> Along our route the *amorpha* [false indigo] has been in very abundant but variable bloom—in some places, bending beneath the weight of purple clusters; in others, without a flower. It seems to love best the sunny slopes, with a dark soil and southern exposure. Everywhere the rose is met with, and reminds us of cultivated gardens and civilization. It is scattered over the prairies in small bouquets, and, when glittering in the dews and waving in the pleasant breeze of the early morning, is the most beautiful of the prairie flowers. The *artemisia*, absinthe, or prairie sage, as it is variously called, is increasing in size, and glitters like silver, as the southern breeze turns up its

leaves to the sun. All these plants have their insect inhabitants, variously colored; taking generally the hue of the flower on which they live. The *artemisia* [also called wormwood] has its small fly accompanying it through every change of elevation and latitude; and wherever I have seen the *asclepias tuberosa* [butterfly weed], I have always remarked, too, on the flower a large butterfly, so nearly resembling it in color, as to be distinguishable at a little distance only by the motion of its wings.

The Planter's House was the hotel of choice for St. Louis's visitors, although Charles Dickens thought its long whitewashed halls resembled London's Middlesex Hospital when he made his visit in April of 1842. Dickens was delighted by the room service, however, especially the abundance of the food. "The inns in these outlandish corners of the world would astonish you by their goodness. . . . They had a famous notion of sending up at breakfast-time large glasses of new milk with blocks of ice in them as clear as crystal. Our table was abundantly supplied indeed at every meal. One day, when Kate and I were dining alone together, in our own room, we counted sixteen dishes on the table at the same time." In the bustling hotel bar, where the famous punch had been concocted, political and business deals were regularly consummated.

3

Dickens was not going to be spared the city's April mud, and the river was swollen and dark. Between lectures, he was taken to swank parties and escorted through the city like a diplomat. He was also given a whirlwind tour of the city's most impressive and (at his insistence) unsavory sites. He visited the St. Francis Xavier Cathedral and witnessed the poor sanitary conditions of East St. Louis. After a day of sightseeing in the French Quarter and viewing the wharves and warehouses in the newer, strictly American sections of the city, Dickens expressed an interest in seeing a bit of the great American plains. An overnight expedition was promptly arranged to the Looking Glass Prairie outside of Lebanon, Illinois. By the time Dickens arrived in St. Louis, which was the final stopping point of his 1842 lecture tour, he had already formed his opinion of Americans—"intensified bores." But among his party to the prairie was William Greenleaf Eliot, a man Dickens managed to admire: "a gentleman of great worth and excellence." On the whole, though, Dickens found us "pretty rough and intolerably conceited. All the inhabitants are young. *I didn't see one grey head in St. Louis.*"

On the way, Dickens crossed the Mississippi by ferry, judging the "hateful river" to be a "dismal swamp . . . a slimy monster hideous to behold," but he was intrigued by the stories he was told about "Bloody Island," which he passed midstream, a popular site for duels because it escaped the legal jurisdictions of both Illinois and Missouri. He was then escorted through Belleville where he had lunch and was ogled by the unimpressed locals, who found his "face and nose profusely ornamented with the stings of mosquitoes and the bites of bugs." The "intensified bores" seemed to have their

own opinions. After Lebanon, Dickens reached the Looking Glass Prairie in time to enjoy the sunset.

Dickens carried about with him an always active social conscience, though he claimed that the arguments concerning slavery he found himself engaged in were forced upon him by his hosts, and in St. Louis he was particularly exasperated by a judge who dared to pity England's ignorance of the subject. "They say the slaves are fond of their masters," Dickens wrote to his friend John Forster, practicing his sarcasm: that was why the newspapers were full of advertisements for runaway slaves; why nine out of ten such notices described the sought-after slave as chained, manacled, mutilated, maimed or branded; "and of course their attachment to us grows out of their deep devotion to their owners."

When Dickens published *American Notes*, the *New York Herald* called it "the essence of balderdash," but that was hardly more than a drop in the storm of indignation that blew from the press. South Carolina considered banning the book (it was the slavery issue again), and lies worthy of a novelist were invented to defame Dickens. During the tour his celebrity had been unmatched, and the adulation he received was greater than any citizen or foreigner had been granted before. His own mood, when he returned, was euphoric; that is, it was until he read the newspapers. He had complained, while here, that American copyright laws were allowing reprint publishers to enrich themselves at his expense. Dickens was "a mere mercenary scoundrel," our press replied, and this quarrel over money darkened Dickens's heart, changed his mind and poisoned his pen.

If Mark Twain, Matthew Arnold, Oscar Wilde and Charles Dickens came to town it wasn't to admire the Indian Mounds, it was to make money. William Makepeace Thackeray, hearing about steamboats blowing up or running aground, at first declined to visit, but he eventually came anyway, spoke at the Mercantile as most did, and took home a handsome fee.

If Dickens's estimate of us in *American Notes* was disagreeable, the American chapters of *Martin Chuzzlewit* were venomous against New York. About St. Louis Dickens concluded:

> No man ever admits the unhealthiness of the place he dwells in (unless he is going away from it), and I shall therefore, I have no doubt, be at issue with the inhabitants of St. Louis in questioning the perfect salubrity of its climate, and in hinting that I think it must rather dispose to fever in the summer and autumnal seasons. Just adding, that it is very hot, lies among great rivers, and has vast tracts of undrained swampy land around it, I leave the reader to form his own opinion.

Prescient if not profound, Dickens's diagnosis would prove true just a few years later—a cholera epidemic ravaged St. Louis in 1849, claiming thousands of lives.

Francis Parkman was in and out of town during April of 1846, and just missed the disease, which had already swung its scythe through the city in 1832, when it had come, like a regular visitor, through Pittsburgh and Cincinnati down the Ohio to Cairo. The miss was more than fortunate, since Parkman was making the journey west (fresh out of Harvard) with the hope of improving his health, which was frail. Parkman was neither a missionary nor a member of the military, but he found his guide for the Oregon Trail in St. Louis as his predecessors had. That guide was a mountain man named Henry Chatillon, whom Parkman came to admire greatly and whom he returned to St. Louis to visit in Carondelet a few years later:

> When we were at St. Louis, several gentlemen of the Fur Company had kindly offered to procure for us a hunter and guide suited for our purposes, and on coming one afternoon to the office, we found there a tall and exceedingly well-dressed man, with a face so open and frank that it attracted our notice at once. We were surprised at being told that it was he who wished to guide us to the mountains. He was born in a little French town near St. Louis, and from the age of fifteen years had been constantly in the neighborhood of the Rocky Mountains, employed for the most part by the company, to supply their forts with buffalo meat. As a hunter he had but one rival in the whole region, a man named Simoneau, with whom, to the honor of both of them, he was on terms of the closest friendship. He had arrived in St. Louis the day before, from the mountains, where he had been for four years; and he now asked only to go and spend a day with his mother, before setting out on another expedition. His age was about thirty; he was six feet high, and very powerfully and gracefully moulded. The prairies had been his school; he could neither read nor write, but he had a natural refinement and delicacy of mind, such as is rare even in women.... He had, moreover, a keen perception of character, and a tact that would preserve him from flagrant error in any society.... No better evidence of the intrepidity of his temper could be asked, than the common report that he had killed more than thirty grizzly bears. He was proof of what unaided nature will sometimes do. I have never, in the city or in the wilderness, met a better man than my true-hearted friend, Henry Chatillon.

When Parkman got back to Boston he collapsed; his eyesight, always weak, almost wholly failed; and he had to dictate *The Oregon Trail* from his amazing memory and messy notes. The only other dictated books associated with St. Louis are those of Patience Worth.

Cholera was St. Louis's evil companion, a by-product of its growth, and the most deadly years for the disease were 1832-33 when upwards of 280 died, and in 1849 when the first cases appeared in January, the sickness soon showing a virulence that gradually grew till 145 corpses were counted in one July day and 722 for a whole week. No U.S. city was harder hit. Again, though poor sanitation and St. Louis's notorious drinking water sustained it, immigrants had brought it—the famous Forty-Eighters, Germans mostly, and some Dutch—and they were its principal victims. Cholera came another time, in 1850-51, killing 1,728; then, in the aftermath of the Civil War, in 1866, 3,527 died.

Improvements on the sewer system were undertaken, but nothing, it seemed, would improve the disposition of the city's citizens. In 1849, this watershed year, there were serious riots and a great fire, too. Catastrophe ran after catastrophe as if there were a race to reach perdition. These were, in a way, land and water wars: the natives who owned land and had deep roots and settled ways were against the water-borne arrivals. They welcomed their labor, which was cheap and needed. If only they didn't bring their revolting views and customs with them. And their diseases.

The city was essentially a harbor. The long lines of four-stacker steamboats, though besmirching the sky, managed to look picturesque, bustling and drowsily monstrous all at once. The 1849 fire began on the steamer

5

White Cloud and then spread to other boats, twenty-three altogether. The goods stacked on the landing began to smoke, the shanties on Front Street went up like the kindling they resembled; next, the buildings on Main Street caught because a strong wind blew the entire night, then those on Second, Market, Elm, Myrtle, Locust and Olive. Fire breaks were created by blowing up yet other structures.

Riots continued off and on (as is the nature of riots) through the fifties, but the Nativist Riot of 1854 surpassed itself in stupid carnage and brutality. Irish arrivals had tended to slide north upriver from the landing, while the Germans collected in the south. They frequently took to bashing one another. On this hot election August, however, the Protestants who felt they owned the city and tried to control the polling places were incited by an Irish knifing. Soon the Irish were being besieged in their saloons, Saint Louis University was surrounded, and the offices of the *Anzeiger des Westens* attacked.

Reporting the lynchings, the arsons, the demagoguery and the strife were the newspapers where many of the writers mentioned in this volume would work; the newspapers that incited hate, misreported many events and tried to suppress public knowledge of others; the newspapers, fearless and cowardly, partisan and public spirited, greedy and charitable, that poured paragraphs at one another like pitch and drew up their rhetoric like men in ranks.

During the Civil War these religious and ethnic antagonisms redefined themselves, mostly in terms of allegiance to the Union and attitudes toward slavery. After the war the Eads Bridge was built, reattaching Missouri to the nation and redefining the river for the city. Barge and boat traffic had been seriously disrupted, and, as Mark Twain observed, would never be the same again. The romance of the river, even for writers, was on the wane.

One admirer of the Eads Bridge was Walt Whitman, who stayed at the home of his brother, Thomas J. Whitman, for three months during 1879. Thomas was an engineer for the St. Louis Water Department and had designed the spectacular water tower on North Grand, completed in 1871. "I have haunted the river every night lately," Whitman wrote, "where I could get a look at the bridge by moonlight. It is indeed a structure of perfection and beauty unsurpassable, and I never tire of it." The journal notes the poet kept while in the city were published in 1882 in *Specimen Days*. Whitman remarked on the bad water, as so many visitors did, but judged the wine to be "very fair" and the beer, found in "inexhaustible quantities . . . the best . . . in the world." He continued:

> The points of St. Louis are its position, its absolute wealth, (the long accumulations of time and trade, solid riches, probably a higher average thereof than any city,) the unrivall'd amplitude of its well-laid out environage of broad plateaus, for future expansion—and the great State of which it is the head. It fuses northern and southern qualities, perhaps native and foreign ones, to perfection, rendezvous the whole stretch of Mississippi and Missouri River, and its American electricity goes well with its German phlegm.

In 1892 the Eads Bridge would have its painter. Frederick Oakes Sylvester was twenty-three when he arrived in St. Louis from New England to become the art director for the newly built Central High School. He gave instruction there as well as at Principia, a new school founded in 1898, where Sylvester taught art in the late afternoons, following his other classes, until 1915. He began his studies of the river and its bridge shortly after leaving New Orleans for St. Louis.

> Then I came to St. Louis. St. Louis hardly knew there was a river. What it knew was that there was an evil-smelling stream lapping along the Levee and that it was muddy, treacherous and unsightly. I was laughed at when I began to paint it as I saw it. Cornoyer [a fellow painter] had told me that no one would buy a painting of a Mississippi River scene. St. Louis seemed to be ashamed of the stream.

During the terrible tornado that struck the city in 1896, destroying much of Lafayette Square, Sylvester nearly lost his "motif," because the great wind gave Eads's engineering its severest test, blowing away three hundred feet of its eastern approach.

Although renderings of the Mississippi stirred little public interest, one of Sylvester's post-impressionist paintings of the river won a medal at the 1904 World's Fair. He was a far better painter than a poet, but poetry was also a passion, and he published two books of his own Arts and Crafts design. The first was *Verses* from 1908, and the last was *The Great River*, 1911.

Well enough known in the city as an educator to have his caricature appear in William Marion Reedy's *Mirror*, Sylvester frequently complained that the Museum of Fine Arts did not sufficiently support local artists. This was true, Halsey Ives, the director, said, because St. Louis artists "counted for nothing, had done nothing and are nothing; and . . . the purchase of a picture from an artist is an act of charity." Sylvester responded in verse:

> **Everywhere within this town**
> **The Guild starts kicking its art around.**
> **It makes no difference if it ain't quite sound,**
> **It's gotta quit kicking its art around.**

Easily the most important St. Louis painter of his period, with skills growing in sophistication, Sylvester died of pneumonia at the age of forty-five, and an important connection between painting, poetry and place was prematurely lost.

Walt Whitman was not well-enough known to be asked to lecture at the Mercantile Library, but it was, for downtown and for a long time, the focus for literary and intellectual activity in St. Louis. All over America for many years, in small towns and large, there were platforms from which humorists, moralists, adventurers, sages and other notable public figures described, amused, admonished and explained things. Even the most modest farming communities liked to boast an opera house often built between the hardware and the feed store. So everyone could measure the height of its civic stature, the appellation, OPERA HOUSE, was often painted in big bold yellow letters on its roof. In addition to Jenny Lind and assorted preachers, speakers on scientific oddities were sought, and in more populated, less distant places, it was customary for the speaker to move almost daily from town to town giving one lecture or reading in each locale; but "because St. Louis was the one place in Missouri for lecturing (Bayard Taylor called the rest of the state 'the Missouri wilds'), it had to give those lecturers who visited it unusually firm support," according to Carl Bode in *The American Lyceum*.

The lyceum system (organizations that sponsor cultural presentations to the community, and named for the grove in whose shade Aristotle paced while he lectured) began to flourish after 1828, and the immediate merit of its offerings was the relief they provided from political argumentation, for such partisan and inflammatory subjects were banned by common consent. A spirit of optimism—a widespread belief in the educability of man, that education should be open to all—persisted for decades until it was dampened if not quashed by the Civil War.

6. *Mercantile Library, 510 Locust Street, 1892*

The movement began in New England—in Salem, Concord, Boston— and sank to New York before heading west. In Boston alone, during the winter of 1837-38, twenty-six courses of lectures (at least eight sessions for each course) were delivered to a total attendance of thirteen thousand. Then churches, clubs, societies of all sorts, began to do the same; finally, individuals—professors, phrenologists, mesmerizers, every kind of quack— would simply hire a hall, sell tickets, promote their passion, hope to have an audience and make a profit. It was the era of the lecture slam.

The Franklin Society, dedicated to the useful arts, opened in Philadelphia in 1824, and the American Lyceum was organized in 1831. At the heart of their activities was the acquisition of books and the establishment of a library. The St. Louis Lyceum, which was active by 1832, had a collection of "Indian curiosities," and it sponsored addresses on Indian history, which it managed to publish in due course. After a few years the organization was allowed to languish, but it was revived in 1838. "Its object was 'the intellectual improvement of its members by means of debates, essays, and lectures.' Early lecture topics included 'The Age of Physical Science,' 'Scepticism,' 'Geology,' and 'The Peculiarities of American Character and Duty of American Citizens.' Science was always the most popular subject, followed by travel, history and what the St. Louis Lyceum called 'morality.'"

The Franklin Society had a short life, but it was made notable through a speech by the Reverend William Greenleaf Eliot, founder of Washington University, which caused quite a stir when it was given in 1835. His topic was "The Obligation Which Rests upon the Present Generation to Establish Literary Institutions in the West." Eliot flirted with an idea popular in some circles right up to the Civil War that Missouri and its river valley comprised a kind of great nation in itself and could be a mediator between east and south, possessing their virtues without paying for them with their customary sins and corruptions. (Actually, it became a battlefield.) This goal could be attained only through education.

> If lyceums or literary societies were erected throughout the West, in every considerable village, they would excite many a young man to obtain a solid, useful education; they would exert a purifying influence upon public morals and tastes, and serve to remind many who are engrossed in money-getting that they have an intellectual treasure within them which ought not to be entirely forgotten.

To St. Louis, Ralph Waldo Emerson had blazed a trail, though at first it was a tentative one. On his return from a lecture tour in 1850, Emerson put up at the Planter's House, only to find the guests dying of cholera. Prudence put him on a boat to Galena upriver in Illinois, but the plague pursued him on board and flourished during the four-day journey. During another stay in 1852, however, he gave six lectures at the Mercantile Library on "The Conduct of Life" and then threw in one more talk on "Anglo-Saxon." In the president's report for 1853, Emerson was said to be "one of the best furnished literary men of America"—a description more appropriate, perhaps, for a drawing room.

"'The lyceum is my pulpit,' Emerson once said. . . . When Starr King was asked what he lectured for he answered 'FAME—Fifty And My Expenses.' . . . Oliver Wendell Holmes remarked to Herman Melville and some others that 'a lecturer was a literary strumpet, subject for a greater than whore's fee to prostitute himself,'" Carl Bode reports.

The St. Louis Mercantile Library Association had received its charter in 1846. After a few rough years its lecture series began to flourish, and though, in the 1850s, the YMCA began to offer its own programs, the library was soon not only attracting many important figures, it was also turning a profit. Due in part to the energetic efforts of its founder, James E. Yeatman, it acquired 2,282 volumes and as many members as days in that first year. In 1854 it boasted a new building at Fifth and Locust Streets. By then its membership had grown to 944 and the number of its books to 10,565. When economies forced the library, in 1998, to move to new quarters on the campus of the University of Missouri–St. Louis, it held a priceless store.

The library has been blessed by librarians who served there for a long time, and it is from them (William Henry Harrison Anderson, sixty years, and Clarence E. Miller, fifty-five years) that we learn that although William T. Sherman donated valuable books to the library he frequently asked for their return when the volumes he presently wanted were not made immediately available; that James Eads insisted that the library purchase books

only he would ever read; that Carl Schurz treated Mr. Anderson as though he were deaf; that Denton Snider and William Harris insisted on discussing philosophical obscurities at the issue-desk, thereby holding up the loan line; that William Reedy was regarded as the country's handsomest fat man.

7

Among the writers on the circuit who lectured at the Mercantile were Henry Ward Beecher, Horace Greeley, Bret Harte, Gerald Massey, Harriet Beecher Stowe, William Makepiece Thackeray, Artemus Ward and Oscar Wilde.

A civic boosterism, which has since disappeared, made St. Louis a world-class city by the 1880s and carried it through the century's turn. The meeting chambers of the library were busy playing host to political conventions (of splinter parties to be sure) and other important gatherings. One of the loudest voices was that of an Illinois newspaperman, Logan U. Reavis, who said of St. Louis that it was "the Babylon of the New World, not standing on the Euphrates, but on the banks of the great Mississippi." Voices of agreement could be heard from as far away as New Orleans and Chicago. St. Louis was the geographic center of the country and would shortly stand in the middle of its burgeoning population. The nation's capitol should be where the center of its power had coalesced. In New Orleans,

De Bow's Review insisted that "St. Louis with its healthful climate, beautiful highlands, and metropolitan character, with its central situation in the midst of our greatest industries, and equally accessible to all parts of the country . . . should be made the Capitol of the United States."

The city had already built a courthouse that rivaled Washington's capitol. Many times rebuilt, remodeled and revised, from its modest beginnings in the 1820s to its completion in 1864, it was ready to serve as the center of the nation. The cast-iron dome, added last, was a model for that other one put on later in D.C.

To consider such a move, in October of 1869, and at the invitation of the Merchants' Exchange, "governors and delegates from twenty-one states and territories, including most of the middle-western and border states, Pennsylvania, Oregon, Alabama, Louisiana, and the territories of Colorado, New Mexico, Utah, Montana, and Alaska met at the Mercantile Library . . . to discuss capital removal." But power and population remained stubbornly in the east, and Reavis's efforts were widely ridiculed. In 1870 Reavis wrote a book to defend his position, though we may include it here as a work of utopian fiction. *St. Louis, The Future Great City of the World* argued that civilization was following the fortieth parallel west from the Tigris and Euphrates Rivers across Europe into North America, where "two waves of civilization, the one rolling in from the Celestial Empire, and the other from the land of Alfred and Charlemagne—will meet and commingle together in one great swelling tide of humanity, in the land of Hiawatha."

There were some citizens—the esteemed scientist George Engelmann was one—who had inadvertently given substance to such grand claims by making St. Louis an important center of scientific activity (as it was in philosophy) by the middle of the century. Because of Engelmann's encouragement, botanical specimens were gathered here for study from all over the west. He became Henry Shaw's principal advisor at the Missouri Botanical Gardens and, with others, founded the St. Louis Academy of Science in 1856. He wrote to Asa Gray, the Harvard scientist with whom he collaborated, that St. Louis was "the center of North America, if not the world and of civilization! We burn one third of our steamboats, destroy one tenth of the wealth of our citizens in one night, kill one tenth by cholera . . . all only to show how much we can stand without succumbing."

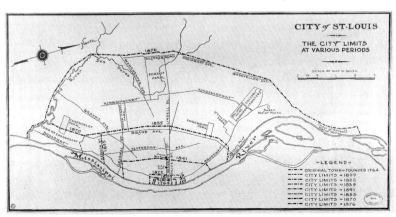

8

8. Map of City Limits of St. Louis, 1820-1876

Too bad less extreme and more successful measures could not have been found.

Now that the bridge was in place, across the river came the train. Union Station was dedicated in 1894. Twenty-two different lines came together in its vast shed. No longer by river, but by rail, then road, the writers would arrive. Dreiser, for instance, saw St. Louis first by standing outside the station and peering up and down Market Street. In 1902 an editor of *McClure's* magazine rode across the bridge and into Theodore Link's Grand Hall in the station. His name was Lincoln Steffens, and St. Louis would take up two of the seven chapters he otherwise devotes to Minneapolis, Pittsburgh, Philadelphia, Chicago and New York in *The Shame of the Cities*, his muckraking classic published in 1904, just in time for the World's Fair.

Perhaps it would be wise not utterly to forget at least three of the views Lincoln Steffens promotes in his "hard-hitting exposé." The first was that it was useless to throw out the "bad" guys to put in the reformers—the "good" guys—because it was the practice of "good" business and the behavior of "good" businessmen that corrupted politicians causing them to govern badly, and these men of commerce would simply continue that practice with any new arrivals; the second was that every big American city needed a Boss like Tweed or Daley to run it because businessmen didn't like to deal with a motley lot of officials who came and went with every election, and said seventeen different things simultaneously; the third was expressed by Steffens in this characteristic passage:

> It's all a moral weakness; a weakness right where we think we are strongest. Oh, we are good—on Sunday, and we are "fearfully patriotic" on the Fourth of July. But the bribe we pay to the janitor to prefer our interests to the landlord's, is the little brother of the bribe passed to the alderman to sell a city street, and the father of the air-brake stock assigned to the president of a railroad to have this life-saving invention adopted on his road. And as for graft, railroad passes, saloon and bawdy-house blackmail, and watered stock, all these belong to the same family. We are pathetically proud of our democratic institutions and our republican form of government, of our grand Constitution and our just laws. We are a free and sovereign people, we govern ourselves and the government is ours. But that is the point. We are responsible, not our leaders, since we follow them. We *let* them divert our loyalty from the United States to some "party"; we *let* them boss the party and turn our municipal democracies into autocracies and our republican nation into a plutocracy. We cheat our government and we let our leaders loot it, and we let them wheedle and bribe our sovereignty from us. True, they pass for us strict laws, but we are content to let them pass also bad laws, giving away public property in exchange; and our good, and often impossible, laws we allow to be used for oppression and blackmail. And what can we say? We break our own laws and rob our own government, the lady at the customhouse, the lyncher with his rope, and the captain of industry with his bribe and his rebate. The spirit of graft and of lawlessness is the American spirit.

Steffens would become an editor of the *American* and then of *Everybody's* magazine, and the articles he wrote for them piled up into books. *The Struggle for Self-Government* (1906) and *Upbuilders* (1909) were two among many, because there seemed always to be a plentiful supply of muck. Still, we can proudly say he got his start as a raker with ours. After all, we live at a confluence of the stuff.

The Eads Bridge figured prominently in one of the worst race riots in the nation's history, a riot of such murderous consequences it drew many a writer's horrified eyes and directed their pens. White workers at the Aluminum Ore Company in East St. Louis had been on strike for weeks and during that time black scabs, unaware of any threat, had been imported to continue the production. On July 2, 1917, an attack upon the black community in East St. Louis by whites of every sex and age began. Nearly a hundred persons were killed, other hundreds wounded, as police and National Guardsmen participated. Hundreds of black men, women and children fled across the bridge, protected, it must be said, by the St. Louis police force.

Among those who wrote of this calamity (apart from the heroic reporting of Paul Anderson of the *Post-Dispatch* and Russell Froehlich of the *Globe-Democrat*) was Carl Sandburg, who held big industrialists accountable, though many others blamed the labor unions:

> Two interests are responsible. One is Armour & Company and the other packing houses who make a specialty of importing southern Negroes to work alongside of white men in the north. The other is an East St. Louis aluminum factory, which has hundreds of white men on strike for months and is using Negroes freshly imported from the south to fill the places of the strikers.

Downtown would eventually be dotted with the rooming houses where writers like Dreiser and Inge stayed, or dwellings where Grant tried to make a go of it and Reedy lived, as well as buildings where the newspapers were written and published, or offices like those in the Security Building where Reedy presided and Winston Churchill collected material for his novels. Zoë Akins hung out at the Old Post Office, where her father worked, while her friend Orrick Johns could be found at the St. Louis Public Library. The Downtown YMCA offered a room to Joseph Pennell, who got even by lodging the protagonist of *Rome Hanks* there, while the Hotel Jefferson furnished the site for two famous poker games, one described in Richard Jessup's novel *The Cincinnati Kid* (though the movie makers moved the game to New Orleans), and the one which cost Tennessee Williams's father part of his ear and maybe his career.

In the 1960s, Paul Metcalf's character Michael Mills crosses the Mississippi to visit his brother, Carl:

9

9. Security Building, 319 North Fourth Street, c. 1906

All at once, I understood why Carl had come here, to St. Louis, of all places; why California had been only a stopping place, and this, the Mound City, had become his inevitable destination. I could see ahead, in the distance, some elevations of earth: I couldn't tell whether these were part of the original Indian mounds, or railroad embankments, or perhaps part of the levee system. In any case, the contour was low, level, and smooth; with the knowledge of the location of the city on the river, and the river's place in the face of the land, I realized that St. Louis was "home," the very eye and center of centripetal American geography, the land pouring in upon itself. I thought of China, and recalled that Carl's journey from there, from all that had happened there, was an eastward voyage, across half the globe; and, perhaps like Ishmael on board the *Pequod*, he was hunting back toward the beginnings of things; and, like the voyage of the *Pequod*,—or of any of the various caravels of Columbus that struck fierce weather returning from the Indies—perhaps Carl's eastward voyage, his voyage "home," was disastrous . . .

We entered East St. Louis, and the train slowed, as we passed through mile after mile of factory, tenement, dump, and slum, an abandoned industrial desolation . . .

Rising over the earth mounds, the tracks entered a bridge, and we approached the river. The cold rainy wind blew waves onto the surface—dark black and purple, the wind squalls rushing across it, here and there turning a white cap. Through the steel girders I watched the water as long as I could see it. When we reached the other side, I felt that we had passed over a great hump.

Because Metcalf's *Genoa* is a collage novel based on texts taken from Columbus's logs, Kansas City newspapers and his distant relative Melville's works, he uses a wonderful passage from Melville's *The Confidence Man* to describe the river and the landing for his contemporary character, but as it was in Melville's day, nearly a hundred years before—thus uniting two different times in a single present. It is April 1 when this "ship of fools" (ironically named *Fidèle*) leaves St. Louis headed for Cape Girardeau and the south.

As among Chaucer's Canterbury pilgrims, or those oriental ones crossing the Red Sea towards Mecca in the festival month, there was no lack of variety. Natives of all sorts, and foreigners; men of business and men of pleasure; parlor men and backwoodsmen; farm-hunters and fame-hunters; heiress-hunters, truth-hunters, and still keener hunters after all these hunters. Fine ladies in slippers, and moccasined squaws; Northern speculators and Eastern philosophers; English, Irish, German, Scotch, Danes; Santa Fé traders in striped blankets, and Broadway bucks in cravats of cloth of gold; fine-looking Kentucky boatmen, and Japanese-looking Mississippi cotton-planters; Quakers in full drab, and United States soldiers in full regimentals; slaves, black, mulatto, quadroon; modish young Spanish Creoles, and old-fashioned French Jews; Mormons and Papists; Dives and Lazarus; jesters and mourners, teetotalers and convivialists, deacons and blacklegs; hard-shell Baptists and clay-eaters; grinning negroes, and Sioux chiefs solemn as high-priests. In short, a piebald parliament, an Anacharsis Cloots congress of all kinds of that multiform pilgrim species, man.

As pine, beech, birch, ash, hackmatack, hemlock, spruce, bass-wood, maple, interweave their foliage in the natural wood, so these varieties of mortals blended their varieties of visage and garb. A Tartar-like picturesqueness; a sort of pagan abandonment and assurance. Here reigned the dashing and all-fusing spirit of the West, whose type is the Mississippi itself, which, uniting the streams of the most distant and opposite zones, pours them along, helter-skelter, in one cosmopolitan and confident tide.

Finally, the English philosopher and novelist Iris Murdoch, who, with her husband John Bailey, lectured at Washington University, included a few St. Louis observations in her fiction of 1977, *Henry and Cato*, by situating one protagonist, Henry, in St. Louis, where he learns to his delight of his hated brother's death.

When the great news reached him Henry had been in St. Louis, sitting in O'Conner's [*sic*] bar eating a hamburger. He had opened a copy of the London Evening Standard which a jet-propelled visitor had left in the lounge of his small hotel and which he had idly picked up. Private Henry shunned university acquaintances in St. Louis, preferring modest hotel life, while trotting to and from the picture galleries and the zoo. Munching, he opened the paper and scanned the news of strikes, trade deficits, Labour Party feuds, rows about education, rows about new roads, rows about new airports. No interesting murders. Everything seemed much as usual in his native land which he had left nine years ago intending never to return. . . .

The local metropolis was weird majestic St. Louis beside the journeying Mississippi. T. E. [*sic*] Eliot's city. Henry, who detested New York, loved St. Louis. Sperriton [Illinois] was tiny and lonely. St. Louis was vast and lonely, and lost Henry delighted in its besieged loneliness. He loved its derelict splendours, the huge ornate neglected mansions of a vanished bourgeoisie, the useless skyscraper-tall steel arch through which the citizenry surveyed the view of shabby warehouses and marshalling yards on the Illinois shore. The empty palaces beside the immense eternal river: what an impressive image of the demise of capitalism . . . Eventually he got onto the trail of Max Beckmann whom a fate even stranger than Henry's had exiled to St. Louis in his later years. Henry had been told by the head of his department that he must write a book, any book. He decided to write about Beckmann.

Such passages as this one from Iris Murdoch's novel should remind us that writers—whether they just drop in or faithfully reside—write; that what they write often contains views and descriptions of the places they've been, opinions frequently expressed with skill and passion; that what they write is more and more webbed, thus read all over the world in less than three instants; so it is always wise to bow to writers when you meet them, offer them free lodging, ample drink, fine food, continuous flattery; otherwise they may do a Dickens on you, and you certainly don't want that.

The newspapers were rarely partisan about poetry, but they grew hot over slavery, free soil and free labor, over God, righteousness and its rewards. In the fierce disputes leading to and following the Civil War, freedom of expression was always one of the combatants. Elijah Lovejoy became a martyr to the First Amendment. His father was a Congregational Minister, his education came at Baptist hands, and Maine was his terrain. Lovejoy came out of Colby College (then called "Waterville") unhappy, though at the head of his class, because he had not yet received his revelation and the kind of conversion he longed for. Poetry was his avocation in the absence of a calling. In the following lines, he described himself:

> Of all that knew him, few but judged him wrong;
> He was of silent and unsocial mood;
> Unloving and unloved he passed along,
> His chosen path with steadfast aim he trod,
> Nor asked nor wished applause, save only of his God.

It says much about his stubborn idealistic character that, lacking funds, Lovejoy decided to walk to Illinois, though the famous command was "Go west, young man!" not "Go slow!" Months from Maine he reached New York, where, to ease his feet and acquire coin, he got a job pounding its pavements selling magazine subscriptions. The president of Colby College took pity on his graduate and lent Lovejoy enough to break his hike by hitching or buying occasional rides on boats and wagons. Malaria made much of the trip a wearing affair, and at one point he wrote:

> . . . now had he come
> To the far woods, and there in silence knelt
> On the sharp flint-stone in the rayless gloom,
> And fervently he prayed to find an early tomb.

When Lovejoy arrived in St. Louis in 1827 its population of six thousand seemed huge, and made of significant national groups—the French, the Spanish, the English and the Irish—mostly engaged in river traffic, furs and farming. The city was Catholic and uncongenial to his religious roots, and he disliked the considerable profanity, drunkenness and public prostitution he was forced to observe.

Clearly, this frontier town needed culture. There were no public schools in St. Louis then, so when Lovejoy founded his it was welcomed and did well. Soon he found himself surprised to be both admired and in funds. However, his ambitions grew along with his bank account, and in a couple of years, when the financially troubled *St. Louis Times* offered him a half-interest, he accepted the ring. As former senator Paul Simon remarks in his biography of Lovejoy, *Freedom's Champion*, "Editing a newspaper at this time required not only the ability to write but also the ability to fight." The *St. Louis Beacon* called the new publisher a "little animal," and Lovejoy responded by describing the *Beacon*'s editor as "a mere inflated bladder." This deserved the phrase "contemptible parasite" which he soon received.

The abolitionist sentiments that would later lead to Lovejoy's murder were not evident in the pages of the *St. Louis Times,* which ran a great many advertisements for slaves or offering rewards for runaways:

> FOR SALE—A likely NEGRO WOMAN with six children. The woman is between 30 and 35 years of age, and the two oldest children, twins, are between 10 and 11 years old. They will be sold for CASH. Apply at this office.

> 30 DOLLARS REWARD—Ranaway . . . a negro named JOHN. He is about 5 feet high, well proportioned, and has a large dent across his nose. . . . I will give for apprehending the above negro $10 if taken in St. Louis, $20 if in the State of Missouri, and $40 if taken in the State of Illinois and delivered to Mr. L. Deaver, St. Louis, or secured in any jail so I can get him again.

A widely admired revivalist preacher, David Nelson, converted Lovejoy to abolitionist ideas and committed him to Presbyterian ways. Resolving to become a minister himself, Lovejoy gave up the paper and went back east to Princeton to study theology. The Fates timed it so that shortly after Lovejoy graduated from the seminary, he received an invitation from a group of St. Louis businessmen, headed by Hamilton Rowan Gamble, a future governor of the state, to manage and edit a newspaper that would promote religion, morality and education.

No temptation could have been more alluring to ambition, enlarging it to weakness, or more fatal to a future than this one that Lovejoy accepted with alacrity. In addition, he became pastor of the Des Peres Presbyterian Church (the "Old Meeting House") so he would have a double pulpit.

Lovejoy's *Observer,* as it was called, immediately mounted intemperate sectarian attacks upon the Catholic Church, whose members he never tired of denouncing; indeed, he had vitriol left over for Baptists, Episcopalians,

10

Disciples of Christ and any other group pretending to a different relationship with God.

At first the paper rather ignored the slavery issue, and then it began cautiously to creep in the direction of abolition, first espousing the Colonizer's cause (they would have freed the negroes and sent them to Liberia), then supporting Gradualism, before finally coming out flatly for Emancipation. Nevertheless, for some time, the *Observer* seemed to regard smoking, drinking, gambling and whoring with more repugnance.

Lovejoy was clearly a man whom heat and hammer tempered. The newspaper's position grew more militant and outspoken, meanwhile incidents of mistreatment of the negro came repeatedly to light, each requiring the restatement of the issue, a rekindling of rage, and an increase in the kind of indignation required to conceal deep stirrings of guilt. If the bite of prejudice is painful, equally uncomfortable is the ache in its bitter jaws. Almost daily there were threats upon Lovejoy's life, but now his zeal had more than a narrow sectarian target. A mulatto cook and porter from the steamboat *Flora* had failed to assist police in chasing a fleeing sailor on the docks and was immediately arrested and threatened with five years in jail, whereupon, in a panic, he wounded one officer with a knife and, with a wild swing, cut the throat of another. The freeman, named Francis McIntosh, was tied to the trunk of a locust tree by a mob of thousands who pried him out of jail and burned him alive, leaving his charred corpse smoldering overnight to be stoned in the morning by idle bunches of small boys for their amusement.

The *Observer* condemned this barbarism in the strongest terms, and outcries came from all over the country. Although no one appeared ready to defend the mob, many were willing to silence those who wished to write about it. The newspaper's equipment was damaged. Anonymous voices threatened to burn any negro who sailed into town. As Senator Simon remarks in his account, the judge who presided at the grand jury investigation could not have been better named by Gilbert and Sullivan. A slave owner who had done time for contempt of court, Judge Luke Edward Lawless, though admitting the lynching was unfortunate, could find no one on whom to fix the blame but Elijah Lovejoy, whose editorials, he argued, had inflamed the negroes and seduced them into disobedience. The legislature should "punish, if they cannot prevent, those exhortations to rebellion" with new laws. The response of the press was predictable. The *Emancipator*, whose morality was only minute by minute, even suggested lynching the judge if a large enough mob could be found to ensure that no one would be blamed for it. The irony was meant but so was the message.

Elijah Lovejoy, while riding the high horse the evil of others had provided him, nevertheless was compelled to notice that Lawless was a papist, and if the judge were to point toward Lovejoy as a cause, he would point in turn at the pope. There were more attacks on the paper's printing presses, even after Lovejoy decided to move the paper to Alton and the greater safety of a free state. There he became the pastor of what is now the College Avenue Presbyterian Church. By February of 1837, Lovejoy had reached the limits of his position, calling the "repatriation" of the slaves "utterly inadequate." It was well that the *Observer* was now on the free side of the Mississippi, since Missouri's legislature passed a law forbidding the publication, promulgation and distribution of anti-slavery views. But madness was not confined to Missouri. When the economy took a dramatic slide, Lovejoy was inclined to blame slave-holders for incurring the wrath of God, whereas the citizens of Alton were inclined to blame Lovejoy.

On one occasion a mob parted to allow Lovejoy to pass, unbloodied, as though it were the Red Sea, but attacks on the presses continued, and pieces of them were tossed into the river to the applause of St. Louis's *Missouri Argus* and *Missouri Republican*. Ill and pregnant, Lovejoy's wife was threatened often enough, and even face to face, that she took to her bed. Meetings were disrupted, and when it was known that still another press was expected, manifestations of rage became the sport and alcohol its energy. The mobs would not allow another press safe passage. At last a meeting was called to find a compromise, or, rather, to suppress Lovejoy's views while maintaining some semblance of justice and due process. At the end of that meeting, whose participants were largely hostile to him, Lovejoy spoke, and these words are why his story deserves the space of these pages on St. Louis's literary history:

> Mr. Chairman, I do not admit that it is the business of this assembly to decide whether I shall or shall not publish a newspaper in this city. The gentlemen have, as the lawyers say, made a wrong issue. I have the right to do it. I know that I have the right freely to speak and publish my sentiments, subject only to the laws of the land for the abuse of that right. This right was given me by my Maker, and is solemnly guaranteed to me by the constitution of these United States and of this state.

> What I wish to know of you is whether you will protect me in the exercise of this right; or whether . . . I am to continue to be subjected to personal indignity and outrage. . . .
>
> God, in his providence—so say all my brethren, and so I think—has devolved upon me the responsibility of maintaining my ground here; and Mr. Chairman, I am determined to do it. A voice comes to me from Maine, from Massachusetts, from Connecticut, from New York, from Pennsylvania—yea, from Kentucky, from Mississippi, from Missouri—calling upon me in the name of all that is dear in heaven or earth, to stand fast; and by the help of God, I will stand. I know I am but one and you are many. My strength would avail but little against you all. You can crush me if you will; but I shall die at my post, for I cannot and will not forsake it.
>
> Why should I flee from Alton? Is this not a free state? When attacked by a mob at St. Louis, I came here to be at the home of freedom and of the laws.

11

11. *Pro-Slavery Riot at Godfrey & Gilman's Alton warehouse, November 7, 1837*

The mob has pursued me here, and why should I retreat again? Where can I be safe if not here? Have I not a right to claim the protection of the laws? Sir, the very act of retreating will embolden the mob to follow me wherever I go. No sir, there is no way to escape the mob, but to abandon the path of duty. And that, God helping me, I will never do. . . .

If in anything I have offended against the law, I am not so popular in this community that it would be difficult to convict me. You have courts and judges and juries; they find nothing against me. And now you come together for the purpose of driving out a confessedly innocent man, for no cause but that he dares to think and speak as his conscience and his God dictate. Will conduct like this stand the scrutiny of this country? Of posterity?

Pause, I beseech you, and reflect. The present excitement will soon be over. The voice of conscience will at last be heard. [The time will come] as you review the scenes of this hour, [that] you will be forced to say: "He was right. He was right." . . .

I have counted the cost, and stand prepared freely to offer up my all in the service of God. Yes, sir, I am fully aware of all the sacrifice I make in here pledging myself to continue this contest to the last.

[A moment of silence.]

Forgive these tears—I had not intended to shed them. And they flow not for myself, but others. But I am commanded to forsake father and mother and wife and children for Jesus' sake; and as His professed disciple I stand prepared to do it. The time for fulfilling this pledge in my case, it seems to me, has come.

Sir, I dare not flee away from Alton. Should I attempt it, I should feel that the angel of the Lord with his flaming sword was pursuing me wherever I went. It is because I fear God that I am not afraid of all who oppose me in this city. No, sir, the contest has commenced here; and here it must be finished. Before God and you all, I here pledge myself to continue it—if need be, till death. If I fall, my grave shall be made in Alton.

Socrates reminded his accusers that those facing death have the power of prophesy, and so it was: on the night of November 7, 1837, Elijah Lovejoy was murdered by a mob angered by the arrival from St. Louis of yet another printing press—the fourth. It was housed in Godfrey & Gilman's stone warehouse for safe keeping; however, the roof was made of wood, and when the mob tried to set the roof afire, Lovejoy was hit by five blasts from a double-barreled shotgun while trying to push away a ladder carrying an attacker who bore a smoking pot of pitch. The crowd, which had been hurling stones through the warehouse windows and dodging a return fire of clay pots, was cheered. They rushed the building, broke up the press and dumped its pieces, as before, into the river. Lovejoy was carried away the next day and buried quietly in an unmarked grave on November 9, his thirty-fifth birthday. Years later the body was removed to an impressive monument erected on a suitable height in Alton. The Latin inscription on the memorial reads: "Here lies Lovejoy—Spare him now the grave."

Although both defenders and attackers were placed on trial, all were found innocent, and no one was ever punished or fined, unless we imagine that the pieces of the four substantial presses, still buried in the silt of the river, continue to suffer for their service to the word.

12

During his tenure as editor of the *St. Louis Times* Elijah Lovejoy employed a printer

WILLIAM WELLS BROWN
1814 — November 6, 1884

whose services were offered by his owner. John Young, a physician, had acquired his slave, whom he called Sanford, in a real estate deal that included the mother and six other children. His mother named him William; his white father was probably the brother of his Kentucky master. William would later append the middle and surname of Wells Brown in honor of the Quaker that helped him escape to the free state of Ohio in 1834. William Wells Brown was born on a plantation near Lexington, Kentucky, around 1814 and brought to St. Louis in 1827. His mother, Elizabeth, and his siblings lived on Dr. Young's farm in Montgomery County northwest of St. Louis. He started out as a house servant but soon became adept at several tasks and so was hired out like a Kelly Girl. After his stint as a printer's assistant to Elijah Lovejoy, Brown worked as a gang boss for a slave trader, James Walker, and traveled up and down the Mississippi to New Orleans for the regular shopping sprees:

> On Landing at Natchez, the slaves were all carried to the slavepen, and there kept one week, during which time, several of them were sold. Mr. Walker fed his slaves well. We took on board, at St. Louis, several hundred pounds of bacon (smoked meat) and cornmeal, and his slaves were better fed than slaves generally were in Natchez, so far as my observation extended. At the end of a week, we left for New Orleans, the place of our final destination, which we reached in two days. Here the slaves were placed in a negro-pen, where those who wished to purchase could call and examine them. The negro-pen is a small yard, surrounded by buildings, from fifteen to twenty feet wide, with the exception of a large gate with iron bars. The slaves are kept in the buildings during the night, and turned out into the yard during the day. After the

12. Elijah Lovejoy, memorial silhouette

best of the stock was sold at private sale at the pen, the balance was taken to the Exchange Coffee House Auction Rooms, kept by Isaac L. McCoy, and sold at public auction. After the sale of this lot of slaves, we left New Orleans for St. Louis.

13

Along with the daily shock of seeing human beings living out the legal definition of chattel, Brown received an education on the streets, widening his world through his movement from job to job. After an aborted attempt to escape with his mother from St. Louis in 1832, Young sold "Sanford" to a steamboat captain, Enoch Price, who made the mistake of docking in Cincinnati on January 1, 1834, and promptly losing his investment to the fleet-footed god Mercury. Brown made his way to Cleveland where he emulated his final owner by working on a steamboat, assisting other fugitive slaves.

William Wells Brown became a sought-after speaker in the United States and abroad (he delivered more than one thousand anti-slavery lectures in England) and, though his slave narrative was published in 1847, two years after Frederick Douglass's famous one, it went through four American and

13. *Frontispiece from* Narrative of William W. Brown, a Fugitive Slave, Written by Himself, *1847*

five British editions by 1850. He would go on to write what is considered the first travel book written by a black author, *Three Years in Europe; Or, Places I Have Seen and People I Have Met* (1852), the first drama, *The Escape; Or, A Leap for Freedom* (1858) and the first novel, *Clotel; Or, The President's Daughter: A Narrative of Slave Life in the United States*, "a panoramic story of the fate of a mixed-race daughter of Thomas Jefferson," published in 1853:

The auctioneer commenced by saying, that "Miss Clotel had been reserved for the last, because she was the most valuable. How much, gentlemen? Real Albino, fit for a fancy girl for any one. She enjoys good health, and has a sweet temper. How much do you say?" "Five hundred dollars." "Only five hundred for such a girl as this? Gentlemen, she is worth a deal more than that sum; you certainly don't know the value of the article you are bidding upon. Here, gentlemen, I hold in my hand a paper certifying that she has a good moral character." "Seven hundred." "Ah, gentlemen, that is something like. This paper also states that she is very intelligent." "Nine hundred." "Nine fifty." "Ten." "Eleven." "Twelve hundred." Here the sale came to a dead stand. The auctioneer stopped, looked around, and began in a rough manner to relate some anecdotes relative to the sale of slaves, which, he said, had come under his own observation. At this juncture the scene was indeed strange. Laughing, joking, swearing, smoking, spitting, and talking kept up a continual hum and noise amongst the crowd; while the slave-girl stood with tears in her eyes, at one time looking towards her mother and sister, and at another towards the young man whom she hoped would become her purchaser. "The chastity of this girl is pure; she has never been from under her mother's care; she is a virtuous creature." "Thirteen." "Fourteen." "Fifteen." "Fifteen hundred dollars," cried the auctioneer, and the maiden was struck for that sum. This was a Southern auction, at which the bones, muscles, sinews, blood, and nerves of a young lady of sixteen were sold for five hundred dollars; her moral character for two hundred; her improved intellect for one hundred; her Christianity for three hundred; and her chastity and virtue for four hundred dollars more. And this, too, in a city thronged with churches, whose tall spires look like so many signals pointing to heaven, and whose ministers preach that slavery is a God-ordained institution!

What words can tell the inhumanity, the atrocity, and the immorality of that doctrine which, from exalted office, commends such a crime to the favour of enlightened and Christian people? What indignation from all the world is not due to the government and people who put forth all their strength and power to keep in existence such an institution? Nature abhors it; the age repels it; and Christianity needs all her meekness to forgive it.

William Wells Brown wrote other Clotel books, a history of black Americans and a book of poetry called *The Antislavery Harp*. He insisted that he had not learned to read until after his escape. If this is true he made up for it with a prolific and distinguished career, arising out of one of the most inhospitable environments, in which a river was a boon accomplice.

14

I hear that at St. Louis a parish is getting together; is it true, and what about it? . . . if I come, I come to remain, and to lay my ashes in the valley of the Mississippi.

—William Greenleaf Eliot

In 1853 Wayman Crow, a state senator, introduced a charter for the establishment of an institution of higher learning in St. Louis. Without consulting its namesake, Crow called it "Eliot Seminary" after the preacher in his church, the Unitarian Church of the Messiah. William Greenleaf Eliot, however, declined to lend his name while offering support otherwise, as his religious belief had to "show itself in good works," and so a race to name the institution was on. In 1853 it was the Eliot Seminary, in 1854 the Washington Institute of St. Louis, in 1855 the O'Fallon Institute and, in 1857, by amendment of the original charter, Washington University.

William Greenleaf Eliot was born in New Bedford, Massachusetts, and was to attend a Quaker Academy but for financial reasons entered Columbian College—later George Washington University—in the District

14. Washington University and Smith Academy by
Thomas Easterly, 1857

of Columbia where his parents had moved. He attended Harvard Divinity School and was ordained in 1834, the year he accepted the offer to lead a nascent congregation in St. Louis. "[We] were young and strong and full of hope, and hardships were easily borne," wrote his new wife (and first cousin) Abby (Adams Cranch) of their move to what was then the American frontier. St. Louis would test their fortitude, as it was "not a healthy place. There was no sewer system, and  cellars were full of water; chills and fever everywhere, and scarcely a poor family without some one in bed. Visiting among the sick and poor kept us very busy, and dark streets and muddy ways made life pretty hard for those of us charitably inclined." In the first sermon after his arrival William Greenleaf Eliot set out the three principles that would unite his church: "First, self-improvement, self-education in morality and religion, and the formation of the Christian character; secondly, usefulness by works of kindness and benevolence, charity and public spirit; thirdly, the diffusion of the Christian faith."

"Mr. Eliot, the Unitarian minister, is the Saint of the West," wrote Ralph Waldo Emerson in 1852, and "has a sumptuous church, & crowds to hear his really good sermons. But I believe no thinking or even reading man is here in the 95,000 souls." A classmate at Harvard compared Eliot to "the Day of Judgement." Public service was primary: during the typhoid epidemic of 1840 he visited the sick and took charge of orphans, and with the onset of the Civil War, organized the Western Sanitary Commission, which monitored the medical services of the Northern army and its fleet. His life, he would later recall for Charlotte Eliot, his daughter-in-law, was "broken into fragments by the cares and occupations unavoidable in a new community during the revolutionary days of progress." His revolution meant the abolition of slavery, women's suffrage, education and prohibition. He could not "'take it easy,' for that is to be unfaithful."

After a "continued pastorate of thirty-six years" William Greenleaf Eliot retired from his church in 1870. (He became pastor emeritus.) A year later he became chancellor of the university he helped to found and to fund, whose eponym he refused and whose head he remained until his death. His pulpit also produced Mary Institute (for girls), Smith Academy (for boys), the Manual Training School and the Academy of Science. His pen produced *The Discipline of Sorrow* in 1855 and *The Life of Archer Alexander*, the story of the slave he bought to free— "a fair presentation of slavery in the Border States for the twenty or thirty years preceding the outbreak of hostilities," which was published in 1885, two years before his death while on a rest cure in Pass Christian, Mississippi. In partial fulfillment of his promise, he is buried in Bellefontaine Cemetery. A tablet placed at his church reads:

In Memoriam, Rev. William Greenleaf Eliot, d.d., 1811-1887, Pastor of this Church 1834-1873, and the wise helper and counselor of the church and people until his death. His best monument is to be found in the many educa-

15. William Greenleaf Eliot by Thomas Easterly, c. 1850

tional and philanthropic institutions of St. Louis, to which he gave the disinterested labor of his life. The whole city was his parish, and every soul needing him a parishioner.

After the Church of the Messiah was torn down the plaque was removed to Eliot Hall at the First Unitarian Church at 5007 Waterman Avenue where it remains.

Henry Ware Eliot, the second son of William Greenleaf Eliot, did not follow his father and brothers into the ministry because, he said, "Too much pudding choked the dog." After graduating from Washington University he worked as a wholesale grocer, became a manufacturing

chemist, and then met prosperity as president of the Hydraulic-Press Brick Company, which produced bricks for many of the houses in the Central West End, including his home at 4446 Westminster Place. In 1868 he married the Baltimore-born Charlotte Champe Stearns, who had moved to St. Louis to teach at St. Louis Normal School. They had four daughters and two sons, the youngest of whom, a family member remarked, "was going to achieve greatness" only "they didn't know what form it would take."

16

Nearly deaf from a childhood bout of scarlet fever Henry Ware Eliot nevertheless loved music and played the flute. For his children he drew faces on boiled eggs, made sketches of cats which they treasured, read to them from "The Donkey Book"—*Don Quixote*, with Gustave Dore's engravings—and wrote a book of his own. In *A Brief Autobiography Written by H. W. Eliot, 1843-1919* he described life with his father:

> So absorbed was he in his work—church, public schools, charities, church building and University . . . [that his] attention was drawn to us [only] in times of illness, and in my childish mind he was associated with quinine and castor oil. My feeling towards him was not one of fear, but of reverential awe. . . . He was not a stern man. His eyes were magnificent, and one felt that he could read one's inmost thoughts.

In 1904 Charlotte Eliot wrote a biography of her father-in-law, *William Greenleaf Eliot: Minister, Educator, Philanthropist*, which she dedicated to her children, "Lest They Forget" (a certain impossibility). She also published a book of poems called *Easter Songs*. In a letter to her son, T. S. Eliot, when he was a student at Harvard, she confided in him about her own writing, "I hope in your literary work you will receive early the recognition I strove for and failed. I should so have loved a college course, but was obliged to teach before I was nineteen. I graduated with high rank, 'a young lady of unusual brilliancy as a scholar' my old yellow testimonial says, but when I was set for teaching young children, my Trigonometry and Astronomy counted for nought, and I made a dead failure." Later, as an editor at Faber in London, Eliot published his mother's epic poem about the Dominican monk who ignited a bonfire of vanities in fifteenth-century Florence. Charlotte Stearns Eliot's *Savonarola* came out in 1926 with an introduction by her son.

Girolamo Savonarola succeeded in bringing down the Medicis and restoring freedom in Florence, but went too far with the sitting pope, Alexander VI (Borgia), who had him jailed, tortured, hanged and burned in 1498. This "great moral reformer" must have been the fifteenth century's William Greenleaf Eliot:

> One lesson I have learned, by sorrow taught,
> My life is not my own, and I have brought
> Both life and love to lay upon His shrine
> Who wills that nothing shall be wholly mine.

Later in the poem, when he is in his cell, Savonarola predicts the future of Florence as long as she remains imprisoned by evil.

> A little longer Florence will be free,
> Till faction and dissension, harmony
> Shall overthrow,
> And then a change will come. When at the gate
> The legions of the enemy shall wait;
> They'll see and know
> (Who erst were blind), God's purpose to fulfil
> They must united be and do His will.

They pretend to say that God invented women to be just what they are. I say that He did not, and men have made women what they are, and if they attribute their doings to the Almighty, they lie.

KATE FIELD
October 1, 1838 — May 10, 1896

—Kate Field, age seventeen

Kate Field was the kind of independent woman that theatrical families often produce. Her parents were well-known Shakespearean actors who performed in towns up and down the Mississippi; Kate grew up watching them and stars like Jenny Lind at the St. Louis Theatre at Third and Olive. Joseph Field, her father, built and founded the Varieties Theatre before competition forced it to close. He also founded the *St. Louis Daily Reveille*, which saw its demise in the Great Fire of 1849. He collected his writings for the paper in an 1847 volume, *The Drama in Pokerville*. In its halcyon age, the

Reveille was prominent enough to be the platform for Edgar Allan Poe's defense of his character against a libelous attack in the *New York Evening Mirror*.

"All the mental discipline I received was between the ages of eight and twelve," wrote Kate Field about Mrs. Smith's Seminary. No wonder: she was translating Racine and playing Chopin by age eleven. When her father died, she and her mother moved in with a rich uncle in Boston who later took the twenty-one-year-old Kate to Europe for refinement, but she began sending home abolitionist travel articles to the *Boston Courier*, at which point Uncle Milton disinherited his too-refined surrogate daughter. Kate Field found her true family in Florence, where she was taken in by the illustrious literary circle of the Brownings, the Trollopes and George Eliot. She was "extremely attractive, slim and blue-eyed," also "tall and beautiful, with magnificent hair and a column-like throat," all to an alleged intoxicating effect: Robert Browning looked deep into her blue eyes and divined great ambition; the elderly (and prolific) poet Walter Savage Landor got a kiss a poem; Anthony Trollope, on holiday from the post office (his greatest contribution to English literature may be the pillar box), was smitten. Her response? "Anthony Trollope is a very delightful companion. I see a great deal of him" to "Met Anthony Trollope. Same as ever." They remained lifelong friends, however, and the outspoken, intelligent women in Trollope's *Miss Mackenzie, He Knew He Was Right* and *Can You Forgive Her?* owe much of their character to Kate Field.

Field made a living writing about her literary connections. She published both books and journalism, and gave immensely popular lectures— "Despised and Neglected Alaska," "The Mormon Monster" and "An Evening with Charles Dickens" were some of her titles. She and Eugene Field were friends but not related, though he liked to call her "cousin Kate." A bold journalist, she did Hemingway fifty years before Hemingway, interviewing the president of the Spanish Republic and graphically describing bullfights in *Ten Days in Spain*. She was known as "The Rose of the Rostrum," and her beauty and erudition inspired larger crowds and longer reviews than Mark Twain's wit—much to his chagrin. Perhaps he had reason to dislike her: she had a Boston accent, despite her Missouri origins; she had lost his investment in her women's clothing cooperative in New York; she had acted poorly in the stage adaptation of his book *The Gilded Age*; and she lectured reverently on Dickens, whose serialized novels Twain called "glittering frostwork." They agreed, however, in their dislike of Mormonism—whose practice of polygamy Field fought against. The French gave her the *Palmes académique* for service to literature and the arts, which she refused until the American government removed all tariffs on the importation of art (which it duly did). Like her father, Field founded a newspaper, the humbly titled *Kate Field's Washington*, but since she wrote the majority of the articles, it ceased publication after five years when she became ill. She took her rest cure in 1896 in Hawaii, subsidized in part through newspaper assignments which, eventually, demanded greater investigation than the confines of her hotel room could afford her, so while tracking down a story by the only available means, a horse, she contracted pneumonia and died some days later. "It never occurred to me that this Republic is faultless, and that the way to correct evils is to conceal them or to pretend they do not exist. I have never enjoyed living in a fool's paradise," she wrote. In her obituary in the *Chicago Tribune*, she was hailed as "the most unique woman the present century has produced."

18

I was in Madrid, eating a real breakfast, thousands of miles from home, and not knowing a soul. What had I come for? To look Spain in the face, and see Castelar. As I ate I pondered, and as I pondered I ate. A handsome Italian garzone stood by, and we discussed Spain in la lingua del sì. The hotel—the best in the country—is kept by an Italian, and his most faithful servants are countrymen. What did the garzone think of the republic?

"Ah, Signora, what would you? The Spaniards are ignorant and cruel. They are not republican. Nobody that I see wants a republic. Everybody wants something else; but, as all are quarrelling among themselves, Señor Castelar maintains his position. He is a good man. He writes fine books, and makes beautiful speeches. But the end of it will be that we shall have a king. I am sick of it all, and I'd like to go to America, where people are intelligent and the poor have a chance to rise."

—Kate Field, *Ten Days in Spain*

Genius is no more a matter of accident than the rising of the sun. Though genius dazzle with the unexpected brilliancy of a comet, like the comet it has its regular orbit, and when the science of art has been discovered, as it will be ere the dawn of the millennium, the world will know the cause as well as the effect of human greatness.

—Kate Field, *Charles Albert Fechter*

Early settlers called it the Gravois farm because of the nearby creek of that name, and it was owned by farmers, fur traders and distillers from the early nineteenth century. These people and their neighbors left their names on the regional map—Lucas, Sappington, Hunt—and they fought for power and property in an impressively brutal way. Charles Lucas bore immortal animosities and hounded his enemies "to the doorstep of death." He was pretty tough, too, surviving a duel with Thomas Hart Benton who shot him, during their first fight, in the jugular vein; however, the second, which took place on a small island in the Mississippi, led to Lucas's death, although he did hit Benton in the leg. His widow, Nancy, who later married a Hunt, wanted quiet after "the battle of Bloody Island" and bought the Gravois farm, whose acres lay about ten miles southwest of the city. The Hunts were indifferent farmers, though, and when the local real estate market sagged so badly they were nearly ruined, they moved to a Lucas family property they called Normandy, and rebuilt their fortune. Meanwhile, the Gravois property was bought by the family of Frederick Dent, who would own the farm for sixty-five years and call it "White Haven," as it is still named today.

Hiram Ulysses Grant grew up in southern Ohio simultaneously loving horses and hating his father's tanning business. His father saw to it that his son received a decent education at the Maysville Seminary across the Ohio River in Kentucky. His father furthermore obtained an appointment to West Point for him, although Grant did not immediately dream of a military career. What should the lad see when he gathered his luggage to travel to the east but his monogram in tacks upon his trunk. It spelled HUG, and these initials clearly would not do in the world of boy/men he was about to enter. So "Ulysses" was moved up a notch. Then he lost "Hiram" altogether, luckily, because it was already the name of a rube, and because his chief recommender to the Point had mistakenly included his mother's maiden name—"Simpson"—in the application. William T. Sherman, a classmate, would read U. S. Grant as "Uncle Sam." It was as if Grant's campaign for the presidency had already begun. His West Point roommate was Frederick Dent of Missouri, and this would also prove to be fortuitous.

Sam Grant excelled at mathematics (among generals a widely shared knack), horsemanship (the best at the Point) and drawing and painting, a talent later so hidden its presence is a surprise. After his graduation from the academy, Grant was posted to Jefferson Barracks at St. Louis, at that time the largest military installation in the country. It was natural that he should visit the farm, White Haven, where his classmate's family lived, and where he met Julia Dent, his future wife. He cut a fine, though abbreviated, figure on a horse, and he didn't drink or smoke or swear—then.

Business abilities made him a quartermaster during the Mexican War, but he captured this conflict's set of dingy engagements to best purpose by writing countless fascinating letters to Julia about how he felt and what he

CAPT. GRANT'S RESIDENCE IN AND ABOUT ST. LOUIS.

19

had observed. It was the beginning of a significant literary career. During the Civil War Grant drafted his own reports and wrote his own orders on the battlefield. This meant, sometimes, composing thirty-five separate commands on a single day, often while under fire or in the company of his staff. He became the master of a succinct, clear, direct style, which was identified later as inherently "American."

It has been observed that, among words, the general had his favorites. He begins the Preface to his *Memoirs* by quoting "Man proposes and God disposes." These would make him verbally famous on top of his other fames. "I propose to fight it out on this line if it takes all summer." "Yours of this date proposing terms of capitulation is just received," he wrote to the Confederate general commanding Fort Donelson. "No terms except an unconditional and immediate surrender can be accepted. I propose to move immediately upon your works." Thus Uncle Sam Grant's initials received an additional reading.

Grant did not take up residence at White Haven until after he resigned from the army in 1854. He had married Julia following his return from the Mexican War, and then the couple endured the usual military postings be-fore Grant was separated from his family and sent to the Isthmus of Panama. His first son was born while he was away. Grant's St. Louis existence was mainly that of an im-poverished farmer and wood cutter, and the simple hard family life he lived on the farm (he soon had three children) became a source of praise and ridicule during his political years. He delivered wood to Jefferson Barracks and occasionally played cards with James Longstreet and other old friends.

20

Frederick Dent gave Julia land on Rock Hill Road and there Grant began hewing the logs for a new house. Although his neighbors helped raise the walls as well as fashion the door frames and window sashes, it was Grant himself who laid the floors, shingled the roof, and built the staircase. "Hardscrabble" was the name he gave the place where he would play a few games of checkers before his wife's wishes and her mother's death moved them back to White Haven. Julia hadn't wanted a log cabin anyway. She'd wanted a frame. Grant gave Hardscrabble more space in his *Memoirs* than it was allowed in his life, and the cabin would move as often and as strate-gically as his army: in 1890 to Webster Groves, then to Forest Park in 1903 to be gawked at by fairgoers and serve as an advertising come-on for the C. F. Blanke Coffee Company, and finally it was returned to Dent property, which eventually became what is now misleadingly called Grant's Farm.

Epidemics of typhoid and malaria, as well as the Panic of 1857, drove the six Grants (the number they were now) from the farm, and it appeared for a spell that Grant would be back in his father's tanning business, despite his dislike of it; however, Grant went into St. Louis real estate instead, mov-ing to the home of Harry and Louisa Boggs (cousins of Julia's and Grant's new business partner) on South Fourteenth Street. Unhappily, his first transactions may have been the sale of the Hardscrabble farm and the mortgaging of White Haven. Grant rented a house at Seventh and Lynch until he could buy another at 1008 Barton Street, near Eighth, where the family lived until they left St. Louis for Galena, Illinois, in May of 1860.

According to the myth makers, Grant spent his time in St. Louis har-vesting county taxes, or as an auctioneer, or as a collector of bad debts. In any case, he didn't make a nickel in real estate, so Grant petitioned for the post of county engineer and applied for a teaching position at Washington University. He got neither of these jobs, but hearsay says he did become a clerk in the customs house. However, his boss died and the new boss did not keep him on.

In Galena, Grant assisted his brother at his leather store, the same tan-ning connection he had tried earlier to avoid. He perhaps ducked more cus-

20. The Real Estate Firm of Boggs and Grant at 35 Pine Street, St. Louis, 1886

tomers than he served. The war then rescued Grant (as it did so many) from the futureless indignities of peace.

During the war, Grant's forces operated around St. Louis in order to frighten Sam Clemens into seeking his fortune in the west. Following the war, with Grant's finances in better shape than he could have earlier dreamed, the general made many efforts, most successful, to reconstitute and recombine the Gravois Creek properties. When Grant returned to St. Louis for short periods, he paced over them again, but he also took care to visit with General Sherman, who was living in the city and contemplating the composition of his memoirs.

For some time, President Grant envisioned retiring to White Haven to raise horses, but during his time in that high office, St. Louis gave the general more trouble than support. The "Whiskey Ring" scandal came to light in the city, and the practice of permitting distillers to make additional untaxed whiskey was laid at the feet of Grant's local cronies; moreover, the affair implicated his brother, Orvil, as well as other members of his extended family. If that wasn't enough, St. Louis spawned some of the most scurrilous stories that had surfaced during Grant's election campaigns. They principally concerned his drinking and his habitually penniless condition. Mud slinging is not a recent invention. And St. Louis had mud left over even after making all those bricks.

21

Grant's famous two-year tour of the world was not undertaken to avoid coming back to St. Louis, but it did the trick; in fact, that and his years in the White House had left Grant without a sense of "home." Business lodged the family in New York City, and that is where, through the embezzlements of others, he lost every cent he had as well as a good many that had never known his purse. To support his family Grant agreed to write a few articles on the battles of the Civil War and then undertook his *Memoirs*, which he hoped would stabilize his finances. Later in that same year— 1884—Grant's cancer of the throat was diagnosed.

The Century Company, which had commissioned the articles for their magazine, offered Grant a 10 percent royalty for his life story, but now Mark Twain (by this time an acquaintance of Grant's, and a publisher himself) came to the rescue, giving Grant 70 percent of the net, a deal which was the purist of charities. Moreover, Twain marketed the *Memoirs* successfully, ensuring Grant's widow a livelihood. Grant wrote through pain to the end, sending notes to his doctors since he could no longer speak. Yet he had written so much he felt he had become a part of speech. "The fact is," he scribbled to them, "I think I am a verb instead of a personal pronoun. A verb is anything that signifies to be; to do; or to suffer. I signify all three." Grant died, still a verb, on July 23, 1885.

21. Ulysses S. Grant, 1860

When Matthew Arnold crossed the sea to America in the fall of 1883, he was met at the boat in New York by Andrew Carnegie, his monetary superior if not his cultural equal; and by week's end his host had laid out a lavish party for his visitor at which General Grant was one guest among many of the most distinguished. The floral arrangement spelled out the titles of his major works in brightly glowing blooms. Arnold then gave an inaudible lecture in incomprehensible British to a packed hall while hiding his face behind his manuscript. Grant, who had felt obliged to attend, remarked to his wife that "we have paid to see the British lion; we cannot hear him roar, so we had better go home."

An "elitist" is the most polite name Matthew Arnold would be given now, nor would our cultivated country notice his arrival in such a flamboyant way today; but he didn't fare too well then, either. He found Philistines everywhere, almost as many as at home. His monocle was not admired. Arnold was said to have refused to give up his seat to a lady on a Boston horsecar, but the unanswered question is why he was riding there instead of in a private carriage. The *Chicago Tribune*, whose reporter had read the British press but not understood its stories, accused Arnold of lecturing for "filthy lucre," and a flurry of denials followed; however, why would Matthew Arnold have lowered himself so far as to bandy words with a newspaper?

The lecture which he chose to begin his tour was the first of two he gave at the Mercantile Library in St. Louis. The program on January 30, 1884, was "Numbers; or, the Majority and the Remnant." He followed this less than tactful discussion of the deficiencies of popular democracy with a very critical essay on Emerson on February 1. Newspapers followed his course noting mostly silly irrelevancies (Arnold speaks surrounded by women), by engaging in petty and provincial criticism (Arnold jeers at popular idols and shows contempt for the popular intellect), while making demeaning observations (when Arnold stands to peer at his manuscript, he looks like "an elderly bird picking at grapes on a trellis") and with curses—which were softened sometimes into innuendo (Arnold has no religious belief).

Back home and happy, expecting to enjoy his retirement, Arnold nevertheless took time from his shortening life to review General Grant's recent *Personal Memoirs*. Nowadays, the reader might be inclined to regard Arnold's remarks as generous, even indulgent, but they were seen as supercilious and condescending by Americans whose sense of inferiority, and consequential sensitivity to slight, were as advanced as a fatal disease. Mark Twain, General Grant's publisher, was particularly outraged. Arnold wrote:

> I found shown in them (the two bulky volumes of the *Memoirs*) a man, strong, resolute and business-like, as Grant had appeared to me when I first saw him; a man with no magical personality, touched by no divine light and giving out none. I found a language all astray in its use of *will* and *shall*, *should* and *would*, an English employing the verb *to conscript* and the participle *conscripting*, and speaking in a despatch to the Secretary of War of having *badly whipped* the enemy; an English without charm and without high breeding. But at the same time I found

a man of sterling good-sense as well as of the firmest resolution; a man, withal, humane, simple, modest; from all restless self-consciousness and desire for display perfectly free; never boastful where he himself was concerned, and where his nation was concerned seldom boastful, boastful only in circumstances where nothing but high genius or high training, I suppose, can save an American from being boastful. I found a language straightforward, nervous, firm, possessing in general the high merit of saying clearly in the fewest possible words what had to be said, and saying it, frequently, with shrewd and unexpected turns of expression.

In a speech given at the Annual Reunion of the Army and Navy Club of Connecticut, April 27, 1887, Mark Twain was, if not in great form, at least in high dudgeon. "Matthew Arnold has been finding fault with General Grant's English," he announced to the assemblage that immediately sensed a victim and began to smile. But Twain has found more errors in Arnold's essay than in Grant's big book. Now those smiles were replaced by laughter as anticipation was followed so swiftly by fulfillment. Twain happens to have at home a volume by Henry H. Breen, he says, devoted to the grammatical errors of the masters, and there he has found examples from thirty authors, each of whom Twain then names. The trump next played is a quotation from Matthew Arnold himself which confusedly overuses the pronoun "he." "To read that passage a couple of times would make a man dizzy, to read it four times would make him drunk," Twain observed to great laughter.

The vengeful publisher of Grant's *Memoirs*, warmed by so many beaten palms like a fine cognac in its snifter, extolled not only the General's prose and character but the simple frank style that America, throughout its history, has asked for and admired.

Great books are weighed and measured by their style and matter, not by the trimmings and shadings of their grammar. There is that about the sun which makes us forget his spots: and when we think of General Grant our pulses quicken and his grammar vanishes: we only remember that this is the simple soldier who, all untaught of the silken phrase-makers, linked words together with an art surpassing the art of the schools, and put into them a something which will still bring to American ears, as long as America shall last, the roll of his vanished drums and the tread of his marching hosts. [*Tumultuous applause.*] What do we care for grammar when we think of the man that put together that thunderous phrase, "Unconditional and immediate surrender!" And those others: "I propose to move immediately upon your works!" "I propose to fight it out on this line if it takes all summer!" [*Applause.*]

It is, nevertheless, Matthew Arnold who chose to quote from General Grant, with less chauvinism and more wisdom, the following great moment in American history: important because it concludes the Civil War, but great because two men, who had it in their power to do much harm, displayed, in this signal moment, uncommon decency instead:

When I had left camp that morning I had not expected so soon the result that was then taking place, and consequently was in rough garb. I was without a sword, as I usually was when on horseback in the field, and wore a soldier's blouse for a coat, and with the shoulder-straps of my rank to indicate to the army who I was. When I went into the house I found General Lee. We greeted each other, and, after shaking hands, took our seats.

What General Lee's feelings were I do not know. As he was a man of much dignity, with an impassible face, it was impossible to say whether he felt inwardly glad that the end had finally come, or felt sad over the result and was too manly to show it. Whatever his feelings, they were entirely concealed from my observation; but my own feelings, which had been quite jubilant on the receipt of his letter, were sad and depressed. I felt like anything rather than rejoicing at the downfall of a foe who had fought so long and valiantly, and had suffered so much for a cause, though that cause was, I believe, one of the worst for which a people ever fought.

General Lee was dressed in a full uniform which was entirely new, and was wearing a sword of considerable value, very likely the sword which had been presented by the State of Virginia. In my rough travelling suit, the uniform of a private with the straps of a lieutenant-general, I must have contrasted very strangely with a man so handsomely dressed, six feet high and of faultless form. But this was not a matter that I thought of until afterwards.

We soon fell into a conversation about old army times. He remarked that he remembered me well in the old army (of Mexico); and I told him that as a matter of course I remembered him perfectly, but from the difference in our rank and years (there being about sixteen years' difference in our ages) I had thought it likely that I had not attracted his attention sufficiently to be remembered by him after such a long interval. Our conversation grew so pleasant that I almost forgot the object of our meeting. After the conversation had run on in this style for some time, General Lee called my attention to the object of our meeting, and said that he had asked for this interview for the purpose of getting from me the terms I proposed to give his army. I said that I meant merely that his army should lay down their arms, not to take them up again during the continuance of the war unless duly and properly exchanged.

Shortly following his society wedding to Ellen Ewing in 1850,

WILLIAM T. SHERMAN

February 8, 1820 — February 14, 1891

William Sherman was posted to St. Louis's Jefferson Barracks, and during that summer he rented a small house for the two of them. His wife became pregnant immediately and returned to her family home in Ohio to have the baby, so that many of Sherman's early months in St. Louis were lonely. He fancied the city, however, which was booming and full of life. He had become acquainted with St. Louis while on a posting seven years earlier, when he had counted thirty-six steamers loading and unloading cargo on the levee, and at that time the massive movement of the Mississippi had made a permanent impression on the man who would later fight along its banks and for control of its ports. Soon he was expressing the hope that his wife's entire family might move from the placid town of Lancaster, where he was also born, to this bustling metropolis. But neither the expectant Ellen nor her family was inclined to budge; consequently, Sherman gave up his bungalow for a room in a boardinghouse. He explained her absence from his side in the gentlemanly manner of the time: "She is detained by a cause common to married ladies and will not probably be able to join me till April."

Sherman's first war was with his wife's passionate Catholicism, since his religious beliefs were indolent and vaguely Unitarian; his second was with his wife's formidable father, a local bigwig and powerful congressman whose influence on his daughter was deep and constant. Sherman had to charge into Ohio and almost rudely return his wife and new baby to St. Louis, where he had rented yet another house; moreover, he extracted her in such haste the legislator hadn't time to get back from Washington to see his grandchild. Neither of these conflicts were struggles a green Captain Sherman would win, for until her father's death in 1873, Ellen would spend more time in her family home than in her husband's house; and when he lay dazed on his death bed, his wife would call a priest to perform the last rites; finally, she would see that he was buried in sanctified ground.

Home life did what home life does, especially to those who leave conception, if not insemination, up to God, because Ellen was soon pregnant again, and off once more for Ohio. Meanwhile, Sherman was travelling downriver to his new assignment in New Orleans. These separations, which were to characterize their marriage, troubled Sherman so much that he determined to leave the army, throw in with James Lucas, a St. Louis financier, and go west to open a branch of the Lucas & Turner Bank in San Francisco. He auctioned the family's St. Louis goods for five hundred dollars and traveled as light as a soldier to the coast. He appears to have exercised his visitation rights, even when so far away, since in due course four more children were conceived, though they each arrived in Lancaster, Ohio, as if by mail. Sherman's fortunes did not fare well. He soon had an opportunity to fail on the East Coast as successfully as he had on the West, so St. Louis remained for him a "rising, growing, industrious" place, where "all patient, prudent, honest men can thrive." Like Grant, Sherman would find civilian life un-manageable, and the Civil War a personal blessing.

When war seemed imminent, Sherman began to consider returning to the army, though he had no enthusiasm for it. However, just at this time he received an offer from Henry Turner, whose San Francisco bank he had watched go under, to undertake the presidency of the St. Louis Railroad Company. The name and title were grand, but the company was not—amounting only to the Fifth Street horsecar line. When war broke out, Sherman was angling for one or other pork barrel appointment and was not greatly tempted by his military opportunities, but finally, when shame and family pressure grew too great, he accepted a colonelcy in the Thirteenth Infantry and went to Washington in time to participate in the first fiasco of Bull Run.

In Washington, Sherman began another war, this one with the press, whose account of the battle had enraged him and whom he began to blame for everything that went wrong instead of the politicians. His reasoning was unique. After an engagement he would imagine what the press would say about it and then angrily and publicly respond, often before any account had appeared. Reporters, he said, are "spies catering to the crassest appetite of our People." "I feel loathing towards them. In camp they are fawning syn-chophants [sic] and when your back is turned become libelous or flatterers according to the demand of the Press." By the time he was fighting in Kentucky, the newspapers were saying that Sherman was mad. Journalists then treated commanders in the field the way we speak of managers and coaches now, and were constantly calling for their disgrace and replace-ment. Military leaders were equally cantankerous. Sherman wrote about one reporter: "I had him with my army for a while. I ordered him shot one day, but got soft-hearted afterward and revoked the order. I've wished many times since I'd carried it out!"

Except for the St. Louis newspapers, which followed his career with a concern that rose soon to alarm, St. Louis dwindled in Sherman's life, hid-den by the noise and smoke of the war. Following the conflict, the notori-ously bloodthirsty General Sherman was given command of the army in Washington, where he languished in idleness and minor controversy (he loved too well the fair sex, it was said) until 1874, when the general, fed up with the corruption of the city and Grant's inept administration, cursing the Philistines into whose hands the country had fallen, moved his person and his command to St. Louis, taking a small surprised staff with him. Why not run the Army of Washington from here? "I am . . . prepared to execute any duties which may be devolved on me by proper authority. Here I am centrally located, and should occasion arise, I can personally proceed to any point . . . where my services are needed." "St. Louis with all its smoke & dirt," he wrote, "is far preferable. Like the oyster we are ugly outside, but in-side cozy and comfortable defying the storms that agitate the surface." Although his services were never needed, Sherman spent much of his time on the road, visiting this post or that, especially those near summer resorts where he had stashed his family. He traveled extensively through Europe, spoke frequently at dedications, statue unveilings, and other public occasions, attended weddings, and collected honorary degrees. Actually, his idiosyncratic move to St. Louis preserved him from the scandals that later soiled most of Washington's stuffed shirts, and he hung on in his pointless but centrally located position until he retired from the army in 1883.

Sherman had always been a reader. On his march to Savannah he consumed the novels of Sir Walter Scott as well as the countryside, and when a civilian he read to his children every evening (if they were with him at home), from Shakespeare, Dickens, and Thackeray, as well as Bret Harte and Mark Twain. Like Grant, Sherman had written many letters and reports, and since his wife was rarely living with him, messages to Lancaster, Ohio, often cantankerous, were frequent; but few could have foreseen the quality of the memoirs he would write during the time he found himself at home in the city which had long ago won his loyalty.

It was the much admired historian, George Bancroft, who urged Sherman to write his memoirs, suggesting a motive that was sure to appeal: so that future generations would not "embrace & perpetuate wrong facts and reasons." Certainly, Sherman did not linger on his errors, while he delighted in those of others, but many of his pages will find few equals in military history.

Sherman's loyalty to St. Louis would be tried. The city did what cities do. Sherman spent twelve thousand dollars renovating his Garrison Avenue house. His property was promptly reassessed and his taxes went up. Then, in 1884, the city paved his street, but the work was sloppily done and had to be repeated. Sherman was assessed for both "improvements." One day a water department official noticed a hired man hosing the sidewalk in

22

front of the General's house. He charged Sherman a dollar for each foot of sidewalk so swept, and the Garrison house water bill rose from $80 a year to $225. The homeowner swore he would not pay, and the *St. Louis Post-Dispatch* promptly attacked him for displaying "poor civic spirit." Ellen counterattacked with her lawyer and was required to pay only the original charge.

Loyal he was, but hardly faithful. As if she were one of the general's many women, New York beckoned, and in 1886, with his children scattered and his wife as unhappy in St. Louis as ever, he took up residence where Grant had settled in his old age, and where his wife, now content but impossibly overweight, was carried to a second floor she never left while alive. Nevertheless, the room she rested in was not in St. Louis. The general, who had suffered from asthma his entire life, grew so weak and breathless he could no longer entertain. Erysipelas became another force on the field, and then pneumonia. Hearing of his condition, Samuel Clemens wrote to him: "You have been a good friend to me, & I, like all the rest of this nation, grieve to think that the kindest heart & the most noble spirit that exist today are about to be taken away from us. These words will not come to your eye, but I had to say them for the love I bear you & so long have borne you."

William T. Sherman died on St. Valentine's Day 1891, in the arms of his longtime enemy, his wife's religion. His body was returned to St. Louis where the funeral was held on February 21, officiated by his son Tom. The largest funeral cortege in the history of St. Louis moved slowly through the streets lined with layers of its citizens until it reached Calvary Cemetery, where Sherman was buried alongside his wife, Ellen, whose remains would live in St. Louis after all.

23

About 7 A.M. of November 16th we rode out of Atlanta by the Decatur road, filled by the marching troops and wagons of the Fourteenth Corps; and reaching the hill, just outside of the old rebel works, we naturally paused to look back upon the scenes of our past battles. We stood upon the very ground whereon was fought the bloody battle of July 22d, and could see the copse of wood where McPherson fell. Behind us lay Atlanta, smouldering and in ruins, the black smoke rising high in air, and hanging like a pall over the ruined city. Away off in the distance, on the McDonough road, was the rear of Howard's column, the gun-barrels glistening in the sun, the white-topped wagons stretching away to the south; and right before us was the Fourteenth Corps, marching steadily and rapidly, with a cheery look and swinging pace, that made light of the thousand miles that lay between us and Richmond. Some band, by accident, struck up the anthem of "John Brown's soul goes marching on;" the men caught up the strain, and never before or since have I heard the chorus of "Glory, glory, hallelujah!" done with more spirit, or in better harmony of time and place.

—*Memoirs of W. T. Sherman*

23. *Sherman funeral procession, turning from Pine Street onto Grand Avenue, 1891*

It is commonly
alleged that the
Germans float-

ed down the Mississippi to St. Louis on the lids of grand pianos, and it is
certainly true that German immigrants became major contributors to the
rich musical heritage of the city; however, it was up the river from New
Orleans they mostly came, following the abortive uprisings of 1848 in
France, Germany and Austria. There was already a substantial German-
speaking community in St. Louis when the new refugees arrived; however,
the new people (called Greens) were political, not economic, outcasts, and
mostly professionals whose bitterness over their losses at home was often
mournfully expressed, and whose scorn for a country they had fled to
rather than eagerly chosen, was often loudly announced and arrogantly as-
serted.

In addition to the "natives" then—smooth-shaven Anglo-Americans
who liked to sport polished boots, wear sober black suits and crown their
heads with stovepipe hats—there were the early immigrants the natives had
grown somewhat used to: the potato-famine Irish with their brawling
drunken ways and misguided national pride toward whom the Anglos had
learned to turn a deaf ear and nurture a blind eye, and then the post-
Napoleonic Germans (the Grays), who were still a bit annoying, with their
caps and pipes, their guttural noises, their priests and beer, their cabbage
and sausage culture. Now another curse was to be inflicted upon the good
people of the city: more Germans, this time bearded bohemians shouting
radical slogans and bearing revolutionary emblems, intellectuals with
sneers for the locals and scorn for the church and its clerics, exiles who
brought nothing with them but their moral superiority and useless refine-
ments.

Couldn't speak a word, of course; had no skills for any kind of normal
employment and even less inclination; so they founded German newspapers, wrote German novels, put on German plays, formed musical groups
in support of German music, took over the Schiller Societies, earlier established to honor the freedom-loving poet, and began to make political nui-
sances of themselves, particularly by seizing immediately on the issue of
slavery and fervently denouncing that "peculiar institution." Americans
regularly forget the relentless energy freedom requires for just the motor's
normal maintenance. And this time market forces permitted a greater play
of moral principle, because the continued influx of cheap labor in urban
areas cost slavery its economic utility so that voices raised against the practice could be better heard and more fully appreciated than before.

The Forty-Eighters found the Germans in St. Louis much as they were
elsewhere in the United States—in social, political, religious and economic
disunity—and the energetic new arrivals felt obliged to give their native
community a persistent and powerful voice. In Adolph Douai's novel of
1858, *Fata Morgana*, the United States is seen as an improvement over
Europe, but in a rather unflattering, warlike way. In Europe the downtrod-
den are given no choice but to be trodden down, for there is no path up for

them; whereas in the States citizens can scratch and bite back, because they "have come far enough for a general feeling of equality to reign, and for a relatively large number of people to be able to rise above the average, so that *actual* equality is expanded, not just equality in the abstract, and *progress is possible.*"

The most immediately important émigré figure to arrive—Heinrich Börnstein—was from Paris via Hamburg, where he was born in 1805. If, for St. Louisans, Börnstein became a mixed bag, he certainly began as a mixed breed: his father was Catholic and an actor, while his mother was a Protestant, and the two faiths appeared to cancel one another out, leaving Heinrich a convinced anti-clerical free-thinker. After service in the Austrian

army, which he enjoyed about as much as his compulsory Jesuit education, Börnstein went to Paris in the 1840s, where, following his father culturally if not otherwise, he adapted French plays for German consumption and started a German weekly called *Vorwärts!*, which was to be a liberal reformist review of culture and, of course, politics, and which he edited with his friend Karl Bernays, a collaboration they would continue later in St. Louis.

24

The German authorities did not fancy this Paris poison and frequently banned offending issues, actions which naturally pushed Börnstein further left, so that soon he was publishing Heinrich Heine and Karl Marx. When, however reasonably, his journal began to support assassination attempts against the Prussian king, Friedrich Wilhelm IV, the Prussian king asked Louis Philippe to shut him down, and Louis Philippe, often an assassin's target, happily obliged. Shortly afterward, Börnstein followed his friend Bernays to America, and in March 1850 he was brought to St. Louis to edit the well-established German-language newspaper *Anzeiger des Westens* (The Western Advertiser), which had been founded by Wilhelm Weber in 1835 and had a long and laudable anti-slavery tradition.

Börnstein was an occupational chameleon: translator, drama critic, editor, political pundit, pharmacist (as needed), physician (if necessary), entrepreneur, investment speculator and muckraking novelist. As soon as he sat down in St. Louis he began an anti-Jesuit novel, *Die Geheimnisse von St. Louis*, which was later translated by Friederich Münch as *The Mysteries of St. Louis; Or, The Jesuits on the Prairie des Noyers, A Western Tale*, published in 1852. The book was dedicated to his newspaper's favorite politician of the moment, Thomas Hart Benton. It contains many intemperate attacks upon St. Louis Jesuits, one of whom, the character of Father Antonio, is depicted as a thief, seducer and murderer. The unholy father's just desert is to be buried alive beneath a chest of jewels. The novel also describes the cholera plague of 1849 with great vividness and considerable accuracy. Börnstein sponsored a series of political novels by his pals, notably Adolph Douai's aforementioned *Fata Morgana* and Otto Ruppius's *Der Prairie-Teufel* (The

Prairie Devil). In addition to serializing fiction in his paper, he printed poems, odd squibs and accounts of murders provided they were sensational enough. In the late 1850s he organized a legitimate theatre company, the St. Louis Opern-Haus, located on Market Street. These were boards his actress wife would trod.

Börnstein also founded a "Society of Free Men," intended as a center of anti-Christian polemic, and from almost his first day engaged in heated attacks against both Catholics and Lutherans. His chief companion in this endeavor was Franz Schmidt, the editor of an anti-clerical weekly, the *Freie Blätter*, who said of the so-called Old Lutherans that their works

25

(by which he meant their writings) "stank as badly as the St. Louis levee on a hot summer's day." We can believe the part about the levee at least. Attacks of this kind, from every quarter, were common. Börnstein's particular bête noire was the Catholic daily *Tages-Chronik* (The Daily Chronicle), founded in 1851 and edited by August Böckling. Its inaugural editorial stated its unremitting hostility to "Jews and heathens," both of whom Börnstein insisted had, as citizens, the same rights as everyone else.

But Börnstein shared the Greens' arrogance and anti-clericalism, which he redoubled; he lived as flamboyantly as he talked, looking always for more pies to put his fingers in; and he encouraged in his papers a kind of "yellow journalism" which earned him the enmity of even those whom he had not managed to affront directly.

An editorial in the October 22, 1857, edition of the *Anzeiger des Westens* advised the new arrivals about the best way to become "an American":

> There is a special technique to becoming American. It seems to us that the right way to become American is to evaluate the relationships here correctly, to learn from their errors and derive benefit from them, to avoid their excesses, and to desist from applying one's own narrowly European concepts of order to this young, untrammeled land, but also not to take as granted the injustices and humbug found here just because they have been accepted by earlier settlers and their descendents. The alternative to this is not Americanization; it is ruin and decadence: to give oneself up to the American style of loafing; to wander the streets spangled with gold but with empty heads, hearts, and pockets; to participate in swindles of all descriptions; to waste one's talents and energies on the false values of lotteries; to be obsessed by humbug; and to lose one's own mother tongue and pass the day mangling English instead. . . .

25. *Frontispiece of* The Mysteries of St. Louis, *1852*

Germans are more careful in business and less excessive in their enjoyment than Americans. When immigration was less intense and Germans lived here as isolated individuals rather than as organized groups, the Americans called them "small souls." The American tolerates a peculiar individual only with misgivings, but as soon as such persons reach a certain mass and are present in large numbers, then he does not withhold recognition. For instance, if the majority of the population here were indifferent to religion and there were only a Methodist dolt or some other sectarian here or there, there is no doubt that the population would laugh these fools to scorn. But since this foolishness is held by many and has become a social necessity, they are spared. How much more must German thriftiness and honesty in business compel recognition when not just a few isolated persons but an entire division of the population sails secure and undamaged through a crisis that arises from the reverse of these virtues, from the excessive luxury, euphoria, and irresponsible self-aggrandizement of the natives.

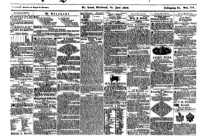

26

When the Civil War began, Börnstein volunteered to be a colonel in the Union Army and was awarded the consulship in Bremen after three months of service. Meanwhile, his newspaper felt the lack of his guiding hand, as did his finances generally, and the *Anzeiger* silenced its presses in 1863. Reconstruction dashed his radical political hopes, and his authority in the German-American community was severely diminished during the ensuing partisan ebb and flow. Ever an opportunist, he remained in Europe as a photographer and then found work as a theatrical manager in Vienna. His memoirs—*Fünfundsiebzig Jahre in der altern und der neuen Welt. Memoiren eines Unbedeutenden* (Seventy-Five Years in the Old and the New World: Memoirs of a Nobody)—did return to annoy the American Germans with its lively but highly partisan and polemical account of "the good old days" when parts of it were published in 1879.

The following is an excerpt from that memoir, a text that deserves to be better appreciated. It incidentally confirms Mark Twain's description of St. Louis's drinking water:

Certainly it took awhile to overcome our qualms and get to like the water as it was then offered in St. Louis. It really had an alarming appearance, and at first we drank it only with misgivings, with a few drops of spirit of fennel or rum. In those days the water works in St. Louis were still of a very limited sort. There was still no talk of clarification or filtration, and when a glass was filled from a hydrant, it looked like chocolate. It had to be let stand for a quarter hour before there was a half glass on top of reasonably clear water, the other half filled with mud sinking to the bottom. I recalled the old saying that every person had to eat seven pounds of mire and filth, but in St. Louis it was even worse, for we downed our seven pounds of mud every month. In later times we came to do well with Mississippi water, finding all alcoholic addition

26. Masthead of Anzeiger des Westens, *June 24, 1856*

unnecessary, and we always felt well, although part of this was due to improvements in the water works with clarification basins and filtration. By continuing our simple European ways in years to come, we all remained healthy. I know that I was only sick in bed once the first year, but otherwise always healthy and strong, and the same was the case with my entire family. We acclimatized ourselves rapidly, and despite many hardships and new, unexpected situations, we had no reason to complain of our condition in America.

The first impression St. Louis made on me was not very positive. The town was already in rapid expansion into a great center of trade, but to me, a spoiled Parisian who was at home on the asphalt of the boulevards, it struck me like a large village. To be sure the main streets had sidewalks paved with bricks placed on end. But the middle of the street was only macadamized, and there was as yet no spraying at city expense. The result was that the streets were like the Sahara in dry weather with thick, swirling clouds of dust, while in rainy weather they became bottomless seas of mire. In wet weather it became an art and a matter of some courage to cross from one side of the street to another without getting stuck in the mire. Granted there were crossing stones at a certain distance from one another, rectangular stones running right across the street so that the wheels of carriages ran between them. This was precisely the same primitive arrangement the Romans had used two millennia before, and which can be discovered in Pompeii, excavated from the ashes of Vesuvius.

A certain dexterity was always called for to get to the opposite side via these stones. One could not make a misstep or his foot would sink into the mire, and continuous rainy weather sometimes brought the mud so high that even crossing stones were covered. Then a person had to step into the unknown, trusting to luck to step in the place where a stone should be. This did not exclude many an error. Once in those days I was in the broad Carondelet Avenue, which then resembled a backwater of the Pontine Marshes in the relentless rain. I made a bad step, landing alongside a crossing stone rather than on it, and my right foot sank up to the calf in mire. I managed to work myself out, but with the loss of my boot, which remained stuck in the mud and was irretrievably lost. The result was that I had to hop on one foot to my apartment, which fortunately was nearby. Such was the condition of the main streets. But in most of the other streets there were neither sidewalks nor crossing stones, and in bad weather one sank in on stepping out of one's own house door. In the streets which ran behind Fourth parallel to the river, there were still no entirely uninterrupted streets constructed, with the exception of Seventh. Instead, large areas of grass, sand or clay lay between scattered groups of houses, the building lots of the future. Who was supposed to be building sidewalks there? Even the streets running to the west from the river were in the same miserable, interrupted condition. Street illumination was in its infancy, and the farther one came from the city's center the poorer it grew, ceasing altogether in the streets running near the outer edge.

There were only a few stone houses. The majority of homes were built with thin brick walls, strongly intermingled with frame houses, and the more one advanced from the center, the more log cabins were to be seen. The bricks for the brick houses, usually only a stone and a half in weight, made the interiors of these houses intolerably hot in the summer, and the heat absorbed in the daytime was radiated by the walls at night, making the heat of rooms even worse after nightfall.

At the Camp Jackson Memorial, now in Lyon Park opposite the Anheuser-Busch Brewery, Heinrich Börnstein's name is misspelled.

> ## CARL SCHURZ
> March 2, 1829 — May 14, 1906

Other Germans would achieve more lasting fame than Heinrich Börnstein, though few would have his literary importance. In 1867 Carl Schurz descended from Detroit to assist Emil Preetorius in editing the *Westliche Post*, a newspaper founded a decade earlier by Carl Daenzer, who had worked for Börnstein before and guided the journal during its first years until 1860. Later Joseph Pulitzer, who had arrived penniless in St. Louis in 1865, also served as an editor. This important liberal daily threw its support to their former employee, Carl Schurz, who had gone public and toned down his radical rhetoric, like any politician, to keep in tune with changing times. The paper argued, as he did, for unrestricted male suffrage, amnesty for ex-rebels, tariff reductions and reform of the patronage-ridden civil service.

Briefly a minister to Spain, a Union general, then a state senator, before becoming the Secretary of the Interior for President Hayes, Schurz was more a speaker of the word than a writer of it; however, his *Life of Henry Clay*, clearly an orator's choice, which he completed in 1887, remains significant. His brief stint as an editor of the *Westliche Post* earned him a nameplate on the monument *The Naked Truth* in Compton Hill Reservoir Park, along with Emil Preetorius and Carl Daenzer.

27

It was Emil Preetorius who was, after 1864, in charge of the editorial columns of the *Westliche Post*. Another radical refugee, this time from the Rhineland, he also began to moderate his views as the success of the radicals increased, and his gift for the middle of the road stood him in good stead for thirty-five years of service as publisher of the *Post*. His work at the paper was ably continued by his son, Edward. When the city held a "German Day" at the St. Louis World's Fair in 1904 (many countries were so honored), a record-breaking 184,000 persons attended. Carl Schurz and Emil Preetorius both spoke. Together they stressed the importance of a continued healthy relation between the United States and the German Empire, and neither could have imagined the animosities that would brazenly show themselves, or the discrimination that would blatantly occur during the First World War. It became persecution, finally, and went a great way toward reducing the influence of the Forty-Eighters on the city's cultural climate, and hastened the city's intellectual and artistic decline.

The importance of the press in mid-nineteenth-century St. Louis cannot be overestimated, and in 1859 Friedrich Münch reported on its flourishing condition:

> The reader will want to know more about the German newspapers in order to be able to form an opinion about the intellectual efforts of his countrymen in Missouri. —The "Anzeiger des Westerns," which appears in St. Louis, was the first German newspaper west of the Mississippi, and from that day to this it has been in capable hands. A bit more than a year ago the "Westliche Post" was founded in the place of other newspapers not worth remembering; both newspapers, though different in tone and attitude, support the cause of progress, of making Missouri a free state, of the rights and interests of the Germans here, and of the reorganization of federal politics, all with equal warmth, and they are not only the most influential German organs in the entire West, but they can be compared directly with the very best of the European newspapers. —The "St. Louis Chronik" is conservative and opposes any alteration of the current system of slavery—it is read mostly by Catholics. —The "Herold des Glaubens" is an utterly Catholic newspaper. The "Mississippi-Handelszeitung" is trying to fulfill its mission with laudable zeal. —The German newspapers in the countryside—the "St. Charles Demokrat," the "Hermanner Volksblatt" and the "St. Joseph-Zeitung" are all on the liberal side.
>
> The newspapers here cannot be expected to preserve the restrained tone of European journals. Not only do they subject the conditions and events of the Old World, of which they are kept well informed through numerous correspondents, to a scathing critique, but the parties hew at one another with a two-edged sword—the President himself is spared no more than the least citizen, and deeds and personalities are discussed which seldom come to be spoken of in public in Germany. Anyone who stands out for any reason must expect to be subjected to public criticism, and few are able to win friends without also gaining open rebuke as well. The searching investigations miss nothing, and a so-called public man had better cover himself well lest he show his weak spots. It is worst of all for a candidate—the opposing party will leave no

artery unslashed. —I would not be so bold as to assert that decency is observed in every case, or that the limits of good taste are not frequently overstepped in the course of this mud-slinging, but until people learn to master their passions, republicans cannot allow themselves to be too touchy. Here people prefer to put up with the abuse of the press rather than give up their unrestricted right to do what they want; people think the evils committed by the press can also be corrected by the press, and only the continuous vigilance of all can preserve freedom and secure progress.

There was little "separation of church and state" in the magazines and newspapers of this period. Religion was politics by different means. While much argumentation was scurrilous and rarely high-minded, some managed to achieve considerable intellectual distinction. For instance, Edward Preuss began his career as a Lutheran lay theologian, the influence no doubt of his

28

German origins, but later became a Catholic intellectual of equal note. He edited the German-language daily, *Amerika*, from 1878 to 1902. His son, Arthur, had an equally distinguished career in theology, publishing the *Fortnightly Review* from 1905 to 1935. In addition, he served as the literary editor for the B. Herder Book Company of St. Louis, a press that published many of his translations of German religious texts, as well as books and compilations from his own pen, among them the unusual *Dictionary of Secret and Other Societies* in 1924.

The publishers of German newspapers realized that although many of their readers read the English-language press and knew what that world was thinking "native Americans" were woefully ignorant of emigrant attitudes and situations; so they established journals in English designed to reflect German concerns. The first of these was the *German-American*, founded by Heinrich Gempp in 1851. Joseph Pulitzer's radical *St. Louis Post* was just such a spin-off, but it quickly showed a wholly independent spirit. In 1879 it swallowed the conservative *Evening Dispatch* when Pulitzer bought the bankrupt paper at auction, and the long and distinguished career of the hyphened pair—the only daily left in St. Louis today—was launched. Magazines followed suit. Frederick Kenkel, the editor of the reform-minded Catholic monthly, *Central-Blatt and Social Justice Review*, gradually shifted its language from German to English.

In nineteenth-century St. Louis, newspapers opened and closed like night-blooming plants, or they merged, or changed their names to increase the confusion, and frequently altered their politics as well.

The *Missouri Gazette and Louisiana Advertiser*, for example, founded in 1808 by Joseph Charless, an Irish printer, was the first newspaper west of the Mississippi. For reasons which escape reason, it became the *Louisiana*

Gazette in 1809, only to emerge as the *Missouri Republican* in 1825 when Charless's son, Edward, took it over. Later on it appeared as the *Republican* and then finally the *Republic* without appreciably shortening its aims. As early as 1823 it said, of that part of the city living near the levee, that the steamboats made smoke "so dense as to render it necessary to use candles at midday." The *Republic*'s building, as well as the offices of the *St. Louis Reveille*, burned during a serious wharf fire in 1849. B. Gratz Brown's *Missouri Democrat* was renamed the *Democrat*, and then became the *Globe-Democrat* when purchased by the *Globe*. On the other hand, Thomas Hart Benton ran the *St. Louis Enquirer*, a paper he founded in 1819, for thirty years without even altering its 'E'.

Pulitzer, long-necked, beaky and gawky as a land bird, was gregari-

JOSEPH PULITZER
April 10, 1847 — October 29, 1911

ous but pugnacious as well, especially in his youth. In 1869, aged twenty-two, he surprised everyone by getting elected to the state legislature. He then exposed in the *Westliche Post*, for which he was still writing, the corruption he found in government, and especially in the County Court of St. Louis, a situation so severe he introduced a bill designed to discharge the court as an administrative body. This did not sit well with Captain Edward Augustine (a Goliath of a man), who was to be the recipient of the court's largess, so he went to Jefferson City to lobby against the legislation. In no time, Pulitzer (our diminutive David, here) and Augustine collided on a carpet of battle. Wallace Gruelle of the *St. Louis Dispatch* (later to be acquired by Pulitzer) wrote the story:

> *Jefferson City, Jan. 27, 1870*—To-night, about half past 7 o'clock, Mr. Pulitzer shot at and wounded Mr. Augustine in the office of the Schmidt Hotel. It appears that Mr. Pulitzer—and, by the way, I am on Pulitzer's side, not because he is a newspaper man, but he is a clever, affable gentleman, whose portrait I intend to paint some day, and he voted right on the Richland County bill—had sent an article to the *Westliche Post*, at which Mr. Augustine took offense, and mildly told Mr. Pulitzer that he was a liar. Mr. Pulitzer cautioned Mr. Augustine against using such strong language. Mr. Pulitzer left the hotel and got a pistol and returned and went for Mr. Augustine. Had not his pistol been knocked down, Missouri would have been in mourning this day for a slaughtered loyal son. As it was, only two shots were fired, one of which took effect in Augustine's leg. Augustine struck Pulitzer on the head with a Derringer, or some other kind of pistol, cutting his scalp and ending the battle. Mr. Pulitzer was arrested and gave bond for his appearance before the City Magistrate of Jefferson City.

A day later, Gruelle could treat the affair with levity:

> I will have to practice him [Pulitzer] at pistol shooting—have to make him understand that when he wants to shoot a gentleman he must take distance at such a pace that the party to be shot cannot knock the pistol down with his hand. Shooting is a science and ought to be scientifically done. I am going to turn the alleyway of Miss Lusk, just back of my room, into a shooting gallery and put Pulitzer under a severe course of training for about two weeks, day and night, and I will bet, at the end of that time, he can snuff a candle at ten steps. If he can't, I now and here pledge you my word of honor that I will shoot myself.

About the affair there was more noise than action. Should the House of Representatives look into it? Of course not. "If a member attended a wine party and happened to kiss a pretty girl there, should the House investigate?" one member rhetorically wondered. Pulitzer was fined one hundred dollars and told not to shoot anybody else, at least for a while.

In December 1878 Joseph Pulitzer bought the bankrupt *Evening Dispatch* for $2,500 at auction on the steps of the Old Courthouse. But the name of the buyer wasn't being broadcast—trumpet blowing would take place later in the history of the Pulitzer empire. Julian S. Rammelkamp wrote about the mystery in his *Pulitzer's Post-Dispatch 1878-1883*:

> Who had actually bought the paper? When questioned, Arnold said he had served as the agent of Joseph Pulitzer, the real purchaser. But when the interested spectators turned to ask him, Pulitzer had disappeared. It was not until evening, in the dining room of the Lindell, St. Louis's leading hotel, that a reporter from the *Globe-Democrat* at last cornered him. Delighting in the role of mystery man, Pulitzer blandly denied that he had had anything to do with the transaction at the courthouse. The reporter persisted, pointing out

that Arnold "told me distinctly that he had purchased the paper for you." "Did he?" was the soft-spoken reply. "Generous man."

Exasperated, the reporter told his editor that "no one better understands the use of language—to conceal one's thoughts—than Mr. Pulitzer. He parries the question like a skillful fencer, and it is as hard to pin him to a point as it is an eel."

The editor of the *Globe-Democrat,* laconic and formidable Joseph B. McCullagh, must have allowed himself an inward smile. Dismissing the frustrated reporter, he turned to his desk and wrote an editorial paragraph for the next morning's edition:

> The fine Pulitzerian diplomacy which has so often shrouded coming events in the dim twilight of uncertainty, is now brought into requisition to hide from mortal vision the fate of our evening contemporary, the Dispatch. But we think we detect the coming journalist behind the evasive interviewee, and behold in Mr. Pulitzer the future wielder of the destinies of that newspaper.

With John Dillon, publisher of the *St. Louis Post*, Pulitzer brought out the first issue of the *Post and Dispatch* on December 12, using the presses of the *Globe-Democrat*. Once Pulitzer possessed both papers he immediately set out to win readers through exposés, lively trivia and moral crusades. The writing in the leading dailies was dull, often deliberately so in order to seem respectable. Pulitzer's pieces were brief, vivid, confident, direct, explanatory. He went after the seducers as well as the seduced, reporting the crimes of the bigwigs as well as those of the petty. Pulitzer founded feuds as though they were investment houses and suffered physical attacks on the street. All news. Across town, William Marion Reedy was reading the competition.

In 1883 Joseph Pulitzer purchased the *New York World* with his profits from the *Post-Dispatch*, and this new challenge drew him eastward. A newspaper empire the equal of William Randolph Hearst's was the eventual result. Some believed Pulitzer was pushed out of town by another shooting. In 1882, while he was out of the city, his paper accused an appropriately named former colonel of the Confederacy, Alonzo Slayback, of cowardice. The colonel was a well-regarded lawyer with extensive contacts who had initiated the Veiled Prophet's parade (and the debutante ball that followed) as a suitable start for St. Louis's autumn social season. Slayback marched into the *Post-Dispatch* offices to demand a retraction. The managing editor, John Cockerill, also appropriately named, shot him dead. Furthermore, Cockerill, accused of planting a weapon on his victim like a contemporary TV cop, escaped indictment. Some wanted to burn the *Post-Dispatch* building down. So while commerce may have lured Joseph Pulitzer to a more glittery city, his journey east was followed by a cloud.

In his will, Pulitzer established the now-famous prizes for drama, fiction, biography, and later, poetry—the call to Parnassus being a bit tardy—which are still administered by Columbia University.

THE FIRST PULITZER PLATFORM:

The *POST* and *DISPATCH* will serve no party but the people; will be no organ of "Republicanism," but the organ of truth; will follow no caucases [*sic*] but its own convictions; will not support the "Administration," but criticise it; will oppose all frauds and shams wherever and whatever they are; will advocate principles and ideas rather than prejudices and partisanship. These ideas and principles are precisely the same as those upon which our government was originally founded and to which we owe our country's marvelous growth and development. They are the same that made a Republic possible and without which a real Republic is impossible. They are the ideas of a true, genuine, real Democracy. They are the principles of hard money, home rule, and revenue reform.

WILLIAM T. HARRIS
September 10, 1835 — November 5, 1909

During the several decades in which St. Louis could call itself a world-class city, it was also the center of philosophical activity in the United States. In 1866 William Torrey Harris founded the St. Louis School of Idealism and originated the systematic study of German thought in this country. His important periodical, *The Journal of Speculative Philosophy* (1867-1893), published the early work of most major American philosophers, William James, Josiah Royce and John Dewey among them, as well as such German philosophers as Hegel, Fichte and Schelling, and was the first professional periodical in the United States to be devoted to philosophy. His seminal book, *Hegel's Logic*, appeared in 1890. He spent a substantial amount of his time in Cambridge, Massachusetts, where (an ardent Emersonian as well) he established the Concord School of Philosophy in 1879.

A Yale dropout, Harris came to St. Louis ostensibly to buy farmland for his father, but he was also seeking personal freedom and desired to become

31. *William T. Harris, 1876*

32

a newspaper reporter—an ambition he soon abandoned when he obtained a teaching position at the Clay School. By chance, he made the acquaintance of an ardent Hegelian, Henry Conrad Brokmeyer (1826-1906), a recent immigrant who had found employment as an iron molder. Brokmeyer was as intellectually unbending as his industrial material, and this inflexibility, which became notorious (it got him expelled from two universities), was parodied by a fellow Idealist, John Gabriel Woerner, in his Civil War novel, *The Rebel's Daughter*. There he can be recognized as Dr. Rauhenfels (or "Dr. Roughrock"). Other members of the group have roles, including William Harris, who performs as Professor Altrue. When Denton Snider (1841-1925) joined the group (and became its chronicler), the St. Louis Idealists were born. Eighteen members signed the society's articles of constitution in 1866. The ambitions of the society can be measured by the invitations they issued, including ones to Ralph Waldo Emerson, Amos Bronson Alcott and Henry James, Sr. Though Harris published a number of books and wrote more then five hundred articles, none of the functioning members was more indefatigable than Snider, who authored more than fifty books through a lifetime that must have been all verbs.

Apart from his specific philosophical work, Brokmeyer published an account of his successful rise from laborer to landowner in *Mechanic's Diary*, while Snider applied his Hegelian views to an understanding of the slavery issue with a book called *Ten Years' War*. Missouri's ambivalence about slavery, its border status and its strategic military location made it a perfect stage for the interplay of Hegelian dialectical forces.

Locally, Harris was esteemed as an educator—appointed University Professor of Philosophy of Education at Washington University in 1876 while he was still superintendent of the St. Louis public schools, then serving as the U.S. Commissioner of Education from 1889 to 1907. It was in these roles that he was honored for his public services by the citizens of St. Louis with the gift of his portrait in full beard and evening clothes on one occasion, with a pewter snuffbox and a sword bearing an etched blade on another, and by three medals, one bronze, one gold, one of yellow metal, on still others. The city even named ten townhouses between 1100-1118 South Eighteenth Street (he lived at 1116) William T. Harris Row. *Sic transit*, however, for histories of American philosophy scarcely mention him now, and one of his portraits leaned against a basement wall in Washington University's Busch Hall for years, unrecognized and ignored.

The Department of Philosophy at Washington University was founded by the appointment of Arthur Lovejoy in 1901. While in this position, he wrote some twenty scholarly papers, several of which became famous, particularly his analysis of William James's views called "Thirteen Pragmatisms." Lovejoy spent the bulk of his career at Johns Hopkins, and his seminal work, *The Great Chain of Being*, influenced a generation of philosophers and literary critics and established the history of ideas as a legitimate subject of study.

If you are the author of the prayer taken by Alcoholics Anonymous as its own, are you thereby a literary figure? Reinhold Niebuhr (June 21, 1892-June 1, 1971) was born nearby in Wright City, though his family moved when he was three to St. Charles on their eventual way to Lincoln, Illinois. Niebuhr received some of his training at Eden Seminary when it was in Wellston, and his image graces a stained glass window in the Seminary Chapel now in Webster Groves. *Moral Man and Immoral Society* made him widely known, and his appearance on the cover of *Time* defined his final fame. William Harris would not have been pleased with the thrust of Niebuhr's thought, which distrusted collectives, doubted the effectiveness of human rationality, disbelieved in progress and the realization of utopias. In the preface to *Moral Man*, Niebuhr puts his position bluntly enough: "In every human group there is less reason to guide and check impulse, less capacity for self-transcendence, less ability to comprehend the needs of others and therefore more unrestrained egoism than the individuals, who compose the group, reveal in their personal relationships."

You will recognize the so called "Serenity Prayer." It is almost hummable: "O God, give us grace to accept with serenity the things that cannot be changed, courage to change the things that should be changed, and the wisdom to distinguish the one from the other."

The first time I ever saw St. Louis, I could have bought it for six million dollars, and it was the mistake of my life that I did not do it.
—Life on the Mississippi

Sometimes Samuel Clemens came to town, sometimes Mark Twain. Sometimes he came from close by, but often from far off, from Hartford where he was living in a proper mansion, making and losing money, remembering the river. In 1845, when he first visited the city, in the company of his father, he was ten and had boated down from Hannibal no more than a hundred miles away and a half-a-day ride. Sam and the city were both starry-eyed. In Hannibal any neighborhood boy who had been to St. Louis became a person of some weight. When Huck Finn and Jim drift by St. Louis during the night of their flight, Huck says "the whole world lit up." Sam's brother, Orion, was working as a printer in the city then, and a bit later his sister Pamela Moffett, and her husband, took up residence. A Clemens presence in St. Louis has been continuous in the city since. The James Clemens mansion at 1849 Cass Avenue is on the Register of Historic Buildings, and Dr. J. L. Clemens lived at 3958 Washington Avenue, a house remarkable for its cast-iron porch pillars. It is now called the Playboy Hotel, a name which carries unfortunate and misleading connotations. Cyril Clemens, a third cousin twice removed, established the International Mark Twain Society and published the *Mark Twain Journal* here, while maintaining his home in Kirkwood as a kind of shrine. He died in 1999 at the age of ninety-six.

With his eighteen-year-old eyes set on New York, where there was a World's Fair and a Crystal Palace, Sam left Hannibal to stay with his sister in St. Louis in their house on Locust, while he earned passage money to the real city. Having worked with Orion a bit in the printing business, he became a printer's devil at the *Evening News and Intelligencer.* St. Louis was a little livelier than New York just then, however. Steamboats and barges by the dozens came and went daily, the town grew almost visibly as though it had eaten out of Alice's hand, and when Clemens returned from the coast it would oblige him with a riot. New York had freaks (he said he saw several), and many in the population were actively resisting the fugitive slave laws, prompting the future Confederate to remark: "I reckon I had better black my face, for in these Eastern States niggers are considerably better than white people." After eight months of long hours, short wages and slim pickings, Sam returned to St. Louis to bed down with the Paveys, whom he'd known in Hannibal. Material for chapter fifty-one of *Life on the Mississippi* was then unpleasantly provided. The city was convulsed by the election riots of the Nativists. Numerous German immigrants came to the city during the 1840s and '50s, and their economic impact, as well as their anti-slavery Unionist attitudes and relaxed manner of living, offended those who dominated city government. The attempt to ban beer and the passage of puritanical blue laws provoked civil disturbances. Mark Twain describes what young Sam Clemens did:

> I spent a week there, at that time, in a boarding-house, and had this young fellow for a neighbor across the hall. We saw some of the fightings and killings; and by and by we went one night to an armory where two hundred young men had met, upon call, to be armed and go forth against the rioters, under command of a military man. We drilled till about ten o'clock at night; then news came that the mob were in great force in the lower end of the town, and were sweeping everything before them. Our column moved at once. It was a very hot night, and my musket was very heavy. We marched and marched; and the nearer we approached the seat of war, the hotter I grew and the thirstier I got. I was behind my friend; so finally, I asked him to hold my musket while I dropped out and got a drink. Then I branched off and went home. I was not feeling any solicitude about him of course, because I knew he was so well armed, now, that he could take care of himself without any trouble.

In 1857 Sam began his four-year apprenticeship as a river pilot and must have docked at St. Louis more times than an hour has minutes. When here, he lived on Locust between Eighth and Ninth Streets (the present site of the Old Post Office). The Civil War put an end to commercial traffic on the river, an end to the steamboat pilot's occupation, an end to his hope he would "follow the river the rest of his days," and therefore an end to his frequent visits to the city. He found himself, without conviction, in Confederate gray because the Union had fired upon his boat and broken the glass in his pilothouse; because he heard that the Union impressed pilots into service at gunpoint; and because his pals in Hannibal were organizing a group of rangers who would fight for Missouri's independence. It sounded like fun.

At General Grant's rumored approach, however, Sam "branched off" and went home again, having enjoyed enough unromantic rain, cold and hunger to unsuit him. Orion (staunchly Union) had managed to squeeze out of Lincoln a bit of prized patronage: an appointment as Secretary to the Nevada Territory; so Sam, the former ranger, contrived to go west as well, serving as a secretary to the Secretary. Since Sam's enlistment had never amounted to much, he never felt his defection amounted to much either.

Samuel Clemens may have been a lukewarm and puzzled combatant, but Mark Twain would see Causes mainly as occasions for coercion. Behind the words that described an enterprise as laudable lay simple self-interest. "From his cradle to his grave a man never does a single thing which has any first and foremost object but one—to secure peace of mind, spiritual comfort, for himself." Behind public-spirited generosity, pushing it ahead, was the force of a mean materialism. "Whenever you read of a self-sacrificing act or hear of one, or of a duty done for duty's sake, take it to pieces and look for the real motive."

Perpetually in need of money, Mark Twain, now notable as a humorist, became a regular on the lecture circuit, and St. Louis was not to be denied the receipt of his favorite speech (he gave it more than one hundred times). Twain arrived in St. Louis in March of 1867 at the beckon and for the benefit of the South St. Louis Mission Sunday School. Could these good people have known who he really was? It was a popular custom, then, to enhance the audience by offering prizes, and Twain, not to be outdone, offered a spavined elephant for the best conundrum; for the best poem on summertime complaints, eighteen hundred auger holes; and for the most convincing essay on women's suffrage, "that splendid piece of property known as Lafayette Park."

The talk was boldly advertised for two nights.

MARK TWAIN
will deliver a
Serio-Humorous Lecture
concerning
KANAKADOM
or,
THE SANDWICH ISLANDS

Tickets were fifty cents.

Adding a few more drum beats, he contributed to the *Missouri Democrat* three articles ridiculing women's suffrage. In them he included made-up letters from imaginary feminists such as Mrs. Zeb Leavenworth, who was the "originator and President of the Association for the Establishment of a Female College in Kamchatka," as well as one from Mrs. Mark Twain, "Secretary of the Society for Introducing the Gospel into New Jersey." Maybe Mr. Clemens was pulling everyone's leg; however, you may perhaps pull a gentlemen's leg safely, but never a lady's. These indiscretions weren't enough. He twice attended church, and thrice his patron's Sunday school, where he entertained a gathering of good citizens by recounting the story of Jim Smiley and his celebrated jumping frog despite a scandalized deacon's efforts to head him off.

The house was reported to have responded enthusiastically to Mark Twain's account of his visit to the islands Captain James Cook had dubbed "Sandwich" when he saw them in 1778, thereby hoping to please the present chief of the British Admiralty who had to bear that name. Fortunately, when we annexed the islands their nomination reverted to "Hawaii." Twain was a man of many jokes, among them several about the island delicacy, "poi," which, he said, "smells a good deal worse than it tastes, and tastes a good deal worse than it looks." The audience pleased Twain as much as he pleased them, for he wrote of St. Louis that it was one of those places "where audiences are jolly, and where they snap up a joke before you can fairly get it out of your mouth." He had to be speaking of opening night, though, because the next night there was a downpour so heavy he had maybe eighty people and "a vast acreage of chair backs" in a hall for a thousand. "It was like lecturing to the disciples on the edge of the Sahara." Nevertheless, he wandered about his topic for a pair of hours, and at the end had the effrontery to applaud himself until an embarrassed crowd joined in.

In 1882, when he returned to St. Louis to renew his memories of the Mississippi for a book he was writing on his pilot's apprenticeship (what would become *Life on the Mississippi*, published in 1883, which he regarded as his best book) by steamboating down to New Orleans, he was Mark Twain for the second time in this city. But the formerly crowded levee was mostly empty and silent and smokeless now; the romance of the river was as dead and chewed over as a concluded cigar; and even a steamboat named for his pseudonym, which he saw a short while after getting underway, failed to improve his mood. The southern habits Sam Clemens had esteemed, Mark Twain angrily rejected. To civilization the South had contributed nothing but the arts of war, murder and massacre, he said. Most of his visits to St. Louis, to Hannibal and the river, would be in memory now, for the old towns, their busy levees crowded with cargo and roustabouts, their seedy saloons and disreputable houses, the gambling dens of *Pudd'nhead Wilson*, could not be found; of the great grand boats, the sand bars, the sluices, the river's former swamps and thickets, there was little to see. Even the drinking water of the hotels, in their carafes, was clear. Only the bluffs had not moved far.

Mark Twain remembered that water:

> Here was a thing that had not changed; a score of years had not affected this water's mulatto complexion in the least; a score of centuries would succeed no better, perhaps. It comes out of the turbulent, bank-caving Missouri, and every tumblerful of it holds nearly an acre of land in solution. I got this fact from the bishop of the diocese. If you will let your glass stand half an hour, you can separate the land from the water as easy as Genesis; and then you will find them both good: the one good to eat, the other good to drink. The land is very nourishing, the water is thoroughly wholesome. The one appeases hunger; the other, thirst. But the natives do not take them separately, but together, as nature mixed them. When they find an inch of mud on the bottom of a glass, they stir it up and then take the draught as they would gruel. It is difficult for a stranger to get used to this batter, but once used to it he will prefer it to water. This is really the case. It is good for steamboating, and good to drink; but it is worthless for all other purposes, except baptizing.

34

There were fewer boats and therefore less smoke, and the outskirts were occupied by fine noble homes on large lots. Twain also admired the parks:
Tower Grove, the Botanical Gardens, Forest Park. These were changes for
the better, but on the levee the situation was nothing but sad.

> Half a dozen lifeless steamboats, a mile of empty wharves, a negro fa-
> tigued with whiskey stretched asleep, in a wide and soundless vacancy, where
> the serried hosts of commerce used to contend. . . .
>
> The pavements along the river front were bad; the sidewalks were rather
> out of repair; there was a rich abundance of mud. All this was familiar and
> satisfying; but the ancient armies of drays, and struggling throngs of men,
> and mountains of freight, were gone; and Sabbath reigned in their stead. The
> immemorial mile of cheap foul doggeries remained, but business was dull
> with them; the multitudes of poison-swilling Irishmen had departed, and in
> their places were a few scattering handfuls of ragged negroes, some drinking,
> some drunk, some nodding, others asleep. St. Louis is a great and prosperous
> and advancing city; but the river-edge of it seems dead past resurrection.

Surrounded by his European fame, Mark Twain returned to the city for
his last visit in June 1902 while coming and going to and from Columbia to
accept an honorary doctorate of law from the University of Missouri.
Greeted by applauding crowds and presented with flowers in both
Hannibal and St. Louis, he frequently had to daub at his eyes, and was often
unable to speak. In St. Louis he attended a ground-breaking for the
oncoming World's Fair in Forest Park and rededicated a familiar boat, the
Mark Twain, as, again, *Mark Twain*.

Like the water of the river, though, when this time he sailed down-
stream, neither Mark Twain nor Samuel Clemens would return.

34. *"Drinking Slumgullion" from* Roughing It, *by*
Samuel Clemens, 1895

Wynken, Blynken and Nod one night
Sailed off in a wooden shoe—
Sailed on a river of crystal light,
Into a sea of dew.
　　　　　—"Wynken, Blynken and Nod"

I do not love all children. I have tried
to analyse my feelings toward children,
and I think I discover that I love them
in so far as I can make pets of them. I
believe that, if I live, I shall do my
best literary work when I am a
grandfather. I give these facts,
confessions and observations for the
information of those who, for one
reason or another, are applying
constantly to me for biographical data
concerning myself.
　　　　　—"An Auto-Analysis"

35

In 1902 Mark Twain unveiled a plaque at 634 South Broadway, telling the assembled crowd that this was the place where Eugene Field, the "Children's Shakespeare" and prolific journalist, was born. Before the end of the ceremony, Roswell Field interrupted Twain to state that, in fact, his brother had been born several blocks north, on Collins Street. "Rose," Twain replied, "whatever the fact may be is relatively unimportant. . . . Officially and for the purposes of the future, your brother was born here."

36

The erroneous plaque remains, reflecting in miniature the story of who Eugene Field was, and who nineteenth-century America wanted him to be.

Eugene Field was born in St. Louis on September 2, 1850, and became one of the most celebrated authors of children's poetry in American literature. Upon his death, the *Chicago Tribune* declared that seldom has the "death of a citizen of Chicago in a private station occasioned such sincere and universal sorrow. On the streets, in the marts of trade, and at the clubs, universal regret was expressed at the loss of such a genius by the thousands who have enjoyed his acquaintance, his writings, and his public readings."

35. Eugene Field House, 634 South Broadway, 1999
36. Samuel Clemens with D. R. Francis at Field House
for unveiling of commemorative tablet, 1902

Field's many volumes of verse include the well-loved poems "Wynken, Blynken and Nod," "Little Boy Blue" and "Jes' 'Fore Christmas." But this prodigious writer could, as one colleague observed, "dip one pen in sugar, the other in astringent."

The "Poet of Childhood" would also become known as the "Father of the Personal Newspaper Column" and its tone his trademark:

PAPA READING

How nice Papa looks sitting by the Fire reading the Police Gazette. He is very fond of Literature. See how absorbed he is. There is a Torpedo on the Mantel Piece. Take it Down and Throw it at Papa's bald Head. That is right. Papa is not so absorbed as he was. He seems to be Hunting for a Strap.

William Marion Reedy, editor of the *Mirror* and Eugene Field's some-time rival, remarked on the confusion over Field's literary character in 1901 in "The Eugene Field Myth":

The Field that people have overdone as an idol came into being chiefly through his cute discovery that the way to reach the public most effectively was through sentiment and not through humor. He set to work deliberately to cultivate the sentimental and he did so with what success the whole world knows. That [these writings] are such a *tour de force* into sentiment by such a rank unsentimentalist, a congenital unsentimentalist, is their chiefest claim to attention.

Reedy knew Field as a fellow journalist in St. Louis before Field went on to greater fame in Chicago. Reedy did not publicly object to the naming of schools after Field, a country-wide trend at the time, but "let us not continue to fool the people by picturing him to them as a sort of Sunday-school seraph."

Field's early life was anything but heavenly. Six siblings died in the house on Broadway. His mother died when he was not quite six, and Eugene and his older brother Roswell were sent to Amherst, Massachusetts, to be raised by his father's relatives. There, he read the *New England Primer*, which he would later adapt for his own: "How many Birds are there in Seven soft-boiled eggs? If you have Five Cucumbers and eat Three, what will you have left? Two? No, you are Wrong. You will have more than that. You will have Colic enough to double you up in a Bow Knot for Six Hours. You may go to the Foot of the Class" ("Mental Arithmetic").

Eugene Field entered Williams College in Massachusetts in 1868 and upon his father's death in 1869 enrolled at Knox College in Galesburg, Illinois, where his guardian, John W. Burgess, was a professor. These are the facts as told by Field himself. Some sources hint that Field was asked to leave these colleges on account of hijinks. We know he escaped expulsion from the University of Missouri–Columbia, even though he failed math and removed some contents of the president's wine cellar. A lifelong prankster, he dressed in a hoop-skirt, bonnet, ribbons and fan, and walked around singing "Old Aunt Jemima, Oh, High, Oh." Later, while employed in

Denver, he got himself up as Oscar Wilde, stopped in at the *Tribune* offices and asked for an interview with managing editor Eugene Field.

Friends and relatives hoped he would practice law like his father—Roswell Martin Field had defended Dred Scott—but he vacillated between professional acting and journalism. After a post-graduation tour of Europe, Field returned to St. Louis and became a reporter on the *St. Louis Evening Journal*. On October 16, 1873, he married Julia Comstock, who was not yet sixteen. They had eight children—three daughters and five sons, two of whom died. He became city editor of the *Evening Journal* and published both his first

37

column and first poem in its pages. In 1875 he went to the *St. Joseph Gazette* as city editor, and then back to St. Louis to work on the *Journal* and *Times-Journal*, and to the *Kansas City Times* (now known as the *Kansas City Star*) before becoming managing editor of the *Denver Tribune*.

In 1883 he settled in "Porkopolis" (Chicago) to write a regular feature of wit, verse and social commentary for the *Chicago Record*, formerly the *Morning News*. Field reviled pretension of all kinds and confronted bureaucratic shams with verses defending the "patriot valour" of political protesters. He also developed a practice of inserting two or three particularly offensive paragraphs into his column for his editors to find, leaving other equally caustic lines to elude censorship. His column "Sharps and Flats" was widely read. His bawdy verses were not:

> He spread her on the verdant sward beneath the starlight dim
> And linked his business end to hers, which she turned up to him.
> Upon her lips with garlic moist, his amorous lips were glued
> And while his foaming tongue the husky harlot chewed.
> Around the hollow of his back he felt her two legs twine,
> Ah! That was glorious bangin', good bangin' on the Rhine.

Like Mark Twain's scatological verse, Field's Rabelaisian poems about Lady Lil, Fair Limousin and the Medieval Maiden were printed for the private amusement of his male friends and journalist colleagues.

"I am neither a poet nor an author. I am simply a newspaperman," he wrote, and once called his nursery rhymes "mother rot." He saw himself as a thistle in a bleak but fertile prairie: "But, presently advancing culture will root up the thistles and then more beautiful flowers will bloom in our stead; that conviction pleases me most." Field finished the columns that make up *The Love Affairs of a Bibliomaniac* just hours before he died of a heart attack in the middle of the night on November 4, 1895.

In 1934 Field's residence at 634 South Broadway was saved in a civic campaign that collected pennies from school children and admirers and converted into a museum in 1936. The Eugene Field House and Toy Museum, a paean to childhood, replete with dolls (he was an avid collector), original manuscripts and other Fieldiana, was added to the National Register of Historic Places in 1975.

Surely the author of *The Clink of Ice, The Holy Cross and Other Tales, A Little Book of Western Verse* and *Echoes from the Sabine Farm*, an adaptation from Horace done with his brother, as well as the privately printed *Libidinous Facetiae* must have known history would come to know him better through his not-so-secret, wicked sense of humor.

Extinct Monsters

Oh, had I lived in the good old days,
   When the Icthyosaurus ramped
     around,
When the Elasmosaur swam the bays,
   And the Sivatherium pawed the ground,
Would I have spent my precious time
At weaving golden thoughts in rhyme?

When the Tinoceras snooped about,
   And the Pterodactyl flapped its wings,
When the Brontops with the warty snout
   Noseyed around for herbs and things,
Would I have bothered myself o'ermuch
About divine afflatus and such?

The Dinotherium flourished then;
   The Pterygotus lashed the seas;
The Rhamphorhynchus prospered when
   The Scaphognathus perched in trees;
And every creature, wild and tame,
Rejoiced in some rococo name.

Pause and ponder; who could write
   A triolet or roundelay
While a Megatherium yawped all night
   And a Hesperonis yawped all day,
While now and again the bray sonorous
Of Glyptodon Asper swelled the chorus?

If I'd been almost anything
   But a poet, I might have got along:
Those extinct monsters of hoof and wing
   Were not conducive to lyric song;
So Nature reserved this tender bard
For the kindlier Age of Pork and Lard.

Not to know Reedy argues yourselves unknown.

—Reedy's portrait caption in *Town and Country*

A newspaper appears daily and disappears in a week. Heedless of its yellow journalism, its fibers yellow without intending any insinuation. The magazine appears weekly or monthly and will remain alive until the next issue renders superfluous its last. Magazines are made of better stock, but they are bulky, and soon tossed. Libraries feel they must subscribe and hate them because periodicals are unreliable, hard to bind, expensive and most of them are of momentary importance. So the journal's choices and designs, the editor's point of view, its reports, its praise, its exposés, its digs, as well as its errors and its lies, are like shouts in a gale, and soon gone. Successful contributors gather their pieces up and preserve them in bound collections. Sources will be acknowledged with a wave. So long.

Except for a few fancy small volumes put out by friends, William Marion Reedy's work remains where he put it—in the issues of his magazine, the *Mirror*. That work, however, concerned more than his own words; it very much dealt with the words of others; and authors whom he encouraged bore that influence around the world. Mr. Reedy went to Washington to dine at the White House. Mr. Reedy was elected honorary mayor of Greenwich Village. Mr. Reedy served on literary juries. Mr. Reedy covered party conventions—with scorn. Mr. Reedy ran a magazine with a national circulation—32,000—that exceeded the *Atlantic*'s and the *Nation*'s. It was available to the homesick in foreign hotels in ten countries. Overly ardent "followers" suggested that Reedy run for the Senate. His political "enemies" put him up for president as a disfavorite son. In any case, he was for a while, as Edgar Lee Masters put it, the "Literary Boss of the Middle West."

The Civil War had barely begun when William Marion Reedy was born in an Irish section of north St. Louis called the Kerry Patch. His father was a cop (of course), and he grew up with tough Irish kids in a neighborhood held together by chauvinism and racial hatred. Literary folks in America must very often find cracks in rocks from which to sprout, but they rarely choose to bloom or go to seed in their birthplace. Reedy was an exception to the latter half of that rule, and remained in St. Louis despite lifelong misgivings and the dislike of many of its respectable people. He once said of the city that it had a soul that sang small if it sang at all and characterized its leading citizens as having "no desire to make the city great and beautiful." They suffered from a "dismal respectability." "Dismal respectability" is a fine phrase, an accurate phrase, but more powerful were the words he used to describe the bedizened ladies of an antebellum society he'd never seen: women who "wore a nigger on every finger," and merchants and bankers who drank their own blood-money away in the houses of the whores.

Reedy's mother saw to it that he had a proper Catholic upbringing and had him prepped at Christian Brothers College—prepped so well he entered Saint Louis University as a student of the classics at fourteen. After all, Latin was a perfect choice as it was the language of the Church. Young as he was, Reedy did not immediately shine, so his impatient father, looking for an excuse to set his son on the financially wide and rewarding rather than on the righteously straight and narrow, ordered him into commercial studies. After that, Reedy was certain to become a follower of Walter Pater and Oscar Wilde, to display the generosity of the spendthrift, imbibe with the best, flaunt his increasingly radical politics and allow himself to be smiled upon by disreputable women.

Reedy became a downtown man while he was still a kid and caught a job as a fledgling reporter on the *Missouri Republican*, a paper which fancied itself, in 1880, as a protector of family values and a cherisher of southern de-

38

mocratic sympathies, despite its name. He was posted to Carondelet, then a suburb, and even from there, although only eighteen, Reedy was able to file a fine anti-establishment story about a fight between a priest and a school teacher which got him favorably noticed, so that he found himself suddenly in the city room, a space of mythological grandeur and importance. A decade later, Theodore Dreiser, another brash young man but in training as a cynic, described the space in less flattering terms:

> The windows were tall but cracked and patched with faded yellow copy paper; the desks, some fifteen or twenty all told, were old, dusty, knife-marked, smeared with endless ages of paste and ink. There was waste paper and rubbish on the floor. There was no sign of paint or wallpaper. The windows facing east looked out upon a business court or alley where trucks and vans creaked by day but which at night was silent as the grave, as was the entire wholesale neighborhood.

Oscar Wilde arrived in St. Louis to entertain the yokels in February 1882, and Reedy was told to interview at least the author's velvet knee breeches where they hung out at the Southern Hotel. The *Post-Dispatch* and the *Globe* also covered the visit, their cartoonists depicting Wilde—no surprise—as a poseur and dandy, or as the monkey he had presumably made of himself. Reedy found Wilde full of horse sense instead of the stuff Wilde was usually described as being full of, and got on well with the esthete, whose speech at the Mercantile Library had also been forthright, unmannered, and reasonable in Reedy's view. It was as if the young reporter had received a slap. He learned not to trust public preconceptions, to see past appearances, and to judge issues independently. He saw a brave man behind the fop, a wily fox inside the furs. Wilde carried the message of the Arts and Crafts movement to America, urging the revival of handicrafts, the pursuit of a simpler life, and a dedication of one's mind and hand to the loveliness of the ordinary and everyday. Reedy's conversion, though pronounced, was incomplete because, when it happened, he was already halfway there.

The Mercantile Library was the forum for most of the famous who came to town, but it was also a treasure house of books, where Joseph Pulitzer could be found feasting furiously, and where Reedy spent many hours getting his extensive, though hit or miss, education. Reedy liked to drag his friends there and stuff them with decadent texts: Baudelaire, Verlaine, Villon, Pater, Yeats, Swinburne, Fitzgerald, Henry George. The library's spiritual value was immeasurable, and it was very likely St. Louis's most important cultural institution at that time.

In the line of journalistic duty, Reedy claimed to have witnessed twenty hangings, which he wrote about with appropriately touching details and moments of compassion and piety. Of course he covered political contretemps, too, as well as society balls and parties, class collisions, rapes and robberies, trials, street fights, scandalous carryings-on, and the occasional setting of the sun over the muddy Mississippi; but after four years of drinking and reporting, reporting and drinking, Reedy was ill and worn out. He took a leave and a boat upriver to Minnesota where the cold air was clean. There he did indeed recover, coming back to the *Globe* in 1886, only to leave again, and return once more, being hired and fired repeatedly between drinking bouts, and fulfilling the myth of the boozy reporter until a sudsy head had formed.

Eighteen ninety-three found Reedy sufficiently down and out that he took a seat at the city editor's desk of the *St. Louis Mirror*, then little more than a society scandal and gossip sheet and a feeble imitation of many other "mirrors" in many other cities, especially *Town Topics* of New York, which held up the glass of vanity in front of the faces of the vain and reported their smirks. Soon St. Louis's little *Mirror* was broken and bankrupt. The owner gave it to Reedy as a gift. After a decent interval it was renamed the *Mirror*, and on February 25, 1894, began its long, arduous elevation and a life of twenty-nine years. In the *Mirror* was reflected sanctimonious givers of bribes, salesmen of favors, vulgar show-offs, ruthless power brokers and oily liars. It celebrated—Reedy liked to rhyme—the "wistful, tristful spirit" of that English fellow, Walter Pater. In St. Louis, that would be: who?

A competitor, who certainly never thought of himself as such, Alexander Nicolas DeMenil, published and puffed the *Hesperian*, a magazine far too dedicated "to the higher literature" to publish stories. Now that William T. Harris had taken his lofty *Journal of Speculative Philosophy* into eastern air, the *Hesperian* had a corner on all decorous activities of the spirit. Reedy had no wish to resemble such respectability (nor could he have, with so little experience of what it was); instead, he would outrage it, look at its pretensions and laugh. Envy sees even excellence as a flaw. But both magazines had one thing in common: keeping their distance from the mob.

DeMenil published two volumes of verse, *Songs in Minority* (1905) and *Forest and Town* (1910), as well as a study of writers whose history could convince him that they belonged to one of the fourteen states of the Louisiana Purchase. This survey he titled, appropriately, *The Literature of the Louisiana Territory* (1904). "I have blazed the trail through old book-shops and public and private libraries from Minnesota to Louisiana, hunt-ed in many a virgin field hitherto unexplored, and used the newspaper re-porter's art of interviewing."

Indeed, DeMenil discovered for us writers like Edmund Flagg, who came to St. Louis to study law in 1836 and ended up editing the *St. Louis Daily Commercial Bulletin* as well as the *Evening Gazette* a few years later. Two of his plays (*Blanche of Valois* and *The Howard Queen*) were performed in several cities, including St. Louis. James D. Nourse gave up both medi-cine and law (a field more readily given up than most apparently) to edit the *Daily Intelligencer* here, where he also wrote two novels, *The Forest Knight* (1846) and *Leavenworth* (1848). The law was not always abandoned. J. Gabriel Woerner served as a judge of the St. Louis Probate Court from 1870 to 1894, but he managed to complete a number of books, among them a novel, *The Rebel's Daughter*. In Webster Groves, DeMenil found Mary Nixon Roulet, who was the literary editor, around the turn of the century, for the *Church Progress*. She wrote children's stories and historical ro-mances. One of the *Hesperian's* authors was R. E. Lee Gibson, who issued a number of booklets in the 1890s containing recognizable poems while con-tinuing as clerk of the St. Louis Insane Asylum for fifteen years. Lelia Hardin Bugg aimed at edification, and among her many works of Catholic instruction was a novel called *Orchids* (1894). Finally there was William Vincent Byars, who wrote a great deal of verse (*New Songs to Old Tunes*, for instance) and edited twenty volumes of *The World's Best Essays* and *The World's Best Orations*. Many of DeMenil's own poems were published in St. Louis magazines and newspapers, though none by Reedy, who loathed DeMenil's deference to convention and his conservative stance.

For ideas, Reedy retained the journalist's low threshold, and he took delight in lampooning the Hegelianese of the St. Louis philosophers and the moral seriousness of the transcendentalists. Though his own opinions may have been born in a bar, he had them looking sober and sprightly enough to be called, in his *Mirror*, "Reflections." They took up three or four pages at the front of every issue. He archly signed them "Uncle Fuller," or "Marion Reed."

Now that he was actually choosing material for a magazine, and now that he had successfully adopted an esthete's standpoint in order to separate himself from his delinquent background, it became both prudent and com-fortable to return his taste to its blue collar origins. "Naturalism," not "sym-bolism," better fitted his form, and he embraced both Stephen Crane and Thomas Hardy, as well as Theodore Dreiser, when that realist came on the scene. James Joyce was acceptable, but he was Irish, after all, hadn't written *Ulysses* yet, and his epiphanies had the merit of offending Dublin from sa-loon to sacristy. Reedy had more than an intellectual quarrel with the Church. He blamed the priest who had married him to a baud for imple-menting his mistake.

Although Reedy's skeptical view of the Spanish-American War brought the *Mirror* national attention, his expressed dislike for the two fat-vested Williams who had been put up for president—Bryan and McKinley in

1896—cost him readers and revenue. The *Mirror* went bankrupt and was auctioned to satisfy its creditors. This proved to be a stroke of luck, because the magazine was bought by Reedy's millionaire businessman friend, James Campbell, who rearranged the books, stood the *Mirror* up to reflect again, and turned its editorial affairs over to its former owner. After all, in the *Mirror*, wealth and individual initiative had always looked pretty good. Now firmly underwritten, Reedy cut each issue's price from a dime to a nickel and drove up his subscriptions to thirteen thousand. The magazine's opposition to the war (not its literary merit), especially after the *Maine* sank, brought sales to a 32,250 peak. He also felt able to marry again.

Reedy's second wife was a respectable woman, not a baud, for her name went two French letters farther than that: it was "Eulalie Bauduy," and she came from a fine medical family of esteemed Catholic standing. They cannot have enjoyed the *Mirror*'s continued attacks on the Church, nor Reedy's ardent campaign on behalf of the St. Louis World's Fair, which was mainly directed against those whom Reedy felt weren't doing enough—namely, "the better sort." In a "Reflection" called "What's the Matter with St. Louis," he said it was "too much matter, too little mind" that was the matter. "The people who predominate lack vision." His provocations were printed as a pamphlet, the pamphlet sold widely, and the response to it was largely positive. Reedy liked to think that the Fair's success was assured on the day in November 1899 that his piece appeared.

The Reedys, meanwhile, moved to a small house on Spring Avenue, but Reedy's happiness in his new marriage was to be exactly as short-lived as his wife, who died suddenly at thirty of a heart ailment exacerbated by a severe thyroid condition. Reedy threw himself into preparations for the Fair as if he hoped to drown in one of the yet-to-be excavated lagoons.

Elbert Hubbard, of Roycrofter fame, pirated a few of Reedy's essays and had them beautifully bound in red suede. The volume's full title was *The Law of Love: Being Fantasies of Science and Sentiment Inked into English to Cheer Up the Gloomsters* (1905). Hubbard's Arts and Crafts influence in St. Louis was considerable, in part because of Reedy's devoted championing of Hubbard's causes. When Hubbard came to St. Louis to lecture, Reedy (in demand as a public speaker) would introduce him. In 1912 the Roycroft Press printed a little tribute to Hubbard's upstate New York community written by Reedy as "A Little Journey to East Aurora" in imitation of Hubbard's famous series, *Little Journeys to the Homes of the Great*.

39. Cover of the Mirror, *December 7, 1899*

Late in 1900, Reedy received in the mail a copy of *Sister Carrie*, a novel by the hardly known Theodore Dreiser, who had spent sixteen months in St. Louis (1893-94) cadging little journalism jobs and, too shy and lowly to approach him, dreaming of the kind of glory enjoyed by Mr. William Marion Reedy, then a feature writer at the *Globe-Democrat*. Without any sense he was doing something special, Reedy had published an article of Dreiser's back in 1897, but *Sister Carrie* was another matter; it was a story, for all its immaturity otherwise, that had, as Reedy thought, "a grip." That grip was, in fact, to be Dreiser's great gift, and Reedy supported his newfound author with letters and reviews throughout his entire career.

The *Mirror* ran a column of society gossip called "Blue Jay's Chatter." Reedy was the blue jay of course, but he had collaborators, one of them the fresh face at the Odeon who collected juicy items for him at a great rate, and a young woman for whom William Reedy had a widower's designs:

> There's a new girl in the Odeon stock who excites much interest, Zoë Akins. She's the daughter of Chairman Akins of the Republican State Central Committee, United States Sub-Treasurer. . . . He's a banker, a friend of the President, and he is to be in the head-set at the inauguration. Well, this Zoë Akins is the weirdest girl. She affects dresses very simple and severe, and won't wear plumes in her hats. She is preternaturally bright. . . . She writes exquisite impressionistic verse, and has the oddest views upon things. She's very young but is as wise as a centenarian, and very girlish withal. She's up on music and art, and is in brief an Admirable Chrichtonness. I haven't said that she is beautiful, but she is, at times, and is always interesting, with a slight suggestion of pose.

Passion ignited Reedy's pen, and he shot letters at her like cupid's darts. But Akins was ambitious as only those of eighteen can be. She let him print her, praise her, pursue her, but possess her never, and used her father's qualms to disengage when it seemed their two forces might collide. Akins soon gave up her post as the *Mirror*'s drama critic to do plays of her own in New York. She was replaced by another youngster, Orrick Johns, just back in town from the University of Missouri. He took Sara Teasdale driving in Forest Park so they could speak of poetry in private. Akins, Johns and Teasdale were each a frequent image in the *Mirror*'s pages. Just as a superb periodical is supposed to do, the magazine created unlikely but fruitful connections, among them Sara Teasdale's brief fling with the work of Fiona McLeod, a mysterious Irish writer of the period that James Joyce caustically called the "cultic toilette," and a person the *Mirror* had been publishing since 1900. ("Fiona McLeod" was actually the pseudonym of one William Sharp, so the mystery was deserved.) Yeats and others wildly praised her work, especially *The Washer of the Ford*, a figure whom Joyce transformed into the Anna Livia Plurabelle of *Finnegans Wake*.

The *Mirror* survived the Panic of 1907 with the help of Reedy's mistress, Margie Rhodes, the madame of a House of Notoriety, who loaned the magazine five thousand dollars in its darkest time; and when she sold her house and moved into the country, thereby becoming as respectable as a chicken, Reedy married her and moved there too. Max Putzel, Reedy's biographer, reports that "the newspapers treated Reedy's career as a farmer with glee, and he himself found that cows made excellent copy." The scandal shook subscribers from the magazine like leaves. In 1911 the farmhouse burned down, but, miraculously, not the marriage.

Another one of the wars which the *Mirror* fought involved a search for, and defense of, a native poetic tradition. This pitted reviewers of books from across the country against one another. Reedy felt that Eugene Field's most popular poetry was insincere and puerile, and he was most upset when the St. Louis Board of Education decided to give a public school the rhymester's name. But he didn't admire the nation's most popular poet either. This was Edwin Markham. His "Man with the Hoe" had appeared in 1899 to general acclaim. Good host that he was, Reedy waited until Markham came to St. Louis and otherwise remarked upon his "genius" before he called the poem's central symbol false. The man with the hoe might exhibit poor posture himself, but Reedy's stance was to be that of common sense. "There is no man with a hoe, as Millet painted him, in this country. There is no oppressor bending the back, flattening the brow, dulling the eye, of the American laborer, or any other laborer, while in France 'tis not the weight of centuries that gives him his stoop, but the very simple fact that the hoe handle is short."

40

The *Mirror* did more than foster homegrown talents (Reedy's "nest of singing birds" included Fannie Hurst, in addition to Akins, Teasdale and Johns); it gave a great deal of space to rambunctious literary journalists like James Huneker, Percival Pollard and George Sylvester Viereck, or to unknown but nearby Chicagoans, Harriet Monroe and Carl Sandburg, as well as those poets of the long names, Edward Arlington Robinson and Edna St. Vincent Millay. Reedy would not feel proud, but history could boast that the *Mirror* had published three poems of Ezra Pound before 1915; that Reedy himself (showing a fondness for fancy words—"esurient" and "obnubilated" for instance) had praised Pound in an editorial that particularly applauded the poet's "contempt for mere verbal upholstery"; and that Babette Deutsch had been persuaded to review his work favorably and at length as early as December 1917.

Vachel Lindsay may have been odd, but he was not esoteric, and more to Reedy's taste, who published many of Lindsay's overheated love poems (some to Sara Teasdale) in the *Mirror*; however, it was Edgar Lee Masters who grew close to his heart. Like Lindsay and Sandburg an Illinois poet, Masters was a lawyer in Clarence Darrow's Chicago offices, and at first Reedy was more interested in him as an author of legal and political pieces than a writer of verse or closet plays. Still, the *Mirror* had printed five of Masters's earlier efforts, although without enthusiasm, before it launched the poet's career by putting seven of his new "spoon river" poems in one issue. Perhaps one of them reminded Reedy of his youthful enthusiasm for François Villon:

> Tell me where, or in what land
> is Flora the lovely Roman,
> or Archipiada, or Thaïs
> who so resembled her,
> or Echo speaking when one called
> across still pools or rivers,
> and whose beauty was more than human.
> But where are the snows of bygone years?
>
> —"Ballade (of the Ladies of Bygone Times),"
> François Villon, translated by Anthony Bonner

> Where are Elmer, Herman, Bert, Tom and Charley,
> The weak of will, the strong of arm, the clown, the boozer, the fighter?
> All, all, are sleeping on the hill.
>
> —*Spoon River Anthology*, Edgar Lee Masters

While World War I broke out in Europe, the *Mirror* published significant bites of what would become the *Spoon River Anthology* in its next two issues. The tone, diction, energy and subject-matter of the poems were acclaimed as uniquely American. Before 1915 was over, the completed volume was as big a hit as a long-running play.

Reedy enjoyed a melee, even if it was only one made by poets, and his magazine managed to remain in the middle of things throughout its life. There was Hamlin Garland (whom Reedy detested) on the right, Amy Lowell and Ezra Pound on the left (whom Reedy cautiously defended), Witter Bynner (who felt the *Mirror* had forgotten him) in the rear, and Carl Sandburg and Edgar Lee Masters up ahead where the future was most bright. As a part of the controversy, Bynner (and an Iowa poet and lawyer, Arthur Davison Ficke) created a fraudulent movement of their own called the Spectrist school. Soon, sure enough, a poet from the spirit world began writing and making herself known in St. Louis by means of a Ouija board managed by Mrs. John H. Curran. Anticipating James Merrill's semi-pseudo whirl with the Ouija, a seventeenth-century maiden named Patience Worth, now a wraith who wrote, came in through a carelessly left-open window. Her inscribings were immediately and immensely popular. There were soon so many ghosts flapping about that the supply of pillowcases was threatened. A novel by Mark Twain, really deceased this time, was the opportune work of a board supervised by one of Mrs. Curran's impressionable friends.

A hoax is often hokum's worst enemy. To send a fake to visit fakes is what Bynner intended, and soon others fell in with the fraud, as still others fell for it. It also became a parlor game and oft-told joke. Majorie Allen

Seiffert was locked in her bedroom while her dinner guests waited to be served and required to produce a bit of Spectrist verse, which, under the nom de plume of Elijah Hay, she did, before the soup grew cold or was even served.

Emmanuel Morgan (Bynner) wrote lines like these:

> If I were only dafter
> I might be making hymns
> To the liquor of your laughter
> And the lacquer of your limbs.

A couplet by Anne Knish (Ficke) came together this way:

> If bathing were a virtue, not a lust,
> I would be dirtiest.

Editor Reedy "scented a trap, announced that it looked like a trap, and then plunged rashly into it." These poems, he unwisely wrote, "have the beauties and the oddities of Chinese landscape painting." Other magazines followed suit, and Bynner enjoyed a popularity as Emmanuel Morgan he hadn't known as himself. Conrad Aiken, new to the scene and presently praised by the *Mirror*, was writing a version of surrealism that might easily have been mistaken for more fooling, but Aiken was sincere, which perhaps makes all the difference.

Although Reedy had reduced his drinking after an attack of nephritis in 1915, he still suffered from hypertension, and that condition finally caused a retinal hemorrhage so serious his eye had to be removed. It wasn't the state of poetry that had pushed his pressure up, he felt, but the usual sorry state of the Republic and its politics. While recuperating, Reedy wrote one-eyed reviews. Shortly afterward, again on account, he felt, of his one-eyedness, he was proposed as a candidate for the Senate. Perhaps, if entirely blind, he would have been a presidential prospect.

In addition to old hands like Edwin Arlington Robinson and Carl Sandburg, the poets appearing in the *Mirror* now were Conrad Aiken, Maxwell Bodenheim and Edna St. Vincent Millay. Reedy knew he had another prize in the latter poet and published, first of all, twenty of her sonnets, five weekly from April 29 to May 20, 1920, and then *Aria da Capo*, a poetic play within a play which Millay had written for the Provincetown Players. Not every issue scored runs, of course. On June 3, one Silas Bent, an inherent error, concluded that Henry James was a snobbish exquisite. Perish the thought.

It was election time again, politics and corruption were afoot, and Reedy was on the road: in Chicago for the Republican convention, in San Francisco to watch the Democrats, and there, though he still had one eye, the Missouri delegation nominated him, as their favorite son, for president of the United States. William Jennings Bryan was pushing for a dry plank in the platform, and for a dry candidate to stand on it. When James Cox, governor of Ohio, was chosen after a long floor fight, Reedy was happy enough, for a non-entity was better than an entity, he said. Afterward Reedy vacationed in Hollywood and boated out to Catalina, dined with friends and filed stories out of San Francisco, and thought about returning home via Canada. Angina, with its customary suddenness, felled him, and he died a day after on July 28, 1920. An announcement appeared in the *Mirror*, out the next day, along with his account of a two-hour battle with a giant tuna. He had published the weekly for twenty-four years. It would linger, as if ill, three more months, never to be successfully revived.

Stricken, in pain and short of breath, Reedy had managed to insist that it wasn't dying he was afraid of, but of not being able to. However, as he had so often, he managed.

His body was returned to his wife in St. Louis and, with some help from a handsome young Irish archbishop, John Glennon, the funeral service was held at Saint Louis University and Reedy was buried in Calvary Cemetery.

His big person matched his voluminous production and flashing style. He was a macrostomatous [*sic*] man. In youth he had been handsome, with a mass of dark, waving hair, broad jutting brows, a finely chiseled mouth, and large, limpid eyes that defied description. When I knew him the shock of hair had grayed and thinned out, the lower face and body had become a mass of flesh, but the eyes had lost none of their darkness and light. Masters said of them that they "were luminous as if they had convex lenses behind the irises." The voice still boomed. In contrast to the rest of his body, his hands were the smallest and most delicate I have ever seen on a man, tapering at the end of a thick arm. Thinking of his hands, one also remembers the tiny, regular, legible writing with which he poured out his daily stint.

—Orrick Johns, *Time of Our Lives*

Writers published in the *Mirror*, some for the first time, some for the first time in America, some whose writing Reedy simply admired:

Max Beerbohm	John Galsworthy	Robert Louis Stevenson
Hillaire Belloc	Maxim Gorky	J. M. Synge
William Rose Benét	Thomas Hardy	Leo Tolstoy
Ambrose Bierce	Nathaniel Hawthorne	Ivan Turgenev
William Blake	William Ernest Henley	Louis Untermeyer
Rupert Brooke	William Dean Howells	John Hall Wheelock
Robert Browning	Rudyard Kipling	Oscar Wilde
Anton Chekhov	Amy Lowell	William Butler Yeats
G. K. Chesterton	Walter de la Mare	
Joseph Conrad	Walter Pater	
John Donne	Christina Rossetti	
Fyodor Dostoevsky	Carl Sandburg	
Anatole France	George Bernard Shaw	

In the light of the world's attitude toward women and her duties, the nature of Carrie's mental state deserves consideration. Actions such as hers are measured by an arbitrary scale. Society possesses a conventional standard whereby it judges all things. All men should be good, all women virtuous. Wherefore, villain, hast thou failed?

—Sister Carrie

According to W. A. Swanberg, one of his biographers, Theodore Dreiser "was reared in superstition, fanaticism, ignorance, poverty and humiliation." Three boys had died before him, and he was so frail at birth his pagan-minded mother consulted a woman thought to be a witch. By the time the family had washed up on the shores of Terre Haute, Indiana, it had suffered a series of serious reverses which only strengthened the religious beliefs of Dreiser's fanatical father. God had snatched success from his father's hard-working hand and given him the shame of debt and failure in its stead. It must be on account of some hidden sin, and was a certain sign of eventual damnation if penance were not faithfully performed and debts paid to the penny.

The family was large despite the deaths which had reduced it, and although father wielded the strap freely and with the bigot's brutality, he couldn't keep up with five sons and five daughters who had learned to seek safety by scattering in all directions. Next to last in line, Theodore was his mother's weak witch-saved baby who sobbed to see the holes in his mother's shoes, who stayed skinny on a diet of milk and mush, cried at a fly, stuttered through protruding teeth, and fled in terror from the nuns who were his teachers. He was a perfect target for bullies; he was a soft sock-and-shake doll.

Poverty split the family. Dreiser's mother took her three youngest to live with a friend in Vincennes, the wife of a fire captain who offered them a small apartment over the station, from which, however, she was running a brisk bordello business, and where Theodore experienced a few post-primal scenes. Poverty pushes the poor from place to place, and there were certain to be losses along the way with older children running off, the boys to ride rails and get drunk in strange towns, the girls with men who of course lied to them and left them in more than the lurch. Sent home from school for being barefoot, Dreiser delivered bundles of clothes his mother had washed and cadged coal in the train yard. His life might have suited a melodramatic protest novel, and later it would admirably serve more than one of his own.

41. Theodore Dreiser, c. 1890

The family was rescued momentarily by Dreiser's prodigal oldest brother, Paul, who wrote lyrics and composed tunes for a minstrel show he also starred in, calling himself Dresser for theatrical purposes, and arriving out of nowhere with a momentarily fat wallet. The mother's wing of the family was transported to Evansville where Paul lived, and lived well, with a celebrated madam, Sallie Walker, and where young Teddy got a few more lessons in the business side of sin. Paul, who tended to sample the goods his mistress purveyed, was soon given the boot and sent back on the circuit with his show. This put the Dreisers of Evansville into another spiral of misfortune until they were united with the Dreisers of Chicago where the eldest girls had gone, although history does not read as if the frying pan were much better than the fire.

The crowded Chicago apartment was Dreiser's tenth residence and fifth town in his life's twelve years, but only a stop on a longer list, because his father soon joined them, jobless and in bitter cantankerous despair, a financial burden that broke the family up again, so that Dreiser moved out with his mother, this time to Warsaw, Indiana, a peaceful, tree-shaded town that the Dreisers quickly scandalized. Even a saucer of ambition would overflow in Warsaw, and the adolescent Dreiser was abrim with it. Chicago would be a town he could toddle to. There he worked as a dishwasher for a few months, in a hardware store for a few hours; he sized canvases for a week, and lasted one day as a boxcar tracer. No better skilled as a stockboy, he was fired, wept in the office of his boss, got rehired, and hung on then by poverty's thread until a former teacher (out of the blue: the same region from which Paul had come with his wallet), because she'd seen promise in him, offered to pay his tuition to Indiana University, which he was able to enter (in those days) with only one year of high school. To get ready, Dreiser read *Tom Brown at Rugby*.

With no background but misery, he was lucky to scrape by at Indiana for one year. He refused further subsidization. Instead, he went back to work canvassing for a failing real estate agent in Chicago, from whom he was soon receiving no pay. His mother finally fell ill from the disease that was her life and died while Dreiser was helping her sit up in bed. A priest called to her side by a devout if not devoted husband refused to give her absolution on account of her irregular attendance at church. Only begging got her buried. Without the mother's grip the family flew apart, nothing in common but their miserable past and their hatred of clerics. Dreiser now drove a laundry truck—until a customer recommended him to her husband for a collections job. At his best pay ever, he collected time-payment and delinquent accounts from "dancing or singing, or even naked or doped, whores and their paramours" who had purchased the gaudy overpriced trinkets his employer stocked.

Dreiser read Eugene Field's column in the *Chicago Daily News* with a pleasure infused with longing and began to compose his own pieces about the city. A greedy desire for a spiffy overcoat he couldn't afford caused him to skim from his accounts, and he got caught, then he got fired. To impress a girl, though out of work at Christmas, Dreiser told her he was a reporter for the *Herald* and tried to make an honest man of himself by haunting newspaper offices until they all knew the scrawny young man they were turning away. But extra hands were needed at the Democratic Convention in Chicago. Dreiser caught on with the poorly regarded *Daily Globe*, whose cynical reporters represented the stereotype.

Dreiser had drive; he was used to insults; he knew the slummiest parts of the city; he could connive; he was being taught about the ubiquity of political corruption and beginning to understand what his copy editor once told him: "Life is a goddamned, stinking, treacherous game, and nine hundred and ninety-nine men out of every thousand are bastards." By now he believed mostly in money and power. Although not exceptionally intelligent, he was street smart; he had an eye, and a willingness to open it on other people's business. In addition, he had no compunction about cutting moral corners. In short, he seemed a good prospect for a future in journalism.

Opportunely, the new city editor of the *Chicago Globe*, John McEnnis, was a good newsman from St. Louis, brought low by liquor, who saw something in Dreiser despite his wretched prose, and finagled a position for him on the *Globe-Democrat*:

YOU MAY HAVE REPORTORIAL POSITION ON THIS PAPER AT TWENTY DOLLARS A WEEK, BEGINNING NEXT MONDAY. WIRE REPLY.

The time was November 1892. St. Louis, as I stepped off the train of a Sunday evening, having left Chicago in cold, dreary state, seemed a warmer clime. The air was soft, almost balmy, although St. Louis could be cold enough too, as I soon discovered. The station, then at 12th and Poplar (the new Union Station at 18th and Market was then merely building), an antiquated affair of brick and stone, with the tracks stretching in rows in front of it, and reached by board walks laid at right angles with them, seemed unspeakably shabby and inconvenient to me after the better ones of Chicago. Such mild standards of comparison as I had thus far acquired were being brought vigorously into play—and to the disadvantage of St. Louis, of course. It was not as good as Chicago, I said to myself, as dynamic, as interesting. Chicago was rough, powerful, active. St. Louis was sleepy, slow. This was because I had entered it of a Sunday evening and all its central portion was still. I made my way to the Silver Moon Hotel, recommended to me by my mentor and sponsor, John T. McEnnis, and found it all he had said it would be, a simple, inexpensive affair—a room for a dollar, a meal for twenty-five cents. I recall the strangeness—the loneliness.

St. Louis was, for Dreiser, freedom city—the first stop on his journey away from his family:

42. *Globe-Democrat Building, Sixth and Pine Streets, c. 1892*

eye—the right,—which was turned slightly outward from the line of vision, and a set of upper teeth which because of their exceptional largeness were crowded and so stood out too much, I had no particular physical blemish except a general homeliness of feature to which I freely admit. It was a source of woe to me all the time because I imagined that it kept me from being interesting to women, which apparently was not true—not to all women at least. This same protrusion of the teeth, by the way, was cured a few years later by the loss of one of them, which gave the others freedom to spread.

Here in St. Louis, as in London, or Paris or Vienna . . . girls walked the streets for hire, and the section where they walked, Olive Street between 6th and 12th about the post office, was quickly pointed out to me by my fellow craftsmen, who were youthfully interested in these matters. Again there was a truly amazing bagnio district, stretching from 12th and Chestnut to 22nd or 23rd and Chestnut, occupying both sides of the street and literally lined with "houses" where the sexually restless and unsatisfied were free to repair and for a comparatively modest price satisfy their needs. . . . Of a spring and summer evening, walking out Chestnut Street on one errand or another, I have seen scores of these women—most diaphanously, or I might even say gorgeously, arrayed—seated on their doorsteps, at the windows or walking up and down the sidewalk, not necessarily soliciting, although they may have been, but rather, I think, taking the evening air after a hot day in the house. (And it could be stifling in St. Louis, as I can testify.)

Dreiser resisted the lures of the whores but not the near-at-hand charms of his new landlady, with whom he was soon on familiar terms.

Dreiser did obtain some interesting interviews: with Ed Butler, the Irish boss of the city; with John L. Sullivan, who was drunk and sparkling with diamonds in his suite at the Lindell; with one Peter McCord, a fallen Catholic, who would at least try to answer Dreiser's earnest questions about the meaning of life; and the theosophist, Annie Besant, eager to do the same.

He covered the murders, by husbands and fathers, of mothers with their children; he attended parades, parties, balls; he tried to estimate the degree of senility in a bishop; he rushed to the side of burning oil tankers that made up a train, wrecked near Alton, and inveigled from a man, who was ablaze, his name; he also got a scoop and a raise; he hung out in the long lobby of the Lindell Hotel, with its line of rocking chairs, observing the goings and comings of its clientele, and trying not to feel lonely, while rocking up and down in one of them, pretending to be going and coming. The manager began to feed him like a stray, and soon Dreiser was filling one of the regular columns of the *Globe*, "Heard in the Corridors," with fictitious gossip about visitors whose names he had weaseled out of friendly clerks.

Those who are young, sad, lonely and ill-fed fall into poetry as though it were a ditch at their feet, and one day, while Dreiser was trying to write a few lines, a colleague named Robert Hazard, who, with another reporter, Arthur Grubb, had co-authored a novel called *Theo* some months before, happened to observe his struggles. "There's no money in that sort of thing,"

Hazard said, "you'd better be putting your time on a book or a play." Plays made money. The example of Thomas Augustus was held out to him, a former cartoonist for the *St. Louis World* who had written big hits and made a fortune with *Alabama*, *In Mizzoura* and *Mrs. Leffingwell's Boots*. Dreiser's head filled with dreams of literary glory. And if he hadn't plays of his own to brag about just yet, perhaps he could write about the performances of others.

While reviewing Pinero and Wilde as well as a host of now unknowns, and admiring every winsome soubrette that came along, he was composing his own play—a fantasy about the Aztecs—entitled, biblically but regally, *Jeremiah 1*. Dreiser's career seemed to be lifting off. At Exposition Hall he heard a Negro singer, Sisseretta Jones, headlined however as "the Black Patti"—a reference to the opera diva—and was so entranced he let his rhetoric run away:

> What is so beautiful as the sound which the human voice is capable of producing when that voice is itself a compound of the subtlest things in nature? Here we have a young girl, black, it is true, who comes up from the woods and fields of her native country, blessed with some strange harmony of disposition which fits her to represent in song that which we know to be most lovely. The purling of the waters, the radiance of moonlight, the odour of sweet flowers, sunlight, storm, the voices and echoes of nature, all are found here, trilling forth over lips which represent in their youthfulness only a few of the years which wisdom requires.

Despite the condescension in Dreiser's praise, the *Post-Dispatch* would have none of it, and made great fun of the review's extravagance, and of the fact that this "mere singer of songs" was black. The worst of it was that the *Post* pretended that Dreiser's editor, the rough, tough Joseph McCullagh, was "the great patron of the black arts," and the lover of "purling streams," who had done the deed.

The rebuke Dreiser received was a mere knock, by disaster, on his door. It was a Sunday night in April of 1893, a big night in the theatre as it turned out because three new plays were to open that evening, and Dreiser was to cover all of them, a not infrequent impossibility.

> In this case I might have given both Dick and Peter tickets and asked them to help me, but I decided, since this was a custom which had been practiced by my predecessor at times, to write up the notices beforehand, the facts being culled from various press-agent accounts which were invariably sent in beforehand, and then possibly comment on the plays more succinctly later in some notes which I published midweek. It was my intention to go about afterward, a little while to each one, and verify these press-agent impressions.

However, Dreiser's editor sent him into the city's western suburbs to investigate a street car hold-up, and when he returned it was too late to look in on anything dramatical. His notices ran in the *Globe*, nevertheless, to the amusement of all but his bosses, when spring rains and flooding prevented all three theatrical troupes from arriving, as the *St. Louis Republic* reported

Monday morning, while the subscribers to the *Globe-Democrat* were reading that "a large and enthusiastic audience received Mr. Sol Smith Russell" at the Grand.

As with the singer's story, other papers made fun of the *Globe* at McCullagh's expense. Dreiser swept the office of his things and went into hiding until, after a week, his money ran out. Then he took himself to the second-rate *Republic,* whose offices were in a building barely standing at Third and Chestnut. He was taken on and told to write like Zola and Balzac.

By now Dreiser had relocated to a pleasant neighborhood on Chestnut Street beyond Jefferson. It was a rooming house managed by an attractive widow upon whose agreeable bosom his head would shortly rest. No change there, but shortly a silly newspaper contest would alter everything. The *Republic,* to increase the paper's circulation, staged a popularity contest among the schoolmarms of Missouri. The twenty winners would have their way paid to the Chicago World's Fair. A fox was chosen to accompany the chickens to the city and write of their adventures in the fair wide world. The homely spinsters that Dreiser feared he'd be ciceroning proved to be mostly young attractive women in light summery dresses. One of them would become his wife—Sara Osborne White—who had gone to school at a seminary in O'Fallon and was presently teaching in Florissant. Miss White was attractive, agreeable and enticingly demure. Her sister Rose soon joined them, and she was even more delightful. Dreiser's emotions flew about in greedy confusion.

He wrote "Sally" lengthy letters and courted her assiduously when she returned in the fall to teach, but he was unable to make his sort of time with her. He was being lured, then demurred, to death. So he proposed. And became engaged. And was fortunately too poor at the moment to be married. His brother Paul, riding a high horse of popularity—his songs "My Gal Sal," "I Believe It for My Mother Told Me So" and "The Bowery" were big hits—brought his melodrama to St. Louis, but incidentally stirred Dreiser's desire to be famous, which had lain for a while like quiet ash, into fresh flames. Like Paul, he wanted to dance away. Meanwhile, his landlady was found to have another beau beside him—the trollop.

Dreiser accepted an absurd proposal and an absurder position at a rural Ohio newspaper called the *Wood County Herald,* whose broken down equipment was housed in a loft above a feed store in a town full of hayseeds and horses. This journal had five hundred—he thought—sleepy subscribers. Dreiser may have been disgruntled, and made immediately aware of his mistake, but he had popped out of the bottle, and after sojourns in Toledo, Cleveland and Buffalo, he would find himself in New York where, all along, he had needed to go.

Dreiser would return to Missouri to woo Sally, who eventually became one of his unhappy wives, but, except for Esther Van Dresser, a woman from St. Louis whom he hired as a secretary in 1928, the St. Louis in Dreiser's future would come mostly through William Marion Reedy—the *Mirror*—and be mostly in the mail.

*I'm afraid the
child's going to be
extravagant.*

—Sarah Akins

Although Zoë Akins was a native of the Midwest, the plays and screenplays for which she is best-known draw upon another background, that of the upper-class societies of New York and Europe. Throughout her long and varied writing career, excess was her inspiration and grand passions her theme. Classical references imbue both the poems of her youth, which are replete with odes on beauty and tales of Zeus, Helen and Calypso, and the plays and novels written in her adult life.

Zoë Byrd Akins was born in 1886 in Humansville, Missouri, a small town in the Ozark Mountains, to prosperous parents with a large family library. Thomas Jasper and Sarah Elizabeth Green Akins moved their family to St. Louis in 1898, when he was named Republican State Chairman. He would hold other prominent political positions, including Assistant United States Treasurer under Roosevelt and Postmaster under Taft. At age twelve, Zoë Akins entered Monticello Seminary, a school for girls in Godfrey, Illinois, two years early, an experience she treasured as an adult—in her 1941 novel *Forever Young* the protagonist attends Huntly, a young women's school thirty miles from St. Louis, and is asked to sit at the principal's table at mealtime, an honor the author herself had enjoyed.

43

During her teens, Akins worked as secretary to her father, whose office was located in the southwest corner of the Old Post Office on Olive Street, where she composed poems on the backs of mailing circulars and completed the novel *Déclassée*. Akins began publishing her poetry at age fifteen, first in the *Globe-Democrat* and then in William Marion Reedy's *Mirror*, which also promoted the work of young local poets Sara Teasdale and Orrick Johns. The three would meet occasionally to discuss their poetry, but Akins's ambition was different: "It was from [Zoë's] office in the dingy old Federal Building that most of our plans for improving the universe emanated. She wrote more prolifically and with greater ease than any of us, and soon the big eastern monthlies [*Forum, Harper's Monthly, International, Theatre*] were publishing her work," noted Orrick Johns, who succeeded Akins as theatre reviewer for the *Mirror* following her departure

43. Zoë Akins, c. 1907

for the first of several periods she would spend in New York before establishing herself there as a playwright in 1919.

Akins and Teasdale attended school at Hosmer Hall, located at 4296 Washington Boulevard. Both traveled in Reedy's celebrated circle, but were never fast friends. Akins's theatricality offended Teasdale's prudish reclusiveness; even as a young woman Akins cultivated the European sophistication and jazz-age antics she would later thread throughout her plays—a pretension Teasdale both ridiculed and admired. Teasdale described a party given by a Comptesse de Venturini (*"she's* a decadent looking creature— small, dark, with a very pale green skin and a brilliant vermilion mouth, evidently painted. . . . all dreadfully Baudelairish"*) and Zoë Akins, who, "with a cigarette, legs crossed in a delicately revealing fashion and her most Frenchy manner . . . quite rivaled Madame la Comptesse." During this evening Akins produced some suppressed poems of the aforementioned

44

Frenchman, which the countess translated. Teasdale observed that "Zoë was quite ready with the unpleasant details," which, despite their Sapphic content, Teasdale "glanced at" later.

While their moral standards diverged, they shared artistic passions, and Teasdale assisted in preparing Akins's first book of poems, *Interpretations*, for publication. Zoë Akins and William Marion Reedy had become engaged a few years earlier. (One can almost believe it. Reedy wrote to her, "Oh, Zoë, the youth of you, the dawn-spirit of you, the fresh, free, poetry of you.") The proposed union was later rescinded by Thomas Akins, who decided against marrying his seventeen-year-old daughter to the forty-two-year-old Reedy. In Teasdale's opinion, Reedy felt "a very fatherly love for the poems" and had not provided the sort of objective editing the manuscript required. Teasdale recognized that Akins had a tendency to "swim in Greece" and persuaded her to "take out half a dozen of the weakest poems, and scores of poor lines." Teasdale pronounced the final version of *Interpretations* "vastly improved over the mss. . . . As it stands, the volume is a perfect beauty. . . . I can only hope that mine compares with it."

This professional admiration was reciprocated in a series of critical essays on contemporary poetry which Akins wrote for the *Mirror* in 1915, titling the collection *In the Shadow of Parnassus*. "Every line that has ever come from her pen has been distinguished by careful technique . . . and a clear, delicate beauty somewhat like candleflame," Akins said of Teasdale's lyric verse. And later, when asked about Missouri authors in a 1926 interview, she queried, "Who's written anything worth talking about except Sara Teasdale?"

Zoë Akins developed an early love for the theatre and regularly attended Saturday matinees at Hosmer, where she met actress Sara Bernhardt. Akins acted the role of Pheobe in a private production of *As You Like It*, produced on the front lawn of the Bixby estate on Lindell Boulevard, and joined the Odeon Stock Company, the leading theatrical group in St. Louis, at age seventeen, while her parents were traveling on the East Coast.

In 1905 Thomas Akins finally allowed his daughter to leave St. Louis for New York to attend college, but almost immediately upon arrival she wrote home to ask if she could "get on with the career I mean to have as a playwright," rather than "'waste time' studying at Columbia." Her father assented, and Akins continued writing, eventually making the acquaintance of Willa Cather, then an associate editor at *McClure's* magazine, who suggested that Akins write for the stage. Akins spent the next decade honing her dramatic skills through various small productions of her plays, including, in St. Louis, a 1915 presentation of *Such a Charming Young Man*, performed by the Tea-Party Players at Cicardi's Restaurant at Delmar and Euclid. Another, *The Magical City*, premiered in 1916 with the Washington

45

45. Main dining room, Café Cicardi, c. 1914

Square players at New York's Bandbox Theatre. Critics called this one-act melodrama in verse a fine example of modernism and a successful effort in experimental theatre.

Zoë Akins's breakthrough in New York theatre came with her stage adaptation of her first novel, *Déclassée*, starring Ethel Barrymore as Lady Helen, the "last of the mad Varricks," who, penniless and betrayed by her lover, gallantly leaves her last pearl on a restaurant check. The enormous popularity of this English society drama led to a string of Broadway successes over the next ten years, most notably *Daddy's Gone A-Hunting* (1921), *A Royal Fandango* (1923) and *The Furies* (1928). Akins received the Pulitzer Prize in 1935 for her dramatic adaptation of Edith Wharton's novella *The Old Maid*, though some critics argued that an original work should have won, such as Lillian Hellman's *The Children's Hour*.

Akins set her plays in penthouses, castles and casinos, and concerned herself primarily with matters of high-society romance, of heroines, lovers, opera singers and artists. She described her work as written "from the heart for the great collective heart," and many reviewers agreed. Alexander Woollcott deemed Akins "the chief romancer on Broadway," and she won praise from others for her witty dialogue. But she was also frequently viewed as sentimental and lacking substance—George Nathan accused her of "suffering from a suppressed desire to have a butler."

In 1928 Akins moved to California, and began a prolific and lucrative career as a screenwriter. She worked for Paramount, RKO and MGM, writing an astounding six screenplays during 1930 and 1931 and contributing original stories or plays for three others. Akins's work during the 1930s includes *Working Girls*, *Morning Glory*, which provided Katharine Hepburn with her first Academy Award for Best Actress, George Cukor's *Camille*, starring Greta Garbo, and *Zaza* with Claudette Colbert. Her 1930 play *The Greeks Had a Word for It* was made into the wildly popular film *How to Marry a Millionaire* in 1953, starring Marilyn Monroe, Lauren Bacall and St. Louis–born Betty Grable.

Like the social elite who peopled her films and plays, Akins lived in a grand manner in the "rarified air of Pasadena." She put off marriage until the age of forty-six, when she wed Captain Hugo Rumbold, a painter and scene designer, and son of the very refined Sir Horace Rumbold, a former British ambassador to Austria-Hungary. Rumbold died within the year of lingering war wounds, and Akins never remarried, citing a long list of unmarried women writers whom she admired. She once noted, "When I was fourteen I decided never to marry. 'It's all some girls can do,' I said, 'but I can write.'"

Akins wrote poetry throughout her life. In 1937 at age fifty-one, she published her second collection of poems, *The Hills Grow Smaller*, with a dedication to Willa Cather. Her favored themes are evident in her descriptions of Apollo and other habitués of Olympus, but there are other poems that let us glimpse a young woman in St. Louis:

> Ah wayward, sad, and diffident you were
> When you beheld the world beyond your door—

The great strange world which waited with its store
Of mysteries for you; and now a tear
Lay on your cheek; now some prophetic fear
Made you yearn backward; and the spoken lore
Of those, your elders who had gone before,
Was like a tale you would not even hear. . . .

One night you took the ribbon from your hair
And held it for a long time in your hand;
Then folding it away, you left the land
Of your first youth forever. You would wear
Your hair, so bound, no more. . . .

—"Seventeen"

Zoë Akins came of age artistically after the turn of the century, when post-Civil-War themes and European dramatic forms defined the American stage. She left New York in the 1920s, as this genre turned to more distinctly American subjects as found in the plays of Clifford Odets, Robert Sherwood and Thornton Wilder, leaving Akins and her grandiloquent stories behind. As Alexander Woollcott observed, "The poetess of Humansville, Missouri, wanted her woe well-dressed."

Willa Cather wrote Zoë Akins following Sara Teasdale's suicide in 1933: "Can you imagine anyone's *wanting* to leave this thrilling world?" Akins could not. She died on October 29, 1958, at the age of seventy-two.

In 1925 Zoë Akins, on a brief visit to her family in St. Louis, gave an interview to the *St. Louis Globe-Democrat*. The paper quoted Akins's description of St. Louis as a "melancholy, gloomy and sorrowful city." Akins, concerned that the interviewer had created a false impression from her words, wrote directly to the paper, which issued a retraction:

We regret that Miss Zoë Akins was misquoted in Tuesday's Globe-Democrat, and we are glad to learn, from her own written statement, that our famed expatriate does not consider St. Louis a gloomy or melancholy city. It was the St. Louis climate, Miss Akins explains, that she was discussing in the interview.... Having made this distinction between the climate and the city itself perfectly plain, she remarks, as if to mollify us, that "the same climate one finds here is also found in England, where some of the greatest literary geniuses of the world lived and worked; in fact, the thought occurs to me that depressing atmospheric conditions may tend to stimulate the inhabitants toward literary and other efforts."

—*St. Louis Globe-Democrat*, February 13, 1925

This assessment of the city's atmospheric conditions riled more than a few inhabitants, and the *St. Louis Post-Dispatch* printed its own "short and snappy" retort:

Miss Zoë Akins has done St. Louis a service. This city, with its gloomy climate, is a ready-made incubator of literary genius. Look at London, Miss Akins says. London, gloomy, melancholy and sorrowful like St. Louis, has a glorious literary tradition. Londoners brood a while, gloom a while, and sorrowfully turn out melancholic masterpieces. We have been wasting this literary climate of ours. We have been making boots and shoes, iron and steel, bartering, trading and doing nothing about the gloom.

Never mind. We shall reform. We shall brood, let the climate soak us with inspiration. Our traffic cops will soon be writing odes. Our city hall politicians will fashion tragic dramas. We shall permit the gloom to turn our stenographers from shorthand writers into Edith Whartons and Zoë Akinses. The teamster will become a Robert Burns. Janitors will become bards and chauffeurs will hail their fares with merry lyrics.

Last Saturday night, Miss Akins says, was lovely but it was also poignant. Should one dance on a night like that? No, she says, one should write a poem. Very well. On lovely Saturday nights we shall write poems, poignant ones. St. Louis will be the breeding place of genius. Conversation will be in blank verse, and the short and snappy retort will be in the form of a heroic couplet.

Next time Miss Zoë Akins comes we'll be wearing vine leaves in our hair and sandals on our feet. We will be passionate, poignant and everything. We will outbrood the Slav, and make Russian despair look hilarious. We will be 100 per cent literary.

—*St. Louis Post-Dispatch*, February 14, 1925

*The best and most
durable acts of
mankind are the
ideals and emotions that go to make up its books . . .*
—Shelburne Essay III

T. S. Eliot regarded him as one of the two wisest men he had known. He has been compared to Samuel Taylor Coleridge, Charles Sainte-Beuve and Samuel Johnson, and his work has been called "the most ambitious and often the most penetrating body of judicial literary criticism in our literature." Paul Elmer More wrote twenty volumes of essays on literature, social criticism, philosophy and religion, collected in *Shelburne Essays*, *New Shelburne Essays* and *The Greek Tradition*. He published a biography of Benjamin Franklin; a book on Byron; an anthology of seventeenth-century religious literature; and translations of Plato, Aeschylus and Sanskrit epigrams. He was also the author of a book of poems, two novels and a bounty of uncollected literary journalism. He was editor-in-chief of the *Nation* from 1909 to 1914, and in both 1930 and 1934 he was on the short list for the Nobel Prize for Literature. In the 1920s and '30s he was considered to be, with Irving Babbit, a founder of New Humanism, which defended classical traditions such as Platonism when relativism was the triumphant philosophy and individualism was de rigueur. In his later years More acknowledged that it was "a desperately hard thing to go all one's life against the current of one's age":

46

> Can or cannot art be divorced from ethics? . . . it is perfectly possible, and may be valuable, to study a work of art, or a movement of art, from the purely aesthetic point of view. Only, in my opinion, it should be remembered that such a study is abstracting for a special purpose what in practice cannot exist separately. . . . I would not for a moment deny that technique and aesthetic enter into the criterion of art and are factors of tradition. . . . But I think you will find that of the two, aesthetic is far more changeable than ethic, and that the continuity of taste depends more on the latter than on the former— though I would not press this point too far. But, after all, the great enduring things are the primary emotions, and about all I would say is that the higher emotions feed the better and more enduring art.
>
> —Letter to William Mode Spackman, February 16, 1929

Paul Elmer More's parents, Enoch Anson More and Katherine Hay Elmer, married in 1846. They followed their minister, James H. Brookes, from Dayton, Ohio, to St. Louis in 1859, where they rented a small brick house on Papin Street. On December 12, 1864, Paul Elmer, the seventh of

46. Paul Elmer More at Washington University, 1887

eight children, was born. He was christened by the Reverend Doctor Brookes on April 16, 1865, at the Sixteenth Street Presbyterian Church.

More went to Stoddard School at Lucas Avenue and Twenty-Eighth Street. His father, a Civil War veteran, took his two youngest sons, Paul and Louis (born in 1870), hunting and fishing. His mother read the Bible to her children, instilling in them a strong sense of religion as well as a love for reading. His older sister, Alice, also read to him and his brother—from Milton, Shakespeare, Southey, Bunyan and the Bible—so passionately that Louis at times would burst into tears.

Around 1872 More's family moved to a three-story house in what was considered the suburbs of St. Louis, at 3113 Washington Avenue. Influenced by his parents, More was sermonizing at the age of ten:

47

> Ther are 2 ways to do every thing, they are the right and the rong . . . we must pray 3 times a day. . . . we must not talk to Jesus as we would to the winds and the waves but we must talk to him like we would to one of our friends . . . (so there are two way to love) loving god and loving the devil. a sinner loves the devil and a christian loves god. a cat loves meat and a bird loves bread or crumbs. there are to ways to do every thing the GOOD and the EVIL.

More also invented special games, cutting out words from old magazines and giving them new definitions, until at last he compiled a dictionary with a new vocabulary and a complex grammar. When he was thirteen, he created a shrine to the goddess Khâla, who, speaking through her expositor, the stern priest Paul, led the service and asked young Louis about his previous day's conduct. After the goddess heard the confession, Paul would then toss a short rod into the air, guided by Khâla's omniscient hand. If the blue end landed first it was a sign of her pleasure with his report. If the red end landed first, the goddess was offended and would demand that an offering be slipped through the slot on top of her temple in order to absolve Louis. Cents and sweets were accepted, but Khâla was partial to maple sugar. Louis found that kindness and sharing, particularly with his brother, were apparent virtues of Khâla's cult.

More went to Branch High School Number One on the corner of Seventh and Chestnut Streets for two years and spent his third at the Old Public High School, at Fifteenth and Olive Streets. He graduated third in his class and in 1883 entered Washington University, financed by an inheritance from his maternal grandfather. When

48

47. Stoddard Branch, St. Louis Schools, c. 1870

48. Old Public High School, 1870

his father, Brigadier-General More, fell on difficult times, he sold the house on Washington Avenue and rented a smaller brick house on the east side of Lay (now Euclid) Avenue.

More began college with aspirations of becoming a poet. He wrote prose and poetry for the student magazine *Student Life*. Due to his passion for study, he would experience temporary blindness periodically during college, and during these times, Alice read his assignments aloud to him, in English, Latin, French, possibly German, as well as some Greek. He would also spend time with his classmate, Clara Sherwood, discussing Spinoza, Hume and Kant. He began to question his beliefs. This came to a climax during a Sunday morning service when he made "a final and so far as Calvinism was concerned, irrevocable decision." More "saw the folly of it intellectually . . . I hid my face and cried. That was the end. . . . Perfect faith, which nothing can replace, passed from my life."

This crisis of faith resulted in an anonymous article, "Quasi Deus," in the December 1886 issue of *Student Life*: "Philosophy must conceive God as infinite, and hence without attributes, an unknowable force informing a creation not distinguishable from the creator. Thus it inevitably falls into pantheism, avowed or unavowed."

More graduated from Washington University cum laude in 1887, traveled to Europe with "a morbid introspection," and then taught at Smith Academy. In 1892 he received his master's degree from Washington University, and then acquired another in 1893 from Harvard, where he taught Sanskrit. His first book, a translation of Sanskrit epigrams, was published in 1898. He was the literary editor of the *Independent* and the *New York Evening Post* before becoming the editor of the *Nation*. More would never settle on one discipline, however. He remained interested in poetry, combined his religious search with his philosophical studies and, throughout, wrote essays. His encyclopedic learning, critical insight and didactic conservatism at once infuriated and alienated his readers, as each volume of his Shelburne essays was published. (The title is taken from the town in New Hampshire to which he retreated, Thoreau style, in 1898.) Francis Hackett, in his review for the *New Republic* of the *Shelburne Essays* ("Mr. More Moralizes"), commented that "it was men like Paul Elmer More who gave Socrates the hemlock." More himself said that he was "at once the least read and the worst hated author in the country." In 1921 he became a lecturer in Greek philosophy and Christian thought at Princeton, where he taught until his retirement in 1933.

Catholicism eventually beckoned, as he believed it supported his humanist philosophy and the grander, spiritual extension of Platonism—he called the Eucharist the greatest philosophy ever created by the mind of man. But he spent his last days with Homer, reading the *Odyssey* in Greek alongside a French translation. No hypocrite, he refused last rites, and died of prostate cancer on March 9, 1937.

> The commonplace or the small may in its own sphere be commendable and may afford a true relish to the finest palate; and, indeed, one of the functions of criticism is to set forth and so far as possible rescue from oblivion the inexhaustible entertainment of the lesser writers. But the humble is another thing than the false, the false is noxious just in proportion to the elevation of the genius to which it adheres. There is nothing mutually exclusive in the complete enjoyment of both Milton and Crabbe; it is at least questionable whether the same man can heartily admire both Milton and Shelley.
>
> —"Shelley," *Selected Shelburne Essays*

Behold the friendless boy as he stands in the prow of the great steamboat Louisiana of

WINSTON CHURCHILL
November 10, 1871 — March 12, 1947

a scorching summer morning, and looks with something of a nameless disgust on the chocolate waters of the Mississippi.

—The Crisis

If, in the 1940s, you went to visit the novelist in the small New Hampshire town to which he had retired, you had to promise in advance never to mention the name of that other Churchill, then so much in the news. But if, as reporters sometimes did, you went to visit anyway, you would likely find the novelist painting watercolors and smoking his pipe. Did he know the other Winston watercolored too? and swallowed much unhealthy smoke? Had he understood the overshadowing to come, he would not have run as the Progressive Party's candidate for governor of New Hampshire, which drew his doppleganger nearer, nor would he have allowed President Woodrow Wilson to use his grand old mansion as a summer White House, increasing the chances of confusion. Nor would he have been so interested in history his whole life, nor been so committed to political movements, nor would he have chosen to end his life as a neglected sage—an immensely popular writer the fickle populace finally tossed aside despite his triumphs.

The Churchills came from old New England stock, and it was a stock that Winston regularly inventoried. His great grandfather made a fortune

in Cuban sugar and shipbuilding and was elected mayor of Portland, Maine, in 1844. His son Edwin, because his father could afford it, developed a taste for the good life, which passed, as such pleasant things usually do, easily into the character of Winston Churchill's father, an "Edward," to mark the small difference. Robert Schneider, Churchill's biographer, characterizes the father as spoiled, lazy and a proficient drinker, although handsome and charming as well. The latter qualities attracted one Emma Bell Blaine of St. Louis, though there is no mention in the record of how they met.

49   After the couple's marriage, they planned to make their home in Portland; however, Mrs. Churchill preferred to have her first child "at home" in St. Louis (as many women did—Ellen Sherman, for instance). Emma died (as all too often sadly happened) scarcely two weeks after Winston was born on November 10, 1871. He was only briefly in the care of the poor mother's mother, for she herself succumbed in two more years, whereupon Winston was taken in and raised by James and Louisa Blaine Gazzam, Emma's half-sister, in a house at 2810 Pine Street.

The child doubtless did not know he was brought up in genteel poverty, though he later thought of his foster father as saintly and his foster mother as a self-effacing Southern Puritan who believed in bearing life's trials (and life was surely nothing else) with cheerful fortitude and forbearance. Success was to be sought, but success lay in strength of character, not in simple social esteem or wealth. This type of triumph is harder to measure than most. Churchill wrote in an unpublished, third-person autobiography:

> The prospect of growing up a nobody, an unsuccessful man whom nobody thought much of, alarmed him. An unsuccessful man meant a poor man. Now his mother was far from a snob; her ambition was not that he should make a large fortune. She wanted to give him culture, and he inevitably connected culture with work; and work was doing something you didn't want to do, in order to be somebody you didn't want to be.

Guilt grew along with all his other inner organs. If Winston lied, played sick in order to avoid going to school, spent his streetcar money on candy, he fell into evil's endless pit, a hole down which no rescuer's ladder could be lowered. He felt that his mostly absent father was finally a fundamentally worthless person, self-indulgent and superficial, and later in life Churchill omitted his father from any mention as thoroughly as his father had omitted himself from his son's life. At the same time, his other relatives saw in the boy his father's looks and other traits, whose presence they did not fail to remark on.

When Winston was twelve his father suddenly called him to spend his summer vacation in Maine with his father's new bride (a widow who brought four kids of her own to the family), and although that stretch seems to have gone off well enough, it was enough, and Winston never saw his father again.

So in 1879, Churchill was enrolled in Smith Academy, a local private school, and he remained there until he graduated with honors in 1888. He was thought to be "a polite and elegant little fellow." A schoolmate, James Yeatman, who would become a well-known St. Louis philanthropist, described him as "a bright boy, a good boy and a frank, manly little fellow," but he "was not precocious and gave no sign of possessing the talent which he . . . developed" after he grew up.

The Gazzams got Winston through private school, but they could not afford college, so when his schoolmates went east to finish their education, he remained in St. Louis where a job was secured for him as a clerk in a wholesale paper store.

"Was I . . . to be denied the distinction of being a college man, the delights of university existence, cruelly separated and set apart from my friends whom I loved?"

Churchill felt neither fish nor fowl nor landsman either. In his third-person autobiography he wrote:

> He thought himself better than the other clerks and the porter with whom he was obliged to associate. His friends, with whom he had been brought up, went off to college. He pictured them in a new and bright and larger world, with other fortunate boys, while he had to go to the store at eight every morning, into that detested business district, and wait on people whom he was really ashamed to wait on, and make out bills and stamps.

Fortune smiled its wry smile. Churchill bumped into a boy who had been forced to give up his appointment to the Naval Academy on account of poor health. He immediately waited upon his congressman, F. G. Niedringhaus, and persuaded him to nominate the eager and articulate young man Winston appeared to be as a replacement. After all, Winston came from a shipbuilding family, had loved building balsa boats as a child, and was under the romantic spell of the sea.

Annapolis, however, stands on dry land; it is only near the ocean; and the academy's concerns were academic and military. Winston worked hard, and after ups and downs which did not resemble the movement of the bounding main, he graduated thirteenth in his class. But he saw the navy as a place for time servers, which he did not wish to be. He had, in addition, "no aptitude for mathematics, mechanics, seamanship or fighting." Instead, Churchill had drifted almost imperceptibly into the world of the writer's profession—in his case, a world more workmanlike than literary. The editor of the *Army and Navy Journal* offered him the naval half of its editorship. It was a job that paid poorly but took little of his time.

He was immediately bored by this job, however, and unhappy with the reaction of his adopted family to his abandonment of a naval career, so when fortune smiled again, and *Century* magazine took a story, and then the new *Cosmopolitan* magazine offered him a position, he began to think seriously of marriage to a wealthy St. Louis woman, Mabel Harlakenden Hall, whose position in life much resembled his own, since she was also without parents and in the care of a guardian.

However, Churchill could not stomach the *Cosmo* staff, and now that he had married his wife's fortune, he could afford to be particular. Afterward, he never left his desk, except, of course, to travel or to walk around the grounds of his cottage on Lake George or his mansion in New England.

Churchill's first novel, *The Celebrity* (1898), a lightly seasoned satire, was followed by a child, a baby daughter whom they took to Baltimore while he worked on the background for his next book, a historical novel, *Richard Carvel* (1899), a commercial success that sent Churchill properly on his way. In October of 1897 the family returned to St. Louis because his wife was slow recovering from childbirth and their daughter fragile. Here he wrote in an office in the Security Building. As soon as his wife's health was restored, they went back to upper New York.

Churchill set *Richard Carvel*, his story of derring-do, during the Revolutionary War and fed it to a public hungry for fictional history, especially military, because this was the time of America's conflict with Spain over its colonies. The book sold wildly; his bio popped up in papers all over the country; teenage girls penned him worshipful letters; women's clubs put on programs centered about his thrilling tale. The bemused British confused him with another young Winston, a confusion neither the American nor the British publishers did anything to dispel. Moreover, their Churchill had just published his own novel, *Savrola*, and was happy to receive congratulations on his masterful yarn spinning, only to have his pleasure extinguished when he learned these letters were directed to a namesake. Then their Churchill wrote ours to say that henceforth he would add his middle name, "Spencer" to the title page of his books; but our Churchill, though appreciative of the gesture, was a simple Winston, and could not follow suit. He also decided against the suggestion that he place a characterization such as "The American" below his name. Meanwhile, secure in the public's impervious ignorance of any mix-up, our Churchill became the sort of celebrity satirized in his own *Celebrity*.

An enterprising entrepreneur (read, "scoundrel") named Major J. B. Pond, who ran lecture tours, thought it a splendid idea to have our Churchill appear on the platform with their Churchill when their Churchill did his American tour. The American Churchill would then introduce the British Churchill to his American audience. "It will be a magnificent and unique occasion." One brilliant notion followed another. Perhaps Mark Twain could be persuaded—he could—to introduce our Churchill, who would then, after the laughter had subsided, introduce theirs. But our man said, repeatedly, no dice.

However, when their Churchill was lecturing in Boston, ours met theirs in their hotel, the cigar-chewing Winston receiving the pipe, puffing Winston while reclining—was it insolently?—on his bed. Later, they had dinner together. Robert Schneider writes that "a relationship of quiet hostility was established—a relationship that never changed."

While the construction of a grand mansion in Cornish, New Hampshire, was proceeding, Churchill returned to St. Louis and sat again at his desk in the Security Building to gather material for and compose his next novel, which was to be set in Civil War St. Louis. For the German background, he leaned upon *Revolution and Counter-Revolution in Germany* by Friedrich Engels, but for life in St. Louis he drew from the first-hand reminiscences of friends, or others recommended to him, who had lived in the city through his story's time. The St. Louis libraries—the Public and the Mercantile—were also an essential source.

The Crisis (1901) had a story that couldn't miss: it recounted the conflict between Blue and Gray and told of the love which would bring harmony to those colors. "At the conclusion of the novel the North and South are reconciled as the Union officer and his Confederate lady, Virginia Carvel, proclaim their love for each other in President Lincoln's office."

The glorification of both sides—a strategy that had proved profitable in Churchill's novel about the Revolutionary War—worked equally well for this one, and reviewers from every region of the country praised it. It may be of some interest that Churchill's odd understanding of the Civil War resembles the view promoted by Heinrich Börnstein and other Germans, who imagined the conflict to be the continuation of a European one:

> Two currents flowed across the Atlantic to the New World. Then the Stern men found the stern climate, and the Gay found the smiling climate.
>
> After many years the streams began to move again,—westward, ever westward. Over the ever blue mountains from the wonderland of Virginia into the greater wonderland of Kentucky. And through the marvels of the Inland Seas, and by white conestogas threading flat forests and floating over wild prairies, until the two tides met in a maelstrom as fierce as any in the great tawny torrent of the strange Father of Waters. A city founded by Pierre Lacleada [*sic*], a certain adventurous subject of Louis who dealt in furs, and who knew not Marly or Versailles, was to be the place of the mingling of the tides. After cycles of separation, Puritan and Cavalier united on this claybank in the Louisiana Purchase, and swept westward together. Like the struggle of two great rivers when they meet, the waters for a time were dangerous.

If our Churchill hadn't at first feared a confusion of identities, he would now, for on his next trip to England the mix-up was pronounced, and although their young MP invited our young best-seller to his club, our man thought theirs acted "like a cad"; moreover, it wasn't just the *Manchester Guardian* that couldn't keep them straight, American papers like the *Chicago Chronicle* began to congratulate the Winston who was Spencer on his understanding of our country.

A new novel on the acquisition of the Louisiana Territory began to occupy Churchill's mind (he was also campaigning for governor of New Hampshire), and this brought him back to St. Louis, where he traveled down the river to New Orleans. His friendship with Pierre Chouteau proved invaluable, since Chouteau was himself occupied with a bibliography of materials on the territory. The novel that resulted, called *The*

Crossing (1904), was another success, although perhaps not as huge as his previous ones. It is not clear when he decided to include the letter "C" in the title of his books, though it became an almost uniform practice. Maybe he did it just for luck, having by chance begun that way, or in order to leave the mark of his name on more than one bit of the title page. But there it was, for after *The Celebrity*, *Richard Carvel*, *The Crisis* and *The Crossing* (1904), there arrived *Coniston* (1906), *Mr. Crewe's Career* (1908), *A Modern Chronicle* (1910), *The Inside of the Cup* (1913) and *A Far Country* (1915).

Churchill would return to St. Louis to visit Joseph Gazzam from time to time and continue to use the city as a fictional location, but his principal interests were now elsewhere—in New England politics, and in his writing concerns:

> I have no patience with literary cant. Writing, it appears to me, is a business, and a direct means to the end. If people read, they want to read for their own entertainment or instruction and not to serve the author's pleasure or hobby. The lawyer prepares his brief to secure a verdict; so must the author. The judgment must be passed from a standpoint entirely apart from that of the author.
>
> I make a business of writing. Action and atmosphere, bone and blood are the things I try to put into books.

If critics ever trouble themselves to remember Winston Churchill, they might hold these remarks against him. As it is, fate's wry smile became sardonic, since Fulton Missouri's Winston (and the celebrated "Iron Curtain" speech he gave there) have, by now, quite eclipsed St. Louis's once popular novelist and his output of some seventeen books, including poems and plays. For twenty years Churchill was the king of fiction in this country; his ten novels sold about 500,000 copies each and went into fifty-four editions as well as being translated into several foreign languages. Then, except for the publication of a philosophical and religious work, *The Uncharted Way* in 1940, he was silent, increasingly engrossed by his painting and in the semi-private solution of philosophical issues.

Churchill's Cornish, New Hampshire, life did not change much for twenty-five years (except that he was alone at its end). He wintered in Florida, and on March 12, 1947, when he took his customary mile walk through the woods in Winter Park to visit Mary Semple Scott, an old friend, it was another day of quiet routine. He seemed to Miss Scott quite animated and in good spirits. They were speaking of his plans to visit St. Louis when he simply sank back silent in his chair with so little change of expression his companion thought him lost in though; consequently, she waited a bit before calling a doctor.

There are those who claim that Winston Churchill died in St. Louis. Not exactly. He was merely thinking about going there. When he did.

I R M A R O M B A U E R	
October 30, 1877 — October 14, 1962	

*But, Irma, who will
buy your book?
All our friends have
these recipes.*
—Rombauer friend

According to her family, Irma Louise von Starkloff Rombauer was not a very good cook, much better at what she would subtitle

50

the most famous cookbook in the world (if not for its contents, its title)— *The Joy of Cooking* and its alliterative description: *A Compilation of Reliable Recipes with a Casual Culinary Chat.* If T. S. Eliot changed the course of twentieth-century poetry, it was another St. Louisan who changed the course of American cuisine: aspics, blankets, charlottes, divinity, endive, fairy lemon tart, golden glow salad, Hurry-Up cake, ice box cookies, Japanese persimmon salad, kisses, lady finger sandwiches, Malaga and Tokay grapes salad, Nesselrode pudding, onion cases, paradise jelly, Queen Mary's sponge cake, rosettes, sea foam icing, tutti-frutti conserve, uncooked pudding, velouté, whips, yaeger torte, zwieback custard pie—as if its contents were props in *A Midsummer Night's Dream.*

Dr. Maxmilian von Starkloff was part of the *Deutschtum*, a cosmopolitan group of upper-middle-class German-speaking Americans, the children of the Forty-Eighters. Out of this culture would come the nation's first kindergarten, music,—particularly for the piano—beer, and, of course, spaetzle, streusel, stollen, sauerbraten, blitzkuchen, bund kuchen and kugelhopf. Von Starkloff lived and worked at many different addresses on his way to becoming a distinguished surgeon. After service in the Civil War as a physician, he opened an office in Carondelet, which was incorporated into St. Louis in 1870. He married Emma Kuhlmann in 1876, the same year that St. Louis seceded from the county, placing the city in critical care in perpetuity. Their first child, Elsa, was also born this year, and then Irma on October 30, 1877. St. Louis, writes biographer Ann Mendelson in *Stand Facing the Stove,* "would be Irma's universe all her life"—and her residence, with the exception of five years when her father served as American consul in Bremen.

The *Lebenkunst*—a not easily translated term for a melding of art and life—of the von Starkloff household meant lots of music (played inside and also organized outside the home), reading aloud from all of literature and talk. The whole family participated and their guests, too. Irma developed a knack for drawing, was a fair musician and read voraciously. When Irma's father was posted in Bremen she was able to meet her German relatives, travel in Europe sampling the various cuisines in search of *Gemütlichkeit*, and read Goethe and Schiller in the land of her ancestors. After their return to St. Louis, she took art classes at Washington University and visited her Indianapolis cousins frequently. There she met Booth Tarkington, who went giddy over her. She replied by marrying Edgar Rombauer, a member of the inner *Deutschtum*.

Irma von Starkloff and Edgar Rombauer led parallel lives. Their fathers were good German Republicans opposed to slavery, in support of women's suffrage and interested in public service. Edgar's father was a judge. His son attended Washington University law school, entered the bar in 1892 and moved to Chicago where he had the first of many "nervous breakdowns." They married on October 14, 1899, and moved into a rented apartment on Botanical Avenue, where they had no servants, not even a cook. Their first child, Roland, died within a year of his birth. Their second child, Marion, was born on January 2, 1903, and Edgar Roderick Rombauer, Jr., ("Put") in 1907. As Edgar, Sr., noted, "our happiness seemed complete."

Irma began to entertain. She also threw herself into civic concerns, such as improving the quality and safety of milk, working on the reduction of infant mortality—she was, after all, the daughter of a doctor—and with Edna Fischel Gellhorn (the mother of Martha Gellhorn) set up a clinic to test and treat venereal disease among prostitutes. She became involved in the St. Louis Symphony in 1911, and with The Wednesday Club, becoming its president in 1923.

The family vacationed in Bay View, Michigan, where Edgar would do the cooking. Marion later recalled that for her mother "cultural indoctrination knew no season," and all were enrolled in Chautauqua classes. Among these were cooking lessons—cake decorating, for example—at which Irma became particularly adept.

After Marion's graduation from Vassar in 1925, she became a stringer for *Women's Wear Daily* and began to see a childhood friend, John Becker, who had obtained his degree in architecture from Washington University. By now the Rombauers were living in a big third-floor apartment on Waterman Avenue and having parties with amusements, such as shadow plays, by Marion. After attending one of these parties a Wednesday Club acquaintance, Caroline Risque Jones, a sculptor, offered Marion a job in the art department at John Burroughs School.

On February 3, 1930, Edgar Rombauer killed himself with a double-barreled shotgun. Irma had to do something both to assuage her grief and to make money: Edgar's estate was not large, and Marion's salary was quite small. They moved to 5712 Cabanne Avenue, and Irma Rombauer began to write:

> Whenever I leave home and begin to move about, I am appalled to find how many people with a desire to write feel impelled to share their emotions with the general public.
>
> Time and again I have been told with modesty and pride, or with both, that I was entertaining a literary angel unawares, until one day, recognizing a

glint of authorship in a man's eye and anticipating his imminent confidence, I forestalled him by saying rapturously, "Oh, do you know, I am a reader!" And now, after all, I am a writer—of a kind.

The Joy of Cooking, with Marion Rombauer's silhouette illustrations, was published in 1931. They engaged a company that had mainly printed labels. Marion recalled their naïveté in 1966:

> We simply called in a printer. I remember the Saturday morning he arrived, laden with washable cover fabrics, type and paper samples. In a few hours all decisions were made, and shortly afterwards we signed a contract for 3,000 copies, complete with mailing cartons and individualized stickers. Then came the new experience of galleys, proofreading and preparing an index.

Their timing, as in great cooking, was exquisite. The depression had deprived many households of their cooks, leaving the homemaker, usually a woman, to learn how. Irma Rombauer admitted that it was her husband who taught her. It was Mrs. Rombauer who told us in a recipe for something sounding very much like Quiche Lorraine:

> In Switzerland we had a vile tempered cook named Marguerite. Her one idea, after being generally disagreeable, was to earn enough to own a small chalet on some high peak where she could cater to mountain climbers. While she was certainly not born with a silver spoon in her mouth—although it was large enough to accommodate several—I am convinced she arrived with a cooking spoon in her hand. If she has attained her ideal, many a climber will feel it worth while to scale a perilous peak to reach her kitchen. The following Cheese Custard Pie was always served in solitary state. Its flavor varied with Marguerite's moods and her supply of cheese. It was never twice the same, as she had no written rule, but I have endeavored to make one like hers for it would be a pity to relegate so good a dish to inaccessible roosts.

The Joy of Cooking was a hit—not because it was great but because of its banter and its incipient claim as the cookbook of record.

Shortly after its debut, Rombauer was at a dinner given by her cousin in Indianapolis; she met D. Laurance Chambers, an editor with Bobbs-Merrill Publishing Company, and in 1935 enlisted his help for the second printing. Which Chambers did. He also helped himself to a cash cow fatted by owning the copyright for the 1936 publication as well as the original, self-published 1931 version. Rombauer and her heirs lost thousands if not millions of dollars in royalties, for by 1940, *The Joy of Cooking* had been number one on the bestseller list for two years running. The story of the war between a tiny German woman in St. Louis and a big publishing company is told in *Stand Facing the Stove*, a biography of this particular group of *Deutschtum* and also a history of publishing in America.

Eventually Irma Rombauer was able to renegotiate her copyright, demand more editorial control, name her successors for the writing of the book, and with Marion, revise and improve subsequent editions. (Irma Rombauer also brought out *Streamlined Cooking* in 1938, which never took off the way *Joy* did, and in 1946, *A Cookbook for Girls and Boys*.)

Marion Rombauer moved to Cincinnati in 1932 with her husband, John Becker, who designed "Cockaigne," their modernist home. She planted a large garden and from her test kitchen there worked on the other versions of the cookbook until her death in 1976.

Without Marion's interest in the evolution of what we put on the table—in international cuisines, enlightened ingredients and new knowledge about the science of nutrition—*The Joy of Cooking* according to Irma Rombauer, with its Campbell soup recipes and Kitchen Bouquet, would have not survived to become the standard cookbook that it is today. But with the original 1931 edition, reissued in facsimile in 1998, we can read again about:

Cocktails

Most cocktails containing liquor are made today with gin and ingenuity. In brief, take an ample supply of the former and use your imagination. For the benefit of a minority, it is courteous to serve chilled fruit juice in addition to cocktails made with liquor.

GIN COCKTAILS

$\frac{1}{2}$ cup gin $\frac{1}{2}$ cup orange juice

$\frac{1}{4}$ cup lemon juice   A few drops of bitters

Apricot or other fruit syrup to sweeten and flavor the cocktail as desired.

These proportions may be varied.

Serve the cocktail iced, with hot Cream Cheese Canapés—Page 6, or with some other appetizer—or prepare $\frac{1}{4}$ cup of cocktail for each person, chill it in the refrigerator and pour it over skinned, chilled and slightly sweetened grapefruit sections, in fruit cocktail glasses—Page 2. Use chilled orange juice over prepared grapefruit for those who do not like liquor in cocktails. Serve the fruit cocktail as the first course of a dinner with, or without, some kind of appetizer.

51

Irma Rombauer died on October 14, 1962, and is buried in Bellefontaine Cemetery. Marion Rombauer Becker brought out the very successful 1963 edition of the cookbook. When the 1975 edition was published, food writers agreed that *Joy* was a supreme achievement of traditional and new cooking. The latest edition of *The Joy of Cooking* was published in 1997. Its authors represent three generations of Rombauers: Irma S. Rombauer, Marion Rombauer Becker and her son, Ethan Becker.

Some will wonder why we are treating a cookbook as literature. They will never understand, but they can take solace in the fact that Irma Rombauer's struggle to regain control of her work is important to anyone who writes, and a cautionary tale. As for the conclusion of the cocktail recipe—well, a writer without gin is like a lawyer without sin, one has no crime, the other no motive.

Irma Rombauer received a star on the St. Louis Walk of Fame in 1998.

Why, I have walked daily across the same stones on which Percy Bysshe Shelley and Sir Walter Raleigh must have walked. I have loitered in the same gateway where the young Sam Johnson is said to have amazed his fellow students. I have stood on Mrs. Bracegirdle's grave in the Abbey and walked down Olive Street in St. Louis with a battalion of whores hailing on the windowpanes and beckoning through the windows.
—The History of Rome Hanks

52

"A strange book is published today, a powerful, eloquent, lusty and lyrical book that is also an irritating, perplexing, overwritten and inchoate book," wrote Orville Prescott in the July 17, 1944, edition of the *New York Times*, in his review of *The History of Rome Hanks*. *Time* magazine called its reception "the most thunderous salvo that has welcomed a first novel since *Gone With The Wind*." This Civil War novel was written by Joseph Stanley Pennell—not Joseph Pennell the photographer, his father, or Joseph Pennell the engraver, biographer of Whistler and judge of the art competition at the 1904 World's Fair. The Pennell under consideration here hailed from Junction City, Kansas, attended the University of Kansas, but decided he preferred Oxford University. In the fall of 1926 he showed up at the gates of Pembroke College. "And by God, sir, do you know, they wouldn't have me," he cabled an old professor—who nonetheless managed to get him in. Upon graduating three years later, Pennell became a journalist at the *Denver Post* before making his way to St. Louis, where he worked in radio, writing advertising copy and continuity for KMOX, taught at John Burroughs School and acted in summer stock theatre: "My biggest part was clerk of the court in *Ladies of the Jury*." Like Lee Harrington, the narrator of *The History of Rome Hanks*, Pennell was a young man in St. Louis during the depression:

> I was to step into the Great Drama of Civil Life and work myself up into a Responsible Position. I could have chosen any one of a number of other cities, but there were the words Mississippi and Mark Twain and Old St. Louis—and besides I knew people in Kansas City—people to whom I did not want obligation, people I did not really like. I did not wish to be watched while I Made Good.
>
> Oh, I found a job alright. I found a good many. I found Christa—and I finished with St. Louis. I wiped it off the map of my Great World.

Pennell wrote his novel "just, well, from a feeling of wanting to do something, you know, to leave something, I guess." Discouraged by publishers' rejections, however, he tried to enter the Canadian army in 1941 and later joined the U.S. forces. After reading the manuscript, Scribner's famous editor Maxwell Perkins wrote to him, saying that he thought it the most remarkable piece of writing he had seen in years, in particular the description of Pickett's Charge, which he considered better than Tolstoy's battle scenes in *War and Peace*. (Pennell was lieutenant in an anti-aircraft battery in San Francisco when his novel was finally published.)

"Mr. Pennell, like [Thomas Wolfe], commits just about every sin known to literary man and, again like Wolfe, thinks up a few of his own," wrote George Mayberry in the *New Republic* in another salvo, the thunder from which resounded in an overnight sellout of the first edition. The noise intensified when the book got itself banned in Boston because of its "raw vulgarity." *Rome Hanks* remained on bestseller lists throughout the year and was nominated for that year's Pulitzer Prize. The film rights were reportedly sold for fifty thousand dollars.

"From so simple a beginning endless forms most beautiful and wonderful have been evolved," writes Darwin in *The Origin of the Species*, which Lee Harrington's great grandfather, Rome Hanks, reads aloud. During the five years he worked on his novel, Pennell read some thousand books and studied all 128 volumes of the *Official Records of the Civil War*. The book's many characters, unconventional narratives and reverse chronology are launched by the novel's opening line: "Yes, I'm sure your Grandfather must have been a fine southern gentleman," Christa Schell utters, indifferent to Harrington's family history and Civil War past:

> You know St. Louis? [Grandpa Harrington] said. You know the river? The levee where the Eads bridge is now? I shan't forget the day we marched through those dingy little streets of warehouses to the boat. We weren't long out of Keokuk, and we expected something more than we got in the way of a sendoff. We had a regimental band of sorts. The drum-major, a Viennese, I think, struck up a Strauss march—but it was no good. There was hardly a dwelling house along our way—narrow streets and high buildings, wet cobblestones, puddles and not a single mean balcony from which a beautiful young girl could wave a snowy-white handkerchief—a square of lace and fine-linen—if there was anybody in that district but broadfaced underbred brewers' daughters.

Cut to Harrington walking back to his "arsenic colored room" in the YMCA, meditating on the whores and houses of St. Louis:

> Ah! That's it! Lee said aloud, a battalion of whores. He smacked his lips over the phrase. A lost battalion of whores.
>
> And bloody lost they were too! Those houses—the sixty years abandoned mansions of the bourgeoisie. Stiff and straight and high they were, with curlicues. Dark hallways and marble fireplaces. Brick, painted and repainted. St. Louis moved westward, leaving its most respectable warren to the whores. Ah, yes, said Lee, bloody lost.

That was during the depression—thirty or thirty-one or two it was. And you couldn't say that they were St. Louis whores or Olive street whores (though perhaps some of them had been born there). They were just anonymous women who had rented these empty former houses in Olive and Locust streets and in little cutoff, choppedout streets near Grand avenue. Former what? I was going to say of the bourgeoisie again, but let us say just former houses. Maybe it would be better to say that the women along that street were first former women and then former whores. They were hard put to it in these years to eat; and those houses weren't much shelter—broken windows, leaky roofs, bleak and sooty in the streetlights. It was as if Doré had turned Lunapark operator to show the bourgeoisie—who had moved farther west into halftimbered houses out by Washington University or even into the country—what they had escaped by having got money.

There were two or three miles of slumproperty—not all filled with whores, for how many could buy an orgasm even then—even at fifty cents a crack? Occasionally there would be a swapshop or a surgical appliance shop with Venus-in-a-truss—or Love Lies a-Ruptured, in the window, or a radio repairshop—or four or five to a dozen houses just bloody empty. . . .

In any winter St. Louis seems an inescapable hell of darkness. Living there gives you a special claustrophobia whether you are indoors or out. It is as if you were locked in the smoky glass trainshed at Lyons with a thousand deaf mutes. It is as if you were lost in the catacombs of a dimenovel unable ever to see the sun. It is a scabrous, diseased city, looking like a peepshow with dirty lenses in a penny arcade. . . .

In 1945 Pennell married artist Elizabeth Horton in St. Louis, and they eventually settled in Junction City, where he wrote the second book in his planned trilogy. *The History of Nora Beckham: A Museum of Home Life* was published in 1948 to considerably less fanfare than *Rome Hanks*. A dispute over the noise made by a merry-go-round across the street from Pennell's office caused a rift between him and his hometown, so the Pennells moved to Seaside, Oregon, in late 1947. Two years later Elizabeth Horton killed herself with an overdose of sleeping pills, fearing she had cancer. Pennell married her sister, Virginia Horton, shortly after. The final installment of Pennell's "Junction City trilogy," *The History of Thomas Wagnal*, never appeared, and apart from *Darksome House* (1958), a small volume of collected poems, Pennell had no more major publications. In the heady days after *Rome Hanks*, Pennell was asked about his future writing program. "If I write all the books I have in mind I'll live to a ripe old age." He died in obscurity in 1963 at the Veterans Hospital in Portland, Oregon.

*I had seen another Caucasian board the train at Shaokwan and made a bet
with U. C.*
　　'Bet you 20 dollars Chinese he comes from St. Louis.'
　　'Why?'
　　*'I think it's a law. When you get to the worst farthest places, the
stranger has come from St. Louis.'*

—Travels with Myself and Another

Martha Gellhorn entered the fray of feminine firsts (a
femme fearlessness) when she was born in St. Louis on
November 8, 1908, the only daughter of a prominent
gynecologist, George Gellhorn, and Edna Fischel,
whose father was a doctor. Edna Gellhorn became
a social reformer and civic leader; she founded the
St. Louis chapter of the League of Women Voters
in anticipation of suffragette success and took her
daughter to the rallies: Martha was one of the tini-
est members of "The Golden Lane," the seven
thousand women with yellow parasols—and sashes
saying VOTES FOR WOMEN—who greeted the
Democratic conventioneers in St. Louis in 1916.

The family, including Martha's brothers,
George, Walter and Alfred, had "a loving, merry, stimulating"
home at 4366 McPherson Avenue with much consultation of books to
prove points. Martha's great-grandparents were Jewish—they are buried in
Mount Sinai Cemetery—but her grandparents and parents became active
in the St. Louis chapter of the Ethical Society. (Ethical Society Sunday
school wasn't much different from other Sunday schools, as Martha played
hooky and bought candy with her donation money.) George Gellhorn
shared his wife's civic interests: he established free prenatal clinics and provided medical services for the poor. He decided against joining a country
club when he discovered that membership just enabled one to play golf.
The only club Edna joined was The Wednesday Club, which her mother
and Martha's namesake, Martha Ellis Fischel, helped organize.

Martha attended Mary Institute, as did her mother before her, and
took dancing lessons at Mr. Mahler's Ballroom, located at Washington and
Euclid Avenues. Because there was not a coeducational private high school
(this was decades before Mary Institute and Country Day School merged),
Edna Gellhorn determined to establish one in time for Martha to enter. A
site was chosen in 1922, "close to nature and free from pollution," and John
Burroughs School, named after the naturalist, was dedicated on October 12,
1923 at 755 South Price Road. Martha sat in on the organizational meetings

53. Martha Gellhorn's graduation portrait,
John Burroughs School, 1926

for the school that would prescribe art history, symphony concerts and art studio classes along with French, Latin, mathematics and science. During her senior year she was one of ten students to found the *John Burroughs Review,* in which forty-two of her poems were published. She wrote Carl Sandburg after meeting him during his visit to Washington University and sent some of her poems, enclosing an SASE for RSVP. Sandburg returned the poetry and, according to Gellhorn biographer Carl Rollyson, responded that "if writing is a necessity, nothing can stop a person from doing it."

Carl Rollyson's *Nothing Ever Happens to the Brave: The Story of Martha Gellhorn,* published in 1990, is the only biography devoted to Martha Gellhorn the writer, rather than Gellhorn, one of a triad of St. Louis wives of a famous American writer. The book came out while Gellhorn was still alive; she did not cooperate, as they say, and she didn't want her friends to, either.

> I'm writing around asking anyone he might approach to tell him to sod off. I hate modern biographies of writers who are not public figures and not fair game. The only thing biographers are interested in are your love affairs and your eccentricities. A writer should be read, not written about. I wish to retain my lifelong obscurity.

After Gellhorn graduated from Burroughs in 1926 she entered her mother's alma mater, Bryn Mawr, continued to write poetry and was published in the university's literary magazine, the *Lantern.* Inspired by her family's European travels she decided to switch her major from English to French; her *Wanderjahre* would become her personal and literary calling card. She embarked after her junior year to the dismay of her highly educated parents, vowing to make her own way—journalism would be her ticket. Her first job was at the *New Republic,* which didn't call for much writing, so she went to the *Albany Times Union* as a cub reporter—her beats were social events (natch) and the morgue (better). She also started to file stories for her hometown newspaper, the *St. Louis Post-Dispatch.*

In 1929, when she was not yet twenty-one, she went to France and in between freelance assignments wrote her first novel, published in 1934. The *New York Times* called *What Mad Pursuit* "palpably juvenilia"; Gellhorn did not list this book among her titles later in life.

She returned to the United States in 1931 to travel around America. During a visit to St. Louis she met Joseph Stanley Pennell, who was writing for the *St. Louis Post-Dispatch*; soon after he was writing her sonnets, and soon after sad, when Gellhorn decided to marry Bertrand de Jouvenel, a French journalist and the stepson (and lover) of Colette. Marriage did not seem to suit Gellhorn—hers with Jouvenel was brief, but she would wed twice more.

She took a job working as a field investigator for the Federal Emergency Relief Administration and wrote about these experiences in *The Trouble I've Seen,* a book of novellas published in 1936, to better reviews than her first book. That same year she met Ernest Hemingway in a bar in Key West while vacationing with her mother. At the time Hemingway was married to his second St. Louis wife, Pauline Pfeiffer, having left his first, Hadley Richardson, for her—"I think if one is perpetually doomed to marry people from St. Louis it's best to marry them from the best families," he would later say. Gertrude Stein, of course, said it another way: "A man who had married three women from St. Louis couldn't have learned much."

Martha Gellhorn married Ernest Hemingway in Cheyenne, Wyoming, in 1940, and for a while their writing lives and their political causes overlapped. They had both reported on the Spanish Civil War—Hemingway for the North American Newspaper Alliance and Gellhorn for *Collier's* magazine. It was in this setting, of observing and describing a war and its effects with another writer whom she admired, that Martha Gellhorn fell in love with Hemingway. It was her desire to continue to cover the world that marked Gellhorn's tenure as his last St. Louis wife, but not his last wife. She did not want to publish under his name or to sit at home. She had been the first woman correspondent during the Spanish War, she was damn well not going to say no to a world war, which Hemingway did not want either of them to cover. She left him during the war and asked for a divorce after he accepted the only front-line correspondent post from *Collier's*, destroying her "chances of covering the fighting-war [in an official capacity]."

Gellhorn continued to report on wars from the front lines and to write fiction. Her wartime articles are collected in the 1959 *The Face of War* (reissued in 1988):

> When I was young I believed in the perfectibility of man, and in progress, and thought of journalism as a guiding light. If people were told the truth, if dishonor and injustice were clearly shown to them, they would at once demand the saving action, punishment of wrong-doers, and care for the innocent. How people were to accomplish these reforms, I did not know. That was their job. A journalist's job was to bring news, to be eyes for their conscience. I think I must have imagined public opinion as a solid force, something like a tornado, always ready to blow on the side of the angels.
>
> During the years of my energetic hope, I blamed the leaders when history regularly went wrong, when cruelty and violence were tolerated or abetted, and the innocent never got anything except the dirty end of the stick. The leaders were a vague interlocking directorate of politicians, industrialists, newspaper owners, financiers: unseen, cold, ambitious men. "People" were good, by definition; if they failed to behave well, that was because of ignorance or helplessness.
>
> It took nine years, and a great depression, and two wars ending in defeat, and one surrender without war, to break my faith in the benign power of the press. Gradually I came to realize that people will more readily swallow lies than truth, as if the taste of lies was homey, appetizing: a habit. (There were also liars in my trade, and leaders have always used facts as relative and malleable. The supply of lies was unlimited.) Good people, those who opposed evil wherever they saw it, never increased beyond a gallant minority. The manipulated millions could be aroused or soothed by any lies. The guiding light of journalism was no stronger than a glow-worm.

I belonged to a Federation of Cassandras, my colleagues the foreign correspondents, whom I met at every disaster. They had been reporting the rise of Fascism, its horrors and its sure menace, for years. If anyone listened to them, no one acted on their warnings. The doom they had long prophesied arrived on time, bit by bit, as scheduled. In the end we became solitary stretcher-bearers, trying to pull individuals free from the wreckage. If a life could be saved from the first of the Gestapo in Prague, or another from behind the barbed wire on the sands at Argelès, that was a comfort but it was hardly journalism. Drag, scheming, bullying and dollars occasionally preserved one human being at a time. For all the good our articles did, they might have been written in invisible ink, printed on leaves, and loosed to the wind.

The companion volume to *The Face of War* is *The View From the Ground*, a collection of "peace-time" writings. Martha Gellhorn wrote six novels, six collections of short stories and a book about a 1942 trip to Asia, *Travels with Myself and Another*, "another" being the Unwilling Companion ("U. C."), her second husband.

"I wrote fiction because I love to, and journalism from curiosity which has, I think, no limits and ends only with death." Her death came on February 15, 1998. The *New York Times* headline read: "Martha Gellhorn, Daring Writer."

Martha Gellhorn and all of her husbands, including her third, editor T. S. Matthews, visited St. Louis on many occasions, though she never wanted to linger. She called it "the St. Louis horrors." But in a 1996 interview she described a party in London at which she and T. S. Eliot tried to outdo one another by reciting the names and stops of all the streetcar lines in the city.

She watched Tippy with a practiced, almost a scientific, eye. She had seen this happen so often: the male blooming, expanding, flowering, and not because one took any real trouble, simply because one listened. Years of successful experiment had taught her that she need, in fact, hardly listen at all. It was done with a gleaming, approving look, while thinking of whatever one chose to think about; with an encouraging or admiring smile—you could always sense, whether by their expressions or the note of their voices, when the moment had come to enlarge the smile into a delighted laugh; with an occasional frown of sympathetic agreement. It was unbelievable that women actually went to bed with men to get what they wanted, when all you had to do to ensnare the gentlemen was listen or seem to listen. Heavens, Rose thought, while Tippy's voice droned senselessly around her, *how* I listened to darling Alan. It was a completely safe and infallible method, and the first thing mothers should tell their daughters.

—"For Richer For Poorer"

What the Sam Hill are you doing in New York—anyway?
—Vachel Lindsay in a letter to Sara Teasdale, 1913

54

The Teasdale family produced prominent ministers, judges, the founder of Concord, Massachusetts, two presidents of Harvard, signers of the Declaration of Independence, a Mississippi steamboat baron, a St. Louis street name and poet Sara (born Sarah) on August 8, 1884. Sara's father, a prosperous importer of dried fruits, beans and nuts, owned J. W. Teasdale & Company at 806 Spruce Street. "I was the flower amid a toiling world," she said of herself, as in her early years she was considered frail and weak. Cough and she was thought to have pneumonia—and in need of a private nurse. Housebound, she would sit in the bay window of her room at 3668 Lindell Boulevard (now the campus of Saint Louis University) and day-dream about the lame older boy who lived across the street. "It was long be-fore I knew how to read, so you see I fell in love very early.... he played sev-eral instruments . . . out under the trees. Sometimes the sheet-lightning would be shining fitfully—it always used to frighten me—but still he kept playing."

In 1909 Sara was sent on holiday when the family moved into their new house at 38 Kingsbury Place, which Sara's mother designed with the help of an architect. On doctor's orders, Sara took rides in Forest Park, sometimes with Zoë Akins or Orrick Johns, in her "little phaeton" with a monogram of her own design. She had a suite of rooms (southwest corner) where she wrote many of the poems for her first three books. "Sara lived the life of a

54. Teasdale home, 38 Kingsbury Place, 1999

Princess in her Tower, as far as I could see," said her friend Williamina Parrish, but Teasdale did not particularly enjoy the charmed life her parents afforded her:

I built a little House of Dreams
And fenced it all about,
But still I heard the Wind of Truth
That roared without.

I laid a fire of Memories
And sat before the glow,
But through the chinks and round the door
The wind would blow.

I left the House, for all the night
I heard the Wind of Truth;—
I followed where it seemed to lead
Through all my youth.

But when I sought the House of Dreams
To creep within and die,
The Wind of Truth had leveled it,
And passed it by.
—"The House of Dreams"

In 1904 Teasdale joined the Potters, a group of artistic young women who gathered each week to drink wine and talk art (usually at a member's house on Thornby Place). The Potters also produced the *Potter's Wheel*, a monthly magazine of their poetry, prose, photos and paintings. It was in these pages William Marion Reedy, editor of the *Mirror*, first read her poems, which he went on to publish in 1906, marking her debut. Sara eliminated the vestigial "h" from her name soon after (more Bernhardt and less Bible). The Potters disbanded in 1907, but most of them went on to careers in the arts—a rare and notable achievement for women at the turn of the

century. In 1908 Sara Teasdale's parents paid $290 for the printing of a thousand copies of her first book, *Sonnets to Duse and Other Poems*, which she sent to writers and actresses she admired. The *St. Louis Republic* did a feature story on Teasdale: "Poetesses are precious," its author mused, and should be considered a public asset like "an eminent baseball player, a splendid police force, an adequate garbage plant, [and] a superb sanitary system." When *Helen of Troy and Other Poems* came out in 1911, Reedy sent her a note: "It's beautiful—that's all. St. Louis ought to be proud of you." "It almost made me forgive him for weighing 260 pounds," Teasdale wrote to a friend.

55

55. *Cover of* Potter's Wheel *1, no. 1, by Caroline Risque, November 1904*

She also sent a copy to A. E. Housman, who replied that he read it "with a great deal of pleasure." She was asked to join the newly formed Poetry Society of America, where she met the East Coast literati and fell in love with New York. "That a girl could live in St. Louis and produce such verse has been a world wonder," opined the *St. Louis Post-Dispatch.*

Sara Teasdale concurred. "It is deadly to come back to this place where poetry is an unknown art, as dead as the embalming of the ancient Egyptians," she wrote. "There is scarcely anybody in St. Louis except my family that I'd give a straw for. Everybody has gone away to live or travel indefinitely in Europe. Sometimes I long to try to earn my own living. If I were a bit stronger I'd go for it. . . ." She signed up for French and ancient philosophy at Washington University, but dropped the one and left the other course incomplete. "St. Louis is a howling wilderness. I don't know how I'm going to stand it."

In her Midwest exile, Teasdale discovered the poetry of John Hall Wheelock. She fell in love with his poems and then the poet, upon meeting him in New York. "I'd rather be with him than see a procession of Irish players stretching from Cork to Killarney," she wrote, after turning down an invitation to a play by W. B. Yeats. "I am wearying my soul out for Broadway and my boy." Wheelock, however, was in love with someone else. "The Most Wonderful was looking handsomer than ever last night," wrote Teasdale, "and we had an endless walk on the east Side—but no love whatever. . . . in my case Eros has no wings." Even so, several men courted Teasdale around this time, among them Ernst Filsinger, a St. Louis businessman in awe of her literary gift. Teasdale preferred the handsomer, funnier and more passionate Wheelock, but Filsinger broke the monotony of St. Louis. And the two men looked remarkably alike: "Every now and then I can almost believe that he is Jack—just for a second."

It is widely and wrongly believed that Sara Teasdale and the Illinois poet Vachel Lindsay were lovers, and their suicides related. True, Lindsay courted Teasdale with long, exuberant letters: "The only place I would have a legitimate right to kiss you would be on the edge of a wheatfield—the thermometer at 108 degrees." He also visited her in St. Louis three times: in February 1914 he "shook her house and her nerves" reading aloud his poems "The Congo" and "The Kallyope Yell"; in April he took her to the movies ("Why do I always feel so bold in Springfield and so timid in St. Louis?" he wrote later); and in June he read at a salon sponsored by one Mrs. Pettus, to which Teasdale brought Filsinger. Sara and Ernst married in December of that year in a small ceremony at Kingsbury Place. Lindsay was devastated—"You shall be my Beatrice." He dedicated three of his books to her, including his *Collected Poems.* Sara was the "Chinese Nightingale" of his famous poem: "Deep in the ages, long, long ago/ I was your sweetheart."

Louis Untermeyer described Filsinger as "a little like the head-usher in a funeral parlor," but Sara's new husband worshipped her and her art and allowed her the time to write. The newlyweds lived in St. Louis for two years, at the Arthur Hotel (Pershing and Skinker) and the Usona (Kingshighway and Waterman), where Sara was at leisure to dwell on the beautiful. During this time the British poet John Masefield visited her when he came through the city on his celebrity lecture tour. "For the first time in years," she wrote, "St. Louis seems really a good sort of place." She published *Rivers to the Sea* in 1915, which established her as a major poet (the title is taken from a Wheelock poem). In 1918 *Love Songs* was awarded the first Pulitzer Prize for Poetry.

56

Sara Teasdale did not have children. The Puritan and the Pagan, as she called them, were constantly at war within her, a conflict which she saw as the source of her poetry. She called her first week of marriage a "fiasco." Yet there was a time when she and Ernst were very happy, even jointly composing poems. However, when she became pregnant in 1917, she chose to have an abortion, which she kept secret from him. She wrote about it in an unpublished poem, "Duty": "The seed is sown,/ the evil stands. . . . Out of the web of wrong" the poet must still weave her "thread of song."

Teasdale saw Vachel Lindsay again two and a half years later, after she and Ernst had moved to New York, when they threw a dinner party in his honor. Lindsay, whom Ernst came to like, later moved to the northwest and married a schoolteacher, Elizabeth Connor, in 1925, but epilepsy, exhausting reading tours, a failing career and mounting schizophrenia proved too much for him. He drank a bottle of Lysol and died December 5, 1931, in Springfield, Illinois. "I did not realize how constantly I should miss him. He was the last knight errant," she wrote. "In Memory of Vachel Lindsay" echoes his poem to her: "You are deep in the ages, now, deep in the ages." She dedicated her unfinished biography of Christina Rossetti to him.

Teasdale is known today as a proponent of the "genteel" tradition in poetry, with its smooth meters, predictable rhymes and mythic subjects. But Teasdale was also on the cusp of the "new poetry" and was a resolute supporter of its best practitioners. As a Pulitzer Prize judge, she forced the other two to include Carl Sandburg in a split prize. She lobbied for Theodore Dreiser when his novel *The Genius* was banned by the Western Society for the Prevention of Vice. She admired Frost, liked "the occasional verbal magic and the fine music" in Wallace Stevens, and was great friends with Amy Lowell. She considered Ezra Pound a "wobbly blond youth." John Reed, the journalist-activist, exchanged poetry volumes and letters with Teasdale. "There is no better living writer of delicate lyrics!" he wrote her. "I loved your book. . . . Why on earth should people like you bother with injustice and dirty things? The merest drudging machine can tend to that. You go on and sing. I'll never depress and brow-beat you with 'social reform' again." Teasdale even wrote erotic limericks and showed them to her friends, but unlike Eugene Field, never had them printed. For a time, Sara Teasdale was one of the most popular poets in America.

56. Sara Teasdale, c. 1910

In 1929 Teasdale divorced Filsinger, citing his frequent business trips as grounds. But her sense of freedom was short-lived: her literary production slowed considerably, her illnesses increased, and her poetic voice, which had always been 'tragic,' gained the eerie feel of real tragedy. "I have sometimes thought that if I ever had to support myself, I should commit suicide," she had written twenty years earlier. "It is so hard for a woman to make even enough to keep soul and body together—and if one is hampered by ill-health one might about as well give it up altogether." Two days before her death, a blood vessel broke in her hand, which she determined to be a sign of imminent death. On January 29, 1933, Sara Teasdale was found in her bathtub, dead of an overdose of sleeping pills which she had been hoarding for the occasion. Her death was ruled accidental by the chief medical examiner.

"Her spirit remained fixed at the stage of romantic love," wrote Vine Colby, a member of the Potters. "One could no more imagine her otherwise than one could imagine Isolde planning Tristan's dinner or getting the children off to school. She lived and breathed poetry." *Strange Victory*, her final book, was published posthumously in the year of her death. Her *Collected Poems*, edited by John Hall Wheelock, was published in 1937, the year Ernst Filsinger died. Her ashes are buried in Bellefontaine Cemetery, at an angle to his, whose name she chose to keep.

THE SONG.

I·MADE· MY·LOVE· A·LITTLE·LAY,
AND·SANG· IT,·SANG· IT· ALL·THE·DAY.
AT·EVE· WE· READ·A· QUAINT· OLD· BOOK-
"O·STRANGE", I· CRIED; "OUR· SONG·LOVE; LOOK!"
AND· VERILY· WE· FOUND·IT·THERE,
OUR· SONG;—A· THOUSAND· TIMES·MORE·FAIR-

OUR· LITTLE·SONG· THAT·FIRST· HAD·COME"
FROM· SINGER'S· LIPS· HOW· LONG· SINCE· DUMB!
I·THOUGHT· THAT· IT· WAS·ALL· MY· OWN,
I· WAS· NOT· GLAD·THAT· IT· HAD· BLOWN,
LIKE· SOME· WINGED· SEED· FROM· VERY·FAR,
WHERE· POET'S', RARE; DIM· GARDENS· ARE.

I· SOMETIMES· THINK· THAT· I·SHOULD· MAKE
ANOTHER· SONG· FOR· HER· DEAR· SAKE,
HAD· OTHER· MEN· NOT· LAID· BEFORE
SUCH·"GOLDEN· FULNESS"·AT· LOVE'S· DOOR,
AND·BROUGHT· MUCH· MORE·THAN·I· COULD·
    BRING,
AND·SUNG·MUCH· SWEETER· THAN· I·SING.

S.T.T.

57

57. "The Song," by Sara Teasdale, appearing in the
Potter's Wheel 1, no. 2, December 1904

Sara Teasdale and T. S. Eliot might have met without knowing it. Teasdale attended Mary Institute for one year, at its old location on Locust Street. Eliot, who lived next door, was four years her junior. He used to venture into the schoolyard after the girls had left for the day and walk the chalk and cedar-scented corridors. Teasdale often lingered after school to avoid the crowds on the streetcar. Many years later, Eliot recalled an encounter: "I remember, when . . . I saw [several girls] staring at me through a window, I took flight at once." Was one of those faces Teasdale? In any case, Sara transferred to Hosmer Hall and went to school with fellow Pulitzer Prize winner Zoë Akins. Teasdale disliked *The Waste Land* (she thought it pompous, willfully obscure, weakly vaudevillian and lacking an integrated design), but she may have liked his "Preludes," which bear a striking resemblance to her 1911 poem "City Vignettes":

Dawn

The greenish sky glows up in misty reds,
  The purple shadows turn to brick and stone,
The dreams wear thin, men turn upon their beds,
  And hear the milk-cart jangle by alone.

There is no record of Eliot's opinion of Teasdale.

How we thrilled to those rolling syllables, and how confidently we looked to that abstract thing called 'beauty' to solve all problems.

ORRICK JOHNS
June 2, 1887 — July 8, 1946

—Time of Our Lives

In 1894, a trolley car on Vernon Street mauled Orrick Johns, age seven, while he was playing tag on his way home from school. One of the few blessings of St. Louis's notoriously sharp January cold—in this case—was its dilatory effect on blood flow, which saved his life but not one of his legs. And so, like Sara Teasdale, another housebound child of St. Louis, Johns began to compose poetry and to develop a style which his friend Zoë Akins would later call "sheer music" filled with "poetic ingenuousness":

Flowers

Gorgon-head and Golden-tongue—
I'll name the flowers that none has sung.

Henna-flame and Blackamore—
Flowers that never bloomed before.

Mirth-maker and Madhair Queen—
These are the flowers you have not seen.

Fire-in-dew and Dream-awake—
Flowers no living hand shall take.

Star-desire and Lady's Breath—
Flowers that lead a man to death.

Orrick Johns was the second of five sons born to newspaperman George Sibley Johns and Minnie McDearmon; the family lived on Compton Avenue. After the trolley accident, the family moved to Maple at Cabanne, and Johns attended Dozier School: "It was home, our own back-

yard, friendly, liberal and encouraging. . . . It made for unforced, harmonious, decent rearing of kids, and for real democracy and fair play," he writes in *Time of Our Lives*, a combination autobiography and biography of his father, editor of the *St. Louis Post-Dispatch*, published in 1937. The book is also a history of St. Louis.

58

Like Fannie Hurst, Johns went to Central High School, the only public one at the time. The school

brought the whole town of the burgher and professional classes together, and some offspring of workingmen. Four years of it was an education in the social history of the town. We all met there, north, south and west end girls and boys, Germans, French, Jews and the descendants of the old South . . . . The business was to make the average American, Western style, according to a local lineage long recognizable. There were more exclusive schools in St. Louis than Central High. Smith Academy for boys and Mary Institute for girls were tops. We played our Thanksgiving game with Smith Academy; there was some feeling of snobbiness on both sides, only overcome years later when grown men met in the life of the city without distinction of class. Some well-to-do boys preferred to go to the High School.

Following graduation, Orrick Johns enrolled at the University of Missouri, declining his acceptance into Princeton, his father's alma mater:

58. Dozier Branch, St. Louis Schools, 1893

The relative expense had an influence on my decision, but much more it was the wish to identify with the state, with the regional character I felt I had inherited, and for which my first two schools had prepared me. . . . It was a genuine experience to meet men from all over the state—log cabin boys by inheritance—from the small towns and farms. They were a shrewd, able type, often well read, thinking for themselves. They talked willingly of what they knew; and they knew much more at first hand, about life, politics, character, than my St. Louis friends did.

In 1908, during his junior year, Johns was elected editor of the humorous monthly the *Missouri Oven,* and at one point he was suspended for poking fun at two professors—one was missing a few fingers and the other had a speech impediment. After the deliberation of Johns's suspension, however, one member of the disciplinary commission pulled him aside: "You fellers are too fresh, well, I guess writers have to be fresh to get anybody to read 'em. Go home," he winked, "and come back."

He did, graduating in 1909, and went on to work as a deputy city marshal: "While on the job I wore a star and carried a six-shooter, and the culmination came when I was arrested, in the middle of the Eads Bridge, for 'impersonating an officer.' My papers counted for nothing. There was a feud between the St. Louis police and the East St. Louis police." In the spring of the following year, after nearly a year of "illegally" enforcing the law, he joined the staff of the *Mirror* at the invitation of William Marion Reedy. Although initially accepted into this circle because of his surname, his creativity, critical insight and boyish charm (at twenty-three he was three years younger than any other member of Reedy's staff) would ultimately win him the respect and affection of his colleagues.

Johns befriended several staff members, including future literary lights Zoë Akins and Sara Teasdale. Under the critical eye of these poets Johns practiced and perfected his poetic style. In 1915 Akins reviewed some of Johns's poems in an essay appearing in the *Mirror*: "Neither Poe nor Verlaine, nor Keats nor Chapman had a greater gift for the suggestive sensitive phrase, the imaginative mood, than Orrick Johns." But, she concluded in candor, "He writes only fragments of poems within poems, for the most part, and he seems incapable of the care and diligence necessary to make much of his work intelligible and competent." In this review she called "Dirge" his "loveliest poem," which concludes:

> By and by,
> We shall lie
> You and I,
> Long together
> In all weather;
> I shall die
> By and by!

The position on the *Mirror* not only gave Johns free time to work on his poetry, it also gave him "a chance to know the bigger world of the city,

ORRICK JOHNS

and the people who figured in the news." He reviewed plays, books, music and fine arts and began to frequent the theatre and restaurant district, between Fourth and Ninth Streets, where "they fed the well-to-do and smart people of the town, the famous actors, lecturers and writers. It was still possible to meet, evening after evening, all the prominent people of the city." He went on to describe St. Louis, circa 1910:

> At the Odeon I heard Caruso in Aida, and the youthful, dazzling Geraldine Farrar, when she set the whole country humming the airs of "Madame Butterfly."
>
> The established old restaurants were still there: Faust's, the Southern Hotel, the Planter's House, mentioned by Dickens in his travel notes, and McTague's, the favorite headquarters of William Marion Reedy. . . . St. Louis was not yet a sprawling metropolis of many strangers and no common gathering places. Before a handful of years had passed the restaurants would disappear, driven out of existence by war and prohibition, and the habit of hurried eating. The theatres would be altered or torn down because of the decline of the road show and the rise of the movies.

Johns and his friends on the *Mirror* helped create a literary character unique to St. Louis, one which eventually migrated to New York. Johns followed Teasdale and Akins there in 1911 and a year later was given an award, from *Lyric Year,* a prestigious New York publication, for his poem "Second Avenue," in which he portrays immigrants drawn by freedom and opportunity, pouring onto the streets of New York City:

> In gutter and on side-walk swells
>   The strange, the alien disarray,
> Flung from the Continental hells,
>   From Eastern dark to Western day.
>
> They pass where once the armies passed.
>   Who stained with splendid blood the land:
> But bloody paths grow hard with years,
>   And bloody fields grow rich and grand. . . .
>
> Are you, O motley multitude,
>   Descendants of the squandered dead,
> Who honoured courage more than creeds
>   And fought for better things than bread?
>
> —"Second Avenue"

He published his first book of poems, *Asphalt and Other Poems* (containing "Second Avenue"), in 1917, the year he moved back to St. Louis. His father had become a landowner in Kirkwood: "I call the three poplars at my door the Brothers Karamazov. One is straight as a die, the other leans, but the third, Ivan, is crooked as a dog's hind leg." During this period he wrote most of the poems he would later publish in his 1926 poetry collection *Wild Plum,* named for one of the kinds of trees in his father's backyard.

St. Louis was feeling the effects of World War I, and Johns found parts of his former bustling city very grim: "War time hysteria came over [St. Louis] like a blanket of terror. . . . on the flimsiest pretext, good citizens of German name were denounced, persecuted, and either arrested or beaten." He took a job at Gardner Advertising Agency for thirty-five dollars a week and remained for three years before returning to New York to ply the same trade. He edited the *New Masses* and became the director of the Federal Writers' Project of the WPA. He visited again in the summer of 1933, to witness the brutality of St. Louis's particular manifestation of the Great Depression. "I had never seen such stark destitution as that on the river front of South St. Louis. The people

were practically imprisoned there, discouraged by police and watchmen from going into the city. . . . Some got baskets of vegetables from the welfare bureau . . . Most of them lived on Mississippi cat fish."

Johns's book ends in 1936, and much of his biography, too. We know he married Caroline Blackman and they had a daughter, Charis, born in San Francisco December 23, 1930; that he lost Caroline to madness in 1933; that he married again in 1937 to Doria Berton; and that in 1946, at the age of fifty-nine in Danbury, Connecticut, he took his own life by taking poison.

Orrick Johns was part of the first generation of writers to be raised in the twentieth century. He was its chronicler, its advocate and its poet:

> I have seen nothing but wars in my time: labor wars, national and international wars, slave insurrections, civil wars, cultural wars, and literary wars. Sad, but necessary to great change. I was exempted from military service by physical disability, but have had a modest share in two civil victories: the revolution in American arts and literature, their release from the anaemia of my boyhood days; and the awakening of labor and social consciousness in America.

The selection of Johns's poem "Second Avenue" from more than nine thousand other poems for the *Lyric Year* first prize of five hundred dollars was controversial. Jessie B. Rittenhouse, a friend and travel mate of Sara Teasdale's, wrote about the incident in her book *My House of Life*:

> It is not strange . . . that a social poem should have received attention wholly out of proportion to its poetic merit. It was a time-spirit product, and solely for this reason, we must believe, the first prize was given to 'Second Avenue' by Orrick Johns.

> To be sure, such a judgement is indefensible, and otherwise wholly inexplicable when a poem like 'Renascense' [by Edna St. Vincent Millay] was in the

---

field, but having been long associated with Mr. Wheeler [one of the three judges of the competition] in the Poetry Society of America, and knowing his interest at the time in poetry which reflected the modern scene and was, as he termed it, 'dynamic,' I can well understand, though no less deplore, his selection.

Sara Teasdale recalls what her good friend Willard Huntington Wright (whose pseudonym, S. S. Van Dine, wrote mystery stories) reported after the final awards were decided:

> [Mitchell] Kennerley was a man of arbitrary and unpredictable moods; he had a deep and sympathetic feeling for Orrick Johns, a young poet from St. Louis, who as a boy met with a frightful accident which necessitated the amputation of a leg. Kennerley had printed his verses in the *Forum*, and since he was leading a precarious literary life in New York, decided the first prize money would be a boon to him, and insisted it be given for his poem, "Second Avenue."
>
> The judges were somewhat displeased at the maneuver, but revealed no dissent for fear the public confidence of any internal controversy based on such a violation of trust might hurt literary competitions.

Here's the poet's take:

> In the fall of 1912 came the news that "Second Avenue" had won the Lyric Year first prize of $500. Nothing had been further from my expectations, and when the book arrived I realized that it was an unmerited award. The outstanding poem . . . was "Renascence" By Edna St. Vincent Millay, immediately acknowledged by every authoritative critic as such. The award was as much of an embarrassment to me as a triumph. A heated controversy ensued over it in New York, and I received critical letters, and clippings from correspondence columns. T. A. Daly, of Philadelphia, the remarkable poet-interpreter of Irish and Italian immigrants, had won second prize. He warned me through Reedy, not to take part in the newspaper scrimmage. I refrained and I also declined to attend the banquet that was given in New York in honor of the book. I did not want to be the center of a literary dog fight.
>
> The choice of "Second Avenue" had been largely due to one man, the late Edward J. Wheeler, editor of *Current Opinion*. It appealed to him for the same reason that it delighted father; it had a "social content." It was the cry of the *plebs urbana* of my youthful environment, the expression of the "little" middle class of the previous century. Its theme was: economic quality, more leisure, high-thinking—all very romantic and confused, of course, but something that found an echo in the political feeling of the older liberals of that day.
>
> The money went for debts incurred on my small pay at the *Mirror* and for clothes. I loved well-tailored clothes and bright colored neckties, and now I got me them in abundance. I also found that a brief bit of national ballyhoo makes it easier to accomplish things.

FANNIE HURST
October 19, 1885 — February 23, 1968

Please make no mistake. I am very clearly aware that I am not a darling of the critics. I have a vast popular audience—it warms me; it's a furnace.

Fannie Hurst was one of the most widely published and highest paid short story writers in America during the early part of the twentieth century. Robert Hobart Davis, editor of the *Cavalier*, thought he had "discovered O. Henry's successor, a woman at that." In her stories, Hurst recorded the lives and working conditions of lower and middle class women; as a champion of the poor and neglected, she described the poverty of the various ethnic groups on New York's East Side, where she eventually moved. A prolific writer, she also published novels and nonfiction, and saw movies made from her books.

Fannie Hurst was born on October 19, 1885 in Hamilton, Ohio, to German Jewish parents, Samuel and Rose Koppel Hurst, who soon after brought her to St. Louis. Some of Hurst's earliest memories were of the Mississippi, of "walking along a high bluff with my hand in my father's, and pausing with him to look out over the wide Mississippi River as it flowed, slow-moving as molasses, past our city"; and of filtering the Mississippi mud out of the family's drinking water: "I used to beg for the privilege of cleaning ours. The filter stone lifted out of its metal container, covered with a heavy coating of thick yellowish slime which washed off as you held it beneath the faucet and ran thick as gravy into the sink."

Hurst's father made a comfortable life for his family, but "intellectual curiosity," Hurst tells us in her autobiography *Anatomy of Me*, "was languid at our house." Even so, she began writing verse at age seven; started to compose stories at the age of thirteen; became president of the Literary Society; wrote for the school newspaper; performed in the dramatic club; and was a member of the basketball team. Her time at Central High School, where so many of the writers in this tour attended school, "proved providential . . . even these public school youngsters coming as they did from

60

61

60. *Fannie Hurst, c. 1920*

61. *Central High School, 1906*

varied social, economic, and cultural backgrounds, struggling, squirming, pushing, filled me with a kind of pity or warm glow." The building was "a red brick turreted pile remarkably modern for its period, standing on its little eminence between the Odeon on the north, and if I rightly recall, an elegant laundry on the south." She continues:

> When people said, as they were wont, and still are for that matter: St. Louis is a slow town, give me Chicago or New York; it seemed to me they must know nothing about Grand Avenue. Besides Central High, Grand Avenue boasted the Odeon Concert Hall, next door, Christian Brothers' College, and the massive stone entrance to the then exclusive Vandeventer Place.

Her parents became exasperated with their bookish daughter ("I wish you thought as much of your family as you do of that public library. If it isn't books, it's scribble-scribble, and when all is said and done what does it amount to?") and were shocked when she announced that she intended to go to college. They relented though, and she enrolled at the University of Missouri to study journalism. She couldn't bear to be separated from her family after all so she returned to St. Louis in 1905 to attend Washington University, where she began her formal study of literature. Here, she wrote twice the number of required English papers and began submitting work to the *Saturday Evening Post*, only to get rejected. She also acted in plays and, in 1909, the year of her graduation, she wrote *The Official Chaperone*, the first musical comedy performed at Washington University.

Fannie Hurst,
St. Louis, Mo.
College. Thyrsus, '06, '07, '08, '09. Vice-President Thyrsus, '07, '08, '09. Annual Play, '07, '08, '09. Student Life, '07, '08, '09. Hatchet, '08. President McMillan Hall, '09. Captain Girls' Varsity Basket Ball, '09. Captain Girls' Class Basket Ball, '08, '09.

62

Hurst's friends encouraged her to send some of her stories to William Marion Reedy, editor of the *Mirror*. He published "The Joy of Living," in 1909. Thrilled, she began to bombard him with stories until finally Reedy replied: "Dear Miss Hurst: So you are a college girl. Hello, college girl. I am going to print your story, 'Episode.' It is as wobbly as a new calf but there is talent in it. Come into my office and let me meet you." She complied. He spoke, "like a cross between a scholar and a bum," about Ovid, Dreiser and Mencken, while giving capsule reviews of other writers: "Sara Teasdale is a middle-westerner who bathes under a sheet. Most American writers . . . [are] wired with suppressed desires [and] their sex life [takes] place chiefly between book covers." Reedy would reject more of Hurst's work, but he strongly encouraged her to continue writing and to send him stories.

Fannie Hurst went on to do graduate work at Washington University, but eager for other experiences she asked her father to help her get a job in the Lutz Brothers shoe factory. She assumed the name Rose Samuels and for two weeks, working with struggling immigrant girls, she assembled shoes. Appalled at the working conditions, Hurst contacted the *St. Louis Post-Dispatch*, which published the story, emphasizing her advocacy of labor reforms and printing her picture. The Lutz Brothers promptly fired her.

Her parents were mortified, but cooled off enough to take her to a spa in Mount Clemens, Michigan, for her graduation present. There she met and fell in love with a pianist and teacher from Moscow, Jacques S. Danielson, whom her assimilated, prejudiced father called a "kike," due to his Russian extraction, and forbade her to marry. Later, she convinced her parents to allow her to move to New York. In the fall of 1910, at the age of twenty-five, she enrolled at Columbia University and began seeing Danielson again. That same year Reedy accepted another of Hurst's stories, "Prose": "Good luck in the fight," he wrote her (referring both to her parents' dotage and to her writing career), "You'll win some. Wish I could help you to an early win, but I can't. I like your grim=kind [*sic*] view of life. . . . People are just as you see them, a little nasty, a little mean, but good after all."

It was through a friend from St. Louis that Hurst met the editor of the *Cavalier*, Robert Hobart Davis, who made many short story writers famous. He became a great force in Hurst's life, encouraging, editing and printing her stories. With his help, Hurst had a story in the *Saturday Evening Post* in 1912. Davis also began to pressure Hurst for a novel, and in 1921 her first book, *Star-Dust*, was published with a dedication to him.

Hurst continued to write for the *Post* and be well paid for it. With this exposure, she gained greater fame and became an American celebrity. She supported good causes with time and money and befriended fellow activist Eleanor Roosevelt. Hurst was one of the first writers to explore other forms of media: she had her own radio show, and later her own TV talk show. Many of her novels were made into movies, including *Imitation of Life* in 1934 and *Humoresque*, filmed twice, with the 1946 version starring Joan Crawford and John Garfield.

Throughout, she remained devoted to her parents and visited them often. In 1955 the hometown-girl-made-good was asked by the *St. Louis Globe-Democrat* to write an article:

> The St. Louis of today, with its accrued wealth of solid industries, gargantuan department stores, factories, major league baseball teams; its avenues, boulevards, residential streets with stone gates that are locked at night; its meatpacking, shoe, fur, chemical and heavy industries; its staggering brewing interests, its mercantile and manufacturing importance, its family mansions; all this staid conservatism of contemporary St. Louis has a background of trappers, of voyageurs, such as the Chouteaus; of Louisiana Purchase pathfinders; of Lewis and Clark, who blazed a trail into the fur monopolies upon which so much St. Louis history rests.

She went on to sketch the city that we know today:

> Come evening, St. Louis likes to enjoy its comfortable living rooms or glassed-in porches, its television, cards, or social gatherings. Downtown streets are largely deserted, theaters indifferently attended. . . . When St. Louisans who have struck out to seek, or make, name and fame for themselves in far-flung places, feel the nostalgic pull to return for a visit, they will be assured a quiet but undemonstrative welcome.

Fannie Hurst and Jacques Danielson had been secretly married in 1915 in Lakewood, New Jersey. She kept her name, and they lived in separate apartments while they pursued successful, independent careers. Five years later, a reporter for the Associated Press came across the official record and revealed their unorthodox arrangement, which came to be known as a "Fannie Hurst marriage." The couple's union survived this exposure, and lasted until Danielson's death in 1952.

Fannie Hurst created many fictions in addition to those between her book covers—many composed for her autobiography *Anatomy of Me,* published in 1958. Early on in her career she forgot her birth date and where she lived in St. Louis, perhaps because her family moved a lot. (As one discovers in this guide, itinerancy was very common.) By the time the family settled at 5641 Cates Avenue, the only residence we cite for Hurst in our tour, the three of them had lived at ten different addresses, according to Hurst biographer Brooke Kroeger in *Fannie: The Talent for Success of Writer Fannie Hurst,* published in 1999. At the age of fifteen Hurst moved to her first rented home without the company of boarders, facts she failed to mention in her official biography. She called these "snags of circumlocution."

After years of living the American story of fame and fortune, Hurst could not interest her alma mater in her success. Other of the universities with whom she was associated called upon her, but from Washington University she did not receive "encouragement, cooperation, nor exhibitions of interest from either the university or the alumni association. . . . So far as I am concerned, every emotion of mine toward Washington U. may be dead to the frost—except deep down within me—in spite of everything are affectionate memories of days that were dear." Finally, in 1947, the newly appointed chancellor, Arthur Compton, asked her to represent the university in New York, and later, sent congratulations when she was made a member of St. Louis Women of Achievement. When she was sixty-seven, Hurst received the Honorary Doctorate of Letters she longed for. Upon her death in 1968, Hurst made Brandeis University heir to half her considerable fortune—based on only one meeting with its president, Adam Sacher, who spoke with enthusiasm about the great Jewish university he was building. Washington University received the other half, and with it, a yearly Hurst Professorship, whose ranks have included some of the most highly esteemed writers in the world of letters. The English departments of both schools also boast a Hurst lounge, where writers and critics give readings and lectures. From her portrait perch in Hurst Lounge in Duncker Hall on the campus of Washington University, she has heard many great writers, among whom few would place Fannie Hurst. But development offices beware!

Fannie Hurst is buried at New Mount Sinai Cemetery.

> It struck Bea, and for the moment diverted her from grief, that quite the most physical thing she had ever connected with her mother was the fact of her having died.
>
> She found herself, crying there beside the bier, thinking of her mother's legs. Such willing ones. They were locked now, as they lay stretched horizontally down the center of the parlor, in the rigidity of death. The bengaline dress, for which only four dreamlike weeks ago they had shopped together on Atlantic Avenue, now lay decently over those dear legs. Dreadful counterpane to the physical fact that Adelaide Chipley's breasts and loins and femurs lay dead.
>
> —*Imitation of Life*

PATIENCE WORTH
July 8, 1913 — December 3, 1937

I be me.

63

Patience Worth was born in St. Louis on Tuesday, July 8, 1913, in the home of Mrs. John H. Curran, who lived at 6031 Kingsbury Boulevard, and she apparently took sick in the middle of November 1937, after her last communication, when she caught Pearl Curran's cold, and died in the moment her amanuensis did, of pneumonia, on December 3, in Los Angeles. Pearl Curran's companions, on the occasion of Patience Worth's appearance, were Emily Grant Hutchings, almost a midwife, and her mother, Mary Pollard, who wrote down Patience Worth's first words. They were those of a Hollywood Indian: "Many moons ago I lived. Again I come—Patience Worth my name."

Irving Litvag, who lived in St. Louis and worked in the publications office of Washington University, describes Patience Worth's oeuvre in his book about the phenomenon, *Singer in the Shadows*:

> In a literary 'career' of nearly twenty-five years she would produce the astounding total of almost four million words, seven full-length books, thou-

sands of poems ranging from a few lines in length to hundreds, uncounted numbers of epigrams and aphorisms, short stories, a few plays, and thousands of pages of witty, trenchant conversation with the hundreds of guests who came to call on her.

If the average English word were five letters long, then the Ouija board's weary planchette had to have poked about pointing to this letter or that approximately twenty million times, and some scrivener would have had to write down what it pointed to with equal energy and as much zeal. On one evening, it is reported by Caspar Yost (the reporter who first wrote about the phenomenon and who remained to help commercialize it) no fewer than 5,000 words were spelled out in a much admired account of the Crucifixion. Always the letters were indicated with such speed that the chirographic skill of Mr. Curran (who was the usual scrivener) was taxed to the utmost.

No wonder Worth was called "Patience." This mystical author waited to become posthumous before beginning her career. Perhaps the times were not favorable for women when she lived. She was instead a muse herself, and spoke not in some prophet's inner ear, or by finding life in willing fingers, or even, more up-to-date, through a stenographer's or typist's swifter skills, but through an ancient toy, trademarked and sold in this country as "Ouija"—the words for "yes" in French and German.

This door that, to the right sort, will open onto the wide world of the spirit is a piece of wood about half an inch thick, sixteen inches wide, and twenty-four long. The twenty-six letters of the alphabet are shown in two concentric arcs, thirteen in each, and below these the first ten numbers are arranged. At the upper corners "YES" and "NO" have been placed. The pointer has an exaggerated heart-shape and stands upon three legs. These allow it to move about on the board so that sooner or later the heart's sharp end will designate something. The fingertips of two enquirers (two to neutralize bias but not connivance) are placed lightly on top of the planchette, for it would not move otherwise than through such pressure, although these fingertips are presumed to be without a will either of their own or of their owners, but tremble upon the surface of the planchette as some spirit might direct.

The style of her best known book, *The Sorry Tale*, staggers between "The Song of Solomon" and the education of Tarzan. When in Solomon's finery, it is alternatively rhapsodical or ecstatic, lush or lusher:

> Lo, love is the honey-sweet of the locust flower. Yea, and deep within it the sting lieth, like unto the bee that nests within the locust's gold and taketh within its cup its sting. So love. Love is the galley that floateth the sea, and the heart throbs the galley's slaves. Love? Love? Love is the tender morn, split asunder of storm's wrath. Love? Love? Love is the ever-spend—the give of all and take of naught. Love? Love? Love? Ah, love is fleshed even as a lovely maid. Yea, and spelleth flesh-joy. But lo, like unto the dim star of morn that day hideth, so this maid falleth shrunkened, and behold, up from out her flesh floateth, as incense smokes, love, love, stripped of flesh! Love? Love? Love may

turn from out the anguished tears dews of gentleness. Love may touch earth's weary, and behold, they slumber. Love? Love—

The peak of Patience Worth's popularity was reached during the last years of World War I. Two of her books were published in this period, Henry Holt bringing out *The Sorry Tale* in 1917, as well as Caspar Yost's vindication of the phenomenon (*Patience Worth: A Psychic Mystery*) the year before. Imitators tried to muscle in with miracles or at least mysteries of their own, even claiming to have Worth herself spelling for them; however, the poor literary quality of these productions spoke only for their spurious nature. Caspar Yost had Worth's poems printed regularly over three years on the editorial pages of the *Globe-Democrat*, and William Marion Reedy's *Mirror* kept her name before its wider public. Then in July of 1917, the first issue of *Patience Worth's Magazine* appeared, put out by Mr. and Mrs. Curran and Casper Yost from the Curran's house, now on Cates Avenue. And all over the country Ouija boards levitated from their merchant's shelves.

James Merrill, while he was a Hurst Professor in the English department at Washington University, lived for a brief time on Kingsbury Boulevard within a block of the house where Patience Worth's visitation first occurred. Merrill's much-praised book-length poem, *The Changing Light at Sandover*, makes extensive use of the Ouija board; however, his board's first expression was a cry: "Help O save me." And the speaker proved to be Ephraim, a Jew born "AD 8 at Xanthos" in Greece.

Patience Worth chose the right period and place in which to be born. Earlier in our history she might have been burned as a witch. Indeed, her claim to a previous life (1649-94) would make her a Puritan. But as Daniel Shea points out, "Patience Worth's poetry is nineteenth century poetry, no matter its date, and Patience's novel, *Hope Trueblood*, is a fairly convincing imitation of a nineteenth century novel." The latter half of that century in America was rich in rapping, in horses that could count, in personality changing trances, in bottles that smoked and globes that lit up. P. T. Barnum exploited the gifted. Harry Houdini was kept busy exposing frauds.

Pearl Curran wrote a little fiction of her own, and before Patience arrived, had collaborated with her husband (who was the nearly constant scrivener) on some stories done in an Ozark dialect. Finally, she left the Ouija board for the typewriter, perhaps as her husband's health failed.

In the early half of St. Louis's literary history, writers born here soon left, usually for the east. In the latter half of it, the writers, often already renown, arrived from elsewhere to find comfortable and accommodating residence. As one of the most purely local "pens" we can boast of, Patience Worth is perhaps the St. Louis writer par excellence. Still, how can we give a habitation to a spirit, though we have its name? Patience Worth, before she became ethereal, was born abroad and traveled by boat to America. Moreover, she died, not of pneumonia in L.A., but in 1694, at age forty-five, when an Indian's arrow pierced her breast.

The cultural anchors of Midtown are lined up along Grand Avenue: Saint Louis University, Powell Symphony Hall and the Sheldon Concert Hall, earlier the home of the Ethical Society. In 1855 the city pushed its boundaries west to just beyond Grand while widening its length both north and south. In 1871, on North Grand, then only a dirt road, a water tower in the unlikely shape of a Corinthian column went up 154 feet to hold up heaven, while at the avenue's southern end, the Compton Hill Reservoir was built in order to improve sanitation (cholera and typhoid feasted on St. Louisans); also to clarify the drinking water (a persistent "literary" subject); and to provide water pressure for the fire department so that hotels like the Lindell or offices such as the *St. Louis Republican* might not burn down while firefighters stood by waterlessly. Even so, the city didn't get the silt out of its system until 1904, just in time for the World's Fair.

Many nouveaux riches moved to Grand and its environs in order to escape the ladder-shaking beer brewers and other vulgar tradesmen, but elegant Vandeventer Place was promptly threatened by commercial interests the moment electrified streetcars reached the avenue. Saint Louis University had been chartered as a Jesuit school as early as 1832 and had endured its own set of sufferings, with the Medical School the object of an anti-Catholic mob of 3,000 presumably protesting the dissection of human cadavers in 1843, and again under siege during the Nativist Riots of 1854. The university's handsome St. Francis Xavier Church was begun in 1884. It was there that General Sherman, upon his death, was memorialized to the surprise of his spirit. When the university obtained the only complete collection of Vatican Library Documents outside of Rome for its Pius XII Memorial Library, the school's scholarly importance became national.

The Sheldon Memorial had been built in 1912 and named for Walter Sheldon, founder of the St. Louis branch of the Ethical Society. The society brought many notable authors to its acoustically perfect performance hall, including writers Felix Adler, Wytter Bynner, John Ciardi, S. I. Hayakawa, Ernest Hemingway, Julian Huxley, Sinclair Lewis and editors Harriet Monroe of *Poetry* magazine and Norman Cousins of the *Saturday Review*. Thomas Mann visited in March 1939 and in an interview with the *St. Louis Post-Dispatch* on the eighteenth, he warned that Adolph Hitler's annexations would continue until that "very stupid man Chamberlain" and his pro-fascist English clique were replaced by a more resolute government—a change that would mean war. "The world's hope for peace rests on the United States and Russia." On the twentieth, Mann left St. Louis for Kansas City and made this entry in his diary:

Monday, March 20; St. Louis

Overstimulated. Heavy dose of pills. After four before I got to sleep. Today very warm, as was yesterday as well. Silk underdrawers. Got up at ten. Coffee for breakfast. —Yesterday reports of Hitler's triumphal return to Berlin. He looked 'weary and grim.' American boycott. Military preparedness and diplomatic cooperation between England, France, Russia, and the United States. Report today of the Russian note to Germany, excellent. —Autographed books. —With Rabbi Isserman to the admirable zoo. Lunch at the hotel. Then packed. Left around four. The Texas Express. Officials of the rail line at the station. Coca-Cola in our compartment, since I was very thirsty. Radio. German newspapers. Dinner at 7:30 in the dining car. Cigar in the club car. Early to bed.

In July of 1945, deep in the writing of his great late novel *Dr. Faustus*, Mann found time, in answer to the newspaper's query, to write a letter to the *Post-Dispatch* concerning his attitude toward the proposed war crimes trials. So long as such a procedure involved a formal disowning of the fascism he felt was still rampant in the world, "then I honour and support it with all my heart."

Thomas Mann may have lectured to the cognoscenti at the Sheldon, but Midtown was no longer where they lived. After 1900 the rich had begun running to the Central West End, although another effort to create a Grand Avenue enclave was put forth near the Eads's Compton Hill mansion. Only in Compton Heights, as it was called, did the city see streets named for literary figures, "Longfellow," "Hawthorne" and "Milton" for instance. The residents of note were largely beer barons, however, who rarely read and never wrote.

Men on frontiers
whether of time or
space, abandon their previous identities. Neighborhood gives identity.
Frontiers snatch it away.

Marshall McLuhan, media guru and author of *The Gutenberg Galaxy* and *The Medium is the Message*, taught in the English department of Saint Louis University from 1938 to 1944. He had just converted to Catholicism and came to St. Louis specifically for the intellectual atmosphere cultivated among the Jesuits at SLU, which he described as "free from fog at every point." The school's poorly stocked library shocked him, however, and so he was forced to go to Washington University to get the books he needed for his five assigned courses. "Extraordinary how hard work lulls one's critical faculties. It is a drug, an escape perhaps," he wrote in his diary at the residence of the Gerardot family at 4343 McPherson Avenue, where he was a boarder. McLuhan was a forceful presence at SLU, failing students in Freshman Composition but inspiring eager graduates in a course called "Rhetoric and Interpretation." Swiss architect Sigfried Giedion, who wrote *Space, Time and Architecture*, also taught there and was friends with McLuhan, as was Walter Ong, one of his students, who became a professor and the author of *Orality and Literacy* and *The Presence of the Word*.

McLuhan conceived and wrote much of his first book *The Mechanical Bride* here, collecting examples from advertising and cartoon strips such as *Dagwood* to demonstrate the transformation of American manhood. Manhood was much on the young instructor's mind in 1939. He was wooing a young woman from Texas whose family was firmly against her marrying a Catholic convert from Canada. But marry they did, in the university cathedral, the bride-to-be sending her parents a telegram that read: "Am getting married in a few minutes." The newlyweds spent their wedding night at the Hotel Jefferson and then sailed for England, where McLuhan took a year's leave of absence to work on his thesis at Cambridge. The couple returned in the summer of 1940 and moved into a one-room apartment at Cathedral Mansions across from the university. Their son Eric was born during this time.

McLuhan and another professor, Felix Giovanelli, were instrumental in bringing the painter and writer Wyndam Lewis to St. Louis. The archmodernist and his wife were languishing in Windsor, Ontario, when McLuhan wrote a letter introducing himself. "We gradually formed the project to bring [Lewis] to St. Louis," wrote McLuhan, "where we hoped to find him some painting commissions and some lectures." Lewis stayed for six months in 1944, in Giovanelli's apartment (vacated for his benefit), the Coronado Hotel, as well as the Chase Park Plaza. Edna Gellhorn, Martha Gellhorn's mother, gave Lewis forty dollars for her portrait in chalk. "She is very keen to have her Martha (Mrs. Hemingway) painted," McLuhan wrote

Lewis. "And Martha is no mean subject." Lewis was paid considerably more ($1,500) for his portrait of Joseph Erlanger, the Washington University physicist who won a Nobel Prize. There were even plans—which fell through—to paint Archbishop John Glennon. Lewis lectured at the Saint Louis Art Museum on "The Role of Art in Ordering Nature" and at The Wednesday Club on "Famous People I Have Put in my Books and on Canvas." The Central West End matrons had not heard of Lewis and felt a curriculum vitae was in order. In the end, Vorticism was not to their taste, so Lewis, the "ogre of Bloomsbury," returned to Canada, where he recommended McLuhan for a job before suddenly breaking relations with him in a cruelly worded letter—for no reason other than he may not have liked McLuhan much to begin with and disliked the prospect of a deepening friendship. McLuhan was hurt but continued to study and promote Lewis's work; he coined his famous phrase "global village" after reading Lewis's *America and Cosmic Man.*

64

McLuhan left St. Louis in 1944. He had received his doctorate and, since he did not get along with the new head of the department and had recently been classed I-A in the draft, he had good reason to move back home. Thirty years later he wrote a fellow professor that he was "remembering all the wonderful times we had in St. Louis. Your home was the super seminar of all time, in which young instructors were taught the mysteries of cuisine, avant garde music, new liturgy, and metaphysics. It was a very rich and heady brew that formed and was shared by your delighted friends. I pray that other such centres exist even now, and that others will be as lucky as I in sharing them." In 1975 McLuhan and his wife visited the cathedral where they had been married. He died five years later.

McLuhan and another professor were discussing James Joyce's *Finnegans Wake* at a tavern in St. Louis, the book open on the bar. Another patron came up behind them and started reading. After one page, he said "My God, I really am drunk" and staggered off.

64. *Corinne and Marshall McLuhan on the steps of the*
New Cathedral following their wedding, August 4, 1939

CENTRAL WEST END & FOREST PARK

1 Soldan High School, 918 North Union Boulevard—Emily Hahn, Kay Thompson, Tennessee Williams

2 Saint Louis Art Museum, Art Hill, Forest Park—Chester Himes

3 Jewel Box, Forest Park—Tennessee Williams

4 4446 Westminster Place—T. S. Eliot

5 4504 Westminster Place, formerly The Wednesday Club—Josephine Johnson, Marianne Moore, Tennessee Williams

6 4633 Westminster Place—Tennessee Williams

7 4858 Fountain Avenue—Emily Hahn

8 4664 Pershing Avenue—William Burroughs

9 38 Kingsbury Place—Sara Teasdale

10 4605 Lindell Boulevard—Irma Rombauer

11 6168 McPherson Avenue—William Inge

12 6031 Kingsbury Boulevard—Patience Worth

13 5641 Cates Avenue—Fannie Hurst

If Grand Avenue was the north/south corridor for Midtown, Kingshighway served the same function for the Central West End. Along its edge and the northern limit of Forest Park, "places" appeared. Portland Place was drawn as early as 1888, and Westmoreland, Westminster, Windemere, Kingsbury, Lenox and Hortense followed, with Washington Terrace to come. Sara Teasdale lived in a "place," as did the Eliot family. Peter Taylor dined on a "terrace." The grandeur of the mansions, mostly copied from European models, is impressive even now, and gave visitors a sense of opulence they never lost.

William Burroughs was born in a nice but more modest house just east of the great gates. Kate Chopin's West End residence was also unpretentious, which she preferred. In 1897 she wrote: "I like to look out of the window" because "there is a good deal of unadulterated human nature that passes along during the length of a day. Of course I do not live in Westmoreland Place." Her neighbors included a coal merchant, two physicians, a dentist, and an ever-changing population of young men who filled the boarding houses. Nor did her modest circumstances relieve her of the duties of society. Chopin's regular reception day was Thursday, the traditional choice by "ladies in the West End" for gadding and gossip. She envisioned a sort of social clearing house where women could pay off all of their calls in one afternoon, ridding them of the "great incubus a fashionable woman has to carry."

65

Fastened to the northern end of Euclid like a fine fruit, Fountain Park, where Emily Hahn grew up, was grandly conceived (as early as 1857), but its grandeur never arrived, and most of the houses were planted there by developers. Perhaps its tattiness preserved its charm, for it remains, in layout, scale and feel, one of the city's loveliest places.

When Gertrude Stein came to town in 1935, she was struck by the sheer size of everything:

> Then we arrived in Saint Louis. We ate very very well there. I was interested in Saint Louis, and it was enormous the houses and the gardens and every way everything looked, everything looked enormous in Saint Louis. We enjoyed it there.... They asked us what we would like to do and I said I would like to see all the places Winston Churchill had mentioned in The Crisis. They were very nice about it only it was difficult to do because naturally they should have but they really did not know a lot about what Winston Churchill mentioned in The Crisis. The Crisis was a best seller when I read it and naturally I remembered it ... Anthony Trollope and Dickens and Thackeray were

best sellers in the nineteenth century in the twentieth century best sellers mostly are not that thing, The Crisis was not that thing although I can read it again and again . . .

When I came to Saint Louis I wanted to see all the places mentioned by Winston Churchill in The Crisis but they mostly could not find them, we found the Mississippi River and almost where they went to it, and some of the homes and then we gave it up and went on to see something that they could find and that I had not really known was there and that was the house of Ulysses Grant.

Of course, that is what happened to best-sellers in America in the twentieth century: they were forgotten. It was something Gertrude Stein did not intend to have happen to her.

Stein was a great admirer of the general and had already chosen him to be one of her *Four in America* (in 1933), along with Henry James, George Washington and the Wright Brothers. In another of her profound and impossibly strange comparisons, she would imagine Grant as a leader of American religion:

It was a cabin and it had once been lived in, when you read Grant's memoirs it does not quite sound as if that was the sort of place that he lived in. I have just been reading it but there seems to be no doubt about it that was the house he did live in. And then we drove back again and I asked them how could people when now they could not have so many servants how could they live in those big houses that were everywhere in Saint Louis, in London now almost every one has given up living in those big houses but they said yes in Saint Louis yes they did still in Saint Louis live in those houses yes they did, some families did not to be sure families are big families in Saint Louis, they did a great many did still live in these big houses. And we ate very well in Saint Louis and then we flew to Chicago . . .

Stein was properly puzzled by the size of Grant's cabin, of course, because, while he had built it, he had never lived in it, even though the structure traveled to fairs like a curiosity and suggested to the curious that he had.

If the Mercantile was the literary hub of downtown St. Louis, and the Sheldon managed that at Midtown, it was the women of The Wednesday Club who performed such service for the Central West End. Percy Bysshe Shelley should perhaps take some credit. The Civil War as well. Just as women had poured into businesses and factories during World War II and found that they liked their new freedom, the Civil War made nurses out of some and managers of land and shops out of many, who were restless and at loose ends after the shooting ceased. As early as 1867, here and there small groups of women came together for the common study of the Bible or Shakespeare or the Renaissance in general. Under the leadership of Mrs. Edward Sterling these droplets were collected to form a drop called The Shelley Club in 1889. Though a drop, it produced a dram of opposition, first from the husbands of the women, who felt that only men carried clubs, and

66

who tightened their purse strings so that even fifty cents for dues might not pop out; and then by other women, who worried that an organization devoted to an agnostic like Shelley, however idealistic his lines, must be up to some devilment, at least in the rhymes. So in 1890 the women regrouped as The Wednesday Club of St. Louis, which acquired one hundred members by the end of its first year. After all, how many complaints could be reasonably lodged against Wednesday?

The club could no longer fit into a living room, so space was found first in the Union Dairy Building at the corner of Washington and Jefferson, and then at the YMCA at Grand and Franklin. From the start The Wednesday Club's interests were wide and diverse, including art, current topics, education, literature and history, science and social economics. This diversity continues with sections on poetics and dramatic study later added. Meanwhile, it formed ties with state and national women's organizations. In 1908, through the generosity of Mrs. William Bixby, it was able to move into a splendid craftsman-style building of its own designed by the notable St. Louis architect Theodore Link at Westminster Place and Taylor Avenue. The house remains one of the city's architectural treasures. Its rather pronounced overhangs allowed one husband (many remained skeptical) to describe it as "the building of projecting Eves."

Over the years The Wednesday Club's programming became more and more ambitious (its members contributed papers and discussion at first), until now there are two outside speakers draped on either side of lunch. A poetry prize was established, with distinguished judges like Marianne Moore and Josephine Johnson and distinguished winners such as Tennessee Williams.

Most of the celebrated women of the city were officers at one time or other: Phoebe Couzins (the first woman to graduate from a law school in the United States), Charlotte Stearns Eliot, Irma Rombauer, Edna Gellhorn,

66. *4504 Westminster Place, former site of*
The Wednesday Club, 1999

Kate Chopin (who, contrary to myth, was not expelled because of the fuss occasioned by her novel *The Awakening*), honorary members Susan Blow (who founded the first public kindergarten in the United States), Sara Teasdale and Lillie Ernst (who, with Sara Teasdale and Caroline Risque, formed the Potter's Club: eight talented young women who published a monthly literary magazine to which each contributed).

In 1973 The Wednesday Club moved to its present location on Ladue Road, and closer to its membership, although its new building, perhaps in order to fit into its suburban surroundings, lacks any architectural distinction.

Since 1975 the local literary organization River Styx has promoted readings by poets and novelists one Monday in the month at Duff's Restaurant; and Left Bank Books, a West End institution, regularly sponsors literary events, as do most other bookstores and some cafés in the St. Louis area.

The large park, once a forest, that lies just to the south of the mansions of Westmoreland and Portland Places, is what remains of the Louisiana Purchase Exposition of 1904, more popularly called the World's Fair by St. Louisans who have chosen to deem it the city's most glorious moment. If it was, the decision in 1875 to draw the city's ultimate boundary just beyond the park was the most inglorious, for what was drawn was really a noose around St. Louis's neck. After heated debates, the Scheme of Separation between St. Louis City and St. Louis County was brought to a county-wide vote. Although the *Post-Dispatch* called it "The Municipal Divorce Bill," the *Globe-Democrat* insisted that the extension of the city "into the wilderness is a piece of folly which will ruin the most flourishing municipality in the country." At first the proposal appeared to fail, but there were numerous charges of voter fraud, and the decision was left to the Missouri Supreme Court which ruled, on April 26, 1877, that the Scheme had been adopted.

Why should this have mattered to "literary" St. Louis? Because "culture" has always been urban and a function of density. Writers are drawn to cities—in particular, to cities where creativity can be found glowing at its core. St. Louis has been such a literary center only once—during the days of William Marion Reedy's *Mirror*, before the consequences of this fatal separation could be felt.

Much of the forest that made Forest Park was cut down to make room for the Louisiana Purchase Exposition, an undertaking so ambitious as to invite the cliché: "fools rush in where angels fear to tread." Cascades, lagoons and streams were created; the River Des Peres, which inconveniently cut across the park, was buried—in wooden, coffinlike channels; elaborate plans were drawn and redrawn for an Ivory City, and at each new scheme the vision grew grander; fanciful buildings were designed, most of them temporary, of plaster and lath, including twelve huge exhibition palaces; grounds for the new campus of Washington University were included, along with the construction of Francis Field, where the third modern Olympic Games were to be held; the entire shebang to be illuminated as nothing had ever been before. The Fair, when it finally opened, was a year late, and, outside of St. Louis, had little lasting cultural influence, but it was lit, and caused envy among the stars.

Henry Adams, for instance, was an interested visitor:

> The St. Louis Exposition was its [electricity's] first creation in the twentieth century, and, for that reason, acutely interesting. One saw here a third-rate town of half-a-million people without history, education, unity, or art, and with little capital—without even an element of natural interest except the river which it studiously ignored—but doing what London, Paris, or New York would have shrunk from attempting. This new social conglomerate, with no tie but its steam-power and not much of that, threw away thirty or forty million dollars on a pageant as ephemeral as a stage flat. The world had never witnessed so marvellous a phantasm; by night Arabia's crimson sands had never returned a glow half so astonishing, as one wandered among long lines of white palaces, exquisitely lighted by thousands on thousands of electric candles, soft, rich, shadowy, palpable in their sensuous depths; all in deep silence, profound solitude, listening for a voice or a foot-fall or the plash of an oar, as though the Emir Mirza were displaying the beauties of this City of Brass, which could show nothing half so beautiful as this illumination, with its vast, white, monumental solitude, bathed in the pure light of setting suns. One enjoyed it with iniquitous rapture, not because of exhibits but rather because of their want. Here was a paradox like the stellar universe that fitted one's mental faults. Had there been no exhibits at all, and no visitors, one would have enjoyed it only the more.

Sally Benson's book, later overshadowed by the movie, did have an appropriate title—*Meet Me in St. Louis*—because the fair drew 100,000 visitors a day to its grounds, and only some of them had the sniffles. Tommy Eliot went more than once; Billy Reedy was amused and gratified by the crowds; it produced poems, ice cream, the hot dog; much ice tea was made, a clock of flowers was caused to grow, though on floral time, and a full-sized cow was craftily compacted of butter; it attracted entrepreneurs like Thomas Wolfe's mother (and her rooming house) to its edges; Kate Chopin was charmed—she had a season ticket but the Fair's August heat may have done her in; there was a bird cage big enough for birds to fly south in; a ferris wheel that could carry 1,440 people up 250 feet in the air; and a fine, permanent art museum designed by Cass Gilbert.

After the plaster of paris extravaganza was dismantled, a number of real things and buildings appeared in the park: a bronze statue of St. Louis by Charles Niehaus, placed overlooking the lagoon and Art Hill, was unveiled in 1906; the anachronistically named World's Fair Pavilion went up atop Government Hill in 1909; the Jefferson Memorial, on axis with the Art Museum, was dedicated in 1913 to house the Missouri Historical Society; a ten thousand-seat Municipal Theatre was finished in 1917; and a glorious greenhouse called the Jewel Box, which would figure in the work of Tennessee Williams, was opened in 1936.

Emily Hahn wrote fondly that "in the summer—in Forest Park, of course—we had open-air entertainment: *The Bohemian Girl, The Merry*

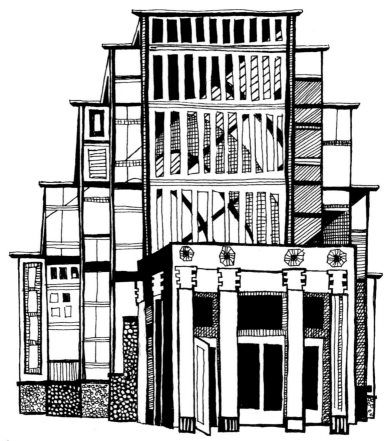

67

Widow, The Bells of Corneville, that sort of thing, and even grand opera. I heard my first opera, *Thaïs*, at the open-air theatre in Forest Park."

Kate Chopin went ice-skating in the park's frozen ponds in its early days, but later Art Hill became the social sledding spot. Hahn adds: "Forest Park was a genuine forest except for the tamed region around Art Hill and, of course, the zoo. In the spring it was full of violets, which, through what must have been a municipal oversight, we could pick. In the fall there were acorns."

The poor resurrected River Des Peres misbehaved in 1923, flooding much of the park, so it was put back in the ground, this time to sneak like some stygian stream through a thirty-two-foot sewer pipe.

The Missouri Historical Society was a major focus of cultural activity in Forest Park from its inception and began to collect many of the objects, documents, manuscripts and graphic work we have made use of here. Charles van Ravenswaay (1911-1990) is best known for his work as a horticulturist and documenter of Missouri's historic buildings, as well as for his service as the first paid director of the Missouri Historical Society (1946-1962), but, in addition, he is important to this guide because, in 1938, he was chosen to oversee the Missouri Writers' Project (a WPA program designed to employ out-of-work writers during depression times). The result was a guidebook, *Missouri: A Guide to the "Show Me" State*, a work deserving a salute.

The Central West End and Forest Park continue to be attractive, not only to the young and the restless, but to the steady and committed. Peter Simpson (1932-1992) was one of the poets who stayed put, flying no farther than three blocks from the neighborhood that hatched him, possibly because his livelihood was always local. He ghost-wrote speeches for politicians and served as a St. Louis alderman himself (1963-1967); he sustained a sports column for the *St. Louis Sentinel* and reviewed regularly for the *St. Louis Post-Dispatch*. These pieces were collected in *Press Box and City Room: Columns*, a book he published jointly with George H. Gurley in 1987.

Simpson could be called a Catholic poet. So raised, he stayed near his spiritual roots, and his faith is frequently reflected in his two books of poems, *Keeping Open* and *Stealing Home* (1985), as well as his confirmed interest in the city and the region.

Present plans for the park indicate that at least some of the reburied River Des Peres may be released to connect and feed the park's restored lakes and lagoons. Boating will be back. Violets too. Sledders will continue to scream down Art Hill's snowy side.

St. Louis by the Mississippi: Urban Eclogue (*Excerpt*)

May—a chilly Sunday morning. Heavy
diesels haul their fright across
Eads Bridge, huff rainbow films
into the wind. They merge with
the smoke that coughs from Switzer's
licorice stoves, dip to sleep, rub
more smudge on the rolling Mississippi's
flat, listless face. The old man's
tired from a winter's wild carouse;
blisters swirl the currents from
the melted snow; the water sucks
the chilly drizzle. Tiny veins
streak out and pump dead blood,
yellows dry Missouri into mud.
                    —Peter Simpson

Having a group of people at my disposal, I thought it might be entertaining (to myself) to throw them together and see what would happen. I never dreamed of Mrs. Pontellier making such a mess of things and working out her own damnation as she did. If I had had the slightest intimation of such a thing I would have excluded her from the company. But when I found out what she was up to, the play was half over and then it was too late.

—Kate Chopin, *Book News*, May 28, 1899

68

America 1899 was scandalized when Edna Pontellier, a married woman, fell in love with another man and had an affair with yet another, someone she didn't even profess to love. "'The Awakening' is too strong drink for moral babes," a letter writer to the *St. Louis Post-Dispatch* cautioned, "and should be labeled 'poison.'" Willa Cather, writing in the *Pittsburgh Leader*, wondered why Miss Chopin would devote "so exquisite and sensitive . . . a style to so trite and sordid a theme." The *Providence Sunday Journal* warned that stories such as this might "fall into the hands of youth, leading them to dwell on things that only matured persons can understand, and promoting unholy imaginations and unclean desires." Kate Chopin would have her defenders, the greatest one being Time, but she would never back away from a battle.

Kate O'Flaherty was born a fighter. As a five-year-old Katie nagged her father so incessantly about where he went each day that he took his daughter to work—down to the Mississippi levee where she saw steam ships, sailors and unsavory sorority sisters. When she was thirteen she was arrested by Union soldiers after tearing down a Union flag from her family's porch in St. Louis. A neighbor, Charles W. Stevens, a Union supporter, promised to vouch for her, and she was released. Missouri had its share of Southern sympathizers, though—the O'Flahertys themselves owned four slaves—who applauded Kate's act and nicknamed her St. Louis's "Littlest Rebel."

Catherine O'Flaherty was born on February 8, 1850, to Thomas O'Flaherty and Eliza Faris, his second wife and twenty-three years his junior. Eliza's family were Creoles who could trace their ties to Auguste Chouteau. With her she brought her mother and four of her siblings to the mansion at 801 Chouteau Avenue, to join Thomas's son George, a teenager. Their first child, Thomas, was born there. Then came Kate and then Jane, who died young.

In *Unveiling Kate Chopin*, published in 1999, the centenary year of *The Awakening*, Chopin scholar Emily Toth speculates that Thomas O'Flaherty may have fathered children by his slaves and that Kate's inquisitiveness was the reason she was sent away at the age of five to board at Sacred Heart Academy, then located at Fifth and Market Streets. Thomas O'Flaherty was an immigrant from Galway with a head for business. He invested wisely in boats and real estate—the land he bought in 1842, on Seventh Street between Franklin and Washington Avenues, provided for his daughter into the next century. His prominence placed him, on November 1, 1855, along with other powerful St. Louis citizens, on the first train to cross the Gasconade Bridge, which collapsed, delivering thirty into the river. He had been instrumental in bringing the telegraph to Missouri, through which instrument it was falsely reported that only two had died in the accident. This story would linger in young Kate's memory and eventually inspire "The Story of an Hour."

When Kate was seven she became a "day scholar" at Sacred Heart and until her graduation would go back and forth as a boarder or day scholar, depending on the family situation and the state of the Civil War. At Sacred Heart "valiant women" received excellent educations—Kate became proficient enough in French to be a translator for hire later in life. Her mother saw to it that she learned to play the piano, at which she was naturally gifted and able to play by ear. When Kate was seventeen Sister Mary O'Meara suggested that she keep a Commonplace Book (which is in the Chopin papers at the Missouri Historical Society). In it she copied passages, reviewed books and ideas, and recorded her own thoughts.

At her graduation on June 29, 1868, Kate O'Flaherty played a duet, read her first-prize winning essay "National Peculiarities," and took a gold medal for "excellence of conduct and proficiency in studies" along with three other students. After such a rigorous course of study Miss O'Flaherty found the life of a belle wanting: "What a nuisance this all is—I wish it were over," she wrote on December 31, 1868. "I write in my book today for the first time in months; parties, operas, concerts, skating and amusements ad infinitum have so taken up all my time that my dear reading and writing that I love so well have suffered such neglect."

Chopin retained her love of music throughout her life—it figures in many of her stories as well as in *The Awakening*. She delighted in the lively musical scene in St. Louis that had been enriched by the German Forty-Eighters, who brought with them a love of keyboard instruments to accompany the mainly stringed ones of the French. She joined a German reading club and otherwise read widely. She took her first trip to New Orleans, where she learned to smoke—which didn't go over well in St. Louis. Shortly after, she wrote her first surviving story, "Emancipation: A Life Fable."

During her debutante year she met Oscar Chopin, a man from a good French family in Louisiana. Chopin was taken with St. Louis, and wrote to his cousin in France that "its delights are as great as those of the Rivoli in Paris . . . the women here are more beautiful than our lovely ladies in Paris. It is charming. . . . There is indeed a vast opportunity for love and I can assure you that the god Eros is not forgotten here." Oscar and Kate were married on June 9, 1870, at Holy Angels Church on St. Ange Avenue. They honeymooned in Europe; saw the houses of Beethoven and Goethe; attended mass at the Fribourg Cathedral as it had "what is considered the finest organ in the world"; and saw Paris just before the Prussian invasion. Back in America they settled in New Orleans. The city enthralled her: she would use its colors, smells, accents, characters and prejudices in her books. The writing would have to wait, though, as Mrs. Chopin was expecting her first child, Jean Baptiste—to be followed by Oscar, George, Frederick, Felix Andrew and their only daughter, Marie Laïza, called Lélia. When Kate Chopin was pregnant with her, Oscar's business went bankrupt, so they moved to Cloutierville where he could work in the family business. In this small town, the country doctor misdiagnosed Oscar's yellow fever as malaria, and Kate Chopin became a widow at the age of thirty-two.

Oscar and Kate Chopin seemed to have been very much in love, unlike Léonce and Edna Pontellier in *The Awakening*. With sadness—and horror, as under Louisiana law she had to petition to be the legal guardian of her children—she set about putting their financial affairs in order and learning her husband's trade. It took her two years to pay off their debts, but not much time to test the mores. It was not only that she was actually running a successful business, horseback riding solo and smoking cigarettes, she was also seeing the handsome, wealthy and married Albert Sampite. There was more than a little of Albert in the character of Alcée Arobin, Edna's paramour in *The Awakening*.

Like Edna, Kate chose independence over romance. She moved back to St. Louis in 1884 to be near her mother (who would die a year later) and to assure her children a proper education. By the 1880s St. Louis had created one of the best free public school systems in the country and opened the nation's first kindergarten. In 1886 Chopin bought a house at 3317 Morgan Street (now Delmar)—far enough from her family for them not to notice she had stopped going to mass—and began her writing career.

Kate Chopin's first publication came in 1888. It was a musical piece, "Lilia. Polka for Piano." Her second was a poem, "If It Might Be," in the January 1889 Chicago-based magazine *America*.

69

That same year, "Wiser Than God," the story of a young woman deprived "for the second time of a loved parent" who throws "all her energies into work," her music, was published in *Philadelphia Music Journal*.

When Lélia was ten and Jean Baptiste eighteen, Chopin was able to establish a routine of writing in the morning and so began work on her first novel. *At Fault* is set in Louisiana and St. Louis and includes St. Louis names, such as Hosmer, and characters, such as Denton Snider, the neo-Hegelian involved with the *Journal of Speculative Philosophy*. She finished *At Fault* in 1890. After one rejection—from Chicago's *Belford's Monthly*—she published and distributed the book herself. It was reviewed locally, at times favorably, but both the *St. Louis Post-Dispatch* and her only national review in the *Nation* balked at an alcoholic wife drinking herself to death and at other crudities, such as calling a railway station a "depot" and a shop a "store." Despite this slang the *St. Louis Republic* conceded that the novel's "local color [was] excellent."

Chopin's reply to the reviewers would be the first of many responses throughout her career, one of the many fights she would fight:

> Will you kindly permit me through the columns of your paper to set the *Republic* book reviewer right in a matter which touches me closely concerning the use and misuse of words? I cannot recall an instance, in or out of fiction, in which an American "country store" has been alluded to as a "shop," unless by some unregenerate Englishman. The use of the word depot or station is optional. Wm. Dean Howells employs the former to indicate a "railway station," so I am hardly ready to believe the value of *At Fault* marred by following so safe a precedent.

Chopin continued to write and send out work, to get rejected and to sketch the stories that would become *Bayou Folk*, published by Houghton Mifflin in 1894, her first book with a major New York publisher. She was forty-three.

Kate Chopin became a sought-after figure in St. Louis. She was a charter member of The Wednesday Club, whose founders included Charlotte Stearns Eliot, the mother of T. S. Eliot and a poet and biographer in her own right. Chopin was a close friend of fellow combatant William Marion Reedy, who published her stories and reviews of her books in the *Mirror*. The Thursday evening gatherings at her house on Morgan Street attracted the cream of the St. Louis intelligentsia, including many on the staff of the *St. Louis Post-Dispatch*.

The controversy surrounding Chopin's writings, particularly *The Awakening*, ignited her popularity in St. Louis. Contrary to the local myth, she was not expelled from The Wednesday Club, but resigned in 1892 in order to have more time to write. The club duly noted her resignation in the minutes. During the height of the controversy over *The Awakening*, the club rallied and invited her for a reading. There she read to a full house of four hundred women, her largest audience ever.

To many, Chopin was too famous to disavow. Frances Porcher wrote in the *Mirror*: "And so, because we admire Kate Chopin's other work immensely and delight in her ever-

70

growing fame and are proud that she is 'one-of-us St. Louisans,' one dislikes to acknowledge a wish that she had not written her novel." In November 1899, the *St. Louis Post-Dispatch*, which six months earlier had published that harsh review of *The Awakening*, ran a full-page article about Kate Chopin titled "A St. Louis Woman Who Has Won Fame in Literature," with a drawing of her first home on Eighth Street and a reproduction of a watercolor painted of her in her workroom by her son Oscar. (He later became a cartoonist for the newspaper.)

The *Post-Dispatch* article succeeded in causing many to believe that *The Awakening* had been banned from the local libraries. Chopin and her children propagated the tale after she went in to the Mercantile Library demanding a copy of her book. When she was told it was not available, she stormed out, her Irish ire up, complaining of the indignities she was forced to suffer as a writer. In fact, they had four copies of the book, which were likely out on loan at the time. (Emily Toth believes the books simply wore out due to over-use.) Both the Mercantile and the St. Louis Public Libraries carried multiple copies of the novel.

The banning myth and the bad reviews didn't assure Kate Chopin success in publishing her next work, *A Vocation and a Voice,* and by the time of her death she was despondent about her career. In 1903 she moved to a smaller rented house at 4232 McPherson Avenue, six blocks from Forest Park. After the World's Fair opened on April 30, 1904, she visited regularly, enraptured by its many shows and novelties. After a particularly hot day there, she suffered a cerebral hemorrhage and died two days later, at the age of fifty-four.

The requiem mass took place at the New Cathedral on August 24, 1904. She was buried in Calvary Cemetery, next to her husband. (All of her children would eventually be buried near her.) Her headstone erroneously lists the year of her birth as 1851. Many of her obituaries did not even mention *The Awakening*, except William Marion Reedy's. Kate Chopin, he wrote, was

> a remarkably talented woman, who knew how to be a genius without sacrificing the comradeship of her children. As a mother, wife and friend she shone resplendent and her contributions to fiction, though few, showed that she possessed true literary genius. [Her books] *At Fault, Bayou Folk, A Night in Acadie* and *The Awakening* [are] literary treasures which she has left and which have afforded many a pleasant hour.

The Awakening was out of print by 1906. Her work was later discovered by the son of a Norwegian feminist scholar while he was working on his graduate thesis at Harvard. In 1969 Per Seyersted published *The Complete Works of Kate Chopin* and *Kate Chopin: A Critical Biography*, rekindling the tale of the banning of her book, assuring it a longer life than its first. In 1990 Emily Toth published the first major biography of Chopin. *A Vocation and a Voice* finally found a publisher in 1991, ninety years after its creation.

Kate Chopin's house on McPherson Avenue was added to the National Register of Historic Places in 1986. In 1990 she received a star on the St. Louis Walk of Fame, about which we think she might not have put up a fight.

When Edna was at last alone, she breathed a big, genuine sigh of relief. A feeling that was unfamiliar but very delicious came over her. She walked all through the house, from one room to another, as if inspecting it for the first time. She tried the various chairs and lounges, as if she had never sat and reclined on them before. And she perambulated around the outside of the house, investigating, looking to see if windows and shutters were secure and in order. The flowers were like new acquaintances; she approached them in a familiar spirit, and made herself at home among them. The garden walks were damp, and Edna called to the maid to bring out her rubber sandals. And there she stayed, and stooped, digging around the plants, trimming, picking dead, dry leaves. The children's little dog came out, interfering, getting in her way. She scolded him, laughed at him, played with him. The garden smelled so good and looked so pretty in the afternoon sunlight. Edna plucked all the bright flowers she could find, and went into the house with them, she and the little dog.

Even the kitchen assumed a sudden interesting character which she had never before perceived. She went in to give directions to the cook, to say that the butcher would have to bring much less meat, that they would require only half their usual quantity of bread, of milk, of groceries. She told the cook that she herself would be greatly occupied during Mr. Pontellier's absence, and she begged her to take all thought and responsibility of the larder upon her own shoulders.

That night Edna dined alone. The candelabra, with a few candles in the center of the table, gave all the light she needed. Outside the circle of light in which she sat, the large dining room looked solemn and shadowy. The cook, placed upon her mettle, served a delicious repast— a luscious tenderloin broiled *à point*. The wine tasted good; the *marron glacé* seemed to be just what she wanted. It was so pleasant, too, to dine in a comfortable peignoir.

She thought a little sentimentally about Léonce and the children, and wondered what they were doing. As she gave a dainty scrap or two to the doggie, she talked intimately to him about Étienne and Raoul. He was beside himself with astonishment and delight over these companionable advances, and showed his appreciation by his little quick, snappy barks and lively agitation.

Then Edna sat in the library after dinner and read Emerson until she grew sleepy. She realized that she had neglected her reading, and determined to start anew upon a course of improving studies, now that her time was completely her own to do with as she liked.

After a refreshing bath, Edna went to bed. And as she snuggled comfortably beneath the eiderdown a sense of restfulness invaded her, such as she had not known before.

—*The Awakening, A Solitary Soul*

Doris: *You'll carry me off? To a cannibal isle?*
Sweeney: *I'll be the cannibal.*
Doris: *I'll be the missionary.*
           I'll convert you!
Sweeney: *I'll convert you!*
           Into a stew.
           A nice little, white little, missionary stew.

—"Fragment of an Agon"

71

"I was brought up to be very much aware of him," T. S. Eliot said of his grandfather, William Greenleaf Eliot, who died in 1887. He remembered him as one who "rules his son and his son's sons from the grave . . . our moral judgements, our decisions between duty and self-indulgence, were taken as if, like Moses, he had brought down the tables of the Law, any deviation from which would be sinful." Sin would hover over Thomas Stearns Eliot so forcefully that his only escape would be to leave its source, a trinity of Unitarianism, a St. Louis brand of conservatism as represented by his family, and the larger world of the United States represented by a melting-pot culture, many of whose ingredients the future Nobel Laureate would find distasteful.

Tom Eliot's parents, Henry Ware and Charlotte Champe Stearns, were both forty-five when he was born at 2635 Locust Street. (A plaque in the sidewalk marks the former site.) There was a nine-year gap between him and his next sibling, Henry Ware Eliot, Jr., and nineteen years between Eliot and his eldest sister, Ada. His three other sisters were Margaret, Marion and Charlotte; they attended Mary Institute next door. Tom and Henry went to Smith Academy, of course. Everywhere was the Eliot history.

The noise, smells and smoke of new industry had turned St. Louis into a seedy semblance of its predicted great future when Tom Eliot was growing up. His father felt obliged to stay close to his mother's house around the corner at 2660 Washington after the death of William Greenleaf Eliot, and so the family lived near newly developed brothels and saloons that were playing a new kind of music called ragtime. "We have lived twenty-five years on the old Eliot place, while all our friends have moved out, and Tom

71. T. S. Eliot in Mary Institute schoolyard, 1896

desires companionship of which he has thus been deprived," wrote Charlotte Eliot in 1905, shortly before her son was to leave St. Louis, in effect, forever.

Because his siblings were so much older, Tom Eliot had few playmates. Also, he was born with a congenital double hernia, which kept him in a truss, out of physical sports and permanently coddled by his family, especially its women. He was greatly attached to his Irish Catholic nurse, Annie Dunne, who would take him to her church at the corner of Locust and Jefferson and wait at the dentist (another weekly affair) while he had his teeth straightened. It was at the dentist, waiting for his turn, that Eliot first read Edgar Allan Poe, devouring his complete works over the course of many visits.

A childhood friend described Tom as "diffident and retiring." His cousin Abigail Eliot considered him a "thoughtful, bright, reserved, mischievous child." The poet described himself as a "priggish little boy." Charlotte Eliot taught her children to improve themselves daily and "to make the best of every faculty and control every tendency to evil."

Animula

'Issues from the hand of God, the simple soul'
To a flat world of changing lights and noise,
To light, dark, dry or damp, chilly or warm;
Moving between the legs of tables and of chairs,
Rising or falling, grasping at kisses and toys,
Advancing boldly, sudden to take alarm,
Retreating to the corner of arm and knee,
Eager to be reassured, taking pleasure
In the fragrant brilliance of the Christmas tree,
Pleasure in the wind, the sunlight and the sea;
Studies the sunlit pattern on the floor
And running stags around a silver tray;
Confounds the actual and the fanciful,
Content with playing-cards and kings and queens,
What the fairies do and what the servants say.
The heavy burden of the growing soul
Perplexes and offends more, day by day;
Week by week, offends and perplexes more
With the imperatives of 'is and seems'
And may and may not, desire and control.
The pain of living and the drug of dreams
Curl up the small soul in the window seat
Behind the *Encyclopaedia Britannica.* . . .

When Eliot was six he went to Mrs. Lockwood's School, a few years behind another St. Louis poet, Sara Teasdale, and in 1898 entered Smith as a "day boy." After school Mary Institute, at Beaumont and Locust, abutting

72. T. S. Eliot, About Twelve Years Old,
by Charlotte Eliot, c. 1900

Eliot's house, was his playground; he would sit under a large ailanthus tree in the backyard, practice his golf swings, or hang on the parallel bars in the school's gymnasium. In a 1959 speech at Mary Institute marking its centennial, Eliot joked that he was the school's "one and only alumnus".

> . . . Issues from the hand of time the simple soul
> Irresolute and selfish, misshapen, lame,
> Unable to fare forward or retreat,
> Fearing the warm reality, the offered good,
> Denying the importunity of the blood,
> Shadow of its own shadows, spectre in its own gloom,
> Leaving disordered papers in a dusty room;
> Living first in the silence after the viaticum.
>
> Pray for Guiterriez, avid of speed and power,
> For Boudin, blown to pieces,
> For this one who made a great fortune,
> And that one who went his own way.

T. S. Eliot the poet had to learn to rhyme in order not to rhyme:
Dear Charlotte,

> Hoping you are better,
> At least enough to read my letter,
> Which I have twisted into rhyme
> To amuse you, I have taken time
> To tell you of the happenings
> Swimming, rowing, other things
> With which I have the time been killing. . . .

Eliot then describes a hike in a province of Quebec in which everyone gets lost. He concludes:

> I suppose now I should desist,
> For I am needed to assist
> In making a raft.
> The family sends
> To you their love and complimen's.
> I must not close without once more a
> Health to you and Theodora.

I am afraid this letter will not please you but I hope you will excuse your brother

> Tom.

While at Smith Academy, Eliot produced his own magazine, the *Fireside*, which promised "Fiction, Gossip, Theatre, Jokes and all interesting" and was edited by "T. S. Eliot, The T. S. Eliot Company, St. Louis." It contained characters with names like Rattlesnake Bob, Gabbie Talker and even a Dr. Sweany. The *Smith Academy Record* published several of his poems and stories and ran a regular advertisement on its back cover for "Prufrock's Furniture Store."

Upon his graduation in 1905 from Smith, Eliot left St. Louis to study at Milton Academy in Boston, where he first learned of his Missouri drawl and tried to correct it. By the time he returned for the Christmas holiday, his high school had changed locations and his parents had moved to 4446 Westminster Place (there is a plaque on the sidewalk) where they stayed until Henry Ware's death in 1919, at which time Charlotte sold the house and moved to Cambridge, Massachusetts. The Eliots are buried in Bellefontaine Cemetery—as are the Prufrocks.

Eliot entered Harvard in October 1906 and took courses in Greek and English literature, elementary German and medieval history. Two months later he was put on probation for poor grades and "for working at a lower rate than most Freshmen," although he apparently had "an excellent record of attendance." He began to publish what he would later call his "minor" poems. He met the poet and critic Conrad Aiken, who would become his best Harvard friend. His junior year he discovered the book that would "affect the course of his life"— *The Symbolist Movement in Literature* by Arthur Symons, which led him to read Laforgue, Rimbaud, Verlaine and Corbière. It was also at Harvard that he first read Ezra Pound, who would later edit his "major" poem *The Waste Land*. Eliot inscribed his copy for Pound *il miglio fabbro* (the better master), but his first response to Pound's work was to call it "rather fancy old-fashioned romantic stuff. . . . I wasn't much impressed by it."

After he graduated in 1910, he took courses at the Sorbonne and roamed around Paris for a year before returning to Boston to undertake a Ph.D. in philosophy on the writings of F. H. Bradley. While doing research in Germany the war began, so he remained in London. "It will be very interesting to hear from you how St. Louis is taking the affair," Eliot wrote his mother. "I can imagine the mob breaking the windows of Faust's Restaurant, and sacking the Anhaüser-Busch, [*sic*] and Mr. Busch giving a million dollars toward national defense." Having completed the poem that would provide the title for his first book, "The Lovesong of J. Alfred Prufrock," and seeing it published in Harriet Monroe's *Poetry* magazine in 1915, Eliot decided against returning to Harvard, which broke his pragmatic father's heart. He died thinking that his son had "made a mess of his life," according to Eliot biographer Lyndall Gordon in *T. S. Eliot: An Imperfect Life*, published in 1998. Moreover, he had married an Englishwoman named Vivian Haigh-Wood after only a few months' meeting. Eliot's father discontinued his allowance. Entreaties fell on deaf ears—even the epistolary

only.
    This ticket is non-transferable and will not be redeemed for any reason.
    Each coupon is good for one admission on any day the Exposition is open to the general public.
    Not good on Sundays.
    This ticket shall be forfeited if presented by any person other than person named, whose photograph appears on inside of cover.
    The person using this ticket voluntarily assumes all risk of accidents and damages.
    Void if showing any evidence of alteration or erasure.
    When tickets are lost, prompt notice must be given the Department of Admissions in order that same may be taken up at the gates when presented.
    Tickets lost will not be replaced.
    I have read the above conditions and accept the same.

73

73. *T. S. Eliot's ticket book to the Louisiana Purchase Exposition, 1904*

intervention from his friend and advocate Ezra Pound, who calculated that $500 the first year and $250 for the second would do to get Eliot started on what was clearly Something Big: gathering the material for *The Waste Land*. To do otherwise, Pound propounded, was "a crime against literature."

And so Eliot took a job at a grammar school (the English poet John Betjeman was one of his charges), gave evening school lectures and wrote book reviews. He tried rather desperately to join the U.S. Navy and then the Army, but every time he tried, "everything turned to red tape in his hands." He finally found work as a bank clerk.

Prufrock and Other Observations was published in England in 1917. With his other work in journals and publication record, Eliot was eventually able to land an editorial position with Faber and Gwyer, later to become Faber and Faber. In time he became the director of Faber's poetry list.

"My urban imagery was that of St. Louis," wrote Eliot, "upon which that of Paris and London have been super-imposed. . . . also . . . the Mississippi, as it passes between St. Louis and East St. Louis in Illinois: the Mississippi was the most powerful feature of Nature in that environment:"

> I do not know much about gods; but I think that the river
> Is a strong brown god—sullen, untamed and intractable,
> Patient to some degree, at first recognised as a frontier;
> Useful, untrustworthy, as a conveyor of commerce;
> Then only a problem confronting the builder of bridges.
> The problem once solved, the brown god is almost forgotten
> By the dwellers in cities—ever, however, implacable,
> Keeping his seasons and rages, destroyer, reminder
> Of what men choose to forget. Unhonoured, unpropitiated
> By worshippers of the machine, but waiting, watching and waiting.
> His rhythm was present in the nursery bedroom,
> In the rank ailanthus of the April dooryard,
> In the smell of grapes on the autumn table,
> And the evening circle in the winter gaslight. . . .
>
> —"The Dry Salvages," *Four Quartets*

Early in his career Eliot decided that "there be no biography" and requested that his friends remain silent on this subject. He destroyed much of his own correspondence. One can understand why. His illiberalism could not be disguised in another country, though he became its citizen; nor his "fear of women" which, if not treated properly, leads to misogyny; nor his anti-Semitism, formed early, or his lazy racism (if they *would* turn in their graves). But does there exist a saintly artist, one who has turned an art form on its head? In response to a group of students who sent him a phonograph record, "You've Come a Long Way from St. Louis," Eliot replied that he particularly liked the last line: "But, baby, you've still got a long way to go!"

T. S. Eliot converted to Anglicanism in 1927, and so there is yet another plaque, with the poet's bas-relief in bronze, at Christ Church Cathedral at 1210 Locust Street. He received the Nobel Prize in Literature in 1948 for what one reporter called *The Entire Corpus*. He remained in England until his death in 1965. His adopted country held a memorial service in Westminster Abbey, and Alec Guinness, who acted in one of Eliot's plays, *The Cocktail Party*, read selections from *Four Quartets*. Eliot's ashes were buried at St. Michael's Church, East Coker, and a memorial stone placed in Poet's Corner at Westminster Abbey on the second anniversary of his death in 1967. Faber and Faber published *The Waste Land: A Facsimile and Transcript* with Ezra Pound's annotations and edited by Eliot's second wife, Valerie, in 1971.

To mark the centennial of his birth in 1988 Washington University held a celebration at which some of America's finest poets read from his work, including Howard Nemerov who, in speaking about "The Lovesong of J. Alfred Prufrock," called him a "strange hero for an age, isn't it? Poor little creep, but he come out all right with them mermaids."

T. S. Eliot received a star on the St. Louis Walk of Fame in 1989.

74

T H O M A S   W O L F E
October 3, 1900 — September 15, 1938

The vast drowsy murmur of the distant Fair,—oh strange and bitter miracle of time—come back again.

—Lost Boy

Thomas Wolfe wrote long, "dithyrambic" autobiographical novels, cataloguing his life in Asheville, North Carolina, the Altamont of his books, and in other parts of the world, including a seven-month stay in St. Louis when he was four years old. This sojourn would haunt his "fiction" for the rest of his short life.

Thomas Clayton Wolfe was born in Asheville on October 3, 1900, the youngest son of a troubled marriage. His alcoholic father, William Oliver

75

Wolfe, was a stonecutter for a tombstone business. His mother, Julia (Elizabeth Westall), left her husband in 1904 to make a livelihood for herself and her children in St. Louis, then frantically preparing for the World's Fair.

They arrived in early April of that year, and Mrs. Wolfe leased a house called The Poquin Home at 5095 Fairmont Avenue (later changed to Cates). She rechristened it "The North Carolina" and took in borders who might visit the nearby festivities.

Thomas Wolfe described his time here during the fair in a 1937 novella, *Lost Boy*. The man who was the four-year-old Eugene in the story—the Eugene in many other stories—Thomas Wolfe, comes back to St. Louis in 1935 to excavate:

> I turned into the street, finding the place where the two corners meet, the huddled block, the turret, and the steps, and paused a moment, looking back, as if the street was Time. . . . it was just as it had always been except the steps were lower and the porch less high, the strip of grass less wide than I had thought, but all the rest of it as I had known it would be. A graystone front,

three-storied, with a slant slate roof, the side red brick and windowed, still with the old arched entrance in the center for the doctor's use.

There was a tree in front, a lamp post, and behind and to the side more trees than I had known there would be. And all the slatey turret gables, all the slatey window gables going into points, the two arched windows, in strong stone, in the front room. The small stone porch, stone-carved, with its roof of gabled slate beside.

And it was all so strong, so solid and so ugly—and all, save for the steps and grass, so enduring and so good, the way I had remembered it, the way I knew that I would not get fooled, the way I knew it would not lie to me, really just the way that it had always been, except I did not smell the tar, the hot and caulky dryness of the old cracked ties, the boards of backyard fences and the coarse and sultry grass, and absence in the afternoon when the street car had gone . . . and the feel of the hot afternoon, and that every one was absent at the Fair.

The novella has four parts, each a point of view of one of the characters: the beloved older brother Grover, age twelve; his ten-year-old sister, Helen; the mother; and Eugene. Grover works at the fair and one day he and Helen travel downtown. Here is Helen:

76

> We got on the car there at King's Highway and rode the whole way down into the business section of St. Louis. . . . We got out on Washington Street and walked up and down. . . . And I tell you, boy, we thought that that was something. Grover took me into a drug store and set me up to soda water. Then we came out and walked around some more, down to Union Station and clear over to the river. . . . And both of us half scared to death at what we'd done and wondering what mama would say if she found out. . . .
>
> We stayed down there till it was getting dark, and we went by a lunch room. . . . an old one-armed joint with one-armed chairs and people sitting on stools and eating at the counter. . . . We read all the signs to see what they had to eat and how much it cost, and I guess nothing on the menu was more than fifteen cents, but it couldn't have looked grander to us if it had been Delmonico's. . . . So we stood there with our noses pressed against the window, looking in . . . Two skinny little kids, both of us scared half to death, getting the thrill of a lifetime out of it.

At this point in the novella the fictional and real Grover fall ill. He has contracted typhoid at the fair and dies, after a quarantine, in the boarding house. In 1923 Thomas Wolfe, writing one of the many long letters he lavished on his mother, recalls the scene:

> I'll never forget it—Grover's sickness and death—I am wakened at midnight by Mabel [Helen in the novella] and she says, "Grover's on the cooling

board." I don't know what a cooling board is but am curious to see. I don't know what death is but have a vague, terrified sensation that something awful has happened—then she takes me in her arms and up the hall.— Disappointed at the cooling board—it's only a table–the brown mole on his neck—the trip home—visitors in the parlor with condolences. . . . Then it gets fairly plain thereafter, and I can trace it step by step.

This is why I think I'm going to be an artist. The things that really mattered sunk in and left their mark. Sometimes only a word—sometimes a particular smile—sometimes death—sometimes the smell of dandelions in Spring—once Love. Most people have little more mind than brutes: they live from day to day. I will go everywhere and see everything. I will meet all the people I can. I will think all the thoughts, feel all the emotions I am able, and I will write, write, write.

Thomas Wolfe published his first novel, *Look Homeward, Angel,* in 1929 and introduced his family to the world. He would continue to write about them, and his friends and lovers, in *Of Time and the River* (1935), the posthumously published *Web and the Rock* (1939) and *You Can't Go Home Again* (1940) and to try to embody the "absence, absence in the afternoon" of a *Lost Boy.*

In 1938, while traveling for the first time west of St. Louis, Thomas Wolfe developed pneumonia. He was sent to Johns Hopkins Hospital in Baltimore where he never recovered from the operation for tuberculosis, which had spread to his brain. He died on September 15, with his mother at his side. He was not yet thirty-eight.

SALLY BENSON
September 3, 1897 or 1900 — July 19, 1972

How will Santa Claus know how to find us? He's so used to coming here.
—Tootie, in the movie version of *Meet Me in St. Louis*

Sally Benson began her writing career interviewing celebrities, mainly authors, for the old *Morning Telegraph* in New York. In 1930 she sent her first short story to the *New Yorker*, which published it, inaugurating Benson's long association with the magazine. A reviewer in Boston called her stories, "brilliant with a knife-like cut, ruthless in their satire, and penetrating often to the point of tragedy." Benson toned down the "knife-like" edge for her stories about a young girl named Judy Graves, which became a popular series published in the 1941 collection *Junior Miss*, a Book-of-the-Month Club selection. A year later she published *Meet Me in St. Louis*, a memoir in the form of a novel based on Benson's childhood in St. Louis during the planning, construction and grand opening of the 1904 World's Fair.

Sally Benson was born Sara Mahala Redway Smith on September 3, 1897 or 1900, to Alonzo Redway and Anna (Prophater) Smith, names she would use in her story. She would use the house in which she was born and grew up, too—5135 Kensington Avenue—but Hollywood, in the form of a librettist, would change the address of the "Boy Next Door" from 5129 to 5133 (there was no 5133) for the movie musical released in 1944, starring Judy Garland as Esther Smith and Margaret O'Brien as Tootie.

For her story, Benson consulted her sister Esther's diary and peopled the book with her family and friends: her parents Mr. and Mrs. Smith, siblings Rose, Lon, Esther and Agnes, and Grandma and Grandpa Prophater. The boy next door, Barton Wagner, was in real life, as they say, Stanley Blewett Wagoncr, who became a building contractor. Benson, of course, is Tootie: "It's only natural that I made myself the smartest member of the family."

Hollywood took other liberties with the book. It was not Tootie who "took" the Waughops on Halloween, it was the older Agnes who "killed" them with flour, making her "the most horrible"—but the precocious child actress Margaret O'Brien got that part. Esther does not have a palpable crush on the boy next door because there is no John Truitt in the book, so no need to sing the Trolley Song; no one counsels us to have ourselves a merry little Christmas, even though we hope you will.

The novel is a date book that begins in June 1903 and serves as a little history of St. Louis and the events leading up to the fair:

> The miracle of the World's Fair in St. Louis, rising as it did out of the wilderness, stunned everyone. It seemed impossible that only two years before, Governor Francis of Missouri had driven in the first stake with a silver ax while crowds walking through the briers and coarse grass to witness the ceremony carried heavy sticks to protect themselves from snakes. The enthusiasm of the press was unlimited, and verses appeared daily in the newspapers.
>
> *The greatest show that ever showed*
> *Will rise beside the Skinker Road.*
>
> The buildings were elegant and formal and were constructed in the approved palatial style. . . . Greek goddesses presided over the domes, classic and beautiful. . . . To the people of St. Louis, the Fair was finished, perfect. It was

the cream of everything in the world. There was nothing better to come. Only the visitors complained of the mud . . .

Unlike Tootie and her family, however, Sally Benson could not talk her father into staying in St. Louis. Mr. Smith took a job in New York and Sally packed up her dolls at the age of eleven (or fourteen). Sally Smith graduated from Horace Mann School, and when she was nineteen (or twenty-two) she married Reynolds Benson. They had a daughter, Barbara, the following year.

In addition to her books Sally Benson wrote for the movies, including screenplays for *Shadow of a Doubt, Anna and the King of Siam* and *Viva Las Vegas.*

Meet Me in St. Louis premiered in the city of its inspiration on November 22, 1944, and the boy next door attended at the invitation of his former neighbor, whose house still stood at 5135 Kensington. Fifty years later, a much less elegant looking home than the one described in the book and portrayed in the movie was torn down and five hundred of its bricks sold as commemoratives.

78

> "It's where we live," Agnes repeated. "We don't have to visit here. We don't have to come on a train or stay at a hotel, or anything. They won't tear it down, will they?"
>
> "No," Tootie said. "They will never tear it down. It will be like this forever."
>
> "I can't believe it," Agnes said. "Right here where we live. Right here in St. Louis."
>
> —*Meet Me in St. Louis*

78. 5135 Kensington Avenue, 1917

Was life flitting fast away? Not so I could notice it. To my mind, in St. Louis, it stood charmingly still.
— "Meet Me in St. *Lewis,* Louie"

EMILY HAHN
January 14, 1905 — February 18, 1997

79

It is not unusual for young artists, in their creative development, to leave their hometowns for other cultural meccas. Emily Hahn took part in this migration, but in her own way: on the eve of Charles Lindbergh's historic flight in 1927, Hahn pledged that should the *Spirit of St. Louis* cross the Atlantic successfully, she would depart the namesake city. Lindbergh landed and Hahn took off for New York, London, the American Southwest, and also to the Belgian Congo, Bombay, Nairobi, Shanghai and Hong Kong. In a lifetime of writing, Hahn traveled ceaselessly and fearlessly, wrote more than fifty books and, as the "Chronicler of her Own Exploits," became one of the world's leading correspondents of the life of her time.

Born January 14, 1905, Emily Hahn was the fifth daughter of Isaac and Hannah Hahn, atheistic Jews of German and Bavarian descent. The family lived at 4858 Fountain Avenue. Isaac was vice president of S. A. Ryder & Company, a purveyor of dry goods and groceries; Hannah, an advocate of equal rights for women, had worked as a stenographer in Chicago before her marriage.

The Hahn daughters—Rose, Dorothy, Helen, Dauphine and Emily (nicknamed "Mickey" by her mother)—and their brother, Mannel, were bright, attractive and outgoing children whose independence was encouraged by their parents. In her youth Hannah created a mild scandal in St. Louis by wearing bloomers while bicycle-riding, and she encouraged her daughters to forsake their school dresses—and public opinion—for the comfort and convenience of knickers. Isaac Hahn was also free thinking: he read "passages from the Bible . . . so that he could point out inconsistencies." Emily Hahn wrote of St. Louis warmly in her 1970 book, *Times and Places,* a collection of essays originally printed in the *New Yorker*:

> Later on, in Chicago, it suited me to mope as if I'd lost a paradise when we moved away from St. Louis . . . There must have been other towns along the Mississippi with a similar charm—places where cement had not yet tamped down everything and nature still showed through—but I thought mine unique. I firmly believed that the little girl from New York who came out every summer to visit her grandparents next door was as miserable, when the time came to return to the brownstone fronts of the East, as Persephone going back to the underworld.

Though Hahn's memory of her childhood was one of Elysian bliss, the city could also resemble Hades:

Late in May, it would begin to heat up. Then we were permitted to go barefoot, outside of school hours—a privilege I did not appreciate, for the sidewalks burned my feet and the asphalt in the streets melted to a mushy consistency, streaking my legs with tar. Wherever potholes in a street were being mended, there was a little heap of soft tar nearby, and I remember—though I hate to think of it—that we filched little pieces of the tar and chewed it. The parched grass of Fountain Park was easier than asphalt on the feet, but if one simply *had* to stay outside, the back yard was best. There we could turn on the garden hose and wallow. When the classroom thermometer at our school rose about ninety, we were sent home.

The Hahn children crossed through Fountain Park on their way to nearby George Washington Public School. They thought of private schools "only as places for children who had something the matter with them—feeble-mindedness or divorced parents," but Emily also augmented her education with Saturday morning classes at Washington University's School of Fine Arts:

The school was housed in an edifice of great, if accidental, distinction. It had been created as a pavilion for the World's Fair of 1904, with an Italian sunken garden and porticoes on all four sides. By the time we got there, it was as romantically decrepit as any real Italian ruin. . . .

St. Louis's bohemians used the school as a center, and put on a pageant there every year—their own Chelsea Arts Ball, or Beaux-Arts. [The Beaux-Arts Ball remains an annual tradition with Washington University art students.] The last year I was there . . . we younger students wore costumes of vaguely Egyptian appearance and danced all together to music from *Aïda*. I was thrilled, especially when somebody took a photograph of me at the dress rehearsal looking dreamy and noble in profile against an empty sky.

Hahn's "unfashionably happy" childhood in St. Louis ended in 1920, when the family moved to Chicago. The relocation came at a difficult time for Emily who, at age fifteen, was enjoying her social and academic life at Soldan High School in the Central West End:

It was almost too outrageous to believe. Live in Chicago—that gritty, high-built town? My parents must have gone crazy, I thought, or were in the grip of some higher power than themselves, mysterious and malign. It was incredible that they should want to go. Taught by them, we thought St. Louis was the best city—with the possible exception of New Orleans, where Daddy had relatives, and Denver, where they'd gone on their honeymoon–in the states; that Fountain Avenue was the most charming part of St. Louis; that our friends in St. Louis were uniquely wonderful; and that St. Louis schools were the best to be found anywhere in the world. That my parents should voluntarily give up all this privilege was inconceivable, unless—as I suddenly thought, for the first time, *might* be possible—they were not, after all, the kindest, wisest people ever born.

Hahn went on to study mining at the University of Wisconsin in Madison, where she was the first woman to graduate from the school's College of Engineering— perhaps only because no one expected a woman to do such a thing. Infected with travel passion, at the conclusion of their sophomore year Hahn and her housemate Dorothy took off on a 2,400-mile cross-country drive from Wisconsin to California in a black Model T Ford, a journey she would later document for the *New Yorker*.

80

Following graduation, Hahn returned to St. Louis to take a position with the mining company McBride Inc., but remained only a year. Discontented with the routine of office work—and frustrated that despite her engineering degree, the only tasks she was given were secretarial—Hahn set her clock by Lindbergh and lit out for New Mexico, where she worked as a tour guide and Harvey Girl for a brief period before moving to New York to begin her writing career.

In her books Emily Hahn tells us about her time in the Belgian Congo in *Congo Solo: Misadventures Two Degrees North* (1933), *With Naked Foot* (1934) and *Africa to Me* (1964); about her seven years in China, during which she was mistress and then wife to poet and publisher Sinmay Zau, overcame an opium addiction, and had a child out of wedlock with British intelligence officer Charles Boxer, in the books *China to Me* (1944), *Steps of the Sun* (1945) and *Hong Kong Holiday* (1946); and about big-game hunting with Indian royalty in *The Tiger House Party: The Last Days of the Maharajas* (1959). Hahn learned to speak both Kingwana, a dialect of Swahili, Mandarin Chinese and other languages during her extended stays. As reporter-at-large for the *New Yorker*—or "Roving Heroine," according to the magazine's Roger Angell—she published more than two hundred pieces over sixty-eight years and worked with the magazine's first four editors— Harold Ross, William Shawn, Robert Gottlieb and Tina Brown.

In addition to the casually elegant and engaging blends of reportage and memoir for which she is best-known, Emily Hahn wrote novels about Aphra Behn and Mata Hari; biographies of Leonardo da Vinci, D. H. Lawrence, the Soong sisters, Chang Kai-shek and Mary, Queen of Scots; nonfiction books on India, Ireland and the Philippines; and histories of feminism, diamond mining and American bohemianism. In her later writing, Hahn did extensive work on primate intelligence and animal communication. A 1982 article noted that "Emily Hahn has written more about practically everything than almost any other writer alive." She was elected to the American Academy of Arts and Letters in 1987.

Her final contribution to the *New Yorker* appeared in the December 2, 1996, issue. It was a poem entitled "Wind Blowing," which she had written in 1917, at the age of twelve:

Wind blowing, wind blowing, looking for a fight,
Looking for a barrier all through the night,
Nothing left to blow against, nothing left to bite!

I can see everything, all round the earth;
Red sun dying, gold sun's birth;
Wind blowing frantically, scouring the earth.

Nothing, nothing anywhere, day and night and day:
Wind blew everywhere, blew it all away.

Nothing, nothing anywhere, night and day and night,
Poor wind blowing, looking for a fight,
Nothing left to blow against, nothing left to bite!

Emily Hahn's affair with Charles Boxer was one of the great scandals of the war. Upon his 1945 liberation from a Japanese prison, Boxer and his British wife divorced, and he was reunited with Hahn and their daughter. The couple had a second daughter, and their marriage lasted until Hahn's death on February 18, 1997, at the age of ninety-two.

Emily Hahn's "partial autobiography" *China to Me*, published in 1944, documented her experiences living there from 1935 to 1943. Her candor placed her in the middle of the growing public debate about China: "Most newspapermen don't know any more about the Communists in China than you do," she counseled her readers.

China to Me became a best-seller:

The Chinese had reinstated a sort of Underground. They were in practice for it, because there had been an active trade in smuggling people across the border into Hong Kong long before Pearl Harbor, when the British authorities were trying to stop immigration from occupied Canton. It was an open secret that Hong Kong's official census fell almost half a million below the actual number of inhabitants in 1940. Now the smuggling had begun again, but it worked both ways. People crept into town without the required permits to enter, they lived there without the necessary permit to stay, and they crept out again without getting permission to do so. The Japanese tried to stop it by means of searching and surprise raids, but as fast as they put it down in one spot it would pop up again in another.

In this way people often received messages from the interior, by word of mouth and even by letter. Letters, of course, were very dangerous. I knew people who corresponded with Free China in that way, but I never did it myself, and nobody sent me letters from outside either. I hoped they wouldn't. I sweated for fear they would, because when such a letter was found by the gendarmes they had a way of reading it, copying it, letting it go through and then, when they had collected enough evidence, pouncing on all the parties concerned.

Hello Mr. Voit this is me ELOISE
kindly forward our mail to Paris France
we're leaving tout de suite which is right away
bon voyage and merci boucoup

—Eloise in Paris

Children's literature usually depicts children as adults see them or would like them to be, but Kay Thompson's *Eloise*, the 1955 book about a charmingly mischievous six-year-old who lives at the posh Plaza Hotel in New York City, does neither. Unlike her colleagues on the tier of most beloved literary heroines—Madeline, whose polite Parisian world was always restored to order, and Laura Ingalls, who learned life lessons on the prairies of the Midwest—overprivileged Eloise never cared to learn from the havoc wrought by her escapades (pouring a pitcher of water down the mail chute, for instance). In producing this "book for precocious grown-ups," Thompson created a star of children's literature and an infamous New Yorker.

81

Kay Thompson was born Catherine Fink in St. Louis in 1909. Her father was a jeweler, and the family lived at 17 Parkland Place. Gifted with both musical skill and parental encouragement, Thompson was a piano prodigy, and in 1928, at the age of sixteen, performed Liszt as a soloist with the St. Louis Symphony. She graduated from Soldan High School and attended Washington University, where she studied English, French and Greek, pledged Kappa Kappa Gamma and was a member of the student theatrical groups Thyrsus and the Quadrangle Club. She served as assistant musical director of the 1931 production *Si, Si Senorita* [*sic*]. The Washington University yearbook *Hatchet* included a review of the show:

> Last night "Si, Si, Senorita," a musical hodge podge produced by the Quadrangle Club, (no relation to this department, thank heavens) opened a four week run at the American Theatre with an awful flop. From the overture to the final curtain the whole concoction was grade A sour goat milk. Otherwise it was awful good fun.

82

Thompson also performed as a vocalist in this production, an interest which led to an early exit from college and her hometown. "I was a stage-struck kid," she would later recall, "and I got out of St. Louis fast."

Thompson took off for Hollywood, where over the next decade she forged a career as a vocalist and musical arranger. She became a singer with the Mills Brothers and with Fred Waring's Band and worked for Metro Goldwyn Mayer, where her innovative vocal arrangements eased jazz rhythms into musicals, and her coaching of the studio's top vocal talent, including Lena Horne and Judy Garland, was highly regarded. (Thompson is frequently credited with assisting in Garland's vocal transition from ingenue to sophisticate, and putting the "sob" in her voice.) She worked as an arranger and songwriter for *The Ziegfeld Follies,* directed by Vincent Minnelli, and *The Harvey Girls,* starring Judy Garland—a connection which led to a lifelong friendship with their daughter, Liza, to whom Thompson was godmother. She also performed in nightclubs, singing with Andy Williams and his brothers from 1947 to 1953. A slim, glamorous blonde, Kay Thompson became as famous for her striking wardrobe of trailing scarves and toreador pants as for her distinctive vocal style.

In 1957 she appeared in front of the camera as flamboyant fashion editor Maggie Prescott in the movie *Funny Face.* In this role, Thompson mugged with Audrey Hepburn and Fred Astaire, but it was her aggressive delivery of frivolous dictates like "Think Pink!" and "It's got to have bizazz!" that stole scene after scene. Thompson toured Las Vegas, Los Angeles and New York as a nightclub singer and in the 1950s opened her one-woman show in the Persian Room of the Plaza Hotel (where she lived rent-free) and famously took to amusing her friends and colleagues with the persona and high-pitched voice of a little girl. This character, Eloise, usually surfaced when Thompson arrived late for rehearsal or when someone in the company misplaced train tickets.

Anxious to "get out of the saloon business," and well-connected with friends in publishing, Thompson started her *Eloise* series in 1955, with illustrations by Hilary Knight. Eloise, the poor little rich girl who lives with her dog Weenie and her turtle Skiperdee at the Plaza Hotel could, with a certain urbane sophistication, call room service while her nanny watched

82. The Quadrangle Club from The Hatchet, *1932.*
Thompson stands in the front row, far right.

the fights on TV and order "three Pilsener Beers for Nanny and one meringue glacée for me ELOISE and charge it please Thank you very much." It was an immediate bestseller. In 1957 Thompson and Knight took Eloise to Paris (with passport photo by Richard Avedon and party frock by Christian Dior). *Eloise at Christmastime* came out in 1958 and *Eloise in Moscow* in 1959.

By 1963 more than a million copies of the book and its sequels were sold and the Plaza Hotel established an Eloise Room. Eloise dolls, dresses and accessories were produced, but Kay Thompson, appalled by a 1956 televised *Eloise* special, eventually suppressed all promotional activity for the books and removed the sequels from publication.

Thompson lived for a time in Rome, working on the books *The Fox and the Fig* and *Eloise Takes a Bawth,* but neither would go to press. Thompson never returned to Eloise, though she did publish again—in 1970, *Kay Thompson's Miss Pooky Peckinpaugh and Her Secret Private Boyfriends Complete with Telephone Numbers* was printed. Upon her death on July 2, 1998, licensing rights for the Eloise stories were turned over to her estate, which authorized the reissue of the previously unavailable titles. These rejoined the publication of the original, which has remained in print for over forty years.

Hilary Knight's portrait of Eloise hangs in the Plaza outside the Palm Court, a tribute to both its fictional subject and Kay Thompson, who, when questioned about the origins of her creation, responded, "Eloise is all me."

A plaque near the entrance of the Plaza reads:

Literary Landmarks Register
The Plaza Hotel
The Home of Eloise

Kay Thompson lived at the Plaza while
writing *Eloise*, first published in 1955.
Miss Thompson and illustrator
Hilary Knight brought this fictitious charmer
to life; an exuberant and
precocious six-year-old who lived on
the top floor of the hotel.
Designated a Literary Landmark,
September 26, 1998.

*I could lift scenes
straight out of Faulkner and put them down in Harlem and all I had to
change was the scene.*
—My Life of Absurdity

Chester Himes, the crime writer, was born in Jefferson City, Missouri, where his father, Joseph Sandy Himes, head of the Mechanical Department, taught blacksmithing and wheelwrighting at Lincoln Institute. "The only memory I have of my life in Jefferson City is of my brother Joseph and myself painting our hair with green paint left by the house painters." The family moved when Chester was four, to one of the many southern towns in which they would live. "My mother was an octoroon, or perhaps whiter. I remember her as looking like a white woman who had suffered a long siege of illness." His mother claimed that she descended from English nobility:

> Much of her nagging and scolding and punishing and pushing us stemmed from her desire for us to live up to our "heritage." . . . My father was the exact opposite . . . a short black man with bowed legs, a perfect ellipsoidal skull, and an Arabic face with a big hooked nose. . . . We all looked like that— like what you are imagining would be the combination of our mother and our father. Only I look more so. My hair is kinky, my complexion sepia, my features might be handsome were my nose not so tiny, and my skull is so flat and misshapen the students of my father used to say he had made it in the blacksmith shop.

As a boy Himes loved the stories of Poe and Homer. He graduated from high school in Cleveland in 1926, and later that summer broke his back when he fell down an empty elevator shaft while working as a busboy at a local hotel. (He wore a brace for several years.) He entered Ohio State University with the fourth highest freshman IQ but didn't study and was expelled. After his parents divorced, Himes took up gambling, pimping, passing false checks, stealing cars, pistol-whipping unworthies and running liquor for a man called Bunch Boy. Ohio State Penitentiary was only a few raps away. One night in 1928 Himes overheard a chauffeur bragging about the money his employer kept in his closet in a safe. Himes made the hit and got twenty-five years hard labor.

During his sentence Himes began to write about prison life and publish his stories in newspapers and magazines around the country, most notably in *Esquire*. "No matter what I did, or where I was, or how I lived, I had considered myself a writer ever since I'd published my first story in *Esquire* when I was still in prison in 1934. Foremost a writer. Above all else a writer. It was my salvation, and is. The world can deny me all other employment, and stone me as an ex-convict, as a nigger, as a disagreeable and unpleasant person. . . . I'm a writer, and no one can take that away."

Chester Himes's family, including his two older brothers, Edward and Joseph, moved frequently when he was a child. In Pine Bluff, Arkansas, Joseph, Sr., worked for Branch Normal College, where he was required to teach black history as well as his mechanical classes, and so likely was one of the first southern teachers of black history. At the end of each year Pine Bluff students would put on a show of what they had learned at school. Chester and his older brother Joseph, whom he adored, planned to perform a chemistry experiment together. Chester misbehaved and was banned by his mother from participating. The

83

demonstration blew up in Joe's face, and Chester fell down a flight of stairs trying to help him. Five days later the family moved to St. Louis, where Joseph, Sr., had bought a house on Taylor Avenue several years earlier and where Joseph, Jr., could receive daily treatment at Barnes Hospital. Joseph attended the Missouri State School for the Blind and his family would visit him there. "Although the public schools in St. Louis were strictly segregated," Chester Himes wrote in the first volume of his 1972 autobiography, *The Quality of Hurt*, "both white and nonwhite males and females attended the school for the blind. Revealing, isn't it?"

According to his autobiography, Chester, now fourteen, enrolled in the one black high school, what he called Wendell Phillips in the book: "I remember St. Louis as a strange big city where I played football, baseball, soccer, basketball, any game that you can name, with suicidal intensity. . . . I broke my right shoulder blade, which healed out of place and still looks deformed; my left ear was half torn from my head; all of my teeth were chipped. . . . I was unpopular with my teachers, disliked by the students; I was lonely, shy, and insufferably belligerent."

The family continued to live in the house on Taylor Avenue, but it was let out to tenants to assist with their dwindling income. In his autobiographical novel *The Third Generation* (1954), Himes describes the place on Taylor as "a huge old house beside a Catholic school in a changing neighborhood. . . . a cold austere house . . . the dead smell of old coal smoke seeped from its ancient flues." The main character is Charles, and his only escape is

> into the cold, lamp-lit attic. . . . [he] read alone . . . fought a thousand duels and saved as many damsels in distress. He was Ivanhoe and Richard the Lionhearted, Alexander the Great and the Count of Monte Cristo, Genghis

Khan and the Scarlet Pimpernel. It was often his face in the iron mask, and his strong back, instead of Jean Valjean's, lifting the carriage from the mud. Most often he was Achilles chasing Hector around the walls of Troy. When all else failed—when he ached with loneliness and Caesar's legions failed to conquer; when Ivanhoe had bad dreams and Horatio couldn't hold the bridge and mud was clinging to his mother's feet—then he was Achilles. There was something apt about being Achilles in Mississippi.

As in fact went fiction. In the story the brother is William, who "was re-hospitalized for a serious operation. . . . They sold the house and bought a rental property in a poorer neighborhood. They moved into one of the flats, taking only the barest necessities." In real life the Himes family was now on Sarah Avenue, Joseph, Sr., could find no employment but as a waiter, and money was so scarce that Joseph, Jr., was sent onto the street to sell copies of a poem his mother had written, "The Blind Boy's Appeal."

Despite Joe's malady, Chester took him bobsledding on Art Hill one winter that was so cold the Mississippi froze over: "once we stayed out so long my toes were frostbitten and I barely escaped losing them." Himes also spent hours at the railroad station watching the trains and at the zoo observing the lions. But after two years "the doctors at Barnes Hospital said they could do no more for my brother's eyes. Scar tissue completely covered the cornea of one eye, but in the other he still retained a little vision." Chester Himes described their exit from St. Louis in *The Quality of Hurt*: "My father was suffering from the frustrations of unemployment and Jim Crow, and as there was no longer any benefit to be had for Joe in St. Louis, he took us to Cleveland, where he had two married sisters and a brother."

In 1936 Chester Himes was paroled from the state pen, having served seven years of his sentence. He married the following year, moved to Los Angeles where he hoped to write for Hollywood, but instead found employment in a bomb factory, an experience captured in his 1947 novel *Lonely Crusade*. He also earned a file at the FBI for his Leftist fulminations in the magazines *Crisis* and *Opportunity*, and won a Rosenwald Fellowship in 1944, which led to his first published novel, *If He Hollers Let Him Go*. Himes and his wife moved to New York City after the war, where they became friends with Ralph Ellison and Richard Wright, and experienced the vibrant cultural life of Harlem. Doubleday, Himes's publisher, promised him its George Washington Carver award "for the best book on Negro life" published in 1945. However, the award and the guaranteed advance sales of ten thousand copies went to another narrative, *Mrs. Palmer's Honey*, by St. Louisan Fannie Cook.

"Nothing in my life hurt me so much as the American rejection of my thoughts . . . What had hurt so much was my discovery that they thought about my thoughts, really thought about them, then went to so much pains to ignore my writing, which was what I lived by. I thought that was a chickenshit attitude," Himes wrote in the second volume of his autobiography *My Life of Absurdity*, published in 1976. He and his wife separated in 1953 and he left for Paris, where he could gather at the Café Tournon with

Richard Wright, James Baldwin, cartoonist Ollie Harrington and painter William Gardner Smith. Himes was poor, but his money troubles improved when he turned his hand to detective fiction. The French version of his first attempt, *For Love of Imabelle*, won him a prestigious prize. Over the next dozen years his Harlem novels, with their memorable duo Coffin Ed Johnson and Grave Digger Jones, were a critical and popular success: "The only time I was happy was while writing these strange, violent, unreal stories." Himes won more prizes, married a second time, and after selling the film rights for *Cotton Comes to Harlem* to Samuel Goldwyn, built a house in Moraira, Spain. In 1972 he was recognized for his literary achievements by the Carnegie Endowment for International Peace. He continued to write, most notably his two-volume autobiography. Chester Himes died in Moraira, with his second wife, Leslie, at his side. In France alone, there were twenty-seven obituaries.

His brother Joseph became a professor of sociology.

"You're my friend, ain't you?" the giant asked.

He had a voice that whined like a round saw cutting through a pine knot.

"What do you need with a friend, as big as you are?" the dwarf kidded.

"I is asking you," the giant insisted.

He was a milk-white albino with pink eyes, battered lips, cauliflowered ears and thick, kinky, cream-colored hair. He wore a white T-shirt, greasy black pants held up with a length of hemp rope, and blue canvas rubber-soled sneakers.

The dwarf put on an expression of hypocritical solicitude. He flicked back his sleeve and glanced at the luminous dial on his watch. It was 1.22 A.M. He relaxed. There was no need to hurry.

—*The Heat's On*

*Through these ori-
fices transmute your
body. . . . The way
OUT is the way IN. . . .
Now I William
Seward, will unlock
my word horde. . . .
My Viking heart fares
over the great brown
river where motors put
put put in jungle twi-
light and whole trees
float with huge snakes
in the branches and
sad-eyed lemurs watch
the shore, across the
Missouri field (The
Boy finds a pink
arrowhead) out along
distant train whistles,
comes back to me hun-
gry as a street boy
don't know to peddle
the ass God gave him.*
—Naked Lunch

84

The stately three-story red brick house at 4664 Pershing Avenue, with its meticulously mown lawn and immaculate flower beds, was the birthplace of one of the most sordid and outlandish imaginations in American litera-ture. The author later known as *el hombre invisible*, then called Young Billy, spent most of his time in a part of the house that cannot be seen from the street. He favored the dark hollow beneath the back steps, where he would convert his mother's cutlery into weapons while transforming his upper-middle-class neighborhood into a perilous make-believe world populated by thieves and pirates. It was here, while attending the progressive Community School, that the precocious eight-year-old composed his first literary work, titled *The Autobiography of a Wolf*. "People laughed and said: 'You mean the Biography of a Wolf.' No, I meant the autobiography of a wolf and still do," he would later recount. It was also at the age of eight that he handled his first gun: "I used to go out duck shooting with the old man and the president of the First National City Bank and the owner of the *St. Louis Post-Dispatch*. You have to get up real early, six o'clock, to catch the ducks. . . . we would put out decoys and then as the ducks came in, all these fat old businessmen would stand up and blast away at them. . . . I used to really enjoy it!"

This fiercely individualistic mind would go on to produce some of the most structurally bizarre and thematically explicit literature of the twentieth century. By combining the colloquial with elements of surrealism and satire he brought brutal insight into the psychological mechanics of human need. Burroughs's graphic depictions of drug abuse and sexuality inject his work with a sensational intensity. In his most famous novel, *Naked Lunch*, he pioneered a technique called the "cut-up," deliberately subverting the chronological narrative by piecing together random fragments, however fantastical. For many readers Burroughs personifies the artist as outsider, whose fiction chronicles a life of self-marginalization to the darkest fringes of the American consciousness.

85

William Seward Burroughs II was born on February 5, 1914, the son of Mortimer, a prominent local businessman, and Laura Lee, a descendant of the famed Civil War general, reported to have a "Victorian distaste for any manifestation of the bodily functions." Burroughs later adopted his mother's maiden name to create the pseudonym William Lee, under which name his first novel, *Junky*, was published in 1953. His paternal grandfather and namesake had invented a more efficient model of the adding machine and founded the Burroughs Adding Machine Company (now called Unisys) to market his patents, providing the family with a comfortable existence. They had a domestic staff—including a maid, nanny, cook and gardener—and a summer home on Lake Huron, but they remained on the periphery of the St. Louis aristocracy. "We were not accepted by old families with ten, twenty, fifty million. Of course we were invited to the larger parties," Burroughs later recalled, "but when the WASP elite got together for dinners and lunches and drinks nobody wanted those ratty Burroughses around. My final inheritance on the death of my mother in 1970 was $10,000 and that doesn't make me a scion of anything."

The family left the Central West End in 1926 for 700 South Price Road in Ladue. He attended John Burroughs School (named after the famous naturalist) where he impressed his classmates with his verbal and trouble-making skills—he once set off an explosion in his family's basement. At age fifteen he was sent to a school in Los Alamos, New Mexico, but returned to St. Louis his senior year to earn his diploma from Taylor High School. Adolescence was particularly distressing for him as his pallid complexion and bony, unathletic build visibly set him apart from his classmates. He was also becoming excruciatingly aware of his homosexuality. During his youth

86

Burroughs developed an attachment to a friend, with whom he spent many Saturday afternoons exploring quarries and fishing in ponds at Forest Park, but his paranoia at being revealed, his sharp intellect and sullen manner all contributed to his alienation. He turned to writing and began to keep a journal, experimenting in several genres: Westerns, gothic horror, and his favorite, pulp fiction.

In 1932 Burroughs entered Harvard and received his bachelor's degree in English in the requisite four years. As a graduation present his parents gave him an allowance and a trip to Europe. He decided to study psychology at the University of Vienna, where he befriended Ilse Klapper, a German Jew whose visa was nearing expiration. They married so that she could immigrate to the United States. Although they never lived together, she and Burroughs remained good friends.

Burroughs returned to work as a cub reporter for the *St. Louis Post-Dispatch* in either 1937 or 1938. Sources vary as to the exact date, but not regarding its two-week duration. Burroughs did not have the stomach for "chasing picture," obtaining photos from the families of those murdered or killed in accidents. He came home again in 1940, to work in the wealthy suburb of Ladue at his parents' new gift shop, Cobblestone Gardens, which Burroughs would later use as the title of one of his books. Over the next eight years, he traveled constantly, dabbling in several careers: studying anthropology at Harvard graduate school, working as a bartender, copywriter, exterminator and private detective. He also served briefly in the army at Jefferson Barracks but was discharged for psychological reasons after intentionally slicing off the joint of a finger with poultry shears in order to impress a friend.

Burroughs moved to New York City in 1944 and shortly after met and married his second wife, Joan Vollmer, an intelligent and free-spirited woman who was friends with many of the principal members of the New York literary scene. She introduced him to Jack Kerouac (then a student at Columbia University), through whom he met Allen Ginsberg; the trio became the major figures in the Beat Movement. Another acquaintance of the group was Herbert Huncke, who introduced Burroughs to morphine. His drug experimentation quickly escalated from recreational use to utter dependency, one he shared with Joan, and his son: William S. Burroughs, Jr.,

86. Class photograph, John Burroughs School. Burroughs stands second from right, c. 1926

was born in 1947 and died of cirrhosis in 1981.

In 1949 Burroughs and Joan fled to Mexico to avoid weapons and drug charges. During a drunken party in 1951 he shot Joan in the forehead. She died instantly. Although it was reported by those in attendance that Burroughs was aiming at a martini glass balanced on her head, he did not speak publicly about the incident until the filming of the documentary *Burroughs*, released in 1984. He also wrote about it shortly after it took place in his novel *Queer*, but the book was not published until 1986. He claimed later in life that they were not playing William Tell, and that the gun went off accidentally. What is certain is that he was released after thirteen days in a Mexican prison and that history will not let him shake the slaying.

Although Burroughs preferred to live as an expatriate, spending much time in Paris, London, Tangier and South America, he always retained an odd affection for his hometown. In 1965 he returned for a brief visit. Documenting some of the changes that had taken place during his absence he lamented: "But what has happened to Market Street the skid row of my adolescent years? Where are the tattoo parlors, novelty stores, hock shops— brass knuckles in a dusty window—the seedy pitchmen—Where are the old junkies hawking and spitting on street corners under the glass lights?"

Other of Burroughs's memories of his youth are filled with an uncharacteristic nostalgia, one of the apparent side-effects of withdrawal:

> In the 1920's the United States, even the Midwest, was a place of glittering possibilities. You could be a gangster, a hard-drinking reporter, a jittery stock-broker, an expatriate, a successful writer. The possibilities spilled out in front of you like a rich display of merchandise. Sitting on the back steps drinking Whistle at twilight on a summer evening, hearing the street cars clang past on Euclid Avenue, I felt the excitement and nostalgia of the '20's tingling in my groin. . . .
>
> Seemed to see West St. Louis, the moving headlights on Lindell Boulevard. Very vivid for a moment. I was in a study with soft lights, an apartment probably. Horrible feeling of desolation.
>
> —*Early Routines*

Burroughs would again write about St. Louis in his 1980 novel *Port of Saints*, creating a character called Audrey Carsons as a version of himself as a child. This experimental quasi-autobiography recounts several incidents from his youth, including a remark made by a schoolmate's father: "That boy looks like a sheep-killing dog." In 1944 he collaborated with Jack Kerouac on *And the Hippos Were Boiled in Their Tanks*, about a fire at the St. Louis Zoo. Many of his works contain references to prominent St. Louis streets, Forest Park, the River Des Peres and the Mississippi. When the documentary on his life and work premiered here in 1984, Burroughs was in attendance. He returned in 1989 for a local gallery exhibition of his bullet paintings (canvases punctured with gunshots). Both times he stayed in his childhood home.

Aside from writing his numerous novels and collections of short fiction, Burroughs strongly influenced music and visual art. *Naked Lunch* coined the phrases "Steely Dan" (the name of a sex toy) and "Heavy Metal." He has been nicknamed the "Godfather of Punk," has produced spoken word albums, written a libretto for an opera and made cameo appearances in several movies. He is also among the medley of famous figures to grace the cover of the Beatles album *Sgt. Pepper's Lonely Hearts Club Band*. In 1983 he was inducted into the American Academy of Arts and Letters.

The last few years of his life Burroughs resided in Lawrence, Kansas, primarily writing in his journal. "'Is it not fine to dance and sing while the bells of death do ring to run on toe and sing hey nanny noo.' Yes I love life in all its variety but at last the bell ringest to eventide." The entry the day before his death on August 2, 1997, reads: "Love? What is it? Most natural painkiller. What there is. LOVE." For a man who lived so long with drugs and guns, he died an old man, of a heart attack. He was eighty-three. He is buried in an unmarked grave next to his grandfather in Bellefontaine Cemetery, along with many other family members, including his parents.

PETER TAYLOR
January 8, 1917 — November 2, 1994

To the annual Veiled Prophet Ball children were not cordially invited. High up in the balcony, along with servants and poor relations, they were tolerated. . . . But generally speaking, children were expected to enjoy the Prophet's parade the night before and be content to go to bed without complaint on the night of the Ball. This was twenty-five years ago, of course. There is no telling what the practices are out there in St. Louis now. Children have it much better everywhere nowadays. Perhaps they flock to the Veiled Prophet's Ball by the hundred, and even go to the Statler Hotel for breakfast afterward.

—"Happy Families Are All Alike"

"To my brothers and sisters, as to my parents, the period in St. Louis represents a relatively brief interlude in their lives . . . They are vague about a lot of things that are very clear in my mind and they will ask me to refresh their memories about people and addresses and even events that took place in that period. For me, of course, almost the reverse is true since I lived there during those years of life when one is taking his measure of the world."

One of Peter Taylor's narrators makes this remark in a short story called "The End of Play," but we have every reason to believe that it also represents the feelings of its author.

And why shouldn't it? Although he was born in Trenton, Tennessee, in 1917, the family moved to Nashville when Taylor was seven, and then to St.

87

Louis in 1926 when he was nine. "Our removals were done always in the most thoroughgoing manner and on the grandest scale. We left behind not a sheet of paper or a picture or a single stick of Mother's heavy, mid-Victorian furniture. Every keepsake in the attic, every old toy any of us children ever had, every coal scuttle or garden tool in the cellar went with us." That could include black servants and dependent kinfolks, the manners and mores of the Old South, as well as a family history of considerable significance and intimidation.

Both of his grandfathers were named Robert Taylor, way ahead of the actor. On his mother's side, Robert Love Taylor of Happy Valley, Tennessee, went up the political ladder like a monkey: a congressman first, governor next, and finally senator—resting on each rung for several terms as if to survey the scene. On one occasion, he ran as a Democrat for governor against his Republican brother, Alf—winning uneasily—while, in the same election, their father stood as a token candidate on the prohibition ticket. Everyone was a lawyer and a politician including Peter Taylor's father, who, as a young graduate of Vanderbilt's law school, was elected speaker of the Tennessee House. His father's given name, "Hillsman," seemed to sum up a history.

First a lawyer for the firm and then its president, Hillsman Taylor came "way up North" to St. Louis to oversee the Missouri State Life Insurance Company and was soon making multimillion-dollar deals. "We lived in a huge, grand house on Washington Terrace, three stories and a basement." In Taylor's second book (the novella, *A Woman of Means*, 1950) the young narrator's life is changed when his father moves to St. Louis and the family fortunes shoot up like fireworks—father finds himself a vice president of his firm; he meets many charming and wealthy women; he joins chambers of commerce and country clubs; he has unaccustomed monies to spend and moves into a fashionable mansion—somewhat in the way Hillsman's world sparkled and brightened. Peter attended Miss Rossman's private school, where his accent provided amusement, and then went on to St. Louis Country Day. Hillsman was unaware that he had been sent to St. Louis by his partner, Rogers Caldwell (familiarly known as the "J. P. Morgan of the South"), so that his nose would have no opportunity to smell the rotten mess Caldwell was busy making in Nashville. The Crash of 1929 struck this flimsy financial empire a mortal blow, and its fall a year later took one hundred and twenty banks in seven southern states down with it. The Taylors were required to move again, this time to Memphis in 1932; meanwhile, Peter had spent six crucial years coming of age here.

Peter Taylor learned to prefer the world of women to that of "deadly practical things" of his father's world which endeavored to ignore "everything clever, gentle, and light." His mother tried to distribute her love among the children equally, but Peter tied himself to her, if not by apron strings, then by wrapping around himself the tales she told, continuing the oral tradition of southern storytelling that has been so vital to its writers. Peter would dedicate his volume of *Collected Stories* (1969) to his mother, Katherine Taylor Taylor, by insisting that she "was the best teller of tales I know" and that it was from her "lips I first heard many of the stories in this book." Naturally, they tended to be accounts of subordination and dispossession. "I found the Blacks being exploited by white women, and the white women being exploited by the white men."

The family's history dictated that Peter enroll in Vanderbilt University with the idea of eventually obtaining a degree in law, but he managed a scholarship to Columbia instead, where he planned to study writing. His father would not support such childish foolishness; Peter would not accept such fatherly tyranny. Father and son stopped speaking, and Peter, most romantically, worked his way to Europe on a freighter. When he returned he got a job on the *Memphis Commercial-Appeal*. Chance interfered with Destiny, because, when he started taking a few English courses at Southwestern University, in a sense across the street, his instructor was the poet Allen Tate, who filled Taylor finally with a sense of the writer's vocation.

I can't teach you anything you don't already know, Tate told him; in any case, I am off to lecture at Columbia, and I suggest you enroll in Vanderbilt after all, because that is where John Crowe Ransom is presently an instructor. Dutiful to his new father, Taylor did, but Ransom was also on the move, shortly taking a position at Kenyon College and founding the *Kenyon Review*. Taylor did another dropout—at which he was becoming accomplished—before finally entering Kenyon and failing the prelaw curriculum so thoroughly Hillsman had to let him make literature the law's new prerequisite. Among his classmates were the poets Randall Jarrell and Robert Lowell, who became his lifelong friends. After he graduated from Kenyon, Taylor visited the graduate program at Louisiana State where Robert Penn Warren and Cleanth Brooks were holding forth—fathers all— but abandoned any thought of scholarship for fiction finally in order to begin unburdening himself of his heritage by writing about it. "I went back years later to visit my sister who lived in St. Louis. The house had been torn down; even the basement was gone. There was just a great hole in the earth." It was as if the family had loaded up his childhood home like a steamer trunk to take it with them when they moved.

Peter Taylor would spend most of his writing life in the obscurity of excellence, though with the admiration of the few who formed his new family, and who called him the American Chekov behind his back, so as not to cause him embarrassment. Although the short story tends to doom one to public extinction, the *New Yorker* kept his work in front of a select set of eyes. Taylor had married the poet Eleanor Ross, and her literary circle enlarged his, so for discrimination's duties there were an ample number. Above all, his career should in no way resemble that of the law:

> I feel so strongly against professionalism, against someone's feeling he has to write a book every year to keep his name before the public. I see people pressing themselves, torturing themselves, for that, rather than writing out of a compulsion some story from their own experience, their own feelings.

Taylor published three collections of short pieces (*A Long Fourth* in 1948, *A Woman of Means* in 1950, and *The Widows of Thornton* in 1954) before he did his first full-length play, *Tennessee Day in St. Louis*, in 1957. Obedient to the classic unities, the play does indeed use up fewer than twenty-four hours. Just as Italian immigrants might commemorate the deeds of Garibaldi in their new country, these Tennesseeans are celebrating General Andrew Jackson's lopsided defeat of the British at the Battle of New Orleans on January 8, 1815, where he had under his command soldiers almost exclusively from the state, while achieving (as at Agincourt) an unbelievable ratio of seven home boys lost to two thousand of the enemy: deaths wholly unnecessary, a victory entirely hollow, since a treaty of peace had been signed in Washington two weeks before.

But the day has much personal significance for Taylor, since his parents were married on Tennessee Day, 1908, and he—a son and heir—was born on the same day in 1917. During the play, an adolescent of the family, Lanny Tolliver (Taylor), relinquishes his search for himself in a legendary past, and, in an ambiguous gesture, blows out the birthday candles numbering his age. The candles are burning in the present, but when the years they represent are extinguished so are their flames. A St. Louis television station did a production of it, which the author missed.

In 1973 Taylor published seven short "ghost plays" in a volume called *Presences*. The first three are set in St. Louis, but the settings are as ghostly as the action. An uncollected memoir story, "The End of Play," describes a political convention which an eleven-year-old imagines for his own amusement, although it is based upon the one he has heard described on the radio during the presidential campaign of 1932. The child invents a blowhard senator from Tennessee through whom he endeavors to dissuade his father from moving back to an ancestral home. Games are lost as well as won, and the game's inventor loses this one. That loss signifies the "end of play."

During a long and distinguished career, medals and prizes notwithstanding, Peter Taylor stayed modestly out of the light and admirably apart from commerce, pursuing his passion:

> I really don't think you should make money writing. Oh, I'm not going to turn down money, but people worrying about how they are going to make a living writing ought to worry about making a living some other way on the periphery, doing something congenial to them like teaching or editing. We hear a lot of complaints from writers now . . . about the situation of the writer—well, it's always been awful! I think you should write for yourself, for the joy of it, the pleasure of it, and for the satisfaction that you have in learning about your life.

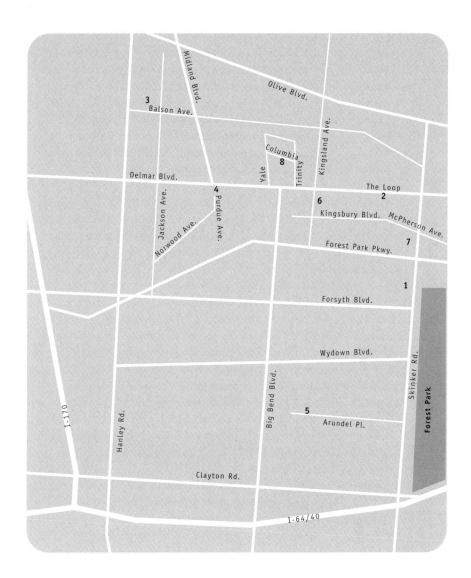

UNIVERSITY CITY & CLAYTON

1   Washington University, One Brookings Drive—Fannie Cook,
    Stanley Elkin, John Gardner, Emily Hahn, Fannie Hurst,
    William Inge, Josephine Johnson, Marianne Moore, John
    Morris, Howard Nemerov, Shirley Seifert, Kay Thompson,
    Constance Urdang, Tennessee Williams
2   St. Louis Walk of Fame, 6200-6600 Delmar Boulevard
3   University City High School, 7401 Balson Avenue—Tennessee
    Williams, Harold Brodkey
4   400 Purdue Avenue—Fannie Cook
5   53 Arundel Place—Tennessee Williams
6   504 Kingsland Avenue—Harold Brodkey
7   6334 McPherson Avenue—John Morris
8   6943 Columbia Place—Constance Urdang

Before the World's Fair had visitors, it had entrepreneurs. About the park's unbuilt edges they began to gather. Edward Gardner Lewis, a scheming dreamer from Connecticut, bought a tract of land to the northwest on Delmar Boulevard in 1902 and built there a publishing plant for his *Woman's Magazine* and several other publications. The present octagonal City Hall was originally the magazine's offices. Lewis was a borrower, and not merely of money. He would build a model city in the spirit of the City Beautiful movement; he would have a ziggurat, a Taj Mahal, a Parthenon; he did erect a gate with a lion atop one pillar and a tiger crouching on another, though the tiger was soon mistaken for the other lion's mate. Through its portals one entered University Heights, a subdivision which Lewis laid out himself, with its houses growing appropriately more modest as they were dotted farther down the hill.

Since Lewis had named his town University City (and not for its proximity to Washington University), its streets were named Cornell, Dartmouth, Princeton, Harvard and so on, but before they could appear— properly degreed, paved and gowned—they supported Camp Lewis, a tent city funded by him to furnish his magazine's subscribers a place to stay while visiting the fair. But Lewis was not the only enterprising opportunist. Julius Pitzman platted Parkview Place at Skinker and Millbrook in 1905, followed by Washington Heights in 1907 and what was called the Catlin Tract in 1909. These neighborhoods, conveniently close to the Delmar Loop, Forest Park and Washington University, became so attractive to writers and faculty that it is safe to say more authors live or lived in these private places than anywhere else in the region: Tennessee Williams for a time, Harold Brodkey, Stanley Elkin, John Morris, Howard Nemerov and Constance Urdang, to mention only a few whose deaths have made them eligible for inclusion in this guide.

Brodkey remembers:

> My mind was largely formed by U. City; my manners derived from the six or seven mansions on a high ridge, the three or four walled and gated neighborhoods of somewhat sternly genteel houses, the neighborhoods of almost all kinds of trim, well-taken-care-of small houses, of even very small houses with sharp gables and fanciful stonework, houses a door and two windows wide, with small, neat lawns; and from districts of two-family houses, streets of apartment houses—we lived in an apartment house—from which rows of trees, the branches of which met over the streets, from the scattered vacant lots, the unbuilt-on fields, the woods, and the enormous and architecturally grandiose schools.

The Delmar Loop in University City is also the location of the St. Louis Walk of Fame, a brainchild of local businessman Joe Edwards, owner of Blueberry Hill.

88

In 1853 Washington University was the Eliot Seminary, and it lived downtown at Seventeenth and St. Charles Streets. By 1894 the university finally convinced itself to become important and planned a campus on high ground just west of Forest Park. An impressive, castle-like building whose central arch was to be the entrance to the campus was built in 1901 and the library, just behind it, in 1902. These structures were initially leased to the Louisiana Purchase Exposition, which used them for administrative offices and meeting rooms. Brookings and Bixby Halls were therefore not occupied by the university until 1905.

Particularly after the Second World War, colleges and universities all over the country began establishing writing programs that served to support poets and novelists of all kinds, and provide pre-professional training in the literary arts. These programs have remained popular, and now there are writers at work at Saint Louis University, Webster University, the University of Missouri in St. Louis, several community colleges as well as Fontbonne and nearby Southern Illinois University at Edwardsville and Carbondale.

It was Washington University, however, that attracted the largest number of authors, either in the bud as students, like John Gardner, Fannie Hurst and Tennessee Williams, or as faculty, such as Stanley Elkin, John Morris and Howard Nemerov. It was also instrumental, over the years, in bringing many writers for readings, lectures and symposia, to the city. In time it established a graduate writing program that Constance Urdang initially directed. Washington University's Olin Library has assembled an important collection of contemporary manuscripts and letters by its faculty and authors as varied as Samuel Beckett, Elizabeth Bishop, Ford Madox Ford, Denise Levertov, James Merrill and May Swenson.

The academic support of literature, through patronage, teaching and scholarship, has been of incalculable value, but the writing and the writers it sustains tend to keep to the campus, so the wider community does not profit as much from their presence as it might.

88. Washington University quadrangle, c. 1920

When you bother about how the Cropperville families will live, you are being a pastor to your people, but when you go out and organize unions and train other men to head them, then you are being a leader for your people. You must think the situation through and decide whether you want to be a Moses or a minister.
—Fannie Cook in a letter to Owen Whitfield, 1942

Writer Fannie Cook was an activist who took on many of the social injustices of her era—and ours—including race relations and, in particular, the mostly black sharecroppers who were being evicted without pay from the land they worked. On January 10, 1939, hundreds of croppers staged a protest by camping along two major highways in southern Missouri. They were led by Owen Whitfield, a black preacher and union organizer. When Fannie heard about the incident, she visited the Urban League of St. Louis, where she met Whitfield, and invited him to a meeting with white and black citizens, out of which they formed the St. Louis Committee for the Rehabilitation of Sharecroppers, electing Fannie Cook, who was white, as their leader.

In the spring of 1939, Cook made arrangements to stay with a family in East Prairie, Missouri, in order to research a book about sharecroppers that would "depict all sides fairly." She witnessed firsthand the terrible conditions in which they lived and wrote about them in her 1941 novel *Boot-Heel Doctor.* She convinced the St. Louis Committee to purchase ninety-four acres of land to be used as a refuge for more than four hundred of the evicted sharecroppers. They called this community Cropperville. Fannie Cook would devote considerable time to this experiment over the next ten years.

Fannie Cook was born on October 4, 1893, in St. Charles, graduated from the University of Missouri in 1912 and received a master's at Washington University in 1916. She published her first piece in *St. Nicholas* magazine when she was seven, and later short stories and verse. Her first novel, *The Hills Grow Steeper,* was published in 1938. A black person's place in the world—and Missouri—would be a recurring theme in her books. Her 1946 novel, *Mrs. Palmer's Honey,* is set in the Ville, which was the premiere black neighborhood in north St. Louis between 1920 and 1950.

> . . . the Ville . . . lay a little north of the exact center. Once it had been Elleardsville, a suburb, but the metropolis had grown around the region as a tree will in time encompass a foreign body, and now no one living there ever thought of it as anything but the Ville, part of the fabric, part of the city.
>
> Few white people ever thought of it at all. Few knew it was there. Though several miles long and several wide, the Ville remained obscure and lived secretly. Streetcars and busses ran along its boundaries as if afraid or too incurious to enter.
>
> Prospering white people lived miles west, where the fabric began to fray into large estates, small farms, emerald golf courses. Vaguely they believed St. Louis had but one colored district, the be-taverned crisscross of shabby

streets near Union Station. Observing that region's slatternly ways, they would at times consider sending their dark-skinned cooks to a clinic for tests and treatment.

Houses in the Ville were low—cottages with slanted attics. Suburban trees were still to be seen, and suburban fences around the small front lawns. . . . Unlike a white folks' neighborhood, however, the Ville did not pivot around a central shopping district. Instead there was a campus worn bare by the great American game of baseball. Flanking the campus were handsome modern brick buildings which the Ville would have regarded with pride had it been able to take pride in a handsome insult.

The buildings were for black folks set aside to live separately. They housed a Negro high school, a Negro grade school, a school for doubly handicapped children—both Negro and blind or deaf or lame—Negro teachers' college, a Negro city hospital. Indoors were jobs and learning and cures, fine gifts ungraciously given and ungraciously received. . . .

The Ville was a city within a city.

Mrs. Palmer's Honey went on to win the first George Washington Carver Novel Award for an outstanding literary contribution that shows "the importance of the Negro's place in American life." Cook won this award over black writer Chester Himes. Her other books are the aforementioned *Boot-Heel Doctor*, which she dedicated to Josephine Johnson "for reasons the Missouri Sharecroppers will understand," and *The Long Bridge*, published in 1949.

Cook continued to head the committee—she even met with first lady Eleanor Roosevelt to discuss the sharecropper situation in Missouri. She resigned ten years after Owen Whitfield led the first protest.

Fannie Cook and her husband, Jerome Cook, a physician, lived at 7068 Maryland, had two sons and later moved to 400 Purdue, where they were living when Fannie suffered a fatal stroke on August 25, 1949.

The following day the *St. Louis Star-Times* published this editorial:

> Courage is the word for Fannie Cook, the St. Louis novelist, artist, reformer who died yesterday. It isn't simply that she dared to be different and to court unpopularity by serving her beliefs, though this

89

she did. It is that she saw so clearly the corroding effects of fear and the galvanizing effects of courage on the human spirit.

Fear, Fannie Cook saw, spawns prejudices, discrimination, injustice, persecution, violence and war. These, in turn, breed more fear and more reasons for fear.

Courage, to Fannie Cook, meant seeing the ugly facts, understanding them, doing something about them.

Owen Whitfield moved to Illinois in 1950, and Cropperville began to shrink. In 1964 the Southeast Missouri Baptist Fellowship purchased thirty-eight acres of Cropperville for only one dollar, and in 1975, with disputes over the proper use of the land, the fellowship acquired the rest of Cropperville for ten dollars. Owen Whitfield's house still stands.

TENNESSEE WILLIAMS
March 26, 1911 — February 25, 1983

Blue is such a delicate piece of paper.
—"Intimations"

In the twenty-eight years that Washington University professor William G. B. Carson taught English XVI, a course in playwriting, approximately eighty-four one-acts were selected for production. Each year three plays were chosen to be staged by Thyrsus, the drama club, the following year. Among "Pop" Carson's 1936-37 academic roster was twenty-six-year-old Tom Williams, who rarely attended class. When he did, he brought with him compelling character sketches of his mother and sister, which Carson would read with great spirit to the class, and with much praise for the author. When it came time to pick that year's plays, it was generally assumed that Williams's entry would resemble the work he had brought in over the course of the semester. Instead, the pre-"Tennessee" Williams submitted *Me, Vashya*:

Vashya: . . . people don't understand my career. Some of them—well, you know!—they call me horrible names. They accuse me of being a war-profiteer. They say I've grown fat off of carrion flesh. They call me a—a vulture! Is that true, Doctor? Haven't I been completely justified in everything that I have done for my country?

Dr.: Your justification, Sir Vashya, is your country's *need!*

Vashya: My—? Yes, my country's *need!* They needed ammunition. I gave it to them, didn't I? They needed tanks, airplanes, gases, subterranean explosives, volcane rockets! I gave it to them! They needed the new death ray, didn't they?

And I supplied them with that. That's my justification, Doctor. I gave them what they needed! (HE BREATHES HEAVILY WITH EXCITEMENT) Yes, that's my justification, my country's need!

Classmate A. E. Hotchner reports that after the play was read aloud there was "considerable half-suppressed laughter." The judges ranked *Me, Vashya* third, but, according to Carson, gave it an honorable mention because they did not think that the role of Mrs. Vashya could be properly cast. Williams, thirty years later, called it "a terrible shock and humiliation . . . a cruel blow. I had always thought I was shy, but I discarded all humility. I stormed into Carson's office. (He was a good professor.) I screamed at him. I surprised myself."

Me, Vashya is not listed among the plays of Tennessee Williams, and he does not mention his year at Washington University in his highly selective *Memoirs*, published in 1975. The St. Louis lacunae have kept his biographers busy: Donald Spoto in his 1985 *The Kindness of Strangers* and Lyle Leverich in *Tom: The Unknown Tennessee Williams*, published in 1995.

90

Thomas Lanier Williams III was born on March 26, 1911, in Columbus, Mississippi, to Cornelius Coffin ("C. C.") Williams and Edwina Dakin Williams, the only daughter of Rosina and the Reverend Walter Dakin, an Episcopal pastor. Edwina gave birth to her first child, Rose Isabel, on November 17, 1909, at her father's rectory, where her second child, Tom, was also born. She moved herself and her children as her parents changed parishes from Mississippi to Tennessee and back to Mississippi. C. C. Williams was a traveling salesman, visiting only on weekends, which seemed to suit Edwina, particularly after a few years of marriage.

The summer of 1918, however, brought the family together, when C. C. Williams accepted a position at the International Shoe Company in St. Louis. After spending a brief period in a boardinghouse on Lindell, Miss Edwina moved the family to 4633 Westminster Place. In a 1955 biographical note, Williams described it as

a perpetually dim little apartment in a wilderness of identical brick and concrete structures with no grass and no trees nearer than the park. In the

90. *Staff of* Eliot Review, *1937. Williams is on the far left, in the front row. A. E. Hotchner stands in the back row, far right.*

South we had never been conscious of the fact that we were economically less fortunate than others. We lived as well as anyone else. But in St. Louis we suddenly discovered there were two kinds of people, the rich and the poor, and that we belonged more to the latter. If we walked far enough west we came into a region of fine residences set in beautiful lawns. But where we lived, to which we must always return, were ugly rows of apartment buildings the color of dried blood and mustard. If I had been born to the situation I might not have resented it deeply. But it was forced upon my consciousness at the most sensitive age of childhood. It produced a shock and a rebellion that has grown into an inherent part of my work. It was the beginning of the social-consciousness which I think has marked most of my writing. I am glad that I received this bitter education for I don't think any writer has much purpose back of him unless he feels bitterly the inequities of the society he lives in.

The place is now called the Glass Menagerie Apartments in his honor, but another of the family residences would be the setting of his famous play.

91

Tom Williams had nearly died of diphtheria just a year before, and having entered first grade at Eugene Field Elementary School on Olive Street, he suffered classmates who made fun of his syrupy southern accent, his size and his excruciating shyness. He was also missing his beloved sister, Rose, who had stayed behind with their grandparents in Mississippi. They all came to St. Louis for the birth of Walter Dakin Williams on February 21,

1919. Things improved slightly. He and Rose could play and, with the onset of summer, he recalled, "We were only a block away from the Lorelei swimming pool and the West End Lyric movie and we had bicycle races about the block." However, his parents' marriage had become a minefield: Cornelius disliked his desk job, Edwina her placement in the social class.

In 1922 the family moved to a "sunnier" apartment on Taylor and Laclede (the Lyndon) and Tom entered Stix School on Euclid. By now his parents had separate bedrooms, Rose was entirely ignored by her father and Tom had retreated to his room to create illustrated stories, which his mother encouraged by buying him his first typewriter.

In the winter of 1924 everyone packed up for 5938 Cates Street, so that Rose could enter Soldan High School and Tom a first-rate progressive school, Ben Blewett Junior High. Tom published his first story, "Isolated," in the school newspaper, *Junior Life*, and later other stories and poems. By the time he graduated he was known as "Tom Williams—Our literary boy." His father thought writing was "a lot of foolishness, especially poetry writing."

The family moved again, into a cramped apartment at 6254 Enright Avenue in University City—now demolished—so that Tom could attend University City High School. This is the apartment building that would serve as the model for the tenement in *The Glass Menagerie*, with its fire escape stoop that was the apartment's front door. He would tap the city and his family further for this 1944 play.

Williams began publishing more seriously and received his first compensation for his literary efforts, thirty-five dollars, when *Weird Tales* published "The Vengeance of Nitocris," a story about the Egyptian queen described for us by Herodotus. Father was not impressed by this first-time publication and also did not like it that Tom was seeing a girl, even though he had called his son "Miss Nancy." His father would continue to be disappointed. An alcoholic, he bullied his wife, ignored his daughter, and pennypinched Tom and his education. Miss Edwina later wrote in her own book, *Remember Me to Tom*, that "Cornelius loved two breathing things: Dakin and the dog in the house."

If the family produced the first tragedy then "The Williamses of St. Louis" had a long run. Rose, pretty as a gin fizz, had gentlemen callers who did not call again; her malady was not a gimpy leg but a bonafide madness which would later be diagnosed as schizophrenia. She, like Tennessee later, would not only do time at Barnes Hospital, but also at the state mental hospital in Farmington on the insulin therapy table, the shock treatment of choice in the 1930s. In 1943 she underwent one of the first lobotomies performed in the United States. It succeeded in subduing her and ensured that she would remain institutionalized for the rest of her life.

Like Laura Wingfield of *The Glass Menagerie*, Rose could not get the hang of typing. They both failed at the Rubicam Business College. Both passed the time they should have been in class in Forest Park "in the art museum and the bird-houses at the zoo. . . . and . . . in the Jewel-box, that big glass house where they raise the tropical flowers." Neither could get a word in edgewise with their mother. Miss Edwina becomes Amanda Wingfield, both of whom are members of the D.A.R. Tom Wingfield is a poet, and the gentleman caller Jim O'Connor is Jim Connor, a colleague of Tom's at the International Shoe Factory—"The play is memory."

Williams graduated from University City High in 1929 and, having written regularly for the school newspaper while continuing to write poetry as well as stories, thought that journalism might be a wise course of study. He entered the University of Missouri in Columbia, the oldest journalism school in the United States, in September, pledged Alpha Tau Omega and impressed not a few on campus with his publishing résumé. In 1930 he wrote his first play, *Beauty is the Word,* and had stories in *Columns,* the student literary journal. He also took ROTC at his father's insistence. He was much more devoted to his writing than to his classes at Mizzou and found the technical side of journalism—layout, for example—not to his liking, but not quite as bad as ROTC, which he flunked.

So began his career in the "celotex interior," the International Shoe Company, where his father, who had forced him to withdraw from school, got him a job—a semi-precious commodity during the depression. Through history's filter, Tennessee would describe the events differently:

> I entered college during the great Depression and after a couple years I couldn't afford to continue but had to drop out and take a clerical job in the shoe company that employed my father. The two years I spent in that corporation were indescribable torment to me as an individual but of immense value to me as a writer for they gave me first-hand knowledge of what it means to be a small wage-earner in a hopelessly routine job.

Williams had Sundays off, and he spent them in the Mercantile Library where he "read voraciously...I would have a thirty-five cent lunch at a pleasant little restaurant. And I would go home in a 'service car'—to concentrate upon the week's short story. Of course all of Sunday was devoted to the story's completion. . . . During the weekdays I would work on verse . . .":

> I have seen them earlier than morning cross the hall,
> serious-eyed and weighted down by schoolbooks,
> as if alarm clocks set at premature hours
> had roused them from sleep before it let them go . . .
> I have seen their pencil-mark distinctions between this thing
> and that one
> their blue angles, sharper than gymnastics.
> In Jack-o'-Lantern's weather,
> their orderly, schoolteachered troop to the Sunflower River
> for an inspection of Flora along these banks
> where blacks in white shifts held springtime baptismals,
> Ha, ha! — shouting . . .
> I have seen them
> never less than azure-eyed and earnest
> tackle
> geometry problems whose Q. E. D.
> is surely speechless wonder . . .

He began to place his poetry nationally in *Poetry, Inspiration, Counterpoint* and *L'Alouette*. He had other stories appear while he tried to crack *Story* magazine and met some of the characters in his plays. Jim Connor, who was a fraternity brother, joined him at the shoe company; Stanley Kowalski worked in the warehouse. Tom took walks in the evening on Delmar, "that long, long street which probably began near the Mississippi River in downtown St. Louis and continued through University City and on out into the county."

In 1933 Tom won First Prize at St. Louis Writers Guild for his story "Stella for Star." The judge was Josephine Johnson, who two years later would win the Pulitzer Prize for her novel *Now in November*. In his letter of thanks, Williams deprecated his effort but said that he had attempted "to create a single, poetic effect and I think I may have succeeded a little in doing that."

Another year, another move, this time to 6634 Pershing, which must have seemed palatial after living on the set of *The Glass Menagerie*. Having suffered a providential heart palpitation episode, Tom was told by his family doctor to quit his job, and so he was finally allowed to attend Washington University. Clark Wills McBurney was taking graduate courses there and introduced Williams to Rimbaud, Rilke and Hart Crane, who became his literary soulmate. He loved him so much that he couldn't part with the university's copy of Crane's collected poems. Through McBurney, who published under the name Clark Mills, Tom met William Jay Smith, and the literary scene was set. The goal was to Get Published, and they did, organizing a chapter of the College Poetry Society of America. He began submitting his poetry to the *Eliot Review*, contributing twenty "perfectly crafted" poems, according to Eliot editor John Pickering, ones that were "deeply felt (in a late adolescent way), conventionally designed, and yet subtly revealing of the themes he was to develop in his plays." He won The Wednesday Club's First Prize for "Sonnets for the Spring" and a prize from the Webster Groves Theatre Guild for his play *The Magic Tower*. Williams's name was now becoming known in St. Louis, and among the theatre folk, too. Willard Holland, the director of the Mummers, mounted the first production of a Williams play, *Candles to the Sun*, followed by *Fugitive Kind*:

> The Mummers of St. Louis were my professional youth. They were the disorderly theater group of St. Louis, standing socially, if not also artistically, opposite to the usual Little Theatre group . . . [which was] eminently respectable, predominantly middle-aged, and devoted mainly to the presentation of Broadway hits a season or two after Broadway . . . Dynamism was what The Mummers had, and for about five years—roughly from about 1935 to 1940—they burned like one of Miss Millay's improvident little candles—then expired. Yes, there was about them that kind of excessive romanticism which is youth and which is the best and purest part of life.

Fugitive Kind was presented at The Wednesday Club on November 30, 1937. The reviews were mixed. Colvin McPherson, drama critic of the *St. Louis Post-Dispatch*, claimed that it "had no plot arising out of its situation and all considered, [it] is a weak play." This enraged Williams who, as in the

Vashya incident, did not take criticism well. (This occupational hazard would prove to be very hazardous indeed.) Other reviews, however, were more generous. "While less intense than his *Candles to the Sun*," wrote Reed Hynds in the *Star-Times*, "[it is] a consistent, vital and absorbing play . . . one making a step forward for the young St. Louisan." (*Fugitive Kind* was originally titled *Battle of Angels*, retitled *Orpheus Descending* for the New York stage production and then changed back to *Fugitive Kind* for the movie.)

Williams finally got his degree in theatre from the University of Iowa in 1938, and shortly after "Tennessee" was born when he sent a play to the Group Theatre contest under this name. He was in Memphis on his way to New Orleans, the city in which he could begin to direct his own fate rather than have it thrust on him by the family of Furies in St. Louis. He would have to return regularly to St. Louis, "the place I dread," however, over the next forty-five years.

92

While visiting during the Christmas holidays in 1944 on his way to Chicago for rehearsals of his new play, *The Glass Menagerie*, the drama critic for the *St. Louis Star-Times*, William Inge, himself an aspiring playwright, interviewed Williams, beginning a stormy relationship that included an intense affair when Inge visited Williams in Chicago for the play's premiere.

Tennessee Williams was out but not in St. Louis: "I was late coming out, and when I did it was one hell of a bang."

The Glass Menagerie was a critical and financial success, and Tennessee Williams would have others with *A Streetcar Named Desire*, which won the Pulitzer Prize in 1948 and in 1955 for *Cat on a Hot Tin Roof*. His lights would burn very brightly in these decades of awards but it would not be repeated, to his extreme disappointment. He would, however, have more of his plays made into movies than any other American playwright. He would also become almost as famous for his chemical dependencies and his hatred of St. Louis, especially as described in his *Memoirs*. In 1968 his brother Dakin checked him into Barnes Hospital:

> I was put in the Queen's division—and I didn't make up that name, that's just what it's called. It is the rather posh division for the "mildly disturbed." I was placed in the "care" of three neurologists and an internist . . . in comes Dakin, grinning with a bunch of yellow flowers. . . . Mother marched in, a little Prussian officer in drag. . . . I lit into her with a vengeance.
>
> "Why do women bring children into the world and then destroy them?"
>
> (I still consider that a rather good question.)
>
> Clutching the flight bag that contained my booze, my vial of speed, clutching it despairingly and tightly. I was strapped into the chair and rocketed out of Queen's Division to Friggins' Violent Ward—there the flight bag was snatched from me, and at this point I blacked out . . . The truth is that I don't really want to go back over the time in Friggins Division of Barnacle Hospital in the city of St. Pollution.

Going cold turkey saved his life but not his love for his brother.

With the success of *The Glass Menagerie*, Williams saw to it that Miss Edwina received half of the play's royalties. This sustained her for the rest of her life and allowed her to move to Clayton. She kicked out C. C., who died an old alcoholic in 1957 in Knoxville. Williams also provided for Rose, removing her from Farmington to a mental institution in Ossining, New York, in 1948. Miss Edwina died in 1980 at the age of ninety-five. For her funeral he imported two thousand English violets to cover her coffin, on which was placed a ribbon that read, "Love from Tom."

After many invitations from Washington University and the refusal of their honorary degree, Tennessee Williams did finally return in 1977 to give a talk in Graham Chapel. He said that his "only happy times . . . [in St. Louis] were at Washington University."

Tennessee Williams died on February 25, 1983, in a New York hotel room. The cause of death was asphyxiation, presumably by a medicine bottle cap found in his mouth. Against his wishes, Dakin Williams buried him in Calvary Cemetery, next to Miss Edwina. His stone reads, "Poet Playwright" and Rose's, who joined him in 1996, "Blow Out Your Candles, Laura."

Dakin Williams continues to live in Collinsville, Illinois.

3. *The Paper Lantern*

My sister was quicker at everything than I.

At five she could say the multiplication tables
    with barely a pause for breath,
    while I was employed
with frames of colored beads in Kindy Garden.

At eight she could play
               Idillio and The Scarf Dance
while I was chopping at scales and exercises.

At fifteen my sister
         no longer waited for me,
impatiently at the White Star Pharmacy corner
    but plunged headlong
    into the discovery, Love!

Then vanished completely—

for love's explosion, defined as early madness,
consumingly shone in her transparent heart for a season
and burned it out, a tissue-paper lantern!

        —torn from a string!
        —tumbled across a pavilion!

flickering three times, almost seeming to cry . . .
My sister was quicker at everything than I.

                —"Recuerdo"

WILLIAM INGE
May 3, 1913 — June 10, 1973

About the time St. Louis–born playwright Zoë Akins quit New York playhouses for the sound stages of Hollywood, a topical shift was taking place in American theatre from drawing room melodramas to stark tales of small-town life as portrayed by writers like Arthur Miller, Thornton Wilder, Tennessee Williams and William Inge. Inge was certainly not the first to move his scenes into kitchens and backyards, but in contrast to the rosy, folksy souls that populate works like Rodgers and Hammerstein's *Oklahoma!*, Inge's midwesterners were scrupulously examined by their creator, and their sociological and psychological pores magnified for audience review.

William Motter Inge was born in Independence, Kansas, on May 3, 1913. The youngest of Luther Clayton Inge and Maude Sarah Gibson's five children, he displayed an early interest in theatre and excelled at recitation. Luther Inge worked in his father's dry-goods business and later became a traveling salesman for the Wheeler and Motter Dry Goods Company of St. Louis, leaving his wife and children alone during the week; now and then he was absent for an entire month. This void, along with the death of three-year-old Irene and oldest son Luther, led to Maude Inge's "nervous matriarchy" over her remaining three children, especially her sensitive and introspective youngest son, whom they called Billy.

As a young man, Inge attended touring plays in Kansas City and acted in theatrical groups during his summers off from college at the University of Kansas, where he studied speech, drama and English literature. He hoped to move to New York to pursue an acting career following his graduation in 1935, but, lacking funds and prospects in the midst of the depression, he accepted a scholarship for graduate school at Peabody Teachers College in Nashville in 1938 and earned a master's degree in drama. Inge then joined the faculty of Stephens College for Women in Columbia, Missouri, where he taught English composition and theatre for five years. As the plays produced at Stephens had more male roles than Stephens had men, Inge acted in numerous productions during his tenure, while writing short stories, poetry and fragments of plays.

Though he found teaching rewarding, Inge's ambition was to write. He moved to St. Louis in 1943 to take a temporary position on the staff of the *St. Louis Star-Times* as the paper's art critic—a vacancy left when Reed Hynds was drafted. (Inge had a deferment.) Inge called his time in St. Louis "probably the best period of my life." He initially took a room at the Coronado Hotel on Lindell Boulevard but soon moved to an apartment at 1213 North Seventh Avenue in Neighborhood Gardens, an architecturally

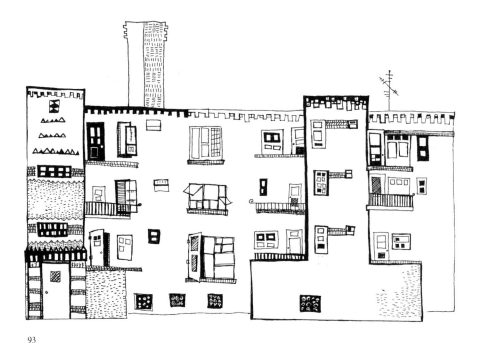

93

distinctive cluster of three-story buildings considered one of the first high-rise, privately developed housing projects in St. Louis.

Inge was industrious as the cultural critic-at-large; he covered plays, musical events, films, art exhibitions, books and even night-club entertainment in more than four hundred signed pieces for the *Star-Times* between June 15, 1943, and February 9, 1946. Liberation from the cloister of Columbia appealed to Inge greatly and, though his colleagues reported that he was usually at his desk by 7 A.M. "working like hell," they also noted that "he always looked like he had a hangover."

Soon Inge began to receive feature assignments. In December 1944 he conducted an interview for a "home-town boy makes good" article on Tennessee Williams, in town visiting his family before Chicago rehearsals for *The Glass Menagerie*. The resulting interview, reports Williams's biographer Donald Spoto, "was full of inaccuracies, half-truths, and Williams's typical alterations of personal history," but it also clearly reflects Inge's admiration for a man with whom he had much in common. While covering the Chicago opening of *Menagerie* over New Year's Eve, Inge and Williams had an affair, and in awe of *The Glass Menagerie*, Inge confided his playwriting aspirations to Williams, who offered him encouragement and a model for his work; Inge knew he could do the same with his own biography.

In his excitement about his new friendship, Inge apparently forgot to report on *Menagerie*'s Chicago run—his review for the *Star-Times* appeared on April 3, four days after the play's Broadway debut. But it was a period of feverish writing nonetheless, for within three months of his visit to Chicago, Inge had composed his first play, *Farther Off From Heaven*, and sent it off to Williams for review. While Williams's response was favorable,

Audrey Wood, the New York agent to whom he forwarded the manuscript, was less impressed, but she encouraged Inge to continue submitting work to her.

By this time Reed Hynds had returned to the *Star-Times*, and so Inge took a position at Washington University, teaching in the Department of English and directing productions of Thyrsus, the student drama club. He moved to 6168 McPherson Avenue and began work on another play, *Front Porch*. His friendship with Tennessee Williams provided him with an introduction to Margo Jones, a theatrical producer based in Dallas who liked his play very much, and included it in her summer season. The Gulf Oil Theatre opened *Farther Off From Heaven* in June 1947, and the production was lauded in New York's *Morning Telegraph*. Inge also negotiated a production of *Front Porch* with the Morse Players in St. Louis's Toy Theatre. This work would later be rewritten, renamed *Picnic* and awarded the Pulitzer Prize in 1955. But it did not go over well in St. Louis: the critic for the *Post-Dispatch*, Myles Standish, called it a "dull drama, one that almost dies on its feet in the first act," upon its opening in February 1948.

In March Inge entered Alcoholics Anonymous. He was thirty-five and his commitment to drama and playwriting had not yet been rewarded with acclaim. The tone and language of A.A.'s tenets resonated with him, however, and he threaded the experience of drying out into a one-act play which became a full-length work, *Come Back, Little Sheba*. This story about a man recovering from alcoholism was "my first experience at the play's writing me instead of my writing the play," Inge said of it later. His confidence was confirmed—Margo Jones, Tennessee Williams and Audrey Wood all loved the work. *Come Back, Little Sheba* was optioned by New York's Theatre Guild. Inge left St. Louis for New York in July 1949.

The gamble of his venture was rewarded, for *Sheba* previewed in Westport, Connecticut, on September 12 to bravos; however, stricken with anxiety about the play's move to Broadway, Inge entered a sanitarium for analysis and treatment for alcoholism—"I knew I was not meeting success in the expected way," he noted later. He exited clean but, showing the strains of a depression that would pursue him throughout his life, could not bring himself to go to the Booth Theatre for the New York opening. He need not have worried. The Drama Critics Circle named him the "most promising playwright" of the season, and *Sheba* won its star, Shirley Booth, a Tony and an Oscar for the 1952 movie version with Burt Lancaster.

Inge's next three plays were also successful. *Picnic* (produced in St. Louis as *Front Porch*) opened in New York in 1953, ran for 485 performances, and won every major theatre award: the Pulitzer, the New York Drama Critics Award and the Outer Circle Award. Inge's next work, *Bus Stop*, premiered in March 1955 and ran for thirteen months. In the filmed version of the play, the character of Cherie became one of Marilyn Monroe's most celebrated roles—given their histories it is not surprising that Monroe and Inge remained friends after the film's completion. *The Dark at the Top of the Stairs*, a work about a wife, her traveling salesman husband and her young, effeminate son (the play originally produced in 1945 as *Farther Off From*

94

Heaven), opened in 1957, directed by Elia Kazan. As Inge expanded Broadway's subject matter to deal with the troubled states of mind and un-realized longings of residents of the rural Midwest, his name began to be linked with Tennessee Williams and Arthur Miller as the premiere play-wrights of the decade. Brooks Atkinson of the *New York Times* wrote in 1953, "Mr. Inge knows his characters so well that you cannot distinguish them from the drama. Inge seems to have no personal point of view, but only a knowledge of people and an instinct for the truth of the world they live in."

These works—all lucrative, highly acclaimed by critics and made into movies—were followed by three plays that failed: *A Loss of Roses* in 1959, *Natural Affection* in 1963 and *Where's Daddy?* in 1966. Inge won his last award, an Oscar for best original film script, in 1961 for *Splendor in the Grass*, but he never regained the praise of theatre critics or the prestige of his former professional position. In 1964 he moved to Los Angeles, taught intermittently at University of California-Irvine, and wrote occasional pieces for television. He published the novel *Good Luck, Miss Wyckoff* in 1970 and *My Son Is a Splendid Driver*, "a novel in the form of a memoir," in 1971. Neither received favorable reviews. The man who began his writing career as a critic died of carbon monoxide poisoning, behind the wheel of his car, on June 10, 1973. On a table in the living room of his house was an unopened envelope containing the typescript of his latest novel, *The Boy from the Circus*, and a rejection from a New York publisher.

94. William Inge outside his apartment at the Dakota in New York City, c. 1950

CHERIE   Where I went to school, we din read no Shakespeare
              till the ninth grade. In the ninth grade everyone read Julius
              Caesar. I only got as far as the eighth. I seen Marlon Brando in
              the movie, though. I sure do like that Marlon Brando.

DR. LYMAN   (*Now that CHERIE has called attention to herself*)
              Madam, where is thy Lochinvar?

CHERIE (*Giggling*)   I don't understand anything you say, but I just
              love the way you say it.

DR. LYMAN   And *I* . . . understand *every*thing I say . . . but privately
              despise the way I say it.

CHERIE (*Giggling*)   That's so cute. (*A memory returns*) I had a very
              nice friend once that recited poetry.

DR. LYMAN   (*With spoofing seriousness*)   Whatever could have
              happened to him?

CHERIE   I dunno. He left town. His name was Mr. Everett
              Brubaker. He sold second-hand cars at the corner of Eighth
              and Wyandotte. He had a lovely Pontiac car-with-the-top-
              down. He talked nice, but I guess he really wasn't nicer'n any
              of the others.

DR. LYMAN   The others?

CHERIE   Well . . . ya meet quite a few men in the place I worked at,
              the Blue Dragon night club, out by the stockyards. Ever heard
              of it?

DR. LYMAN   No, and I deeply regret the fact.

                                                            —*Bus Stop*

JOHN G. NEIHARDT

January 8, 1881 — November 3, 1973

*My friend, I am going
to tell you the story of
my life, as you wish;
and if it were only the story of my life I think I would not
tell it; for what is one man that he should make much of
his winters, even when they bend him like a heavy snow?
So many other men have lived and shall live that story, to
be grass upon the hills.*

—Black Elk Speaks

95

John Greenleaf (later changed to Gneisenau) Neihardt
was born on a farm in Sharpsburg, Illinois, on January
8, 1881. Shortly after, his parents, Nicholas and Alice
May Culler, moved to western Kansas City, then to
Kansas and finally to Nebraska—the state that would
name him its Poet Laureate in 1921. It was in Missouri
that John Neihardt had a fever vision that would make
William Blake proud. It spoke to him of poetry and
produced a literary charismatic of the pantheistic variety. Observing the flooding of the Missouri River with
his father, who had, after all, assigned him his original
middle name after the American poet, led Neihardt to a cosmogony: "I had
caught my first glimpse into the infinite. I was six years old."

He began to compose on the epic model after Tennyson and the
Aeneid. He even wrote of a camp revival meeting in the *Tentiad*. Neihardt
was nineteen when he vanity-published *The Divine Enchantment* in 1900.
Vanity also led him to destroy it as evidence in "the case of posterity"
against John G. Neihardt. Posterity should know that although Neihardt
lived in poverty his early years, because of his great intellect and scientific
mind he was allowed to go directly from elementary school to college in
Nebraska, where he majored in physics.

A budding Herodotus, Neihardt, in his youth, interviewed pioneers
migrating west and visited the Native American settlements on the outskirts of Kansas City. He became obsessed with documenting the frontier
and its inhabitants; this obsession produced more than thirty books of poetry, stories, essays and catalogues of the adventures and misadventures of
explorers, trappers and the Native Americans in the westward expansion.

St. Louis frequently appears as a backdrop to Neihardt's conception of
the definitive American experience. His magnum opus, a five-part epic
poem entitled *A Cycle of the West* (begun in 1912 and completed in 1941), includes this early stanza:

> Behold them starting northward, if you can.
> Dawn flares across the Mississippi's tide;
> A tumult runs along the waterside
> Where, scenting an event, St. Louis throngs.

—"The Song of Three Friends"

95. John Neihardt, c. 1920

Neihardt composed some of the epic during his stay in St. Louis from 1926 to 1938, when he was the literary editor for the *St. Louis Post-Dispatch*. As an outspoken critic of political and social conditions, he rejoiced in the paper's liberal leanings. His editor, George S. Johns (the father of poet Orrick Johns), gave him only one stipulation: not to commercialize. "You could not get me to commercialize for all Pulitzer's money," he replied. He enjoyed working for the paper and wrote many well-respected essays and reviews during his tenure. He reviewed the work of Gerard Manley Hopkins, Willa Cather, Robert Frost, Ernest Hemingway, W. B. Yeats and A. A. Milne, and defended James Joyce against the censors. He confessed to his readers that he was a "mystic" while reviewing the *Prophet* by Khalil Gibran. He also reviewed Orrick Johns's *Wild Plum* and the work of Sara Teasdale and Eugene Field. He was generally good to the locals. Urban life, however, never really suited him—whenever work on the poem came to a standstill he would grumble about the city, branding it a "scurvy civilization" or "damned money-trap."

In 1931 Neihardt requested a leave of absence to travel west and conduct research for a poem about the massacre at Wounded Knee. While in South Dakota he befriended an Oglala Sioux Holy Man called Black Elk, a cousin of Crazy Horse revered by his people as a prophet. Black Elk responded to Neihardt's gifts and inquiries by claiming that he had been sent to transcribe his visions and religious beliefs. Those interviews became *Black Elk Speaks*, completed by Neihardt, "the sender of words," the following year. The novel was greatly admired—Jung wrote a preface for it and it is used as an anthropology text—particularly by successive generations of Native Americans. Today it is widely considered one of the most important outsider accounts of Native American spirituality.

After leaving St. Louis, Neihardt became the Director of Information for the Office of Indian Affairs during World War II until he accepted the position of Poet in Residence at the University of Missouri–Columbia. In 1952 he was named the Midwest regional vice president of the Poetry Society of America, a post which he held until his death in 1973. At his funeral, a group of Sioux performed a traditional ceremony, conducting rites rarely given to a white man. As to this final frontier, if it were at all possible, Neihardt would be writing about it.

> For a little span
> Their life-fires flared like torches in the van
> Of westward progress, ere the great wind woke
> To snuff them. Many vanished like a smoke
> The blue air drinks; and e'en of those who burned
> Down to the socket, scarce a tithe returned
> To share at last the ways of quiet men,
> Or see the heart-reek drifting once again
> Across the roofs of old St. Louis town.
> —"The Song of Three Friends"

HAROLD BRODKEY
October 25, 1930 — January 26, 1996

True stories, autobiographical stories, like some novels, begin long ago, before the acts in the account, before the birth of some of the people in the tale.

—"The Wild Darkness," *New Yorker*, February 5, 1996

Many of the writers who leave St. Louis to seek their fortunes in the wider world leave it early in life, so that the city rarely occupies a significant place in their future work, but the troubled spaces of his youth pursued Harold Brodkey to New York, and where he resided, they resided too. Memory commanded his hand:

> I am only equivocally Harold Brodkey. I was adopted when I was two in the month following my real mother's death, and Harold was a name casually chosen by Joseph Brodkey because it sounded like Aaron, the name I'd had with my real mother. I was told in various ways over a number of years, and I suppose it's true, that my real father blamed me because I became ill at my mother's death and cried and didn't trust him: I had been my mother's favorite; he kept my brother, who was older than me, and more or less sold me to the Brodkeys for three hundred and fifty dollars and the promise of a job in another town. I saw my brother once a year, and he told me I was lucky to be adopted.
>
> The Brodkeys never called me Harold—Buddy was the name they used for me. Brodkey itself is equivocal, being a corruption of a Russian name, Bezborodko. To what extent Harold Brodkey is a real name is something I have never been able to decide.

Brodkey's real parents were Ceil and Max Weintraub, whose cousins Joe and Doris Brodkey lived in an apartment on the corner of Kingsland Avenue and Kingsbury Boulevard. There Harold suffered through his adolescence, aware of his "otherness," and carefully, successfully, disguising it. He graduated from University City High School in 1947.

> We lived in University City, U. City or Jew City—the population then was perhaps thirty-five percent Jewish; the percentage is higher now. St. Louis swells out like a gall on the Mississippi River. . . . St. Louis is an island of metropolis on a sea of land.

During the sultry St. Louis summers, the fire escape became the steps to hell during mid-day when the steel baked, and a sleeping, breathing, smoking, sitting room by night. In 1849 a stack of mattresses caught fire on the levee and soon the waterfront and then the entire downtown were in flames. The lesson of Chicago and St. Louis was that ramshackle wooden buildings burned. Since clay was abundantly at hand St. Louis built itself back out of brick. It made the city seem solid, safe as the sensible pig, but also an oven where a pig might roast.

There is a certain shade of red brick—a dark, almost melodious red, sombre and riddled with blue—that is my childhood in St. Louis. Not the real childhood, but the false one that extends from the dawning of consciousness until the day that one leaves home for college. That one shade of red brick and green foliage is St. Louis in the summer (the winter is just a gray sky and a crowded school bus and the wet footprints on the brown linoleum floor at school), and that brick and a pale sky is spring. It's also loneliness and the queer, self-pitying wonder that children whose families are having catastrophes feel.

I can remember that brick best on the back of our apartment house; it was on all the apartment houses on that block, and also on the apartment house where Edward lived—Edward was a small boy I took care of on the evenings when his parents went out. As I came up the street from school, past the boulevard and its ugliness (the vista of shoe-repair shops, dime stores, hairdressers', pet shops, the Tivoli Theatre, and the closed Piggly Wiggly, about to be converted into a Kroger's), past the place where I could see the Masonic Temple, built in the shape of some Egyptian relic, and the two huge concrete pedestals flanking the boulevard (what they supported I can't remember, but on both of them, in brown paint, was a large heart and the information that someone named Erica loved someone named Peter), past the post office, built in W.P.A. days of yellow brick and chrome, I hurried toward the moment when at last, on the other side, past the driveway of the garage of the Castlereagh Apartments, I would be at the place where the trees began, the apartment houses of dark-red brick, and the empty stillness.

Brodkey has been walking through the Delmar Loop as it looked in 1943; an area called the Loop because it was where the streetcars turned around to return to town; and where the mountebank and dreamer Edward Gardner Lewis, in 1903, founded University City, established his *Woman's Magazine* publishing empire, and where he built the symbolic and utopian buildings that still stand by the Lion Gates on Delmar: the octagonal city hall, the University Masonic Hall and the Trinity-Delmar Building in Egyptian style, as well as the Lewis Center and the aforementioned "gates of opportunity."

In alleys, little ever changes, and the apartments are still there, disfigured by the outside stairs the fire codes require.

> In the middle of that stillness and red brick was my neighborhood, the terribly familiar place where I was more comfortably an exile than anywhere else. There were two locust trees that were beautiful to me—I think because they were small and I could encompass them (not only with my mind and heart but with my hands as well). Then came an apartment house of red brick (but not quite the true shade) where a boy I knew lived, and two amazingly handsome brothers, who were also strong and kind, but much older than I and totally uninterested in me. Then came an alley of black macadam and another vista, which I found shameful but drearily comfortable, of garages and ashpits and telephone poles and the backs of apartment houses—including ours—on one side, the backs of houses on the other. I knew many people in the apartments but none in the houses, and this was the ultimate proof, of course, to me of how miserably degraded I was and how far sunken beneath the surface of the sea. I was on the bottom, looking up through the waters, through the shifting bands of light—through, oh, innumerably more complexities than I could stand—at a sailboat driven by the wind, some boy who had a family and a home like other people.

Harold was "the walking encyclopedia" to his classmates, and he felt their fear of him through an isolation mutually imposed.

> I was fierce and solitary and acrid, marching off the little mile from school, past the post office, all yellow brick and chrome, and my two locust trees (water, water everywhere and not a drop to drink), and there was no one who loved me first.

Until his high marks got him off to Harvard, he would take, through his hometown, the back ways.

> Our apartment was on the third floor. I usually walked up the back stairs which were mounted outside the building in a steel framework. I preferred the back stairs—it was a form of rubbing at a hurt to make sure it was still there—because they were steep and ugly and had garbage cans on the landings and wash hanging out, while the front door opened off a court where rosebushes grew, and the front stairs were made of some faintly yellow local marble that was cool and pleasant to the touch and to the eye. When I came to our back door, I would open the screen and call out to see if my mother was home. If she was not home, it usually meant that she was visiting my father, who had been dying in the hospital for four years and would linger two more before he would come to terms with death.

Brodkey felt himself twice orphaned, and death did seem like a clock that ticked then tocked his days. Writers may choose to remember their early years and their hometown time, but it is those who move to a locale later, when they are established and on their own, who are likely to love it, and turn like a cat cautiously round and round to shape a safe and comfy place. Two years out of Harvard, Brodkey published his first story in the *New Yorker*, whose staff he would later join, and began to develop the style of hyperbolic realism which would make him famous. In 1986 he returned to Washington University as a visiting Hurst Professor and remet a few old friends of his youth including Naomi Lebowitz, a professor in the Department of English. He recognized the irony when he attended a party at Stanley Elkin's house near his old neighborhood. After decades of preparation, he published *Runaway Soul* in 1991, a work whose title (a modification of the descriptive phrase "a runaway slave") tells us a lot about his own flight. In 1993 Brodkey learned that he had contracted AIDS, but he continued to

97

write in the *New Yorker,* most movingly, of the effect of his illness on himself and his wife, the novelist Ellen Schwann, until his own death arrived on January 26, 1996.

Perhaps, as a toddler, then a tyke, in Batavia, New York, John Gardner did not en-

> **JOHN GARDNER**
> July 21, 1933 — September 14, 1982

counter many writers, and it is possible he didn't see any at DePauw University in Indiana, where he enrolled to study chemistry, but he certainly ran into some of the right books, because his interest almost immediately began to shift in the direction of literature. He published a story in the campus magazine and did the book as well as the lyrics for a musical comedy called *The Caucus Race*, though it was performed in February 1954, after he had transferred to Washington University because of his recent marriage. "I saw real writers at Washington U. and I realized I could do the same thing," he said. Gardner spent two years studying with Jarvis Thurston, then also the editor of *Perspective*, and it was while working with Thurston that he began the story that would become the novel, *Nickel Mountain*. He considered Thurston to be one of the best teachers he ever had. Gardner went on to do graduate work at the Iowa Writers Workshop, where he met poets Donald Finkel and Constance Urdang, who would later join Stanley Elkin in the Washington University English department.

After Iowa, Gardner bounced from job to job as he was wont, lasting a year at Oberlin before taking a position at Chico State College (later a university and part of the University of California system). There he edited *MSS.*, an innovative literary magazine that would publish Howard Nemerov and William Gass, eventually Washington University writers, too. Gardner continued to keep various degrees of connection with the university while at San Francisco State, and then at nearby Southern Illinois University in Carbondale, where he had a farm on the romantically named Boskydell Road. He remained at SIU until 1976 and during that period would visit William Gass or Stanley Elkin in St. Louis from time to time. Gardner and Elkin also regularly taught during the summer at the Breadloaf Writers Conference in Middlebury, Connecticut. He was now one of the best-known novelists in America. Gardner concluded his teaching career at the State University at Binghamton, and it was while riding his motorcycle to campus that he was run off the road by another vehicle and killed on September 14, 1982.

JOHN MORRIS
June 18, 1931 — November 25, 1997

> *You have written me. I am*
> *As you have made me.*
> *Though I am in your hand*
> *I live without you.*
>
> — "The Autobiography"

John Morris was born in Oxford, England, and christened in the chapel of Merton College, where his father, Charles Morris, was doing postgraduate studies in English. "The birth was difficult, and my enormous pineapple of a head (with red ringlets to the shoulders) a nurse reshaped by hand," Morris wrote later. "After the Oxford year my father took up a graduate fellowship at the University of Virginia. . . . I think it was now that, as cause not consequence, my father first went mad. From a family visit in the Adirondacks a telegram summoned Mother to Washington, where my father had been working at the Library of Congress. She found him in St. Elizabeth's, straitjacketed in a bare cell."

John Morris's parents divorced in 1938. "The near identity of my parents' names—Charles Morris and Charlotte Maurice—invites me to set the two families in complementary relation: Southerners and Northerners; landowners, lawyers and academics on the one hand, manufacturers and moneymen on the other." Morris would spend the next years living on his grandfather's peach farm in Eagle Springs, North Carolina. In 1940 his mother married John Hammond, son of drama critic Percy Hammond, and they moved to New York. Morris was sent to Augusta Military Academy in Fort Defiance, Virginia.

In October 1947, the family moved to Clinton, New York, after John Hammond bought the *Clinton Courier*. He was the editor, the sole reporter, and also ran the print shop: he died of a heart attack in 1948 at the age of fifty. John Morris worked at the paper while his mother tried to sell it: "At its end, I would not have accepted the editorship of the *Washington Post*."

Morris went on to Hamilton College in Clinton, where he received his bachelor's degree in English in 1953. He then spent two years in the Marines: "'This intelligent young officer's interests are not Marine Corps peculiar.' . . . I would have to make my way inside another sort of institution." Morris investigated graduate schools and entered Columbia University, where he received his doctorate in English literature in 1964. He taught at the University of Delaware, San Francisco State College and Columbia University. In 1967, at the invitation of Jarvis Thurston, chair of Washington University's English department, he came to St. Louis and joined writers Howard Nemerov, Mona Van Duyn, Stanley Elkin, Donald Finkel and Constance Urdang. He specialized in poetry and eighteenth-century English literature.

> Into my office, arrogant and green
>> They stalk to stammer
> Suspiciously of my perhaps obscene
>> Passion for grammar.
>
> Why should I ask them for, or they expend
>> Their morning forces?
> What if they should, with every sense, attend
>> All of their courses?
>
> "Shakespeare certainly had the knack for writing"
>> Is what they'd learn.
> I cannot show them even the "exciting,"
>> For which they yearn.
>
> You'd think they'd try sometimes to catch me out;
>> But never. Look:
> They nod, though I grow dull and wrong about
>> Some perfect book.
>
> —"What the Professor Said"

98

Morris and his wife, Anne, lived in Parkview Place and had three children. In 1995, after almost thirty years at Washington University, John Morris retired and moved to North Carolina, where on November 25, 1997, he died of pancreatic cancer.

"We all adored him," said professor Naomi Lebowitz, a colleague in the English department. "He was old fashioned in a charming way —and very shy—he couldn't stand to answer the phone. He was always writing poetry, but kind of as a secret profession. The other poets adored his poetry — Howard [Nemerov] and Mona [Van Duyn]. Helen [Vendler] loved his poetry. He was also the best writer [of criticism] in the department."

His first book of poetry, *Green Business*, was published in 1970, followed by *The Life Beside This One* in 1975 and *The Glass Houses* in 1980. He was the recipient of a Guggenheim Fellowship and in 1979 an award from the Academy and Institute for Arts and Letters. *A Schedule of Benefits*, Morris's last book, came out in 1987.

"He had a wry sense of humor and was a great storyteller," said his colleague Wayne Fields in the obituary for the *St. Louis Post-Dispatch*. Lebowitz concurs: "He sang old songs hilariously and was famous for his anecdotes, particularly the ones about his goofy relatives. People would come into the Coffee Room just to hear him tell a story. . . . He was always in the library, reading the poetry magazines after hours." A portrait of

Morris hangs on the ground floor in Washington University's Olin Library, in the corner where Morris used to read.

On the List

As Who Isn't? his snobbery protests.
Still, he is pleased to be included.
As if his daily imitation
Of one of the grownups had succeeded,
Here he is among the real
Doctors and other serious persons.
Now he is somebody at last,
And there is his full name to prove it.
And an occupation. Out of the wide
Range of narrow choices the proprietors
Of the list provided he elected one.
He appears in print to be an Educator.

Most of the rest the proprietors
Left entirely to him.
Here he may be born when he chooses
And no one will correct him,
Certainly not his curtly acknowledged parents.
Now he may have as few wives as he wanted.
For a couple of lines his schooling goes smoothly.
Then he begins to rise in his profession,
Arriving at last at his home
Or office address and telephone number.

Every couple of years they ask him again
Who he is. He adds a child, a line
Of honors and awards, the grants
That prove he is a formidable beggar.
Yet it goes without saying that much
Must go unsaid. One principle
Ruling these little lives is omission.
Even the proprietors do not pretend
To offer anything like a full account.
Think how many things there is no room for.
Here everyone is friendless and unbrothered.
And where shall he record his treasured losses?

Someday when they ask their question
He will not be able to return an answer.
Then the proprietors must
Edit him out of the list.
By name. The object of an intention.
Perhaps this confers some distinction:
One dies and has to leave the foolish pages.
As if some purpose had been served at last.
But for now he is one inch tall
Including all his publications,
And he is a little proud of that.
Although he knows it comes to nothing much,
Bound in the color of blood
He soldiers on among his gray companions—
He and all these strangers by the thousand.

CONSTANCE URDANG
December 26, 1922 — October 8, 1996

I'm none of you, Missouri,
With your old-time ebony or high-yaller blues,
Your sternwheeling, gambling, nothing-to-lose,
Your mustachioed, melodrama, flood-stage blues—
Nothing here I can use.

—"Missouri"

In his introduction to *The Picnic in the Cemetery*, published in 1975, poet and translator Richard Howard called Constance Urdang "astonishing among the women poets I know for her egalitarianism, for her coupled measurements of what it is to be fully human. What bothers her into poetry is not resentment but response, not competition but compassion, not replacement but replenishment." Her last book of poetry, *Alternative Lives*, was published in 1990.

On Rereading the Poets

Thinking about the mad poets,
The drunken, the drugged, the dead poets,
The forgotten ones, those half-remembered
For badly remembered lines, misunderstood,
Admired for the wrong reasons, and too late,
I am amazed at the persistence of poetry.
Like the secret writing of children
That becomes visible on paper held over a flame,
Obstinately, the old lines come to life
Letter by letter, stuttering across the page,
Confounding criticism, fanned into breath
Over and over, making themselves new again.

Constance Urdang was born in New York City in 1922 and attended the Fieldston School, where she read the classics. She grew up being read to and reading poetry and was eight when her first publication, a Christmas poem, appeared in a national magazine. She attended Smith College and graduated cum laude in 1944, after which she worked as a military intelligence analyst and then as a copyeditor. She was an associate editor for the 1957 and 1959 editions of the O'Henry Awards *Prize Stories* and the editor of the *Random House Vest Pocket Dictionary of Famous People*, published in 1962, and the *Vest Pocket Book of Great Events of World History* in 1964.

Urdang attended the highly regarded University of Iowa Writers Workshop, from which she received her Master of Fine Arts in Poetry in 1956. There she met poet Donald Finkel; they married in 1956 and lived for a time in Mexico. In 1960 they moved to St. Louis when

99

Finkel took a faculty position in the Department of English at Washington University. They settled in the Heights of University City, at 6943 Columbia Place, where they raised three children. Urdang and Finkel later moved to Lafayette Square.

Urdang published her first book of poems, *Charades and Celebrations* in 1965. This was followed by a novel, *Natural History,* in 1969, another novel, *American Earthquakes,* in 1988, and two collections of novellas, *Lucha, A Novella* (1986) and the tandem volume the *Woman Who Read Novels* and *Peacetime* (1990). Her other books of poetry include *The Lone Woman and Others* (1980) and *Only the World* (1983).

While Urdang was writing her many books she taught at Washington

University's University College. With her husband she helped establish the university's Writing Program and served as coordinator from 1977 to 1989. She received the Oscar Williams and Gene Derwood Award for excellence among poets and artists, the Delmore Schwarz Memorial Poetry Award and the Carleton Centennial Award for Poetry. Urdang died of complications of lung cancer on October 8, 1996.

When Urdang's children were growing up, she kept her study downstairs so she could keep an eye on them. She explained why in an interview for *St. Louis* magazine in 1978: "I've had moments of envying Virginia Woolf who had absolutely nothing to do after breakfast. . . . I prefer this life. I wouldn't have missed it for anything."

The Oracle at St. Louis

> *Many moons ago I lived. Again I*
> *come—Patience Worth my name.*

The perfume of God's garden is wasted on jackals
The fruit of the tree is stamped in the mud
The star shines, steadfast as an angel, in the sky,
    but no eye is lifted up

The god spoke
Not through the lips of a starlet with Hollywood dentures
And penciled lips and eyebrows; not even
In a childish babble (signifying innocence). No.
The oracle
Was sluttish and unwashed, probably stank. Also,
All that smoke made everyone cough.

Similarly,
In St. Louis in 1913,
"A semi-literate housewife"
Wrote a series of astonishing works
Dictated to her by a 17th century spirit.

My light comes from the moon.

STANLEY ELKIN
May 11, 1930 — May 31, 1995

Maybe if Stanley Elkin had grown up in St. Louis he wouldn't have liked it so much, wouldn't have cast the city in major and minor roles in many of his books. Without the Aeschylean tragedy of a Tennessee Williams, the abusive stepfather of a Harold Brodkey or the New York fame graduation party of Akins, Teasdale, Johns and Hurst, St. Louis would prove a perfect place to write his unparalleled prose. Stanley Elkin had published stories, had worked, while a graduate student, on the literary journal *Accent* at the University of Illinois with William Gass, a visiting professor in the philosophy and English departments, before being invited by Jarvis Thurston to join the faculty of the Department of English at Washington University to become part of what was considered by some the most important group of literary writers assembled on one campus; that is, a campus without the now pervasive writing program one finds at most major American universities. That would come later. But at this time, in 1960, a writing faculty was being convened by chair Thurston and would include the poets Donald Finkel, John Morris and Howard Nemerov, joined across the quad by fiction writers Richard Watson and William Gass, faculty members in the Department of Philosophy.

Stanley Elkin published all of his books here. Why St. Louis?

> ... because I'm an American of the vaguely professional class, a tenured academic, the least mobile of men, and you live where they ask you in this business and get maybe two or three solid offers in a working lifetime, and because I've been luckier than most or less brave, perhaps, and have only received one—two if you count the feeler, pursued halfheartedly on both our parts, from the University of California in Santa Barbara ... and we tried it for a summer and didn't much like it, my wife because it made her nervous to go for bread at eighty miles an hour and me because, as I say, I'm not brave and didn't know if I'd like my friends.

> Which is really why I live where I live.

> I live in University City, Missouri, a block from the St. Louis city limits. (The city of St. Louis is self-contained as an island, exists in no county, is, in a way, a kind of territory, a sort of D.C., a sort of Canal Zone, gerrymandered as Yugoslavia, its limits fixed years ago, before the fact, staked out, one would guess, by a form of sortilege, a casting, say, of vacant lots, working farms and nineteen miles of the Mississippi River into the equation, the surveyor's sticks and levels and measures doing this tattoo of the possible, of the one-day-could-be, shaping a town like a stomach, stuffing it with ellipses, diagonals, the narrows of neighborhood.) University City is not so much a suburb as St. Louis's logical western addendum. There are over ninety incorporated municipalities surrounding St. Louis, closing it off like manifest destiny, filling it in like some jigsaw of the irrefutable. Mondrian's zones and squares like a

budgeted geometry. And I live where I live because of the civilization here.

—"Why I Live Where I Live"

Stanley Elkin's final novel, *Mrs. Ted Bliss,* was published in 1995, the year he died, and it received a posthumous National Book Critics Circle Award. He received his first Book Critics Circle Award for his 1982 novel *George Mills.* Originally called *The Griefs,* the book traces the first thousand years of George Millses, all of whom are doomed to a blue collar life. The story begins in England in 1097 during the First Crusade. Because the first George Mills knew nothing about horses or geography he and his master, Guillalume, fail "to hang a right in the Netherlands" and, relying on the navigational abilities of their horses (George's is called "Mills's horse" because horses didn't have names then) miss the Crusade, sparing their lives but not Mills his fated station. Encamped in what is probably Poland, the first George Mills has a dream and confides to his horse what he sees:

"All this I saw last night in my dream . . . We went upstairs. Through the cold scarpéd halls, the parapeted, circumvallated keep and fastness, through miles it must have been of that fortress house. And that's where I saw it. Along one immense stairwell. A hanging, they told me, a tapestry. Woven in Germany, I think, or France, or some such far-off place. Whatever name they used as meaningless to me as the sandpaper syllables of animals.

"Please, sir, may I look for a bit?"

"And one of the men raised his hand as if to strike me, but Sir Guy himself stayed the blow. '*Noblesse oblige,* asshole. Let him. What? The ink not yet dry on the Magna Carta and you'd strike a stableboy for looking at a tapestry? Give Elvin my lance, lad. Thank you for carrying it this far. Take my coin. When you've done, go out quietly.'

"It was like a flag, Mills's horse—only larger than any real flag. And the colors not as bright as they'd been on the escutcheon, for those were the consolidate, idealized, concentrate colors of claims and qualities, the paints of boast and fabled beasts. This was a picture. Not a picture like a picture in a church. No saints with halos like golden quoits about their heads, no nimbuses on edge like valued coins, not our Lord, or Mother Mary, or allegory at all, but only the ordinary pastels of quotidian life. A representation, Horse, in tawns and rusts, in the bleached greens and drought yellows of high summer, in dusty blacks and whites gone off, in blues like distant foliage. Everything the shade of clumsy weather. There were gypsies in it and beggars. There were honest men—hewers of wood and haulers of water. Legging'd and standing behind their full pouches of scrotum like small pregnancies. There were women in wimples. Ned and Nancy. Pete and Peg. It was how they saw us—see us. Shepherds and farmers. Millers, bakers, smithies. Mechanics with wooden tools, leather. Pastoral, safe, settled in the tapestry condition of their lives, woven into it as the images themselves.

"Only I knew *I* wasn't like that . . . Maybe the Germans, maybe the French, but not me, not anyone I knew. We are a dour, luteless people, cheerless, something sour in our blue collar blood."

The contemporary George Mills fulfills the family fate by driving a truck for a man who repossesses furniture in South St. Louis. This George Mills grew up in St. Louis, romanced his wife in St. Louis and danced to the Stan David Orchestra at the Delgado. (Some readers will recognize the riff on the real Russ David, the orchestra leader at the Chase Hotel for many years.)

George is aware of his new clothes, the creamy fabrics like an aura of haberdash, a particular pocket like a badge of fashion. The vaguely heraldic suggestion of his collar, his lapels like laurels, his cuffs like luck. He strolls across the dance floor and, absorbed in all the flying colors of his style, already it is like dancing. He moves in the paintbox atmospherics of the big glowing room, the polished cosmetics of light.

Chiefly he is aware of his shoes, his elegant socks, his smooth, lubricate soles like the texture of playing cards. Always before the earth has resisted, stymied his feet, and he has walked in gravity as in so much mud. There has always been this layer of friction, of grit. Now he moves across glass, ice, the hard, flawless surface of the dance floor packed as snow. He feels swell.

Stan David, his voice augmented by saxophones and clarinets, by drums and bass, calls the room to attention. He is neither seductive nor peremptory but matter-of-fact as someone returned from an errand. He breaks into their mood seamlessly. "The boys and I are awful glad to be playing for you folks tonight. It's an important date for us because it's the first time Mr. Lodt has asked us to do a Saturday night at the Delgado, so first off we want to thank those old friends who've so loyally supported our week-night appearances and who Mr. Lodt tells us have been requesting our engagement for the big one."

Most of the people applaud Stan David's announcement. George, on the strength of his good mood, applauds too.

What this George Mills discovers is that there is no curse, not in England, not, even, in St. Louis. Maybe even especially not in St. Louis.

Stanley Lawrence Elkin was born in New York on May 11, 1930, to Zelda and Philip Elkin, a costume jewelry salesman who moved the family to Chicago three years later. Stanley Elkin started writing, he recalled in a 1981 interview, using his father's stationery: "I would print on that letterhead and for some reason I thought that that was making a book, because all of the pages looked somehow official, authorized by the logo. I must have been eight or nine years old then."

Stanley Elkin attended the University of Illinois and received his bachelor's degree in 1952, his master's in 1953 and his doctorate in 1961. There he met Joan Jacobson, and they married on February 1, 1953; they had three children. Joan Elkin began to paint after the family moved to University City in 1960. She has employed her husband's and their friends' and relatives' images for many of her drawings, watercolors and oil paintings. ("I help her out with the reds and greens," Stanley Elkin once remarked.) Her painting *Jarvis Thurston and His Circle* and another portrait of members of the Department of English faculty hang in Duncker Hall on the

100

Washington University campus. She continues to paint at her home in University City.

Boswell: A Modern Comedy, Stanley Elkin's first novel, was published in 1964, followed by a book of short stories, *Criers and Kibitzers, Kibitzers and Criers*, in 1966 and *A Bad Man* in 1967. *The Dick Gibson Show* came out in 1971 and a collection of three novellas, *Searches and Seizures,* in 1973.

While in London in 1972 Elkin began to exhibit the symptoms of multiple sclerosis: "They said it was my posture. So I went to this gym for an hour a day for perhaps a month. And I was a tiger. I was chinning up walls with my teeth. But the symptoms didn't go away." They didn't for Ben Flesh either, "Mr. Softee," in his 1976 novel *The Franchiser*:

> He'd been driving for hours, on his way from his St. Cloud, Minnesota, Dairy Queen to his Mister Softee in Rapid City, South Dakota—his milk run, as he liked to call it. His right hand had fallen asleep and there was a sharp pain high up in the groin and thigh of his right side.
>
> Mornings he'd been getting up with it. A numbness in his hand and hip, bad circulation, he thought, which left these damned cold zones, warm enough to the touch when he felt them with the freely circulating blood in the fingers of his left hand or lifted his right hand to his face, but, untouched, like icy patches deep in his skin. Perhaps his sleeping habits had changed. Almost unconsciously now he found the right side of the bed. In the night, sleeping alone, even without a twin or triplet beside him, the double bed to himself, some love-altered principle of accommodation or tropism in his body taking him from an absent configuration of flesh to a perimeter of the bed, a yielding without its necessity or reason, a submission and giving way to—to what? (And even in his sleep, without naming them, he could tell them apart.) To ride out the night sidesaddle on his own body. (No godfather Julius he, not set in *his* ways, unless this were some new mold into which he was pouring himself.) Pressing his head—heavy as Gertrude's marrowless bones—like a nighttime tourniquet against the flesh of his arm, drawing a knee as high up as a diver's against his belly and chest, to wake in the morning cut off, the lines down and trailing live wires from the heavy storm of his own body. Usually as

the day wore on, the sensation wore off, but never completely, some sandy
sensitivity laterally vestigial across the tips of his fibers, the sharp pain in the
region of his thigh blunted, like a suction cup on the tip of a toy arrow. Bad
circulation. Bad.

Disease would become a theme, a character and a setting in Stanley
Elkin's life and work; he would spin its scientific facts and its as yet uncon-
quered mysteries into a Rumpelstiltskinned lustre, possessing the language
the way multiple sclerosis occupied his body. (Because all art, he would say,
is contrast.)

In his 1985 novel *The Magic Kingdom* he infects seven children each
with a different disease and sends them on a dream vacation to Disney
World in Florida. The trip is organized by Eddy Bale, whose son Liam has
a terminal illness. After a few days there the kids coax Mickey Mouse into
their hotel room and finally get him to talk.

"You know, it's strange," the Mouse said philosophically. "It is. It really is.
What goes on, I mean. I mean people really do die. Your age. I mean there you
are, you're going along taking pretty good care of yourself. You look both ways
before crossing, you don't accept rides from strangers, you brush after each
meal, then whammo! Whammo and blammo! Whammo and blammo and
pow and zap! Kerboom and kerflooey, I mean. Mayday, I mean! But who's
going to hear you? And what good would it do if they could? No one can
help. All right, maybe they take up a collection, maybe you get to be guests of
honor at the watering place of your choice. Lourdes, the Magic Kingdom.

"But what's strange, what's really strange, is that after the melodrama,
after all the best efforts and good offices of the go-betweens, the mediators,
the maids of honor, the honest brokers, and best men, after the prayers and
after the sacrifices, after the candles and after the offerings, worse comes to
worse anyway. The unthinkable happens, the out-of-the-question occurs, all
the unabashed, unvarnished unwarranted, all the unjustifiable unhappy, all
the unwieldy unbearable. The unbelievable, the uncivil, the uncharitable, the
uncalled-for. The undivided, undignified uncouth. The unkempt, unkind un-
endurable. The uncontrollably uncomfortable. All that unethical, unbridled,
unconditional undoing. All the ungodly unhinged, all the unfriendly unnat-
ural. The unpleasant, the unimaginable, the unprincipled. The unfit, the unsavory, the unforeseen. The unsurpassed, unsightly unruly. The untimely un-
suitable, the unwelcome unutterable. The undertaker, I mean."

"Untrue," Mudd-Gaddis objected. (Because everything has a reasonable
explanation . . .)

. . . and someday science will find a cure for the disease that plagues Liam:

"Well, I'm sure it was very clever of the doctors to let you work out your
cure for yourself. They seemed to be stymied there when *they* had a go at it,
God knows. So what did it turn out to be? The breakthrough? What'd it turn
out to be in the end? When all is said and done, I mean?"

This time he rushes his finger to his lips, admonishing Liam's silence.
The gesture is like an awry slap.

"No," Eddy says. "Hush, Liam. Hush, son. Because if you really *are* dead —not that I think you are, you understand, not for a minute—but just in the event, on the outside chance, I don't want to hear about it. I *won't* hear about it. Nor will I listen to a word about bold cures and new breakthroughs. Not if you're dead, I won't.

How'm I doin?

The Magic Kingdom was followed by *The Rabbi of Lud* in 1987, *The MacGuffin* in 1991, set in a highly fictionalized St. Louis, a book of essays, *Pieces of Soap,* in 1992 and *Van Gogh's Room at Arles* in 1993, which was nominated for a PEN/Faulkner Award—seventeen books including *The Living End* and *Stanley Elkin's Greatest Hits,* not counting the limited editions and *The Coffee Room*, a radio play commissioned by National Public Radio and produced locally with Stanley Elkin starring as himself. From cane to wheelchair, stairs to tram, from university exam booklets to a computer—disease did not deter him: it was his guide and language his life.

Stanley Elkin died of heart failure at Barnes Hospital on May 31, 1995.

In his essay "Where I Read What I Read," he spoke about what books meant to him and what he wanted for his own:

> I would hope that some day someone will read one of my books with just a particle of that sense of occasion that I brought to Flaubert and to Mann and to all the rest. I haven't said it here, am almost ashamed to own up, but once I opened books slowly, stately, plump imaginary orchestras going off in my head, like overtures, like music behind the opening credits of films, humming the title page, whistling the copyright, turning myself into producer and pit band, usher and audience . . .

Stanley Elkin was inducted into the St. Louis Walk of Fame in 1991.

101

101. Stanley Elkin Walking in Parkview Place, *1988*
by Joan Elkin

. . . And the purpose of poesy, as all of us know
Without the sermon, is, by telling the truth,
To disintoxicate and disenchant
By lying like Homer taught us first to do.

—"Drowning the Book"

When Howard Nemerov came to visit Washington University from Brandeis in 1969, it was as the first Fannie Hurst Professor of Creative Literature. He was already one of the most distinguished poets in America, the author of twelve books of verse and prose, with a long teaching career at Hamilton College and Bennington behind him, and he had been a pre-poet laureate as well, serving as the consultant in poetry to the Library of Congress in 1963-64, the same position that was later upnamed to a laureancy—improved in its spelling, richer in reward, redolent of immortality.

But what was most remarkable was the fact that when Howard Nemerov assumed his professorship here, if we reckon by his natal days, he was just a little boy of thirteen. According to Gilbert and Sullivan. When Frederic's buccaneering friends inform him of the real length of his indenture in *The Pirates of Penzance*, they sing "it is a paradox, a paradox, a most ingenious paradox," for Nemerov, like the apprentice pirate, was born on a leap day, February 29, 1920.

By his own description, a "Jewish Puritan of the middle class," critics have frequently noted the oppositions that made up the Nemerov nature, beginning with the alternation, among his publications, of poetry with fiction, and continuing with the brooding melancholy that runs through much of his work, a thoughtful somberness that is nevertheless enlivened by his mischievous, sometimes mordant, wit. They also observed, from his first book (*The Image and the Law*, 1947) onward, how Nemerov habitually set our ordinary sensuous experience over against the colorless, odorless order of ideas found in the mind. It is a poetry that tackles the great issues; it is the product of intense ambition; yet its tone is often flip, dismissive or resigned. One critic, Peter Meinke, said his poetry expressed "a philosophy of minimal affirmation."

Nor was it, when Nemerov arrived in St. Louis, a particularly good time in our nation for any poet of ceremony or irony or erudition or restraint. It was a time for outrage and confrontation, for name-calling and fist-shaking and the deep satisfactions of moral superiority—an occasion for self-importance, not deprecation.

Nemerov came to visit. Then he asked to stay. He was seen, in the east, to be running away. "When I moved here a little snit from Brandeis wrote me a very unconsciously funny letter, in which he said he understood my wish to 'retire from the center of culture into some quiet backwater.'"

At that moment the backwater was becoming one of the literary centers of the United States. Nemerov understood, enjoyed, the irony. To the question, how do you like St. Louis? he replied: "I think of it as the earthly paradise. We've never been so comfortable in our lives. Better not put that in the paper, or somebody'll come and take it away. I don't refer to the city, I don't go down there, in general I don't even get as far as Clayton. In the morning at eight o'clock I walk [to school], at noon I go home and have lunch. A minor poet can afford the real estate here, which is not true if you look around, say, Houston or New York."

It was not just the stroll, of course, the route to his office that became

102

locally famous, it was the state of mind the poet was allowed to enjoy, as he did so, that made it a path in paradise. He could walk to work. And walk back. Morning after morning. And consequently pass from shaded streets of quiet residence through those of traffic, serious business and restless behavior to the calm of the campus, meanwhile observing minute changes in clime, foliage, flower, flow of life. What the poet observed in this paradise was the vigorously earthy. He was a "low-down fellow with lofty thoughts," Nemerov said. Lofty maybe, but firmly tethered.

From 1970 on, his neighborhood, his friends, music, books and art, a few memories, pleasant routines furnished his poetry with its materials: walking down Westgate, observing ginkgoes in the fall, studying a painting, lounging at ease at the edge of a friend's pool, remembering when he made model airplanes as if he already knew he would risk his life in a real one.

Nemerov wore like a uniform the same blue denim jacket every day and carried a book bag slung over one shoulder almost as if the sack and its placement were the gear of a religious order. His haircut was military, which oddly confirmed the head's higher calling. And reminded those who knew him of his history: how he had, after graduating from Harvard at the age of six in 1941, enlisted in the Royal Canadian Air Force, since we were not yet

102. Howard Nemerov with manuscript page and letter from

Thomas Mann, c. 1985

a combatant, and, in the coffinlike cockpit of a Bristol Beaufighter, had flown through the entire horror of the war, strafing shipping in the Dover Straits, chasing a v-1 rocket, dodging Messerschmitt and airborne bullets. In 1944 he transferred to the Eighth United States Army Air Force, which was based in Lincolnshire, and there he met Margaret Russell, an Englishwoman who would become his wife.

After the war, he began writing poetry as an adult and not as an adolescent. First the facts:

> I had one year living in New York on the proceeds of the hostilities until I realized you needed money. In the Air Force that had all been taken care of. I took it for granted that the money came in every month. So I was quite at a loss. I was interviewed for a job that was then Paramount News. Before we had TV we had news programs at the movies. A friend got me the interview but even he couldn't get me the job. The man said, "What can you do?"—a big fat man with a cigar and his sleeves rolled up. I said, "Well, I, I . . ." "Don't tell me about the war, the war is over." I said, "Well, I can fly an airplane." That gave him his chance: "Look around. How many airplanes do you see here?" I didn't get the job. But then as I say, by some happy accident I fell into teaching and found I could sort of do it and stayed.

Then the reality:

> Redeployment
>
> They say the war is over. But water still
> Comes bloody from the taps, and my pet cat
> In his disorder vomits worms which crawl
> Swiftly away. Maybe they leave the house.
> These worms are white, and flecked with the cat's blood.
>
> The war may be over. I know a man
> Who keeps a pleasant souvenir, he keeps
> A soldier's dead blue eyeballs that he found
> Somewhere—hard as chalk, and blue as slate.
> He clicks them in his pocket while he talks.
>
> And now there are cockroaches in the house,
> They get slightly drunk on DDT,
> Are fast, hard, shifty—can be drowned but not
> Without you hold them under quite some time.
> People say the Mexican kind can fly.
>
> The end of the war. I took it quietly
> Enough. I tried to wash the dirt out of
> My hair and from under my fingernails,
> I dressed in clean white clothes and went to bed.
> I heard the dust falling between the walls.

Not only was Nemerov aware the war wasn't over—no more than for Lady Macbeth would washing cleanse the world—he wondered sometimes (as many of the more observant did) just who the enemy was.

> Hate Hitler? No, I spared him hardly a thought.
> But Corporal Irmin, first, and later on
> The O.C. (Flying), Wing Commander Briggs,
> And the station C.O. Group Captain Ormery—
> Now there were men were objects fit to hate,
> Hitler a moustache and a little curl
> In the middle of his forehead, whereas these
> Bastards were bastards in your daily life,
> With Power in their pleasure, smile or frown.

Nemerov was sharply sensitive to the miseries of Man and equally aware of the privileges that furnished his own life with more security, calm and leisure than most. He was the son of a well-to-do New York City merchant who owned Russeks Fifth Avenue. He attended the progressive Fieldston School in the Bronx (as did his sister, Diane, later Arbus) and went to Harvard, continuing a career in school that would last his life— "The day after I arrived at college I found that all the most precious, arrogant, richest sons of bitches said they were poets, so I said, 'That's for me.'" Following a brief vita that Nemerov had supplied to an encyclopedia, he wrote:

> The above somewhat bald chronology convicts me, if we may count the armed forces as a school, of having been at school almost steadily from the age of five; a career which I have heard held to be the worst possible one for a person pretending to imaginative writing. Whether it is so in fact I cannot of course say; I have seen dangers in the academic life, but so are there dangers everywhere; and I think to have seen one advantage, that teaching absorbs a good deal of one's bent for explaining things—a doubtless praiseworthy trait which, however, in my opinion, ought to be allowed the least possible play in writing fictions whether in verse or in prose.

And Nemerov's career was hung with ornaments and stars: ten prizes including the Pulitzer and the Bollingen for poetry, four awards, especially the National Book, five grants and fellowships, as well as medals and trophies, membership in many academies, particularly the American Academy of Arts and Letters, thirteen honorary degrees, the last one from Washington University, a star on the St. Louis Walk of Fame, and finally the poet laureateship of the United States, which he held from 1988 to 1990.

The acclaim accompanied and applauded a prolific production of significant books: twelve novels, stories, essays and collections and nineteen volumes of poetry, including plays in verse.

Nemerov was one of the masters of the "public" or "ceremonial" poem, as the critic Helen Vendler notes: "Nemerov's stunning performance in a vein that few of his contemporaries attempt, let alone succeed in, makes his book [*War Stories*] worth thinking about." However, he could embarrass the powers that be by describing public processes and ceremonies truly, as he did when he wrote (as he was expected to) the Laureate's Inaugural Poem, "The Process," which begins:

> Every four years or every eight,
> A dozen gents and maybe a couple of dames
> Announce they have received the money and the Word
> That fits them for the highest office in the land.
> And so begins The Process . . .

And ends:

> Such is The Process, concerning which a couple of drunks
> In a bar the next night after Election Day
> Challenged each other to say The Pledge
> Of Allegiance they had had to learn at school;
>
> And one drunk said "Mine eyes have seen
> The glory of the coming of the Lord,"
> And the other said "from sea to shining sea,"
> And the first drunk said "you said it, Jack."

Needless to say, the poem was not read at the inauguration. Instead, it was published in the *Post-Dispatch* on January 20, 1989.

After Howard Nemerov's death, Alexander, one of his three sons, wrote a graceful tribute entitled "Modeling My Father" for the *American Scholar*.

> Like Howard, when I was a little boy I used to build model airplanes: Mustangs and Thunderbolts, Spitfires and Hurricanes. Building these planes, I see now, I sought to emulate his heroic flying experience. But I also sought to emulate his creative mind: to craft things, if only in the most rudimentary way. As I got a little older, my brother Jeremy and I collected a few large-scale boxes—big things that contained refrigerators and radar ranges—and took them down to the family basement, where we laid them end to end to make a long snaking fuselage. To either side of this fuselage we place a pair of large fans: four prop engines. In the front box we cut out a couple of squares and over them slapped some Saran Wrap: a windshield. We'd sit down there for hours inside those boxes, operating the little construction-paper controls Howard had helped us fashion. Sometimes, his long legs drawn up to his chest, Howard would sit in there with us—the future poet laureate of the United States sitting inside a Frigidaire box in his own basement. Strange but (happily) true. As I got older, my emulations of Howard changed. I remember he helped Jeremy and me write a story about a ship whose crew members were pieces of fruit. Peter Persimmon was the first mate. My contraptions had become words on a page.

The war, the worries and the wonders of the world—yes—these were among Nemerov's subjects, which he wrote about wryly, sadly, sardonically, always well, but his deepest meditations were occasioned by works of art, by his beloved Bach, by dance, great paintings, novels, poems—poetry itself. One finds him at his finest in a prose poem, "The Measure of Poetry," which compares the movement of poetry to the sea's incessancy. It concludes:

> The rise of the shore shapes the wave. The objects which are to appear in the poem, as they begin to rise beneath the empty periodicity of the pure rhythm, introduce into that rhythm a new character, somewhat obstinate, angular, critical. But in another sense, which technically may be the more useful of the two, the analogy represents the elements of speech itself. The tidal impulse from far away, the wind's generation of force without content, these are the vowels; the consonants are rock and reed and sand, and the steep or shallow slope which gives the wave its form while absorbing the shock of its force, from strength bringing forth sweetness.
>
> The laws of this measure are simple and large, so that in the scope of their generality room may remain for moments of freedom, moments of chaos; the complex conjunction itself raising up iridescences and fantastic shapes, relations which it may be that number alone could enrage into being.

Not yet eighteen, Howard Nemerov left the form of his body on July 5, 1991, a most ingenious paradox.

During a Solar Eclipse

The darkening disk of the moon before the sun
All morning moves, turning our common day
A deep and iris blue, daylight of dream
In which we stand bemused and looking on
Backward at shadow and reflected light,

While the two great wanderers among the worlds
Enter their transit with our third, a thing
So rare that in his time upon the earth
A man may see, as I have done, but four,
In childhood two, a third in youth, and this

In likelihood my last. We stand bemused
While grass and rock darken, and stillness grows,
Until the sun and moon slide out of phase
And light returns us to the common life
That is so long to do and so soon done.

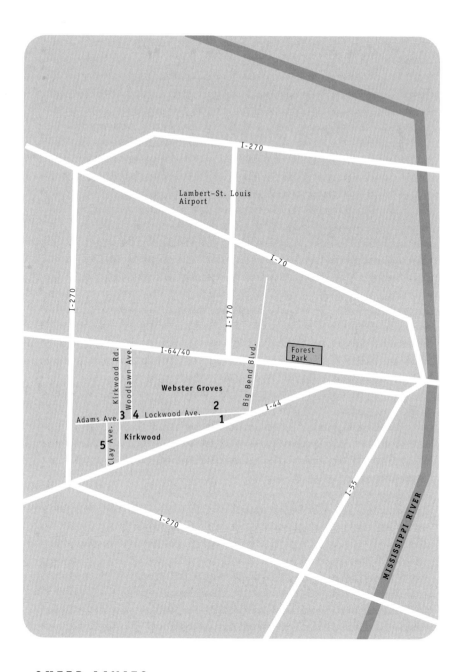

OUTER LIMITS

1. Webster University, 470 East Lockwood Avenue—Harry James Cargas
2. Eden Theological Seminary, 475 East Lockwood Avenue—Reinhold Niebuhr
3. Old Presbyterian Manse, First Presbyterian Church, 100 East Adams Avenue—
    Marianne Moore
4. 203 South Woodlawn Avenue—Josephine Johnson
5. 505 South Clay Avenue—Shirley Seifert

St. Louis has always been an aeronautical city—at least since invention gave it the opportunity. In October 1907 more than 100,000 watched nine balloons take off from Forest Park in a race for distance in which only the Atlantic Ocean halted the winner. Forty thousand watched dirigibles sail over a triangular course laid out in the sky above the park, and then Glenn Curtiss drew 300,000 who hoped to see him fly for forty seconds across the grounds in one of those newfangled airplanes. Hare and Hounds competitions are still an autumn tradition. Later air races would be held at Lambert Field, again before huge crowds; McDonnell Aircraft would begin building war planes; and, of course, Lucky Lindy would fly, all by his lonesome, to Paris and to fame. Who might have imagined he would write such a lively and unlikely book?

Webster University came into being as a Catholic women's college, evolving over eighty years from Loretto (as it was initially called) to Webster College in 1924 and then to a university in 1983. It is notable for its extensions on sixty-eight sites in the United States as well as four abroad. It presently maintains a lively literary and writing program.

Harry James Cargas (1931-1998), who was for much of his career a professor of literature and language at Webster University, bears the meritorious distinction of being the only Catholic ever appointed to the International Advisory Board of Yad Vashem, and a considerable number of his thirty-one books are concerned with the Holocaust or matters related to it. His work on this troubling subject earned him humanitarian awards from the Anne Frank Institute and the United Nations Association. Among the most important books are *Conversations with Elie Wiesel* (1976), *Reflections of a Post-Auschwitz Christian* (1989) and *A Christian Response to the Holocaust* (1990). Earlier, while the director of the Foreign Student Program at Saint Louis University he edited the Christian Critic Series, including a volume on Graham Greene (1979).

The city's sprawl overtook established towns like Kirkwood and Webster Groves, allowing us to claim Marianne Moore and Josephine Johnson as St. Louisans. Those who were born a bit farther away, like Mark Twain and Chester Himes, we'd grab when they came to town for more than the briefest stay. A balloon would do to achieve the limit of our reach, as water, rail and road had certainly sufficed before. But any city must some time wear out its elastic.

I shall purchase an etymological dictionary of modern English
that I may understand what is written,
and like the ant and the spider
returning from time to time to headquarters,
shall answer the question
"why do I like winter better than summer?"

—"Bowls"

103

The poet's mother, Mary Warner, was educated at Mary Institute, a school endowed by the Reverend William Eliot as a memorial to a daughter he had lost. She married an engineer with a poet's name in 1885, but John Milton Moore moved her to Newton, Massachusetts, where he was building a factory designed to produce smokeless furnaces. This project failed, and so did Moore's mind. He was institutionalized in Ohio, where he had grown up, so Mary Warner Moore, pregnant, and her seventeen-month-old son, John, returned to live in Kirkwood, Missouri, with her father, the Reverend John Riddle Warner, who was pastor of the First Presbyterian Church in Kirkwood. There Marianne Moore was born on November 15, 1887, just ten months before T. S. Eliot, whose grandfather was also a preacher— a Unitarian, in his case. The two families didn't know one another, but the grandfathers met at ministerial luncheons, and Marianne Moore reports that after one such occasion her grandfather said, "When Dr. William Eliot asks the blessing and says, 'and this we ask in the name of our Lord Jesus Christ,' he is Trinitarian enough for me."

In Marianne Moore's life men went mad (as her father had) or they died (as her grandfather did when she was seven) or they sailed away (her brother became a Navy Chaplain). Mary Moore was now compelled to move near relatives again, to Carlisle, Pennsylvania, which, however, put her within reach of Bryn Mawr, where Marianne Moore would leave her mother to attend college, the only time the two were separated until Mary died at the age of eighty-five. By that time, Moore was sixty herself. Mother was a formidable woman who, in her youth, had practiced the piano ten hours a day, an instrument her daughter also learned to play. She saw to it that Marianne took voice lessons as well and learned to paint watercolors, an art for which Moore had a copiest's careful talent. The poetry would ex-

103. Remains of Old Presbyterian Manse,
Adams Avenue and Kirkwood Road, 1999

emplify the poet's extraordinary ear and penetrating eye.

In answer to the customary question from an interviewer, Moore remembered writing her first poems when she was at college, but in fact she began her poetic career quite early, about seven, with the rhymes that follow:

> Pussy in the cradle lies—
> and sweetly dreams of gnats and flies.
>
> This Christmas morn
> you do adorn
> Bring Warner a horn
> and me a doll.
> That is all.

Later she would write free, individually formed poems in syllabic verse of extraordinary density and precision and publish them in impressively anorexic volumes such as *Nevertheless* (1944), which contained six poems and ran on for sixteen pages. Astronomical, botanical, zoological terms found themselves, for the first time, and duly astonished, in poems where their meanings were explored and their referents celebrated. Her friends and readers delighted in sending her clippings about the strange doings of rare animals or the odd qualities of exotic plants. Apparently that is what Mona Van Duyn had done when she invited Moore to read at Washington University. Miss Moore replied in a postcard with a poem built on lines that reflect the syllables of Van Duyn's married name:

> Assistance
>
> If unselfish ingenious
> Mona Van Duyn Thurston
>
> could send me on a post-card,
> despite inconvenience and
> a dearth of wild animals—
> a wild moose making its way through
> a Maine lake in deep water—
>
> could I not ignore disability
> and fly to Washington University?

Moore also agreed to judge The Wednesday Club's annual poetry contest, having won the first one the group held in 1926.

She practiced many occupations, none for long—that of the head of the commercial department at the Carlyle Indian School, for instance, where, by most odd chance, one of her students was Jim Thorpe; then that of a librarian; an editor of the *Dial*; a freelance reviewer—before she became a public figure, famous for her tricorne hat, her gnomic pronouncements, her unlikely love of horse racing and baseball, her fashion spread in

104

Life, her appearance on Johnny Carson, her offer to name what became the Edsel, and her four words about poetry ("I, too, dislike it"), rather than for her infrequent, arcane, unfathomable writings.

Miss Moore recieved an honorary degree from Washington University in 1967. She died in Brooklyn on February 5, 1972, and received a star on the St. Louis Walk of Fame in 1996.

---

260 Cumberland Street
Brooklyn 5, 1962 New York

Dear Mr. Guenther:

We all like The POST-DESPATCH.

I don't know that I can answer helpfully but let me try.

When my mother, my brother and I were living with my grandfather, the Reverend John R. Warner and my mother's aunt, Mrs. George Eyestef, in Kirkwood, Missouri, where my grandfather was pastor of the First Presbyterian Church of Kirkwood, ~~our aunt~~ died - 1893; and the following year - 1894, my grandfather died. A cousin, a niece of my mother's mother, had lived in Carlisle, Pennsylvania, and suggested that my mother come to the east to live (Carlisle) where in the course of time my brother could attend Dickenson College, and I also, the college being co-educational. My brother, however, attended Yale (class of 1908) - a graduate of Yale, and I attended Bryn Mawr (1909).

When my brother (not married) became the pastor of the Ogden Memorial Presbyterian Church of Chatham, New Jersey, my

104. Mona Van Duyn and Marianne Moore at Washington University commencement ceremonies, 1967.

mother and I left Carlisle, to assist him in administering the Manse. In 1918 my brother was married, entered the Navy. My mother and I, instead of returning to Carlisle, found an apartment in New York; I was, ~~in 1924 - or was it~~ (1925) - invited by Scofield Thayer and J. S. Watson, owners of The Dial, to join the staff. When The Dial was discontinued in 1929, my mother and I came to Brooklyn to live, my brother having been appointed to duty in the Brooklyn Navy Yard. My mother died in 1947. My brother - forty years in the Navy, then Chaplain of the Gunnery School, Washington, Connecticut, now lives in Washington, Connecticut.

I have fond and admiring memories of St. Louis. My mother attended the Mary Institute, whose bulletins I receive and read with keen interest. I have a veiled Prophet procession Mermod, Jaccard, plate presented me by the Wednesday Club (souvenir of some assistance of mine in connection with a contest). Mr. A. S. Mermod lived in Kirkwood and was an elder in my grandfather's church. I cannot think any city more cultured than St. Louis.

Sincerely yours,
Marianne Moore
i.e. Marianne Craig Moore

Please condone my ragged typing and narrative, disability having prayed upon me this month. I thank you for the enclosed envelope.

Mr. Charles Guenther
2935 Russell Boulevard
St. Louis, Missouri

If my feeling about Brooklyn is of interest, BROOKLYN FROM CLINTON HILL is included in A MARIANNE MOORE READER (Viking), 1961

The Mind is an Enchanting Thing

is an enchanted thing
    like the glaze on a
katydid-wing
        subdivided by sun
          till the nettings are legion.
Like Gieseking playing Scarlatti;

like the apteryx-awl
    as a beak, or the
kiwi's rain-shawl
        of haired feathers, the mind
          feeling its way as though blind,
walks along with its eyes on the ground.

It has memory's ear
    that can hear without
having to hear.
        Like the gyroscope's fall,
        truly unequivocal
because trued by regnant certainty,

it is a power of
    strong enchantment. It
is like the dove–
        neck animated by
        sun; it is memory's eye;
it's conscientious inconsistency.

It tears off the veil; tears
    the temptation, the
mist the heart wears,
        from its eyes—if the heart
        has a face; it takes apart
dejection. It's fire in the dove-neck's

iridescence; in the
    inconsistencies
of Scarlatti.
        Unconfusion submits
        its confusion to proof; it's
not a Herod's oath that cannot change.

*It was a black hour
of a night without a
moon, the month being
July, the year 1763.
Along the dark curve of*

the New Orleans river front no lights showed except in a couple of dark hovels where vagabond boatmen, like bears gorging against a winter's fast, drank and reveled late in anticipation of the lean rigors of the return voyage upstream, now drawing daily closer to them.

—River Out of Eden

Unlike many of the other writers in this book, Shirley Louise Seifert did not depart the town of her birth. She not only remained true to her school, she stayed put and got published. Seifert was born in St. Peters, Missouri, and later moved to Kirkwood. She attended Central High School and graduated from Washington University in 1909, the same year as Fannie Hurst, with whom she was a member of Thrysus, the university's student-run theatrical group. After graduation she taught in the St. Louis public schools, and during World War I she worked in the Liberty Loan office.

105

Shirley Louise Seifert,
St. Louis, Mo.
College. Thyrsus, '07, '08, '09. Annual Play, '07, '08.
Pi Beta Phi.

106

In 1919 Seifert published her first short story in *American Magazine*, "The Girl Who Was Too Good Looking." Her preferred genre, though, was the historical novel, and she published her first, *Land of Tomorrow*, in 1937. In a foreword to her 1940 novel *River Out of Eden*, Seifert offered a précis of her work:

> We know the mighty deeds of our forbears as they made their brave way
> through deep and secret forests, following great rivers that rose and ended no-

---

105. *Cast of* London Assurance *in* The Hatchet, 1909. *Seifert
stands in the middle row, second from left, wearing white.
Fannie Hurst stands in the center, with a rider's crop.*
106. *Washington University graduation photograph, 1909.*

body knew exactly where, living out their lives with danger always dark and close beside them; but of the human frailties and passions and victories and defeats that went with them wherever they moved we know very little. Those stories were left for dreamers, mooning over the old legends, to shape out of bits and scraps and to tell for the pure delight of weaving a tale.

Shirley Seifert's 1938 novel *The Wayfarer* was nominated for a Pulitzer Prize. She conducted extensive research for her books, consulting diaries, newspapers and letters. Some of Seifert's other books include *Captain Grant* (1946), *The Turquoise Trail* (1950), *Let My Name Stand Fair* (1956) and *A Key to St. Louis* (1963). With her sister Adele she wrote the mystery *Death Stops at the Old Stone Inn* (1938) and *A History of the Grace Church in Kirkwood* (1959). She taught fiction writing at Washington University and was active in Theta Sigma Phi, the women journalist's society.

Seifert died in Kirkwood at the age of eighty-three.

CHAPTER

I.   . . . I Am Afraid
II.   Destination–?
III.   "Man, What a Night!"
IV.   ". . . Caught in a Trap"
V.   "Get Lieutenant MacGowan"
VI.   ". . . A Murderer. . . Is a Dangerous Person"
VII.   . . . The End Of The World
VIII.   I, William, MacGowan
IX.   "Seems to Me There Was a Man . . ."
X.   . . . A Suit of Peach-tinted Pajamas
XI.   . . . Alibis Are Tricky Things
XII.   . . . The Weapon
XIII.   . . . Bric-a-brac
XIV.   The Day Was Done
XV.   Chaos Reigned
XVI.   . . . He Scared the Heart Out of Me
XVII.   . . . The Unregistered Guest
XVIII.   . . . The Exquisite, Ruined Handkerchief.
XIX.   . . . A Door Slammed
XX.   "Yes. . . I Knew"

—Table of Contents, *Death Stops at the Old Stone Inn*

St. Louis is a city of winds, and the air above Lambert Field is usually rough.
    —Spirit of St. Louis

CHARLES A. LINDBERGH
February 4, 1902 — August 26, 1974

Like most airports, Lambert was a cornfield first. After Charles Lindbergh graduated at the head of his class from the Advanced Flying School at the U.S. Army's Kelly Field, he had expected to proceed to active duty as a second lieutenant in the Air Service Reserve Corps, but the corps had few openings in their squadrons just then, so the former barnstormer had to look about for employment. He had flown upside-down, demonstrated stalls, chuted toward a flour-outlined target, walked on wings, looped the loop, landed on one wheel or with a "dead stick." On one occasion he had attended the St. Louis Air Meet, which was held October 4-6 in 1923 above the partly cleared cornfield that balloon pilot Major Albert Lambert had purchased a few years before. "The one-hundred-seventy-acre clay sod field had no runways, simply a triangular landing space at its center. In winter the cold, the wind, and the frozen grooves in the ground challenged even the best pilots." The 125,000 people who watched the sky on the last day had not come to contemplate a muddy field but to watch the meet's main event, the Pulitzer Trophy Race which was won by a Navy Curtis biplane that averaged 243.7 miles per hour over the 125-mile course. The *St. Louis Globe-Democrat*, squeezing a few sour grapes, said that such speed was only possible for a military aircraft and that such shenanigans had no commercial value.

Lindbergh picked up a few flying students (one named Marvin Northrop) and barnstormed several Illinois towns, but he always returned to Lambert Field, which was becoming an increasingly important place for planes crisscrossing the country. With St. Louis as his home base, but while performing stunts in Minnesota, Beans (not yet "Lucky Lindy") enlisted in the Air Force, mainly to fly their De Haviland planes. It was natural, then, that after his graduation, and looking for work, Lindbergh should try his luck back in St. Louis. To be close to Lambert Field he chose a boarding-house in Anglum, some ten miles northwest of downtown, a place that has since disappeared from most maps.

Lindbergh took on casuals at first. There was one passenger who wanted to pee upon his hometown, and got his wish. Another time he flew a judge alongside a plane carrying a bride and groom. Aerial weddings enjoyed a brief craze. And there was the manager of a flying circus whose girlfriend and star refused to wing-walk as advertised, and who stiffed him, stealing the receipts. Finally, though, Lindbergh was carrying the U.S. mail between St. Louis and Chicago—a job steady, though dangerous. Once he had to bail out and float blindly through fog into one of those fields of corn. The postman's famous motto, now mostly forgotten and no longer observed, was Lindbergh's and his buddies' creed:

Ploughing through storms, wedging our way beneath low clouds, paying almost no attention to weather forecasts, we've more than once landed our re-built army warplanes on Chicago's Maywood field when other lines canceled out, when older and perhaps wiser pilots ordered their cargo put on a train. During the long days of summer we seldom missed a flight. But now winter is creeping up on us. Nights are lengthening; skies are thickening with haze and storm. We're already landing by floodlight at Chicago. In a few more weeks it will be dark when we glide down onto that narrow strip of cow pasture called the Peoria air-mail field. Before the winter is past, even the meadow at Springfield will need lights. Today I'm over an hour late—engine trouble in St. Louis.

Meanwhile, Lindbergh was beginning to detail his dream of flying nonstop across the Atlantic. That is, he was envisioning the plane and cal-culating the fuel load and spending the posted twenty-five thousand dollar prize. More than that, he was composing his pitch and selecting sponsors in his mind. With a single page proposal drawn up, Lindbergh began his cam-paign by talking to an insurance executive, Earl Thompson, whom he knew was an ardent flier. He buttonholed Thompson in his home, but more often Lindbergh hung out at Louie's lunch stand at Lambert. There, commercial pilots and aviation fans as well as sales reps tended to gather between flights. Meanwhile, the prize, like honey, was gathering other flies: René Fonck, France's World War air ace Lieutenant Commander Richard Byrd, Clarence Chamberlin, Noel Davis and Stanton Wooster, as well as the French team of Charles Nungesser and François Coli.

Eventually, Major Lambert as well as his brother pledged their savings, and Lindbergh's boss, Major Bill Robertson, agreed to adjust mail flight schedules to accommodate preparations. In New York he spoke with the de-signer of the Bellanca-Wright airplane he had chosen, though the availabil-ity of the plane remained doubtful. He also considered raising money from St. Louis citizens, inviting them to support him at ten dollars a head. However, an editor of the *Post-Dispatch* told Lindbergh that they "wouldn't think of taking part in such a hazardous flight. To fly across the Atlantic Ocean with one pilot and a single-engine plane! We have our reputation to consider. We couldn't possibly be associated with such a venture!"

Finally, Slim (when he wasn't string "Bean") went to the head of the St. Louis Flying Club, Harry Hall Knight, and Knight, full of understanding and enthusiasm, made it his business to raise the necessary funds, which he quickly did, enlisting a private pilot, his friend Harold Bixby, who was also a vice president of the State National Bank and the president of the St. Louis Chamber of Commerce, in the project. Later, E. Lansing Ray, owner of the *Globe-Democrat*, was persuaded to come in. More difficulties secur-ing the right plane followed. Finally, Lindbergh went to Ryan Aircraft in San Diego, which custom built his plane for him.

Meanwhile, the competition was demonstrating the flight's degree of danger. Fonck's Skorsky went into a gully at the end of a runway at Roosevelt Field, Long Island, killing two of the crew; Byrd's Fokker crash-

107

landed on its first trial flight, injuring three; during takeoff, Chamberlin's Bellanca (the very plane that Lindbergh had coveted) lost its landing gear; Davis and Wooster were both killed on their last test run; and Nungesser and Coli, who had taken off from Paris, disappeared over the sea.

Lindbergh flew his new Ryan home from San Diego and ate a celebrational lunch of ham and eggs at Louie's. With the fate of his competition still cloudy, Lindbergh flew to New York in seven hours and twenty-two minutes, which, with his time from San Diego, established a new transcontinental record. Weather and repairs delayed the attempt a few days. On the evening of May 19, 1927, learning that by morning conditions should improve, they began filling the plane's tanks.

The rest, as we say, was sandwiches, steering and history. Lindbergh would fly far away from St. Louis, despite the plane's name. But had Lindbergh not succeeded and been captured in the inescapable net of the world's attention, he couldn't have written *The Spirit of St. Louis* either, his own wonderful account of the adventure, or be regarded, ever after, as an author.

In 1954 Charles Lindbergh received a Pulitzer Prize for his autobiography.

107. Charles Lindbergh with reporters outside
Louie's lunchroom at Lambert Field, 1927

Turn back to this quiet acre in the night
And find the cold petals of that pristine star
Which, alone and immaculate and white
Blossoms beyond the temporal hour.

—"The Quiet Flower"

Most writers have obsessions. Josephine Johnson's were nature's landscape and society's sins. These would compel her to write her first novel, *Now in November*, a portrait of a poor farming family, and to advocate for those without advantage and ease—although childhood can be perilous for anyone, even someone born in Kirkwood:

> Twenty years is a long time in one place. I loved that place. I knew every inch of it, and every hour of the day and every season. But I have no will to write about it now. Too much pain. Too long ago. Growing up is a terrible time. A person lives with such intensity you wonder there is anything left to go on when it's over. It's a life assimilated now, used up, written out. A curious life. Mother was left with four girls, two hundred acres, and four living sisters of her own. We all turned out strangely sane in spite of everything, although we wondered sometimes if we would make it. There was lots of sky. I saw more sky there on the farm than ever in my life before. Sky and wind. I had a rolltop desk in the attic under the dormer window (the wind through those dormer windows made an eerie banshee sound), and I wrote. I wrote, if not endlessly, then enormously, fulsomely.

Josephine Winslow Johnson was born in Kirkwood on June 20, 1910, and lived there until 1947. She was named for her maternal grandfather, Joseph Franklin, an immigrant from Tipperary in County Cork, Ireland. Franklin worked his way up to become vice-president of the William Barr Dry Goods Company, a forerunner of the May Company, also known as Famous-Barr. Joseph Franklin moved to Kirkwood in 1883 and built Oakland, "ten acres of great oak trees." The house "stood on a slope above a large pond—a pond with a huge granite figure of Neptune at one end with a gray stone beard and a trident imported from the World's Fair in St. Louis." Josephine Johnson wrote about this house and others in her 1973 book *Seven Houses: A Memoir of Time and Places.* (The family sold Oakland in 1915. It was later bought by the Ursuline order of nuns and converted to a religious academy for girls. The original house was torn down.) Josephine's mother, Ethel Franklin, married Benjamin Johnson at Oakland in 1908, and they settled at 203 South Woodlawn, where their four daughters were born. Later the family stayed with Josephine's aunts at 621 Monroe Avenue while their own house (sky, attic, dormer) was being built just outside of Kirkwood. They moved to Hillbrook in 1922.

108

. . . my father bought a farm and sold his wholesale coffee business in St. Louis. (I can still smell the harsh sweet fragrance of raw coffee, see the brown beans sliding down troughs, and the big rolltop desk in Dad's office, the boats on the Missouri River, the big stones of the levee.) Mother was tired of trees, she wanted a view, and they built a house, a big stone house, on the top of a naked hill, not a tree around, and you could see the lights of St. Louis fifteen miles away. Dad was sixty years old and had worked very hard all his life. He had dreamed of this retirement for many years.

He had a little while of his dream. Grapevines and cows and corn and horses and a good man to do the work. He named the place Hillbrook, a pleasant homely name for the pleasant life he hoped to live. He had money and leisure now, but his health was gone. He had put his dream off too long. In a few short years he died of cancer.

That was in 1926. Benjamin Johnson had lived at Hillbrook for almost four years.

Josephine and her sisters, Mary Elisabeth, Florence and Marjorie, went to Hanover, "a very good school with one teacher"—Blanche Byars, the daughter of Vincent Byars, a Greek scholar, poet and writer on the staff of the *Mirror*. Near the end of World War I, Josephine wrote her first poem, a patriotic one "inspired by a huge newspaper drawing of Liberty, Justice and Humanity striding along in a blaze of sunlight bearing flags and banners. . . . I had found my niche in life." She was seven.

> Out of the light
> Come the conquerors three,
> Liberty, Justice and Humanity.

Johnson entered Lenox Hall after graduating from Hanover. She kept a diary cum sketchbook documenting her thoughts and the natural world as she observed it at Hillbrook and her other houses. Writing and drawing would be her companions throughout her life. She entered Washington University in 1927 and studied in both the art and English departments while continuing to live at home. She also began to publish stories and poems in *Harper's* and *Poetry* and to correspond with Clifton Fadiman, an editor at Simon and Schuster, who had read one of her stories in the *Atlantic*. She left Washington University after three years to write and volunteer, painting murals at the Mission Free School and the Turner School for the Disabled and Delinquent Negro Children. As a new member of the St. Louis Writers' Guild she was asked to judge the short story contest and awarded the prize to Tom Williams who, in his letter of gratitude, included a few poems by Li Po, whose work he had just discovered. In 1934 Johnson won the St. Louis Writers' Guild contest for her poem "Ice Winter," the same year in which she signed a contract for and submitted "Novel As Yet Untitled" to Simon and Schuster.

The book was *Now in November*. It is set on a farm in Missouri and is narrated by a young woman close to Johnson's age whose family is financially ravaged by the depression. Nature threatens to do the same:

> By June things were shriveling brown, but not everything was dried and ugly yet. It was not so much the heat and dryness then as the fear of what they *would* do. I could imagine a kind of awful fascination in the very continuousness of this drought, a wry perfection in its slow murder of all things. We might have marveled and exclaimed and said there was never anything like it, never anything worse, and shaken our heads, recalling all other years in comparison with a kind of gloomy joy. But this was only for those to whom it was like a play, something that could be forgotten as soon as it was over. For us there was no final and blessed curtain—unless it was death. This was too real.

Now in November was published on September 13, 1934, and won the Pulitzer Prize the following year. Josephine Johnson was twenty-four. She used her new fame to tell stories outside of her books: she wrote articles for the *St. Louis Post-Dispatch* about the conditions of the poor; she became a member of the American Civil Liberties Union, the Urban League, the Fellowship of Reconciliation; and, with Fannie Cook, she worked on the St. Louis Committee for the Rehabilitation of Sharecroppers. She also became president of the Co-operative Consumers of St. Louis in the hopes of abolishing the "profit system." She published a book of short stories, *Winter Orchard*, in 1935; her first book of poems, *Year's End*, and her second novel, *Jordanstown* in 1937; and a children's book, *Paulina: The Story of an Apple-Butter Pot*, in 1939, the same year Simon and Schuster rejected her next novel *Inland Ocean* and the year she married her first husband, Thurlow Smoot, an attorney for the National Labor Relations Board (NLRB) in St. Louis. They had one son before divorcing in 1941. A year later she married Grant Cannon and "the real life began," she writes in *Seven Houses*.

Cannon was from Salt Lake City and had come to St. Louis as a field examiner for the NLRB. Their first child was born in St. Louis. Josephine Johnson lived with her two children at Hillbrook while Cannon fought in World War II. He returned, Johnson writes, "during an extraordinary spring and from that hour I was married to an extraordinary man for thirty years. ... [his] mind reminded me of an electric powerhouse full of various engines. He went about revving them up and down, attending to them, neglecting them, returning—but none ever went cold." In 1947 Cannon became the editor of the *Farm Quarterly* and they moved to Cincinnati, Ohio, and then in 1956 to what would become their "inland island," the Summerside area of Clermont County, Ohio. Their second child was born and Johnson continued to write, but not as much. Grant Cannon died in 1969, the year she published *Inland Island*, an essay about the lives of her family and the other inhabitants of their farm in Ohio:

> The fox seems fast and fearless, clever and cunning, and without manners or morals or scruples, a legend of freedom, and I had long found release in this private image in my heart. When harassed by those affairs of life for which I am not well fitted—those which require grace, authority, political acumen, wit and social ease; weddings and meetings, funerals and gatherings; or when, bewildered by the constant domestic matters where the warm maternal wisdom and patience are drawn as though they were from an unfailing spring, instead of a cistern much in need of rain—then, tormented by conflicting voices, by inadequate responses, by lack of wit or wisdom (or even the answer to Who-the-hell-are-you?) the self sought relief in the heart's image of the wild free fox. The fox on the ridge moving lightly, seeing far below her the hound on the chain, the old, slow doorstep hound, whose eyes followed only the boots and the shoes and the beetle's tracks. The wild red-and-grey fox circling the farm lots, free, running the ride, regarding with cold amber eyes the penned white flock, or sleeping in the silence of the ferns.

In 1970 Josephine Johnson was awarded an honorary doctorate of humane letters from Washington University. In 1990 she contracted pneumonia but was too busy to go to the doctor. She died on February 27. "Appreciate the living," she wrote in *Inland Island*. "Live the summers now. That's all you'll ever have. They're all anybody will ever have."

109

LOCATIONS LIST

Existing sites, plaques and memorials are noted with a star; all other locations no longer stand. Sites on maps are keyed to:
St. Louis and Environs [SLE] map p. 3
Downtown [D] map p. 14
Central West End [CWE] map p. 144
University City [UC] map p. 189
Outer Limits [OL] map p. 234

Zoë Akins (1886-1958)
Hosmer Hall, 4926 Washington Avenue, c. 1900
4902 Washington Avenue, c. 1902
★ Old Post Office, city block bounded by Olive, Locust, Eighth, and Ninth Streets, 1900-1903 [D7]
★ 30 Benton Place, c. 1905 [D13]
Cicardi's Restaurant, Delmar Boulevard and Euclid Avenue, c. 1906
4116 Westminster Place, 1910

Sally Benson (1897-1972)
5135 Kensington Avenue, c. 1897

Heinrich Börnstein (1805-1892)
Anzeiger des Westens, 16 North Third Street, c. 1850
Anzeiger des Westens, 15 North Third Street, c. 1860
★ Camp Jackson Memorial in Lyon Park, South Broadway and Arsenal Street [D14]

Harold Brodkey (1930-1996)
★ 504 Kingsland Avenue, University City, c. 1940 [UC6]
★ University City High School, 7401 Balson Avenue, c. 1947 [UC3]

William Wells Brown (1814-1884)
North side of Lucas Avenue, west of First Street, c. 1830

William Burroughs (1914-1997)
★ 4664 Pershing Place, 1914-1924 [CWE8]
★ Community School, 900 North Lay Road, Ladue, c. 1922
Fairmont Hotel, 4907 Maryland Plaza, c. 1926
700 Price Road, Ladue, c. 1926
★ John Burroughs School, 755 South Price Road, Ladue, c. 1926 [SLE5]
★ Taylor High School, 222 North Central Avenue, Clayton, c. 1931

★ 10036 Conway Road, Ladue, Cobblestone Gardens Gift Shop, c. 1940 (now a residence)
★ Jefferson Barracks, 533 Grant Road, c. 1942 [SLE10]
★ Bellefontaine Cemetery, 4947 West Florissant Avenue [SLE4]

Kate Chopin (1850-1904)
801 Chouteau Avenue, birthplace, demolished for the Ralston Purina Complex
1118 St. Ange Avenue, c. 1865
1125 St. Ange Avenue, c. 1884
1122 St. Ange Avenue, c. 1885
Sacred Heart Academy, Fifth and Market Streets, c. 1868
Holy Angels Church, St. Ange Avenue between Chouteau and LaSalle, c. 1870
★ 4504 Westminster Place, The Wednesday Club, c. 1890 [CWE5]
3317 Delmar Boulevard, formerly Morgan Street, c. 1900
★ Mercantile Library, 510 Locust Street, c. 1902 [D3]
★ 4232 McPherson Avenue, 1904 [CWE12]
★ Calvary Cemetery, 5239 West Florissant Avenue [SLE3]

Winston Churchill (1871-1947)
2810 Pine Street, c. 1875
★ Security Building, 319 North Fourth Street, c. 1897 [D2]

Fannie Cook (1893-1949)
★ 7068 Maryland Avenue, University City, c. 1938
★ 400 Purdue Avenue, University City, c. 1949 [UC4]

Carl Daenzer (1820-1906)
Sixteenth and Papin Streets, c. 1867
Westliche Post, 116-118 Chestnut Street, c. 1867
1730 Missouri Avenue, c. 1897
★ Naked Truth Monument, Compton Hill Reservoir Park, Grand Boulevard at Russell Avenue [SLE12]

Theodore Dreiser (1871-1945)
★ Wainwright Building, 708 Pine Street, apartment, 1892-1894 [D5]
Globe-Democrat, Sixth and Pine Streets, c. 1892
Missouri Republican, Third and Chestnut Streets, c. 1893

The Planter's House Hotel, Fourth and
Pine Streets, c. 1893
★ Mercantile Library, 510 Locust Street,
c. 1894 [D3]

William Greenleaf Eliot (1811-1887)
Unitarian Church, Fourth and Pine
Streets, c. 1830
Eighth Avenue between Olive and Locust
Streets, c. 1840
Church of the Messiah, Ninth and Olive
Streets, c. 1852
Church of the Messiah, 508 Garrison
Avenue, c. 1881
2660 Washington Boulevard, c. 1885
★ Bellefontaine Cemetery, 4947 West
Florissant Avenue [SLE4]

T. S. Eliot (1888-1965)
Henry Ware Eliot (1843-1919)
Charlotte Stearns Eliot (1843-1929)
★2635 Locust Street, T. S. Eliot birthplace,
plaque
Mrs. Lockwood's School, 3569 Lindell
Boulevard, c. 1894
★ 4504 Westminster Place, The Wednesday
Club, c. 1890 [CWE5]
William Prufrock Furniture Store, 1104
Olive Street, c. 1900
★ 4446 Westminster Place, c. 1906, plaque
[CWE4]
★ St. Louis Public Library, 1301 Olive
Street, plaque [D11]
★ Christ Church Cathedral, 1210 Locust
Street, plaque [D9]

Eugene Field (1850-1895)
★ Eugene Field House and Toy Museum,
634 South Broadway [D4]
★ Eugene Field School, 4466 Olive Street

Kate Field (1838-1896)
St. Louis Theatre, Third and Olive Streets,
c. 1840
St. Louis Reveille, 22 Olive Street, c. 1845
Mrs. Smith's Female Seminary, 19 North
Sixth Street, c. 1848

Martha Gellhorn (1908-1998)
★ 4366 McPherson Avenue, c. 1910
★ Mahler Ballroom, 4915 Washington
Avenue, c. 1915
★ John Burroughs School, 755 South Price
Road, Ladue, 1922-1926 [SLE5]

Ulysses S. Grant (1822-1885)
★ Jefferson Barracks, 533 Grant Road,
c. 1843 [SLE10]
Fourth and Cerre Streets, c. 1848
★ Ulysses S. Grant National Historic Site
(White Haven), 7400 Grant Road, c. 1854
Seventh and Lynch Streets, c. 1855 [SLE8]
★ Hardscrabble Cabin, Grant's Farm, 10501
Gravois Road, c. 1856 [SLE9]
Planter's House Hotel, Fourth and Pine
Streets, c. 1857
Seventh and Lynch Streets, c. 1859
1008 Barton Street, c. 1860
★ Tucker Boulevard and Market Street,
statue of Ulysses S. Grant

Emily Hahn (1905-1997)
★ 4858 Fountain Avenue, 1905-1920 [CWE7]
George Washington Public School, Euclid
and Fountain Avenues, c. 1910
★ Soldan High School, 918 North Union
Boulevard, c. 1920 [CWE1]

William T. Harris (1835-1909)
★ 1100-1118 South Eighteenth Street,
William T. Harris Row (he lived at 1116),
c. 1875

Chester Himes (1909-1984)
★ Barnes Hospital, 216 South
Kingshighway Boulevard, c. 1923
★ Missouri School for the Blind, 3815
Magnolia Avenue, c. 1923
★ Art Hill, Saint Louis Art Museum,
Forest Park, c. 1924 [CWE2]

Fannie Hurst (1885-1968)
Central High School, Grand and Finney
Avenues, c. 1900
★ 5641 Cates Avenue, c. 1900 [CWE13]
★ New Mount Sinai Cemetery, 8430
Gravois Road [SLE7]

William Inge (1913-1973)
★ Coronado Hotel, 3701 Lindell Boulevard,
c. 1943
★ Neighborhood Gardens, 1213 North
Seventh Street and Biddle, c. 1945 [D6]
★ Musical Arts Building, Olive and Boyle,
c. 1948
★ 6168 McPherson Avenue, c. 1949 [CWE11]

Orrick Johns (1887-1946)
4066 Cook Avenue, c. 1889
5657 Cabanne Avenue, c. 1894
Dozier Public School, 5749 Maple Avenue,
c. 1895
5655 Maple Avenue, c. 1899
Central High School, Grand and Finney
Avenues, c. 1902
★ St. Louis Public Library former location,
Locust and Ninth Streets, c. 1910 (now the
Board of Education Building)

Josephine Johnson (1910-1990)
341 South Sappington Road, "Oakland,"
Kirkwood, home of maternal grandparents
and where Johnson's parents were mar-
ried, now the site of Ursuline Academy
★ 203 South Woodlawn Avenue, Kirkwood,
birthplace [OL4]
Hanover School, 427 N. Taylor, Kirkwood,
c. 1907
★ 621 East Monroe Avenue, home of
Johnson's aunts, where the family lived
while "Hillbrook" was being built,
Kirkwood, c. 1919
★ 1667 North Woodlawn Avenue,
"Hillbrook," Kirkwood, c. 1922
Lenox Hall, Woodlawn and Gill Avenues,
Kirkwood, c. 1922
Mission Free School, 369 North Taylor, c. 1930
★ Turner School, 4235 West Kennerly
Avenue, c. 1930

Charles Lindbergh (1902-1974)
476 South Kingshighway, site of Racquet
Club, c. 1925
★ Lambert International Airport, c. 1926
[SLE2]

Elijah Lovejoy (1802-1837)
St. Louis Observer, North side of Lucas
Avenue, West of First Street, c. 1830
★ Rock House, meeting place of Elijah
Lovejoy's Anti-Slavery Society, 2705
College Avenue, Alton, Illinois, c. 1835
★ College Avenue Presbyterian Church,
1702 Clawson Street, Alton, c. 1837
★ Elijah Lovejoy Monument and Gravesite,
Monument and Fourth Streets, Alton [SLE1]
★ *Alton Telegraph*, yoke from the fourth
printing press, 111 East Broadway, Alton
★ Elijah Lovejoy Memorial Room, Alton
Museum of History and Art, 2809 College
Avenue, Alton

Marshall McLuhan (1911-1980)
★ 4343 McPherson Avenue, c. 1938
★ Hotel Jefferson, Tucker Boulevard and
Locust Street, c. 1940
★ Coronado Hotel, 3701 Lindell Boulevard,
c. 1944
★ Chase Park Plaza Hotel, Kingshighway
and Lindell Boulevard, c. 1944
★ Saint Louis University, 221 North Grand
Boulevard, 1938-1944 [SLE11]

Marianne Moore (1887-1972)
★ Old Presbyterian Manse, Adams Avenue
and Kirkwood Road, Kirkwood, c. 1887 [OL3]

Paul Elmer More (1864-1937)
Sixteenth Street Presbyterian Church,
Sixteenth and Walnut Streets, c. 1859
Papin Street, between Fourteenth and
Fifteenth Streets, c. 1864
Stoddard School, 2840 Lucas Avenue, c. 1870
3113 Washington Avenue, c. 1872
Branch High School No. 1, Seventh and
Chestnut Streets, c. 1880
Old Public High School, Fifteenth and
Olive Streets, c. 1883
1520 Lay (now Euclid) Avenue, c. 1885

John Morris (1931-1997)
★ 6334 McPherson Avenue, 1967-1995 [UC7]

Reinhold Niebuhr (1892-1971)
Eden Seminary, 6700 Easton Avenue (now
Dr. Martin Luther King Boulevard), origi-
nal location in Wellston, c. 1905
★ Eden Chapel, Eden Theological
Seminary, 475 East Lockwood, Webster
Groves, stained glass memorial [OL2]

John Neihardt (1881-1973)
5500 Enright Avenue, c. 1936
★ *St. Louis Post-Dispatch*, 900 North
Tucker Boulevard, 1926-1938 [D10]

Joseph Stanley Pennell (1908-1963)
★ YMCA, 1528 Locust Street, c. 1930

Emil Preetorius (1827-1905)
1145 South Seventh Street, c. 1867
Westliche Post, 116-118 Chestnut Street,
c. 1867
★ Naked Truth Monument, Compton Hill
Reservoir Park, Grand Boulevard at
Russell Avenue [SLE12]

Joseph Pulitzer (1847-1911)

Westliche Post, 116-118 Chestnut Street, c. 1867

★ Old Courthouse, 11 North Fourth Street, c. 1878 [D1]

2920 Washington Avenue, c. 1879

2648 Locust Street, c. 1880

William Marion Reedy (1862-1920)

Twenty-First Street between Washington and Carr Avenues, c. 1864

Saint Louis University, Ninth Street and Washington Avenue, 1876-1880

Missouri Republican, Third and Chestnut Streets, 1882-1886

Globe-Democrat, Fourth and Pine Streets, 1886-1891

Star-Sayings, 105 North Sixth Street, c. 1890

1902 Cass Avenue, c. 1892

1324 North Twenty-Fourth Street, c. 1893

Sunday Mirror, 516 Walnut Street, c. 1893

1327 North Twenty-Seventh Street, c. 1894

204 North Third Street, c. 1896

★ *Mirror*, Security Building, 319 North Fourth Street, c. 1898 [D2]

3501 Washington Avenue, c. 1900

509 North Spring Avenue, c. 1900

Mirror, 915 Olive Street, c. 1910

Mirror, 211 North Seventh Street, c. 1921

Clonmel, Reedy's farm, Manchester and Berry Roads, Rockhill, 1909-1920

★ Calvary Cemetery, 5239 West Florissant Avenue [SLE3]

★ St. Louis Public Library, 1301 Olive Street, bust of Reedy [D11]

Irma Rombauer (1877-1962)

2304 Scott Avenue, 1879

1017 Grattan Street, 1880

2325 Market Street, 1881

7620 South Main Street, 1882

7620 South Broadway, 1886

★ 7619 South Broadway, 1896

3816 Botanical Avenue, 1899

★ 5142 Waterman Avenue, Apartment C, c. 1925

2167 South Spring Street, Marion Rombauer's apartment, c. 1925

5712 Cabanne Avenue, 1931-1955

★ 4605 Lindell Boulevard, the Monticello, Apartment 804, 1955-1962 [CWE10]

★ Bellefontaine Cemetery, 4947 West Florissant Avenue [SLE4]

Carl Schurz (1829-1906)

Westliche Post, 116-118 Chestnut Street, c. 1867

Park Avenue between Mississippi and Missouri, c. 1868

★ Naked Truth Monument, Compton Hill Reservoir Park, Grand Boulevard at Russell Avenue [SLE12]

Shirley Seifert (1888-1971)

Central High School, Grand and Finney Avenues, c. 1904

★ 5774 DeGiverville, c. 1930

★ 505 S. Clay Avenue, Kirkwood, c. 1970 [OL5]

William T. Sherman (1820-1891)

★ Jefferson Barracks, 533 Grant Road, c. 1850 [SLE10]

Harrison Street between First and Fremont Streets, c. 1855

226 Locust Street, c. 1861

912 North Garrison Avenue, 1865-1886

★ St. Francis Xavier, "College Church," Grand and Lindell Boulevards, 1891

★ Calvary Cemetery, 5239 West Florissant Avenue [SLE3]

Peter Taylor (1917-1994)

5 Washington Terrace, 1926-1932

★ St. Louis Country Day School, 425 North Warson Road, c. 1930 [SLE6]

Sara Teasdale (1884-1933)

3668 Lindell Boulevard, c. 1884

Mrs. Lockwood's School, 3569 Lindell Boulevard, c. 1890

J. W. Teasdale and Company, 806 Spruce Street, c. 1885

★ 38 Kingsbury Place, c. 1890 [CWE9]

Hosmer Hall, 4926 Washington Boulevard, c. 1900

★ Bellefontaine Cemetery, 4947 West Florissant Avenue [SLE4]

Kay Thompson (1909-1998)

17 Parkland Place, c. 1909

★ Soldan High School, 918 North Union Boulevard, c. 1922 [CWE1]

Mark Twain (1835-1910)

Ninth and Olive Streets, c. 1857

South side of Locust Street, between Eighth and Ninth Streets, 1859

Evening News and Intelligencer, 76 N. Third Street, c. 1859
★ St. Louis Public Library, 1301 Olive Street, bust of Twain [D11]

Constance Urdang (1922-1996)
★ 6943 Columbia Place, University City, c. 1960 [UC8]

Tennessee Williams (1911-1983)
★ Eugene Field School, 4466 Olive Street, c. 1918
★ The Glass Menagerie Apartments, 4633 Westminster Place, c. 1918 [CWE6]
★ Soldan High School, 918 North Union Boulevard, c. 1920 [CWE1]
★ Lyndon Building, 5 South Taylor and Laclede Avenues, c. 1922
5938 Cates Avenue, c. 1924
Ben Blewett Junior High School, 5351 Enright Avenue, c. 1924
6254 Enright Avenue, c. 1926
★ University City High School, 7401 Balson Avenue, c. 1929 [UC3]
★ Mercantile Library, 510 Locust Street, c. 1930 [D3]
★ 4504 Westminster Place, The Wednesday Club, c. 1933 [CWE5]
★ 6634 Pershing Avenue, c. 1935
Rubicam Business School, Central School, 4931-4933 Delmar Boulevard, c. 1935
★ 1501-1509 Washington Boulevard, International Shoe Company, c. 1935 [D12]
★ 42 Aberdeen Place, c. 1937
★ Hotel Jefferson, Tucker Boulevard and Locust Street, c. 1940 [D8]
★ 53 Arundel Place, c. 1940 [UC5]
★ Jewel Box, Forest Park, c. 1940 [CWE2]
★ Barnes Hospital, 216 South Kingshighway Boulevard, c. 1968
★ 6360 Wydown Boulevard, Miss Edwina's home, c. 1970
★ Calvary Cemetery, 5239 West Florissant Avenue [SLE3]

Thomas Wolfe (1900-1938)
5095 Cates Avenue (formerly Fairmont), boarding house, 1904-1906

Patience Worth (1913-1937)
★ 6031 Kingsbury Boulevard, birthplace [CWE12]
★ 6037 Kingsbury Boulevard, c. 1914

★ "Rosedale Studio," 6040 Delmar Boulevard, c. 1914
1363 Union Boulevard, c. 1915
★ 1395 Union Boulevard, c. 1916
★ 5711 Cates Avenue, c. 1917
★ 5715 Cates Avenue, Apartment A, c. 1918
5714 Vernon Avenue, c. 1919
5641 Enright Avenue, c. 1921
5604 Kingsbury Boulevard, c. 1923

★ St. Louis Walk of Fame, 6200-6600 Delmar Boulevard [UC2]
William S. Burroughs
Kate Chopin
T. S. Eliot
Stanley Elkin
Eugene Field
Ulysses S. Grant
William Inge
Charles Lindbergh
Elijah Lovejoy
Marianne Moore
Howard Nemerov
Joseph Pulitzer
Irma Rombauer
William T. Sherman
Sara Teasdale
Tennessee Williams

Washington University
Washington Institute, Benton School, site of the first classes, 1854
The Academy, Academy Hall, college preparatory school for boys, Seventeenth Street between St. Charles and Washington Avenues, 1856-1880
Mary Institute, college preparatory school for girls, 1417 Locust Street, 1859-1879
Mary Institute, Locust and Beaumont Streets, 1879-1902
Smith Academy, expansion to Nineteenth Street and Washington Avenue, 1880-1917
Mary Institute, Lake and Waterman Avenues, 1902-1930
★ Mary Institute, 425 North Warson Road, 1930-present (Mary Institute officially separated from Washington University in 1949) [SLE6]
★ Washington University, "Just Beyond Tom Skinker's Road," 1905-present [UC1]

BIBLIOGRAPHY

Zoë Akins

Cranmer, Catharine. "Little Visits With Literary Missourians." *Missouri Historical Review* 20 (January 1926): 252-61.

Demastes, William, ed. *American Playwrights, 1880-1945.* Westport, Conn.: Greenwood Press, 1995.

Parke, Catherine, ed. *In the Shadow of Parnassus: Zoë Akins's Essays on Contemporary Poetry.* London: Associated University Presses, 1994.

Schlueter, June, ed. *Modern American Drama: The Female Canon.* London: Associated University Presses, 1990.

Shafer, Yvonne. *American Women Playwrights, 1900-1950.* New York: Peter Lang Publishing, 1995.

Slide, Anthony. "Zoë Akins," in *Dictionary of Literary Biography.* Detroit: Gale Research Co., 1984.

"Some Playwright Biographies." *Theatre Arts Monthly* 11 (July 1927): 531-32.

Sally Benson

Benson, Sally. *Meet Me in St. Louis.* Cleveland: World Publishing Company, 1941.

"Sally Benson, Author, 71, Dies; Wrote 'Meet Me in St. Louis,'" *New York Times*, July 22, 1972.

Heinrich Börnstein

Boernstein, Henry. *Memoirs of a Nobody: The Missouri Years of an Austrian Radical, 1849-1866.* Edited and translated by Steven Rowan. St. Louis: Missouri Historical Society Press, 1997.

Douai, Adolph. *Fata Morgana.* Deutsch-Amerikanische Preis-Novells. St. Louis: *Anzeiger des Westens*, 1858.

Rowan, Steven, ed. and trans. *Germans for a Free Missouri.* Columbia: University of Missouri Press, 1983.

Harold Brodkey

Brodkey, Harold. *First Love and Other Sorrows.* New York: The Dial Press, 1957.

——. *Runaway Soul.* New York: Farrar, Straus and Giroux, 1991.

——. *Stories in an Almost Classical Mode.* New York: Alfred A. Knopf, 1988.

William S. Burroughs

Burroughs, William S. *Early Routines.* Santa Barbara: Cadmus Editions, 1982.

——. "Last Words," *New Yorker* (August 18, 1997): 36-37.

——. *Naked Lunch.* New York: Grove Press, 1959.

——. *Port of Saints.* Berkley: Blue Wind Press, 1980.

——. "St. Louis Return," *Paris Review*, no. 35 (fall 1965): 51-62.

Goodman, Michael B. and Lemuel B. Coley. *William S. Burroughs: A Reference Guide.* New York: Garland Publishing, Inc., 1990.

McGuire, John M. "Billy Burroughs of St. Louis," *St. Louis Post-Dispatch*, August 10, 1997.

Miles, Barry. *William Burroughs: El Hombre Invisible.* New York: Hyperion, 1993.

Morgan, Ted. *Literary Outlaw: The Life and Times of William S. Burroughs.* New York: Henry Holt and Company, 1988.

Passaro, Vince. "The Forgotten Killer," *Harper's Magazine* (April 1998): 71-76.

St. Jorre, John de. *Venus Bound: The Erotic Voyage of the Olympia Press and Its Writers.* New York: Random House, 1994.

Watson, Steven. *The Birth of the Beat Generation.* New York: Pantheon Books, 1995.

Kate Chopin

Chopin, Kate. *The Awakening: A Solitary Soul.* New York: Alfred A. Knopf, 1992.

Toth, Emily. *Kate Chopin: A Life of the Author of the Awakening.* New York: William Morrow, 1990.

——. *Unveiling Kate Chopin.* Jackson: University Press of Mississippi, 1999.

Winston Churchill

Schneider, Robert W. *Novelist to a Generation: The Life and Thought of Winston Churchill.* Bowling Green: Bowling Green University Press, 1976.

Fannie Cook

Cook, Fannie. *Mrs. Palmer's Honey.* Garden City, N.Y.: Doubleday and Company, Inc., 1946.

Cadle, Jean Douglas. "'Cropperville' From Refuge to Community: A Study of Missouri Sharecroppers Who Found An Alternative to the Sharecropper System." Master's thesis, University of Missouri–St. Louis, 1993.

"Fannie Cook," *St. Louis Star-Times*, August 26, 1949.

Hynds, Reed. "St. Louis Woman Author Believes Her Sex Can Stabilize Human Race," *St. Louis Star-Times*, August 20, 1938.

"Mrs. Fannie Cook, University Graduate of 1914 Has Success in Writing," *Columbia Missourian*, December 24, 1938.

Charles Dickens

Dickens, Charles. *American Notes: A Journey.* New York: International Publishing Company, 1842.

Slater, Michael, ed. *Dickens On America and the Americans.* Austin: University of Texas Press, 1978.

Theodore Dreiser

Dreiser, Theodore. *Newspaper Days.* Edited by T. D. Nostwich. Philadelphia: University of Pennsylvania Press, 1991.

Swanberg, W. A. *Dreiser.* New York: Charles Scribner's Sons, 1965.

The Eliots

Ackroyd, Peter. *T. S. Eliot*. London: Hamish Hamilton, 1984.

Behr, Caroline. *T. S. Eliot: A Chronology of His Life and Works*. New York: St. Martin's Press, 1983.

Eliot, Charlotte C. *Savonarola*. London: R. Cobden–Sanderson, 1926.

———. *William Greenleaf Eliot: Minister, Educator, Philanthropist*. Boston: Houghton, Mifflin and Company, 1904.

Eliot, T. S. *The Complete Poems and Plays*. London: Faber and Faber, 1969.

Eliot, Valerie, ed. *The Letters of T. S. Eliot*. New York: Harcourt Brace Jovanovich, 1988.

Gordon, Lyndall. *T. S. Eliot: An Imperfect Life*. New York: W. W. Norton and Company, 1999.

Holt, Earl K. *William Greenleaf Eliot, Conservative Radical*. [St. Louis]: First Unitarian Church of St. Louis, 1985.

Ricks, Christopher, ed. *T. S. Eliot, Inventions of the March Hare: 1909-1917*. New York: Harcourt Brace and Company, 1996.

Stanley Elkin

Cuoco, Lorin. Unpublished radio interviews. St. Louis, 1979-1988.

Elkin, Stanley. *George Mills*. New York: E. P. Dutton, 1982.

———. *The Magic Kingdom*. New York: E. P. Dutton, 1985.

———. *Boswell*. New York: E. P. Dutton, 1986.

———. *Pieces of Soap*. New York: Simon and Schuster, 1992.

Lesniak, James G. *Contemporary Authors, New Revision Series*, vol. 8, 1983.

Ralph Waldo Emerson

McAleer, John. *Ralph Waldo Emerson: Days of Encounter*. Boston: Little, Brown and Company, 1984.

Eugene Field

Conrow, Robert. *Field Days*. New York: Charles Scribner's Sons, 1974.

Dennis, Charles H. *Eugene Field's Creative Years*. New York: Doubleday, Page & Co., 1924.

Field, Eugene. *The Tribune Primer*. Boston: H. A. Dickerman and Son, 1900.

———. *An Auto-Analysis and the Two Friars*. New York: H. M. Caldwell Co., 1901.

———. *The Writings in Prose and Verse of Eugene Field*. New York: Charles Scribner's Sons, 1905.

Thompson, Slason. *Life of Eugene Field*. New York and London: D. Appleton, 1927.

Kate Field

Field, Kate. *Ten Days in Spain*. Boston: James R. Osgood and Company, 1875.

———. *Fechter in Europe, 1824-1869*. New York: Benjamin Bloom, 1882.

Glendinning, Victoria. *Anthony Trollope*. New York: Knopf, 1993.

Moss, Carolyn J., ed. *Kate Field: Selected Letters*. Carbondale: Southern Illinois University Press, 1996.

John Gardner

Chavkin, Allan, ed. *Conversations with John Gardner*. Jackson: University Press of Mississippi, 1990.

Martha Gellhorn

Gellhorn, Martha. *Travels With Myself and Another*. London: Eland Books, 1983.

———. *The Face of War*. New York: Atlantic Monthly Press, 1988.

———. *The Novellas of Martha Gellhorn*. New York: Vintage Books, 1991.

Kert, Bernice. *The Hemingway Women*. New York: W. W. Norton, 1983.

Mellow, James R. *Hemingway: A Life Without Consequences*. New York: Houghton Mifflin Company, 1992.

Rollyson, Carl. *Nothing Ever Happens to the Brave: The Story of Martha Gellhorn*. New York: St. Martin's Press, 1990.

Ulysses S. Grant

Arnold, Matthew. *General Grant with a Rejoiner by Mark Twain*. Edited by John Y. Simon. Kent: Kent State University Press, 1995.

Little, Kimberly Scott. *Ulysses S. Grant's White Haven: A Place Where Extraordinary People Came to Live Ordinary Lives, 1796-1886*. St. Louis: Historic Resource Study, Ulysses S. Grant National Historic Site National Park Service, 1993.

Murray, Nicholas. *A Life of Matthew Arnold*. New York: St. Martin's Press, 1996.

Emily Hahn

Angell, Roger. "Ms. Ulysses." *New Yorker* (March 10, 1997).

Calisher, Hortense. "Emily Hahn: 1905-1997." Presented at the meeting of the American Academy of Arts and Letters, New York, April 8, 1997.

Cuthbertson, Ken. *Nobody Said Not to Go: The Life, Loves, and Adventures of Emily Hahn*. London: Faber and Faber, 1998.

Hahn, Emily. *China to Me: A Partial Autobiography*. New York: Da Capo Press, 1944.

———. *Times and Places*. New York: Thomas Crowell Company, 1970.

———. "Meet Me in St. Lewis, Louie." *American Heritage*, (August/September 1982).

Smith, Dinitia. "Emily Hahn, Chronicler of Her Own Exploits, Dies at 92," *New York Times*, February 19, 1997.

William T. Harris
Leidecker, Kurt F. *The Record Book of the St. Louis Philosophical Society Founded February 1866.* Lewiston, N.Y.: The Edwin Mellen Press, 1990.

Watson, Richard. *The History of the Department of Philosophy, Washington University, St. Louis, 1853-1996,* [St. Louis], 1997.

Chester Himes
Fabre, Michel and Robert E. Skinner. *Chester Himes: An Annotated Primary and Secondary Bibliography.* Westport: Greenwood Press, 1992.

Himes, Chester. *The Quality of Hurt.* Garden City, N.Y.: Doubleday Company, Inc., 1972.

——. *The Third Generation.* Chatham: The Chatham Bookseller, 1973.

Margolies, Edward and Michel Fabre. *The Several Lives of Chester Himes.* Jackson: University Press of Mississippi, 1997.

Muller, Gilbert H. *Chester Himes.* Boston: Twayne Publishers, 1989.

Fannie Hurst
Hurst, Fannie. "In the Crowded Areas of My Memory," in *The Red and Black.* [St. Louis]: Central High School, 37-38, n.d.

——. *Imitation of Life.* New York: Harper and Brothers Publishers, 1933.

——. "Saint Louis," *St. Louis Globe-Democrat,* November 6, 1955.

——. *Anatomy of Me.* Garden City, N.Y.: Doubleday, 1958.

Koppleman, Susan. "Fannie Hurst." *Belles Lettres* (fall 1994): 72-76.

Kroeger, Brooke. *Fannie: The Talent for Success of Writer Fannie Hurst.* New York: Random House, 1999.

Ravitz, Abe C. *Imitations of Life: Fannie Hurst's Gaslight Sonatas.* Carbondale: Southern Illinois University Press, 1997.

William Inge
Inge, William. *4 Plays.* New York: Random House, 1958.

Montgomery, Paul L. "'Sheba' an Instant Success," *New York Times,* June 11, 1973.

Shuman, R. Baird. *William Inge: Revised Edition.* Boston: Twayne Publishers, 1989.

Voss, Ralph F. *A Life of William Inge.* Lawrence: University Press of Kansas, 1989.

Orrick Johns
Johns, Orrick. *Asphalt and Other Poems.* New York: Knopf, 1917.

——. *Wild Plum: Lyrics.* New York: Macmillan, 1926.

——. *Time of Our Lives.* New York: Stackpole Sons, 1937.

Josephine Johnson
Carter, Quentin R. "Josephine Johnson and the Pulitzer: The Shaping of a Life." Ph.D. diss., University of Denver, 1995.

Johnson, Josephine W. *Now in November.* New York: Simon and Schuster, 1935.

——. *Year's End.* New York: Simon and Schuster, 1937.

——. *Seven Houses: A Memoir of Time and Places.* New York: Simon and Schuster, 1973.

——. *The Inland Island.* Cincinnati: Story Press, 1996.

Charles Lindbergh
Berg, A. Scott. *Lindbergh.* New York: G. P. Putnam's Sons, 1998.

Lindbergh, Charles. *The Spirit of St. Louis.* New York: Charles Scribner's Sons, 1953.

Elijah Lovejoy
Simon, Paul. *Freedom's Champion, Elijah Lovejoy.* Carbondale: Southern Illinois University Press, 1994.

Marshall McLuhan
Gordon, W. Terrence. *Marshall McLuhan: Escape into Understanding.* New York: Basic Books of Harper Collins, 1997.

McLuhan, Corinne, Matie Molinaro and William Toye, eds. *Letters of Marshall McLuhan.* Toronto: Oxford University Press, 1987.

McLuhan, Marshall. *The Mechanical Bride: Folklore of Industrial Man.* New York: Vanguard, 1951.

Marianne Moore
Hadas, Pamela White. *Marianne Moore: Poet of Affection.* Syracuse: Syracuse University Press, 1977.

Hall, Donald. *Marianne Moore: The Cage and the Animal.* New York: Pegasus, 1970.

Moore, Marianne. *The Complete Poems of Marianne Moore.* New York: The MacMillan Company/The Viking Press, 1980.

"The Art of Poetry IV." *Paris Review,* no. 26 (summer/ fall 1961): 42-43.

Paul Elmer More
Dakin, Arthur Hazard. *Paul Elmer More.* Princeton: Princeton University Press, 1960.

Lambert, Byron C., ed. *The Essential Paul Elmer More.* New Rochelle: Arlington House, 1972.

More, Paul Elmer. *Selected Shelburne Essays.* New York: Oxford University Press, 1935.

Tanner, Stephen L. *Paul Elmer More: Literary Criticism As the History of Ideas.* Provo: Brigham Young University, 1987.

Warren, Austin. *Connections.* Ann Arbor: The University of Michigan Press, 1970.

John Morris
"John Nelson Morris, 66; Poet, Was Professor at Washington U." *St. Louis Post-Dispatch,* November 29, 1997.

Morris, John N. *Green Business*. New York: Atheneum, 1970.

——. *The Life Beside This One*. New York: Atheneum, 1975.

——. *The Glass Houses*. New York: Atheneum, 1980.

——. *A Schedule of Benefits*. New York: Atheneum, 1987.

——. "A Message to the Fish: A Memoir of Childhood." *Contemporary Authors Autobiography Series*, vol. 13, n.d.

——. "Recollections," *Ideas* 5, no. 2 (1998).

John Neihardt
Aly, Lucile F. *John G. Neihardt*. Boise: Boise State University Western Writers Series, no. 25, 1976.

Deloria, Jr., Vine, ed. *A Sender of Words: Essays in Memory of John G. Neihardt*. Salt Lake City: Howe Brothers, 1984.

House, Julius T. *John G. Neihardt: Man and Poet*. Wayne, Neb.: F. H. Jones and Son, 1920.

Neihardt, John G. *A Cycle of the West*. New York: The MacMillan Company, 1949.

——. *The Giving Earth: A John G. Neihardt Reader*. Edited by Hilda Neihardt Petri. Lincoln: University of Nebraska Press, 1991.

Richards, John Thomas. *Rawhide Laureate: John G. Neihardt, A Selected, Annotated Bibliography*. Metuchen, N. J.: The Scarecrow Press, Inc., 1983.

——. *A Voice Against the Wind: John G. Neihardt As Critic and Reviewer*. Oregon: New Frontiers Foundation, 1986.

Whitney, Blair. *John G. Neihardt*. Boston: Twayne Publishers, 1976.

Howard Nemerov
Cuoco, Lorin. "An Interview with Howard Nemerov." *River Styx* 28 (1989).

Lowes, Robert. "Walking With Howard Nemerov." *Washington University Magazine* (fall 1991).

Nemerov, Alexander. "Modeling My Father." *American Scholar* 62 (1993).

Nemerov, Howard. *The Collected Poems of Howard Nemerov*. Chicago: The University of Chicago Press, 1977.

——. *Sentences*. Chicago: The University of Chicago Press, 1980.

——. *War Stories: Poems About Long Ago and Now*. Chicago: The University of Chicago Press, 1987.

——. *Trying Conclusions: New and Selected Poems 1961-1991*. Chicago: The University of Chicago Press, 1991.
Pace, Eric. "Howard Nemerov, Former Poet Laureate, 71, Dies," *New York Times*, July 7, 1991.

Unger, Leonard, ed. *American Writers: A Collection of Literary Biographies*. vol. III. New York: Charles Scribner's Sons, 1974.

Reinhold Niebuhr
Brown, Susan K. "The Paradoxical Pastor," *St. Louis Post-Dispatch*, June 18, 1992.

Niebuhr, Reinhold. *Moral Man and Immoral Society: A Study in Ethics and Politics*. New York: Charles Scribner's Sons, 1949.

Joseph Stanley Pennell
"Books." *Time* (August 7, 1944).

Burger, Nash K. "The Making of an American." Review of *The History of Rome Hanks by Joseph Stanley Pennell*, *New York Times Book Review*, July 16, 1944.

Mayberry, George. "Two Down," *The New Republic* (August 14, 1944).

"Pennell, Joseph Stanley." *Current Biography* (1944).

Pennell, Joseph Stanley. *The History of Rome Hanks*. New York: Scribner's Sons, 1944.

——. *The History of Nora Beckham*. New York: Scribner's Sons, 1948.

——. *Darksome House*. Coffeyville: The Zauberberg Press, 1959.

Prescott, Orville. "Books of the Times," *New York Times*, July 17, 1944.

Reddig, W. M. "'Rome Hanks' Was a Mystery in Kansas Novelist's Home Town," *Kansas City Star*, September 10, 1944.

T. M. O. (Author's initials.) "An Unconventional Kansan Stirs Critics With An Unconventional Civil War Novel," *Kansas City Times*, July 19, 1944.

Wiley, Bonnie. "Kansas U. S. Army Lieutenant Makes Hit With New Book," *Wichita Eagle*, August 20, 1944.

Joseph Pulitzer
Rammelkamp, Julian S. *Pulitzer's Post-Dispatch 1878-1883*. Princeton: Princeton University Press, 1967.

William Marion Reedy
King, Ethel M. *Reflections of Reedy*. Brooklyn: Gerald J. Rickard, 1961.

Putzel, Max. *The Man in the Mirror: William Marion Reedy and His Magazine*. Cambridge: Harvard University Press, 1963.

Irma Rombauer
Mendelson, Anne. *Stand Facing the Stove: The Story of the Woman Who Gave America "The Joy of Cooking."* New York: Henry Holt, 1997.

Rombauer, Irma S. *The Joy of Cooking*, facsimile of 1931 edition. New York: Simon and Schuster Inc., 1998.

Carl Schurz
Rowan, Steven, ed. and trans. *Germans for a Free Missouri*. Columbia: University of Missouri Press, 1983.

Shirley Seifert
Seifert, Shirley and Adele Seifert. *Death Stops at the Old Stone Inn*. New York: Hillman-Curl, 1938.

Seifert, Shirley. *River Out of Eden*. New York: M. S. Mill Company, 1940.

William T. Sherman
Fellman, Michael. *Citizen Sherman: A Life of William Tecumseh Sherman*. New York: Random House, 1995.

Hirschson, Stanley P. *The White Tecumseh: A Biography of General William T. Sherman*. New York: John Wiley and Sons, Inc., 1997.

Sherman, William Tecumseh. *Memoirs of General W. T. Sherman*. New York: Library of America, 1990.

Peter Taylor
Griffith, Albert J. *Peter Taylor*, rev. ed. Boston: Twayne Publishers, 1990.

McAlexander, Hubert H. *Conversations with Peter Taylor*. Jackson: University Press of Mississippi, 1987.

Sara Teasdale
Carpenter, Margaret Haley. *Sara Teasdale, A Biography*. New York: Schulte, 1960.

Drake, William. *Sara Teasdale, Woman and Poet*. Knoxville: University of Tennessee Press, 1979.

Teasdale, Sara. *The Collected Poems of Sara Teasdale*. New York: Macmillan, 1937.

——. *Mirror of the Heart: Poems of Sara Teasdale*. Edited by William Drake. New York: Macmillan, 1984.

Centennial issue of *From Mary to You*. St. Louis: Mary Institute, 1959.

Lindsay, Vachel. *Collected Poems*. New York: Macmillan, 1946.

Saul, George Brandon. *Quintet*. Paris: Mouton, 1967.

Kay Thompson
Biederman, Marcia. "Eloise, Liberated by Her Author's Death," *New York Times*, November 16, 1998.

Pace, Eric. "Kay Thompson, Author of 'Eloise' Books, Dies," *New York Times*, July 7, 1998.

Thompson, Kay. *Eloise in Paris*. New York, Simon and Schuster, 1999.

——. *Eloise: The Absolutely Essential Edition with Scrapbook by Marie Brenner*. New York: Simon and Schuster, 1999.

Mark Twain
Kaplan, Justin. *Mr. Clemens and Mark Twain: A Biography*. New York: Touchstone, 1966.

Rasmussen, R. Kent. *Mark Twain A-Z*. New York: Oxford University Press, 1995.

Twain, Mark. *Life on the Mississippi*. Edited by Guy Cardwell. New York: Library of America, 1982.

Constance Urdang
Urdang, Constance. *Charades and Celebrations*. New York: October House, 1965.

——. *Picnic in the Cemetery*. New York: George Braziller, 1975.

——. *The Lone Woman and Others*. Pittsburgh: University of Pittsburgh Press, 1980.

——. *Alternative Lives*. Pittsburgh: University of Pittsburgh Press, 1990.

Walt Whitman
Kaplan, Justin, ed. *Whitman Poetry and Prose*. New York: Library of America, 1982.

Tennessee Williams
Leverich, Lyle. *Tom: The Unknown Tennessee Williams*. New York: Crown Publishers, Inc. 1995.

Mead, Shepherd. "The Secret Year of Tennessee Williams," *Washington University Magazine* 47, no. 3 (spring 1977).

Pickering, John H. "Remembering Tennessee," *Washington University Magazine* 53, no. 3 (summer 1983).

"The Return of Tennessee Williams," *Washington University Magazine* 48, no. 1 (fall 1977).

Spoto, Donald. *The Kindness of Strangers: The Life of Tennessee Williams*. Boston: Little, Brown and Company, 1985.

Williams, Edwina Dakin. *Remember Me to Tom*. St. Louis: Sunrise Publishing Co., Inc., 1963.

Williams, Tennessee. *The Glass Menagerie*. New York: New Directions, 1949.

——. *27 Wagons Full of Cotton*. Norfolk: New Directions, 1953.

——. *In the Winter of Cities*. Norfolk: New Directions, 1956.

——. *Memoirs*. Garden City, N.Y.: Doubleday and Company, Inc., 1975.

Thomas Wolfe
Donald, David Herbert. *Look Homeward: A Life of Thomas Wolfe*. Boston: Little, Brown and Company, 1987.

Rubin, Jr., Louis D. *Thomas Wolfe: The Weather of His Youth*. Baton Rouge: Louisiana State University Press, 1955.

Terry, John Skally. *Letters to His Mother*. New York: Charles Scribner's Sons, 1943.

Wolfe, Thomas. *The Lost Boy*. Chapel Hill: University of North Carolina Press, 1992.

Patience Worth
Litvag, Irving. *Singer in the Shadows: The Strange Story of Patience Worth*. New York: The MacMillan Company, 1972.

Shea, Daniel. "A Psychic St. Louis Woman." Lecture delivered at Washington University in St. Louis, 1997.

Worth, Patience. *The Sorry Tale* communicated through Mrs. John H. Curran. New York: Patience Worth Publishing Company, Inc., 1924.

Yost, Casper S. *Patience Worth: A Psychic Mystery.* New York: Henry Holt, 1916.

General

Amster, Kevin. *Final Resting Place: The Lives and Deaths of Famous St. Louisans.* St. Louis: Virginia Publishing Company, 1997.

Andrews, William L., Frances Smith Foster and Trudier Harris. *The Oxford Companion to African-American Literature.* New York: Oxford University Press, 1997.

Bartley, Mary. *St. Louis Lost.* St. Louis: Virginia Publishing Company, 1998.

Bode, Carl. *The American Lyceum: Town Meeting of the Mind.* Carbondale: Southern Illinois University Press, 1968.

Christenson, Lawrence O., William E. Foley, Gary R. Kremer and Kenneth H. Winn. *Dictionary of Missouri Biography.* Columbia: University of Missouri Press, 1999.

Collester, Jeanne Colette. *Frederick Oakes Sylvester: The Principia Collection.* St. Louis: The Principia Corporation, 1988.

Corbett, Katharine T. and Howard S. Miller. *Saint Louis in the Guilded Age.* St. Louis: Missouri Historical Society Press, 1993.

DeMenil, Alexander Nicolas. *The Literature of the Louisiana Territory.* St. Louis: The St. Louis News Company, 1904.

Dillon, Richard. *Merriwether Lewis: A Biography.* New York: Coward-McCann, Inc., 1965.

Faherty, William Barnaby. *St. Louis: A Concise History.* St. Louis: Masonry Institute of St. Louis, 1989.

Fifield, Barringer. *Seeing St. Louis.* St. Louis: Books and Books, 1987.

——. *Seeing Beyond St. Louis.* St. Louis: Books and Books, 1991.

Fox, Tim, ed. *Where We Live: A Guide to St. Louis Communities.* St. Louis: Missouri Historical Society Press, 1995.

Gates, Henry Louis and Nellie Y. McKay. *The Norton Anthology of African American Literature.* New York: W. W. Norton, 1997.

Gill, McCune. *The St. Louis Story: Library of American Lives.* St. Louis: Historical Record Association, 1952.

Gunn, Walter. "The Sheldon." N.p., 1989.

Hart, James D., ed. *The Oxford Companion to American Literature.* New York: Oxford University Press, 1983.

Jacobs, Elijah L. and Forrest E. Wolverton. *Missouri Writers: A Literary History of Missouri 1780-1955 with Suggestions for the Proper Observance of Missouri Writers' Day Required by State Law in all Public Schools.* St. Louis: State Publishing Company, 1955.

Kunitz, Stanley J. and Vineta Colby. *Twentieth Century Authors, First Supplement.* New York: The H. W. Wilson Company, 1955.

Kunitz, Stanley J. and Howard Haycroft. *Twentieth Century Writers: A Biographical Dictionary of Modern Literature.* New York: The H. W. Wilson Company, 1942.

Landmarks Association of St. Louis. *Literary St. Louis: Noted Authors and St. Louis Landmarks Associated with Them.* St. Louis: Associates of Saint Louis University Libraries, Inc. and Landmarks Association of St. Louis, Inc., 1969.

Loughlin, Caroline and Catherine Anderson. *Forest Park.* Columbia: University of Missouri Press and the Junior League of St. Louis, 1986.

Magnan, William B. and Marcella C. *The Streets of St. Louis.* St. Louis: Virginia Publishing, 1994.

McCue, George and Frank Peters. *A Guide to the Architecture of St. Louis.* Columbia: University of Missouri Press, 1989.

Miller, Clarence E. *Exit Smiling.* n.p. 1950.

Mitchell, Edwina W. *The Crusading Black Journalist, Joseph Everett Mitchell.* N. p., Farmer Press, Inc., [1972?].

Morrow, Ralph E. *Washington University in St. Louis.* St. Louis: Missouri Historical Society Press, 1996.

Mott, Frank Luther, ed. *Missouri Reader.* Columbia: University of Missouri Press, 1964.

Patrick, James B., ed. *Washington University Portrait.* Introduction by Howard Nemerov. Little Compton, Rhode Island: Fort Church Publishers, Inc., 1985.

Primm, James Neal. *Lion of the Valley.* 2d ed. Boulder: Pruett Publishing Company, 1981.

Primm, James Neal. *Lion of the Valley.* 3d ed. St. Louis: Missouri Historical Society Press, 1998.

Reps, John W. *Saint Louis Illustrated.* Columbia: University of Missouri Press, 1991.

Rodabough, John. *Frenchtown.* St. Louis: Sunrise Publishing Company, 1980.

St. Louis Walk of Fame. St. Louis: St. Louis Walk of Fame, 1998.

Schild, James J. *House of God: The Historic Churches and Places of Worship of the St. Louis Area.* Florissant, Missouri: The Auto Review, 1995.

Shoemaker, Floyd Calvin. *Missouri's Hall of Fame: Lives of Eminent Missourians.* Columbia: The Missouri Book Company, 1921.

Stiritz, Mary M. *St. Louis: Historic Churches and Synagogues.* St. Louis: Landmarks Association of St. Louis, 1995.

Toft, Carolyn. *St. Louis: Landmarks and Historic Districts.* St. Louis: Landmark Association of St. Louis, 1988.

Upham, Charles Wentworth, ed. *Life Explorations and Public Services of John Charles Fremont*. Boston: Ticknor and Fields, 1856.

Van Ravenswaay, Charles. *Saint Louis: An Informal History of the City and Its People, 1764-1865*. St. Louis: The Missouri Historical Society Press, 1991.

Walker, Betty Boyd. "The History of the Saint Louis Mercantile Library: Its Educational, Social and Cultural Contributions." Ph.D. diss., St. Louis University, 1986.

Webster's Dictionary of American Authors. New York: Smithmark, 1996.

The Wednesday Club. *The Wednesday Club of Saint Louis: The First Hundred Years, 1890-1990*. St. Louis: The Wednesday Club, 1990.

Witherspoon, Margaret Johnson. *Remembering the St. Louis World's Fair*. St. Louis: Comfort Printing Co., 1973.

Wright, John A. *Discovering African-American St. Louis: A Guide to Historic Sites*. St. Louis: Missouri Historical Society Press, 1994.

ILLUSTRATION CREDITS

A. G. Edwards and Sons, Inc., St. Louis, Missouri, Illus. no. 1

Courtesy of Ethan Becker, Illus. no. 50

John Burroughs School, Archives, Illus. nos. 53, 86

Dartmouth College Library, Illus. no. 49

Denver Public Library, Western History Collection, Illus. no. 37

Joan Elkin, Illus. nos. 100 (Courtesy of Washington University's Department of English), 101 (Courtesy of Marilyn and Steven Teitelbaum)

Courtesy of Donald Finkel, Illus. no. 99

Independence Community College Library, Independence, Kansas, courtesy of the William Inge Collection, Illus. no. 94

Orrick Johns, Illus. no. 59 (photograph of Orrick Johns from *Time of Our Lives: The Story of My Father and Myself*, 1937)

Estate of Josephine Johnson, Illus. no. 109

Kansas State Historical Society, Illus. no. 52

Library of Congress, Illus. no. 33

Lilly Library, Indiana University, Bloomington, Indiana, Illus. nos. 41, 79

Estate of Marshall McLuhan, Illus. no. 64

Mercantile Library, St. Louis, Illus. no. 63

Missouri Historical Society, St. Louis, Illus. nos. 3, 4, 5, 6, 7, 8, 9, 10, 11, 12, 14, 15, 16, 17, 21, 22, 23, 24, 25, 26 (used by permission of Steven Rowan), 28, 29, 30, 31, 32, 36, 38, 42, 43, 45, 47, 48, 55, 56, 58, 70, 71, 72, 73, 77 (courtesy of *St. Louis Commerce*, June 1960), 78 (courtesy of *St. Louis Magazine*), 80, 81, 87, 89, 107

Missouri Historical Society Library, St. Louis, Illus. nos. 2, 13, 34, 39

John G. Neihardt Trust, Illus. no. 95

Ohio State University Libraries, Rare Books and Manuscripts, and the Estate of William S. Burroughs, Illus. no. 85

Pack Memorial Library, Thomas Wolfe Collection, Asheville, North Carolina, Illus. no. 76

Princeton University Library, Manuscripts Division, Paul Elmer More Papers, Illus. no. 46

Emily Pyle, Illus. nos. 27, 35, 40, 44, 54, 65, 66, 67, 68, 74, 84, 91, 93, 96, 103

Harry Ransom Humanities Research Center, Photography Collection, the University of Texas at Austin, Illus. nos. 60, 92

Courtesy of Jeff Rombauer, Illus. no. 51

School Sisters of Notre Dame, Photo Collection, St. Louis, Illus. no. 69

Eileen Travell, Illus. no. 97 (Courtesy of Metropolitan Books)

University of North Carolina at Chapel Hill, North Carolina Collection, Illus. no. 75

Ursuline Academy, St. Louis, Illus. no. 108

Washington University Archives, St. Louis, Illus. nos. 62, 82, 88, 90, 102, 105, 106

Washington University, Olin Library, St. Louis, Illus. no. 98

Washington University, Public Affairs Office, Photographic Services Collection, St. Louis, Illus. no. 104

West Virginia State Archives, Boyd B. Stutler Collection, Illus. no. 18

White Haven, St. Louis, Illus. nos. 19, 20 (from Albert D. Richardson. *A Personal History of Ulysses S. Grant*. Hartford: American Publishing Company, 1969.)

Yale Collection of American Literature, Beinecke Rare Book and Manuscript Library. Courtesy of the Van Vechten Trust, Illus. no. 83

INDEX

CONTRIBUTORS

The editors of *Literary St. Louis: A Guide*, Lorin Cuoco and William Gass, founded the International Writers Center at Washington University in 1990.

With William Gass, associate director **Lorin Cuoco** is the editor of four other books published by the International Writers Center: *The Writer in Politics, The Dual Muse: the Writer As Artist, the Artist As Writer* exhibition catalogue and symposium volume, and *The Writer and Religion.*

Director **William Gass** is the author of *Omensetter's Luck, On Being Blue, In the Heart of the Heart of the Country,* the award-winning books of essays *Habitations of the Word* and *Finding a Form, The Tunnel, Cartesian Sonata* and *Reading Rilke.* Gass is the recipient of a Lannan Lifetime Achievement Award and the first PEN/Nabokov Award.

Michelle Komie curated the images in this volume. Program coordinator of the International Writers Center since 1998, she previously served as curatorial assistant for the exhibitions *The Dual Muse* and *Max Beckmann and Paris,* and is a 1997 graduate of Washington University's School of Art and College of Arts and Sciences.

Designer **Ken Botnick** joined the Washington University School of Art faculty in 1997. Botnick has designed over 100 limited edition titles and university press books. His work is in the collections of the New York Public Library, the Bodleian Library and the Getty Center for the Humanities.

Illustrator **Emily Pyle** is a 1999 graduate of Washington University's School of Art where she won that year's Kranzberg Award for Best Book.